ENGINEERING STATICS

THIRD EDITION

Sridhar S. Condoor

Department of Aerospace and Mechanical Engineering
Saint Louis University

ISBN: 978-1-58503-530-4

PUBLICATIONS

Schroff Development Corporation

www.schroff.com

Published by:

Stephen Schroff
Schroff Development Corporation

PREFACE

Statics, which deals with the study of systems that are in a state of rest or uniform motion, is a fundamental course. The concepts in statics serve as the building blocks for future courses in engineering, mechanics of solids in particular. However, from my experience in teaching follow-on courses to statics, mechanics of solids, machine design, aircraft structures, aerospace and mechanical engineering capstone design courses, and finite element analysis, I have found that some of the most popular statics textbooks suffer from three fundamental 'disconnects':

- Emphasis, perhaps overemphasis, on the role of vectors in analyzing structures. This emphasis may result from the strong influence of physics in the texts. Further, the textbooks in mechanics of solids do not even mention vector concepts.

- A lack of physical feel due to an emphasis on structural problems. This omission results from a strong civil engineering influence in the texts.

- A lack of a systematic approach for analyzing statically indeterminate structures.

These fundamental disconnects almost inevitably curtail students' abilities to apply these concepts in their design/analysis of real systems in subsequent courses.

The pedagogical method used in this book is based on the premise that students learn more effectively if the relevance of the exercises and scenarios to real world problems is clear, leading to a systematic improvement in their skill sets. The book uses five teaching instruments: case studies, short design examples, intelligent formulation problems, concept questions, and work sheets. Short examples and case studies address the issue of relevance by presenting (1) good designs that intelligently embody the concepts in statics and (2) engineering disasters that resulted in the loss of human lives. The other three instruments, concept questions, intelligent formulation problems, and work sheets, provide students with focused opportunities to improve their skill sets still further.

Case studies can help students learn from the historic failures and successes, apply previously-tested knowledge, and, finally, realize the intended and unintended social and economic consequences of technology. Most students comment that the "stories" were useful in remembering and recalling the concepts. Thus, they serve as excellent mental cues. Short examples connect the concepts to real-world applications, enabling students to develop an appreciation for the features of everyday products. The insights gained through these examples hopefully plant the seeds of reasoning that will help the student develop intellectual independence.

These problems are designed to nurture the ability to identify alternative approaches to formulating the problem. The problems therefore enable them to step out of the rut and verify results with an alternative method. Conceptual understanding is critical for increasing the retention of the concepts over a long period of time, applying the appropriate concepts to the different situations, and seeing the big picture. In this book, concept questions help to rectify misconceptions and promote conceptual understanding.

Worksheets, a standard teaching instrument for paper-based learning, offer students the chance to systematically improve their skill sets. Introductory worksheets were designed to offer a large number of simple problems that focus on a specific concept. Once the student is at ease with the individual concepts, the challenge worksheets develop their strategic thinking skills. These worksheets initially assist in the strategy by dissecting the problem into discrete steps. As students gain expertise, they work independently. Worksheets offer continual feedback and gradually reinforce the physical reasoning by requiring students to test their results and ensure that they make sense at each step.

It was with an insight into the disconnects between statics and subsequent courses and an understanding of various teaching instruments that I developed this book. The first edition was successfully used for teaching Statics for Aerospace and Mechanical Engineering students at Saint Louis University. The feed-back from the students has been very positive. The second edition extends the extent of case studies and worksheets further. I hope this approach will help students to learn the fundamental concepts and better prepare for their subsequent courses. A special thanks goes to the editor, Dr. Brian Walter, who was instrumental in the development of this book. I would also like to thank Mr. Khoa Nguyen, Dr. Sanjay Jayaram, and Mr. Larry Boyer.

ABOUT THE AUTHOR

Sridhar S. Condoor received his Ph.D. from the Department of Mechanical Engineering at Texas A&M University. He received M.S. from the Indian Institute of Technology, Bombay and B.S. from Jawaharlal Nehru Technological University, Hyderabad, India. His research interests include many areas of Design Theory and Methodology, Computer Aided Design, Cognitive Science, and Mechatronics.

Condoor is the co-author of *Innovative Conceptual Design: Applications: Theory and Application of Parameter Analysis* (Cambridge University Press). He conducted several short-courses for both faculty and practicing engineers on design techniques. He coauthored several papers on various facets of design including design management, design theory, design principles, cognitive aspects of design and design education.

Condoor currently teaches at Saint Louis University – Parks College of Engineering, Aviation & Technology. He initiated the multidisciplinary design program with a strong emphasis on industry participation at Saint Louis University. He works with a diverse range of industries in creating new products, modeling existing products to understand the underlying physics, and developing automated manufacturing systems.

DEDICATION

This book is dedicated to my students.

COMPUTATIONAL METHODS

Computers play an important role in engineering problem-solving. Engineers create simple spreadsheets to sophisticated programs to answer numerical problems with ease. To succeed in the engineering profession, one should be proficient with the analysis using computers and be able to verify the results with hand-calculations. Several problems in the book can be worked out by using spreadsheets. Spreadsheets are easy to understand and troubleshoot. They keep the focus on the fundamental concepts and stop the user from getting lost in the programming aspects. Further, most users are familiar with Microsoft Excel – the most common spreadsheet application. Excel is readily available on most computers. Even though, the CD has the Excel spreadsheets, other software such as MathCAD and MatLab can be used to solve these problems. The reader is encouraged to take advantage of the spreadsheets provided on the CD to solve the problems, verify solutions worked out on paper, and customize them for future use. The CD has the following spreadsheets:

- **CHAPTER I – *CONVERT.XLS***
  This spreadsheet helps to convert quantities from one set of units to another. One can add his/her own set of conversion factors and customize it further. This spreadsheet can become a valuable resource for your future engineering work.

- **CHAPTER II & III – *FORCE ANALYSIS.XLS***
  This spreadsheet has three worksheets to help in solving problems in chapter II. The worksheets perform the following functions:

  1. ***Unit vector and direction cosine worksheet* –** Input the values of the force or position vector. The spreadsheet calculates the unit vector and the direction cosines. ***Problem 2 – Exercise Set III is solved in this worksheet.***

     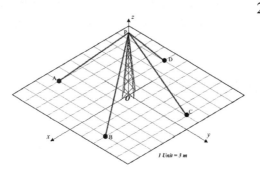

  2. ***Force vector worksheet* –** Input the values of the force magnitudes and the position vectors along which the forces are acting. The spreadsheet calculates the unit vector, force vector, and the direction cosines. Further it calculates the resultant force vector and its magnitude. ***Problem 8 – Exercise Set III is solved in this worksheet.*** Note that the spreadsheet in this example reduces the repetitive task.

  3. ***Dot product worksheet* –** Determines the dot product of two vectors and calculates the angle between the vectors. ***Problem 12 – Exercise Set III is solved in this worksheet.***

Several problems in Chapters II and III can be solved using this spreadsheet.

- **CHAPTER IV – *MOMENT ANALYSIS.XLS***
This spreadsheet helps to analyze the moment due to a set of forces. Input the values of the force magnitude, the position vector along which the force is acting, and the position vector to the line of action of the force. The spreadsheet calculates the unit vector, the direction cosines, and the force vector, and the moment vector. If several force vectors are specified, the spreadsheet computes the moment due to individual vectors and also adds these moment vectors. The spreadsheet shows the solution to **Problem 6 – Exercise Set III**.

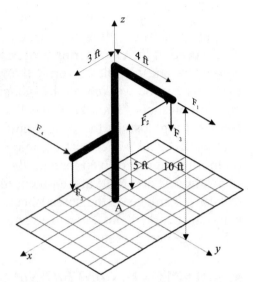

- **CHAPTER VII – *SIMPLY SUPPORTED BEAM.XLS* AND *CANTILEVER BEAM.XLS***
These two spreadsheets help to create the shear force and bending moment diagrams. The simply supported beam analysis is demonstrated in **section 7.8**. This analysis lays the ground work for numerical methods taught in future courses as well as the finite element method. The spreadsheet makes it easy to compute the stresses and deflection of beams with non-uniform cross-section in the mechanics of solids class. "Chapter VII – Cantilever Beam.xls" file shows the solution to **Problem 8 – Exercise Set IV**.

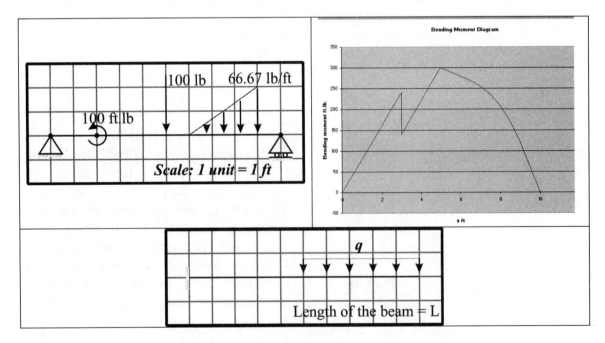

- **CHAPTER VIII – CENTROID AND MOMENT OF INERTIA.XLS**
  This spreadsheet helps to locate the centroid for a composite section and also, determine its moment of inertia about the centroid. The spreadsheet shows the solution to *Problem 6 – Exercise Set I and Problem 10 – Exercise Set II.*

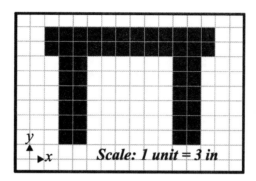

With increasing computational power, the finite element method is playing an important role. Combining the solid modeling capabilities of current CAD software with the finite element method helps to analyze complex structural problems. These software tools are becoming the common in everyday structural design and analysis. To familiarize the reader with these tools, the CD has two tutorials for ProEngineer - ProMechanica. The tutorials are:

- **CHAPTER VI – STRUCTURAL ANALYSIS**
  This lesson takes the user through the step-by-step process of creating a truss or a frame in ProEngineer and analyzing in ProMechanica. It familiarizes the reader with the analysis process and the importance of constraints. Further, it helps in visualizing the differences in deformation patterns between beams and trusses. This lesson can be used to solve any of the trusses in Exercise Set I.

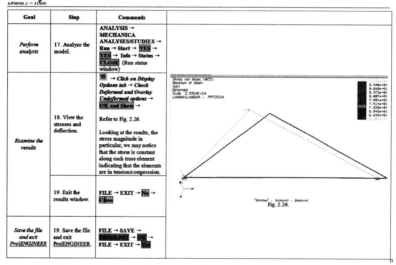

- **CHAPTER VII – SHEAR FORCE & BENDING MOMENT**
  This lesson takes the user through the step-by-step process of creating a beam in ProEngineer and analyzing in ProMechanica. The reader can distinguish between the different type of beams, their shear force and bending moment diagrams, and the resulting deformation.

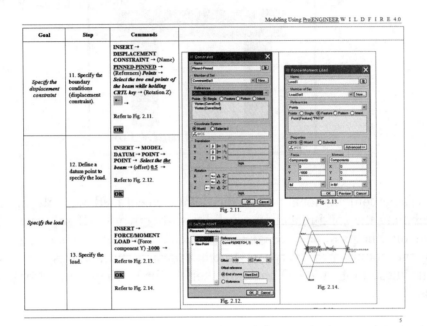

TABLE OF CONTENTS

Additional end of chapter exercises for in class review
or for at home assignments are available at

www.schroff.com/resources/statics

CHAPTER I
INTRODUCTION

Learning Objectives

The material presented in this chapter will enable you to do the following:
1. Develop an overview of engineering mechanics.
2. Understand the relationship between Newton's laws of motion and statics.
3. Distinguish mass from weight.
4. Convert quantities from one system of units to another system.
5. Appropriately round off results in numerical calculations.

1.1. What is Mechanics?

Engineers design and build structures that are stationary and machines that move. During the design process, they synthesize forms by conceiving geometric shapes, assigning materials, and specifying manufacturing methods. They analyze these forms for their suitability to the application at hand. This analysis often includes the estimation of the forms' ability to withstand the loads imposed on them during the operation. The analysis in turn helps engineers to conceive new forms and refine existing forms. Mechanics, one of the oldest branches of physics, provides the basis for such analysis.

Definition: *Mechanics is the science that entails the study of forces and their effects on material systems.*

Mechanics incorporates two branches:
- *Statics* deals with material systems that are subjected to a system of forces and are in a state of rest or uniform motion (constant velocity). For example, the principles of statics are useful in analyzing the forces transmitted by the different members of a bridge.
- *Dynamics* deals with the motion of objects. For instance, dynamics is useful in analyzing the interaction between a tennis racket and a tennis ball. The interaction can change both the path of the ball and its speed. The impetus of motion can always be traced to a set of forces, in this particular example, the force from the tennis racket.

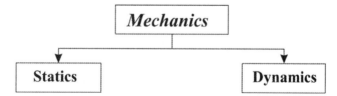

Figure 1. The division of mechanics

This book focuses on statics, i.e. the study of systems that are in a state of rest or uniform motion. The concepts in statics will serve as the building blocks for future courses in engineering, including courses that incorporate dynamics and the mechanics of solids.

1.2. Newton's Laws of Motion

Sir Isaac Newton published his masterpiece *The Mathematical Principles of Natural Philosophy* in 1687. In this book, Newton outlined the relationship between the forces acting on a particle and the motion of the particle. A *particle* idealizes an object by placing its mass at its center and neglecting its physical size. In other words, a particle has mass, but negligible size. In the real world, all objects have both size and mass associated with them. While discussing the concept of a particle, the relative size plays an important role.

Earth – A Planet or a Particle?

Earth is the largest terrestrial planet with a mass of 6×10^{24} kg. At the equator, the diameter is approximately 13,000 km. It orbits around the sun at an average distance of 150×10^6 km. Now on a relative scale, the diameter of Earth is less than one-thousandth of the average distance from the Sun. While analyzing the orbit, Earth can be viewed as a particle of negligible size. Fig. 2 provides an insight into the relative scale of the solar system. Note that most planets are quite small relative to the solar system.

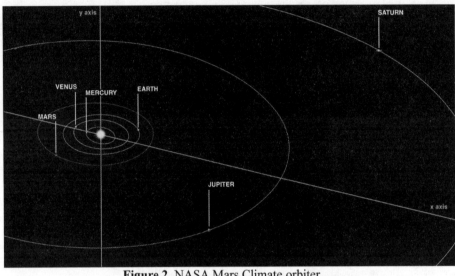

Figure 2. NASA Mars Climate orbiter
Photo courtesy of NASA

Using the idealized concept of a particle, Newton established three laws of motion:

First Law*: A particle in a state of rest or uniform motion will continue to be in the same state when the net force acting on the particle is zero.*

As Statics deals with systems that are in a state of rest or uniform motion, the net force acting on an object is zero. Therefore, this law plays an important role in identifying the systems that can be designed and analyzed using the principles of Statics. This law is also referred to as the *law of inertia* because it describes the *inertia* of an object. *Inertia* refers to the natural tendency of any object to resist a change of its state of rest or motion. Inertia tries to maintain the current state by resisting the action of forces, and depends solely upon the mass. A large object, say a container ship, has significant inertia due to its mass. It is therefore difficult to accelerate or decelerate the container ship and change the direction of motion.

Seatbelts and Airbags

Seatbelts and airbags play an important role in ensuring the safety of the occupants of a car. Together, they constitute the most effective occupant restraint system for reducing fatal accidents. When the car maintains a constant speed on a straight road, the car and its occupants are moving at the same speed. Now, if we view the occupant as particle, s/he continues to be in the same state of uniform motion. According to Newton's First Law, the net force needed to maintain this state is zero. Therefore, the seatbelts do not exert any force on the driver and the airbags need not inflate either.

When the driver applies the brake, the car decelerates while the occupants continue to move at the original velocity in accordance with Newton's first law. As a result, they experience forward motion against the seatbelts, which are designed to restrain the occupants in their place. In the extreme case of a head-on collision, the car comes to rest immediately. At the same time, the occupants maintain the uniform motion, experience a high relative velocity with respect to the car, and tend to make impact the interior of the car. To cushion such impacts of the occupant's upper body against the car interior, the airbags are designed to inflate in a matter of milliseconds.

*Second Law: The net force **F** applied to the particle is equal to the product of the mass **m** and acceleration **a** of the particle.*

Mathematically, the law can be expressed as

$$F = \mathbf{m}a \qquad\qquad 1$$

The term "net force" refers to the sum of all the forces applied to an object. According to this law, the acceleration is inversely proportional to the mass, i.e., a large mass, due to greater inertia, accelerates less. Note that in this relationship, the net force *F* and acceleration *a* are vectors while mass **m** is a scalar. As it provides a quantitative relationship, it is invaluable particularly in the field of dynamics. In Statics, its application is limited to determining the weight of an object.

Dynamics of a Parachute Descent

A closer look at the dynamics of a parachute descent reveals Newton's second law in action, describing the motion from the beginning of the skydiver's descent to the final landing. Prior to the parachute's full deployment, the drag force on the chute is small in comparison to the gravitational pull (total weight of the skydiver and the parachute). The net downward force (gravitational pull – drag force) accelerates the parachute towards the earth. As its speed increases due to acceleration and the deployment of the parachute, the drag force becomes significant and the net downward force diminishes. When the drag force is equal to the gravity force, the acceleration drops to zero and the parachute descends at a constant speed. Finally, when the skydiver touches the ground, the gravity force on the parachute drops suddenly as the ground starts supporting the weight of the skydiver. This contact results in a net upward force on the parachute for a brief period and manifests as a visual flare-up of the parachute.

Figure 3. Parachute – Photo by Tech. Sgt. Arthur Deslauriers – Photo courtesy of U.S. Army

Third Law*: For every action, there is an equal and opposite reaction.*

The third law defines the interaction between two bodies. The interaction always occurs in terms of a pair of forces, "action-reaction." The "action-reaction" force pair is always equal in magnitude and opposite in direction. For instance, when you hit a tennis ball with a racket, the ball experiences a force from the racket (refer to Fig. 4). According to the third law, the racket experiences a force equal in magnitude and opposite in direction. Even though it seems obvious and simple, this third law is of great value in statics. Using this principle, a designer can divide a complex structure or machine into individual components and analyze them by assuming that the force interaction between the components is equal in magnitude and opposite in direction.

Figure 4. The "action-reaction" force pair – Photo by David Preston - Photo courtesy Tara Grant

Helicopter Rotor Design

The motion of a traditional helicopter (see Fig. 5) is governed by the main rotor and the tail rotor. In the absence of a tail rotor, the main rotor will spin the body of the helicopter in the opposite direction because there is no resisting torque to counter the main rotor's torque. To satisfy the requirement for an equal and opposite reaction (torque in this particular case), the traditional design uses a tail rotor to cancel the spinning of the helicopter body. Another solution uses two counter-rotating rotors, a design that inherently balances torques. The Chinook helicopter shown in Fig. 6 uses this two-rotor solution.

Figure 5. Black Hawk helicopter
Photo by Air Force Staff Sgt. Jacob Bailey –
Photo courtesy of U.S. Army

Figure 6. CH-47F Chinook helicopter with two counter-rotating rotors
Photo by Gregory Frye – Photo courtesy of U.S. Army

1.3. Mass and Weight

Mass, a fundamental quantity, is an intrinsic property of matter. It quantifies the amount of matter contained in an object. The mass of an object remains constant, regardless of its location. In other words, an object will have the same mass on the surface of the earth as it will on the surface of the moon. The International System's (SI) unit of mass is the *kilogram* (kg). A metric ton (also spelled as *tonne*) is 1000 kg. In the U.S.'s customary (FPS) system of units, *slug* represents a unit mass.

The weight of an object is the force exerted by the gravitational pull. Mathematically, we can express it as

$$W = \mathbf{m}g \qquad\qquad 2$$

where W is the weight, $\mathbf{m}$ is the mass, and g is the acceleration due to gravity. From this equation, we can see that the object's weight depends on the magnitude of the acceleration due to gravity g.

On the earth's surface, the average value of the acceleration due to gravity g is approximately equal to 9.81 m/s^2 or 32.2 ft/s^2. Therefore, an object with a mass of 1 kg experiences a force of 9.81 kg. m/s^2 or 9.81 N. N stands for Newton – the unit of force in the SI system – same as kg. m/s^2. To given an order-of-magnitude sense of the unit - Newton, the weight of an apple is approximately 1 N.

On the surface of the moon, the acceleration due to gravity is approximately 1.62 m/s^2 , or about 1/6th that on the earth. On the moon, the 1 kg object weighs 1.62 N (1/6th of the weight on the earth). In the FPS system, 1 lb (lb stands for pound – the unit of force in the FPS system – same as slug. ft/s^2) is the force needed to accelerate 1 slug mass at a rate of 1 ft/s^2. Therefore, an object with a mass of 1 slug weighs 32.2 lb or 32.2 slug ft/s^2 on the surface of the earth.

1.4. Working with Units

The International System (SI) of units is the accepted standard throughout the world. However, in the United States, we still use the FPS system of units for several reasons. The reasons include a "physical feel" for the numbers in the FPS system as they are used in everyday life. Also, a vast number of existing designs were created and analyzed in the FPS system. Converting these legacy designs to the SI system of units requires an enormous engineering and financial effort.

In the global business environment, it is therefore imperative that we be fluent in both systems of units. We should be able to convert quantities from one system to another. Even though the unit conversion is simple, when improperly applied, it has significant consequences.

The Loss of the Mars Climate Orbiter

The NASA Mars Climate Orbiter, the first interplanetary weather satellite designed to orbit Mars, was launched on December 11, 1998. It was lost after its entry into Mars occultation on September 23, 1999. An investigation determined that the root cause for the failure was an improper use of units; the design teams were working with different systems of units. While the interface documentation required the thruster performance data to be in the SI system, one of the teams used the FPS system and failed to convert them. As a result, the $125 million orbiter was lost. As Dr. Stone, director of the Jet Propulsion Laboratory, succinctly said "Our inability to recognize and correct this simple error has had major implications."

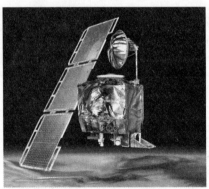

Figure 7. NASA Mars Climate orbiter
Photo courtesy of NASA

Exercise caution in numerical calculations, following these two tips for proper solution implementation:
1. *Use consistent units* when solving the problem. If the information in the problem definition uses multiple units, convert them to one system of units before solving the problem. Focus on the dimensional consistency of the equation. In other words, the units of both sides of any equation should match. For instance, in the equation $W = \mathbf{m}g$, the units of W should be same as the product of the units of $\mathbf{m}$ and g.
2. *Document the units* along with the numbers throughout the work. Make sure that the units are written along with the numbers and that the units match the quantity being calculated.

Table 1 provides the conversion factors for most quantities used in Statics.

Length or distance		Mass	
1 m	100 cm 1000 mm 1.0936 yard 3.2808 ft 39.37 in	1 kg	1000 gm 0.06852 slug
		1 slug	14.59 kg 14594 gm
1 cm	0.01 m 10 mm 0.010936 yard 0.3937 ft 0.0328 in	Weight	
		1 kip (kilopound)	1000 lb 4448 N
		1 ton	2000 lb 8896 N
		1 lb	4.4482 N
1 ft	0.3333 yard 12 in 0.3048 m 30.48 cm 304.8 mm	1 N	0.2248 lb 100×10^3 dyne
1 yard	0.9144 m 91.44 cm 914.4 mm 3 ft 36 in	**A powerful unit conversion excel file - convert.xls - is available on the CD.**	
1 mile	1760 yards 5280 ft 1.609 km 1609 m		

Table 1. Conversion chart

The following examples demonstrate the conversion procedure.

Example 1

Convert 60 miles/hr to inch/second.

$$60\,\frac{\text{mile}}{\text{hr}} = 60\,\frac{\text{mile}}{\text{hr}} \times 5280\,\frac{\text{ft}}{\text{mile}} \times 12\,\frac{\text{in}}{\text{ft}} \times \frac{1}{60}\,\frac{\text{hr}}{\text{minutes}} \times \frac{1}{60}\,\frac{\text{minutes}}{\text{seconds}}$$

$$= 1056\,\frac{\text{in}}{\text{second}}$$

Note that each product in the conversion $\left[5280\,\frac{\text{ft}}{\text{mile}}, 12\,\frac{\text{in}}{\text{ft}}, \frac{1}{60}\,\frac{\text{hr}}{\text{minutes}}, \frac{1}{60}\,\frac{\text{minutes}}{\text{seconds}} \right]$ is essentially equal to one.

Example 2

Convert 150 lb to SI units.

$$150\,\text{lb} = 150\,\text{lb} \times 4.4482\,\frac{\text{N}}{\text{lb}}$$

$$= 667.23\,\text{N}$$

Note that the product in the conversion $\left[4.4482\,\frac{\text{N}}{\text{lb}} \right]$ is essentially is equal to one.

Example 3
Convert 325 m² to FPS units.

$$324 \text{ m}^2 = 324 \text{ m}^2 \times \left(3.2808 \frac{\text{ft}}{\text{m}}\right)^2$$

$$= 3488 \text{ ft}^2$$

Note that the product in the conversion $\left[3.2808 \dfrac{\text{ft}}{\text{m}}\right]$ is essentially is equal to one.

1.5. Accuracy

The advent of handheld calculators and computers in the last few decades of the 20th century made the actual numerical manipulation much easier and more accurate than it had been in previous eras. The ability to perform accurate calculation helped in creating complex designs that depend on fast and accurate calculations. Errors in calculations have serious consequences. A good example of small numerical errors resulting in serious consequences is the failed interception of an Iraqi Scud missile by a US Patriot Missile, resulting in the death of 28 personnel during the first Gulf War. As this example indicates, numerical accuracy is paramount where it is needed with today's advanced technologies.

Accuracy indicates how closely the results match the true value of the measured or calculated quantity. Still, increased accuracy in the representation of the results can give a false sense of confidence. It is important to describe any quantity with an accuracy that reflects the confidence in the measurement and/or estimation. As an example, airlines use the average weight of a passenger as 190 lb in summer and 195 lb in winter. These numbers are not very accurate, as they reflect our inability to accurately describe the average weight. Increased accuracy in specification gives a degree of confidence in the results. For instance, in 1973, engineers designed the Hartford Civic Center, which covers two-and-a-half acres, using a computer model. For typical external loads, such as wind and self-weight, the computer model predicted the loads carried by various members and the deflections with a high degree of accuracy and gave the designers a false sense of confidence. After five years of service, during a snow storm in 1978, the roof collapsed under the weight of snow and ice just hours after a basketball game. These examples illustrate the importance of rounding off numbers to reflect the assumptions made in formulating and solving the problem.

When working with numbers, the following tips help:

1. *Round off numbers:* The ability to round off numbers appropriately depends, to a great degree, on experience. For now, in statics (and particularly in this book), round off to three or four significant figures. The number of significant figures is equal to the total number of digits. While counting the number of significant figures, we include the zero digits that are between non-zero digits. For example, the number 2.007 has four significant digits. Zeros used to set the decimal point are not significant. Thus, the number 5,000 has one significant figure. If a decimal point is followed by trailing zeros, they are significant. For example, 10.00 has four significant figures.

2. *Use an additional significant figure during calculations:* To avoid round-off errors, always carry out the calculations with one more significant figure than the solution requires.

3. *Use an exponent to denote large quantities during calculations:* Use the exponential form $A \times 10^B$ where the exponent B is written in multiples of three during the calculations. This method prevents accidental omissions that result from the use of prefixes.

---

4. *Use prefixes to indicate large quantities ONLY in the final results.* Table 2 provides the six most used prefixes:

Giga	10^9	G
Mega	10^6	M
Kilo	10^3	K
Milli	10^{-3}	m
Micro	10^{-6}	μ
Nano	10^{-9}	N

Table 2. Prefix Chart

Example 4

Find the mass of a person in kg who weighs 150 lb (on the surface of the earth, of course).

Step 1: Convert units

$$150 \text{ lb} = 150 \text{ lb} \times 4.4482 \frac{N}{lb}$$
$$= 667.23 \text{ N}$$

Note that we retain five significant digits (4.4482) in conversion.

Step 2: Determine the mass

We know that $\mathbf{m} = \dfrac{W}{g}$.

$$\mathbf{m} = \frac{667.23 \text{ N}}{9.81 \dfrac{m}{s^2}}$$
$$= 68.01529 \text{ kg} = 68.01 \text{ or } 68 \text{ kg}$$

We can approximate the weight as 68 kg.

Notes:

Concept Questions

Name: _____

1. TRUE/FALSE: Statics is the study of bodies in a state of rest or uniform motion.

2. TRUE/FALSE: The mass of an object is independent of its location.

3. TRUE/FALSE: The weight of an object is independent of its location.

4. What is inertia?

5. TRUE/FALSE: Inertia is a function of velocity.

6. Identify the action and reaction forces in the following case:

Case	Action	Reaction
Gun fire	Force on the bullet	Recoil force on the person
Firing of the rocket		

7. What is the function of a tail rotor in a helicopter?

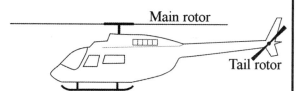

8. What is a particle?

9. If the mass of an astronaut is 6 slugs, what is his or her weight in outer space (in N)?

10. Define the term - accuracy.

Name: _____

1. Determine the number of significant digits in the following numbers:

   56.71   _____

   1000.00   _____

   505   _____

2. Round off the following quantities to three significant figures:

   5.76453 lb/in   _____ lb/in

   1000.04 m   _____ m

   50.567 N   _____ N

3. Represent the results using the correct SI form:

   4.56 N/mm^2 _____

   78.56 MN.cm/ms   _____

   54 kN.μm   _____

4. On the surface of the earth, convert the following:

   1 slug is equivalent to _____ lb

   1 kg is equivalent to _____ N

   1 N is equivalent to _____ lb.

   1 lb is equivalent to _____ kg.

5. If the mass of an astronaut is 6 slugs, what is the mass in outer space (in kg)?

Name: _____

6. Convert 125 in^2 into ft^2 and m^2 to three significant digits.

7. Convert 5 m^3 into ft^3 and in^3 to three significant digits.

8. Convert 100 km/hr into ft/s and miles/hr to two significant digits.

9. Convert 60 miles/hr into m/s to three significant digits.

10. Determine the equivalent of 1 MPa in psi (*hint:* 1 Pa = 1 N/m^2 and psi stands for lb/in^2).

Name: _____

11. Simplify the following expression in terms of both its numerical value and unit consistency:

$$\frac{100 \text{ MN} \times 50 \text{ cm}}{5 \text{ kg}}$$

12. A pressure sensor measures 100 psi (psi stands for lb/in^2). Determine the equivalent pressure in Pascals (*hint:* $1 \text{ Pa} = 1 \text{ N/m}^2$).

13. The weight density of steel is 490 lb/ft^3 respectively. Calculate its density in the SI system (kg/m^3) to four significant digits.

14. The weight density of aluminum is 170 lb/ft^3. Calculate their density in the SI system (kg/m^3) to four significant digits.

15. The weight of an object is 10 MN. Determine its mass in kilograms.

CHAPTER II
POSITION & FORCE VECTORS

Learning Objectives

The material presented in this chapter will enable you to do the following:
1. Distinguish between scalar and vector quantities.
2. Understand position and force vectors, and their classification.
3. Manipulate vectors by scaling, adding, subtracting, and resolving them.
4. Represent and manipulate two-dimensional and three-dimensional force vectors using the Cartesian vector notation.
5. Apply the concept of unit vectors to represent forces.
6. Compute the angle between two vectors and the component of a vector along a specified direction using the dot product.

Quadracci Pavilion - Milwaukee Art Museum

Designed by the Spanish architect Santiago Calatrava, Quadracci Pavilion, a modern architectural marvel, was created to increase space and bring a new image to the museum on lakefront of the Lake Michigan. Immediately after its opening in 2001 at a cost of approximately $120 million dollars, it was recognized as the Times best design of the year. The 217-foot span signature wing structure weighs 90 tons and moves to act as a sunshade (the Burke Brise Soleil). If the wind speeds exceed the critical values, the wings close in less than four minutes. According to Calatrava, "the building's form is at once formal (completing the composition), functional (controlling the level of light), symbolic (opening to welcome visitors), and iconic (creating a memorable image for the Museum and the city)." The 200 foot mast supports a pedestrian bridge which spans 250 ft and weighs 175 tons. A good understanding of vector formulation of positions and forces, the primary concept in this chapter, is a requisite for the analysis of this structural masterpiece.

a   b

Figure 1. a. Quadracci Pavilion b. The cable-strayed bridge

2.1. Scalars and Vectors

a. Scalar

Definition: *A scalar quantity is characterized by a number-unit combination that represents its magnitude.*
Examples: Mass, length, time, area, volume, temperature, pressure, and speed.
A number-unit combination (e. g. 60 mph) completely describes the speed of a car. Therefore, the quantity, speed, is a scalar. A scalar can take positive or negative values. It is independent of the reference coordinate system. In this book, a bold letter (example: **a**) represents a scalar.

b. Vector

Definition: *A vector quantity is characterized by both magnitude (a number-unit combination) and direction.*
Examples: Position, velocity, force, and moment.
A bold italic letter designates a vector. *A,* for example, is a vector whose magnitude (always a positive scalar quantity) is represented by $|A|$. While the magnitude of a vector is the same in any coordinate system; its representation depends on the coordinate system. A vector is graphically shown by an arrow that indicates its direction, sense, and magnitude. Fig. 2 shows vector *A* whose

- Direction is θ to x-axis;
- Sense is indicated by the direction of the arrow head; and
- Magnitude is the length of the line.

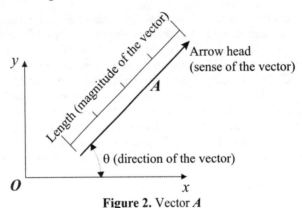

Figure 2. Vector *A*

2.2. Position and Force Vectors

a. Position vectors

A position is a vector quantity that defines the spatial location of an object in relation to a specified coordinate system. We can describe the position of an object using absolute or relative terms. An *absolute position vector* captures the distance and the direction of a point from the origin of the reference coordinate system. In Fig. 3, vectors OA and OB are two absolute vectors which define the positions of points A and B with respect to the reference coordinate system. Vectors OA and OB are referred to as r_{OA} (or simply r_A), and r_{OB} (or r_B), respectively. Note that when there is only one subscript for a position vector, then the vector is an absolute position vector with its tail at the origin.

A *relative position vector* defines the position of one object in relation to another object. Vector AB in Fig. 3 shows the relative position of point B with respect to point A and is denoted as r_{AB}. We can also interpret vector r_{AB} as the displacement or the change in position of an object from A to B. Thus, we can memorize vector AB as vector A to B. Now, let us continue to think of r_{AB} in terms of displacements. We can displace an object from the origin to point B along path OA and then along path AB, or along the direct path OB. Both paths lead to the same final destination, a fact that can be represented as a vector addition

$$r_B = r_A + r_{AB}$$ 1

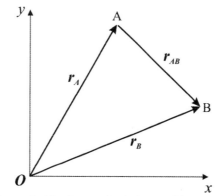

Figure 3. Absolute and relative position vectors

b. Force vectors

A force is a vector quantity that results during the interaction between two objects. For instance, when a tennis racket hits a tennis ball, there is a force interaction. In accordance with Newton's third law, the ball and the racket experience forces which are equal and opposite in direction. The forces act as long as the two bodies are interacting with one another, and they cease to exist when the interaction ends. The key point to remember from this discussion is that *"Forces ALWAYS act in PAIRS during the interaction between two objects."*

Force interactions can be classified into the following:
- *Contact forces* result from physical contact between interacting objects. Frictional forces acting at the interface between two objects fall under this category.
- *Non-contact forces* act on a body without direct contact. Gravitational and electromagnetic forces fall into this category.

Another classification scheme is the following:
- *Internal forces* act within the body i.e., between parts of the same object. For instance, a force interaction occurs between the spring and the body of a ballpoint pen. Even when there is no external force applied on the pen, the internal forces exist and are contained within the pen.
- *External forces* act on a body from objects/environment outside the body. For instance, the two key external forces acting on a high-rise building are gravity and wind loads.

Yet another scheme for classifying force vectors is the following:
- *Point forces* are often used to idealize a force distribution. For instance, as the contact area between the ball-point pen and the paper is quite small, the force on the paper can be viewed as a point force.
- *Surface forces* refer to forces that are distributed on the surface. The distribution can be uniform (example: pressure on the walls of a pressure vessel) or non-uniform (example: pressure distribution on an airplane wing).
- *Body forces* act on the volume of the body. Gravitational and electromagnetic forces are good examples of body forces.

Remember, the units of force are *Newton* (abbreviated *N*) in the SI system and *pound* (abbreviated *lb*) in the FPS system. The graphical representation of the force vectors is useful to understand the direction of the force application on each of the interacting bodies.

2.3. Manipulating Vectors

a. Scaling a vector

Scaling of vector *A* changes its magnitude and sense. Mathematically, scaling is accomplished by multiplying vector *A* with real number **b**. The resultant vector will have the magnitude $\mathbf{b}|A|$ and the sense is the same if the number is positive. If the number is negative, the sense of the resultant vector will change. In practice, devices that provide mechanical advantage, such as levers, pulleys, inclined planes, and hydraulic presses, scale a force vector. Fig. 4 shows several scaling operations on vector *A*.

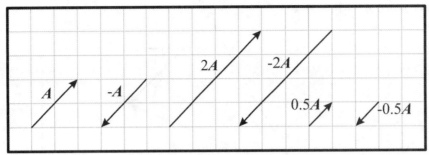

Figure 4. Scaling of vector A

b. Multiplying a vector with a scalar

As we know a scalar quantity consists of a number-unit combination. When we multiply a vector with a scalar, the numerical part of the scalar scales (stretches or shrinks) the vector and results in another vector quantity. The units of the resultant are different from that of the initial vector as they include the units of the scalar quantity. For instance, let us look at the equation:

$$W = \mathbf{m}\,\mathbf{g}$$ 2

In this equation, while the mass $(\mathbf{m})$ is a scalar, the weight of the object (W), and the acceleration due to gravity $(\mathbf{g})$ are vector quantities. Scalar $\mathbf{m}$ scales vector $\mathbf{g}$ and results in the vector W. The units of W include the units of $\mathbf{m}$ and $\mathbf{g}$ and is $kg.\dfrac{m}{s^2}$ or $slug.\dfrac{ft}{s^2}$ in the SI and the FPS systems respectively.

c. Adding and subtracting vectors

To add two vectors graphically, we place the tail of one vector at the arrowhead of the second vector and then draw the resultant vector from the tail of the first vector to the arrowhead of the second vector. This process of aligning the tail of one vector to the arrowhead of the previous vector can be extended to add several vectors (refer to Fig. 5a and b). According to the commutative law of vector addition, the resulting vector R is the same irrespective of the addition order. Therefore, we can add vectors A and B in any order. The difference between two vectors can be found by treating subtraction as addition of the first vector and the negative of the second vector. As subtraction is not commutative, the difference of vector A and B results in vectors S and T with equal magnitude but opposite directions.

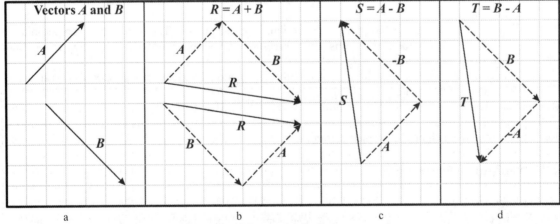

Figure 5. Adding and subtracting vectors

Another common method for adding vectors is the *parallelogram rule*. In this method, vectors A and B form the sides of a parallelogram. The diagonal of the parallelogram originating at the tails of A and B defines the resultant vector R. The second diagonal (connecting arrowheads) constitutes the difference of the two vectors *A* and *B* (*A-B* or *B-A* depending on the direction of the arrowhead). Fig. 6 illustrates the parallelogram rule.

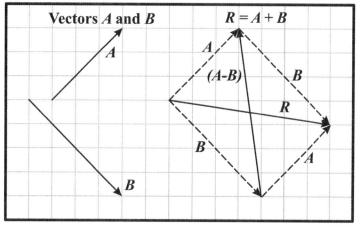

Figure 6. Using the parallelogram rule to add vectors

d. Resolving a vector into components

Resolving a vector is the reverse of vector addition. It breaks the vector into two vector components whose sum it is. The parallelogram rule can be used to resolve a vector into components. Let us say we face the task of resolving vector *A* into two components along the lines OA and OB (see Fig. 7). We construct a parallelogram by drawing lines parallel to OA and OB and passing though the head of vector *A*. Vectors *P* and *Q* along lines OA and OB are the components of vector *A*. Note that a component of vector can be larger in magnitude than the original vector. In this particular case, the magnitude of vector *Q* is larger than that of vector *A*.

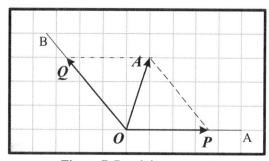

Figure 7. Resolving vector *A*

Resolving Vectors – Bicycle vs. Tricycle

A toddler can take a sharper turn with a tricycle than a kid riding on a bicycle. The secret to this trick lies in force components. In the case of a bicycle, we steer the front-wheel and drive the rear-wheel. We can establish a coordinate system (shown in Fig. 8a) and resolve the force vector moving the bicycle in the required direction (force component along x-axis) and the component pushing the bicycle off its path (force component along y-axis). When turning, the force component along the y-axis tips the bicycle. On the other hand, toddlers steer and pedal the front-wheel. Now, as the traction force acts in the same direction as the motion, there is no force component pushing the tricycle off its path. Further, the low center of gravity of a tricycle prevents potential tipping (refer to Fig. 8b).

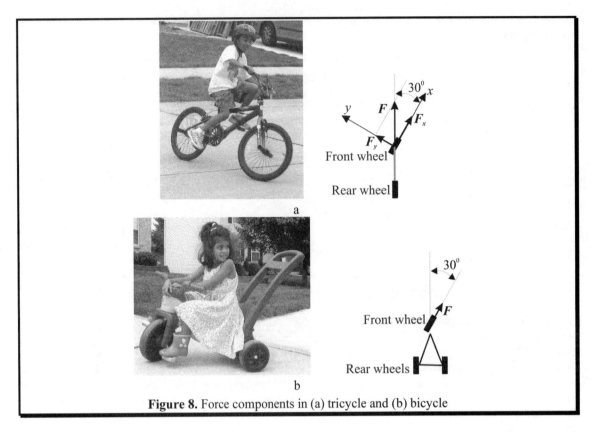

Figure 8. Force components in (a) tricycle and (b) bicycle

Several problems dealing with vector addition and resolution require the use of the sine and cosine laws and knowledge of basic trigonometric relationships. Table 1 summarizes the sine and cosine laws.

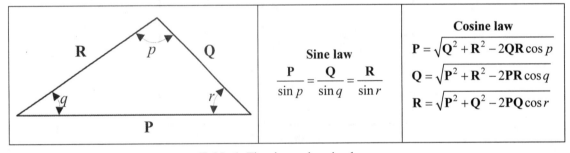

Table 1. The sine and cosine laws

Example 1

A cable on a pulley is under tension of 100 lb. Determine the net force applied by this tension at the pivot.

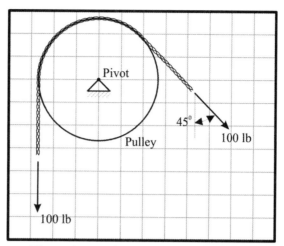

Figure 9. A pulley system with two forces

Assuming the weight of the pulley to be negligible, only two forces act on the pulley. We can add these two force vectors (100 lb. each) graphically by using the parallelogram rule (refer to Fig. 10a) or by aligning the tail of the second vector with the arrowhead of the first vector (refer to Fig. 10b). We end up with the same resultant vector R by using either of these two methods. We can determine the magnitude of the vector by using the cosine rule.

$$|R| = \sqrt{100^2 + 100^2 - 2 \times 100 \times 100 \cos 135}$$

$$\boxed{|R| = 185\,\text{lb}}$$

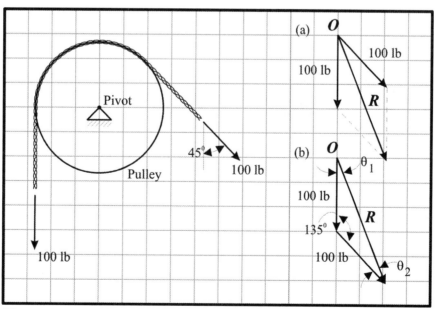

Figure 10. Vector addition (a) using the parallelogram rule (b) by aligning the tail of the second vector with the arrowhead of the first vector

We can compute the direction by using the sine rule.

$$\frac{|R|}{\sin 135} = \frac{100}{\sin \theta_1}$$

$$\boxed{\theta_1 = 22.5^0}$$

Alternatively, we can compute the angle by identifying the triangle formed by the two applied forces and the resultant force as an isosceles triangle (two equal sides), and using the following relations: θ_1 is equal to θ_2, and the sum of angles in a triangle is 180^0.

Example 2

A block rests on an inclined plane. The mass of the block is 100 kg. The angle of the incline (θ) is 30^0. Determine the friction force at the interface.

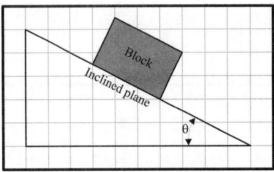

Figure 11. A block on an inclined plane

We can divide the gravitational force on the block into two components: F_x and F_y which are parallel and perpendicular to the inclined plane respectively (refer to Fig. 12). The inclined plane provides the reaction to the normal force F_y. The friction at the interface resists the force parallel to the inclined plane. According to the Newton's third law, this friction force is equal to and opposite of F_x.

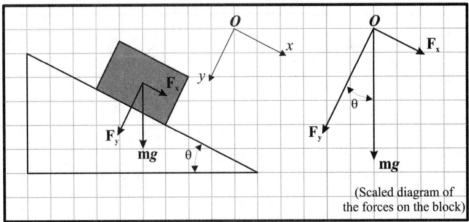

Figure 12. Forces on the block

Step 1: Determine the gravitation force on the block ($m.g$).

$$m.g = 100\,kg \times 9.81\frac{m}{s^2}$$

$$= 981\,N$$

Step 2: Establish a convenient coordinate system.

In this particular case, we can establish the axes to be parallel and perpendicular to the inclined plane.

Step 3: Determine the components using simple geometry.

$$\mathbf{F_x} = \mathbf{m}g \sin\theta$$
$$= 490\,\text{N}$$
$$\mathbf{F_y} = \mathbf{m}g \cos\theta$$
$$= 850\,\text{N}$$

Force $\mathbf{F_y}$ will act along the inclined plane in the downward direction.

Notice that as the angle of the inclined plane increases, the normal force decreases and the force along the inclined plane increases. This makes sense physically as we increase the angle of incline, reaching a point where the block slides down due to this force $\left(\mathbf{F_x}\right)$.

Step 4: Determine the friction force.
The friction will be equal in magnitude i.e., 490 lb in magnitude, directed upward along the inclined plane. This force prevents the block from slipping and keeps it at rest.

$$\boxed{\left|\mathbf{F}_{friction}\right| = 490\,\text{lb}}$$

Example 3
If the x-component of force vector $\mathbf{F}$ is 10 kN, determine the y-component of the force vector and also, the magnitude of the force vector.

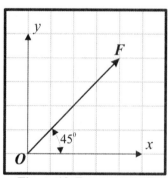

Figure 13. Force vector $\mathbf{F}$

The x-component of force $\mathbf{F}$ is

$$\mathbf{F_x} = \mathbf{F}\cos 45 = 10\,\text{kN}$$

Therefore, the magnitude of force $\mathbf{F}$

$$\left|\mathbf{F}\right| = \boxed{14.14\,\text{kN}}$$

Now, we compute the y-component as

$$\mathbf{F_y} = \mathbf{F}\sin 45$$
$$\mathbf{F_y} = \boxed{10\,\text{kN}}$$

Notes:

Concept Questions

Name: _____

1. TRUE/FALSE: A vector is a quantity characterized by only a positive or negative number that represents its magnitude.

2. TRUE/FALSE: Multiplication of a vector with a negative number changes the sense of the vector.

3. Name two devices that can be used for scaling force vectors.

Give two examples for each of the following:

4. Contact forces:	5. Non-contact forces:
6. Internal force:	7. Point forces:
8. Surface forces:	

9. Add and subtract vectors *A* and *B* using the parallelogram rule.

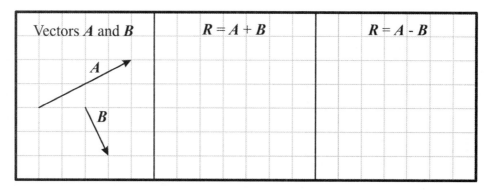

Vectors *A* and *B*	*R = A + B*	*R = A - B*

10. Resolve vector *P* into components along OA and OB directions.

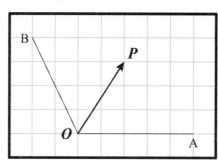

Name: _____

Problem 1

A ship is pulled into the dock by two ropes, which exert 4000 lb and 9000 lb. Determine the resultant force.

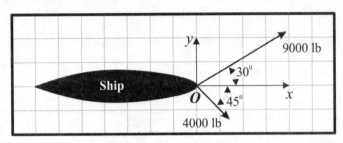

Step I: Determine the resultant of the two forces by aligning the tail of the second vector with the arrowhead of the first vector.

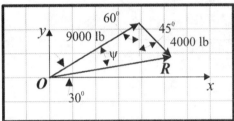

Resultant vector (R):

Magnitude: _____ lb

Direction: _____ degrees to the x-axis

Problem 2

Perform vector operations on the two force vectors and determine the resultants (graphically).

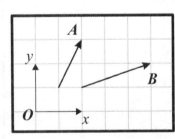

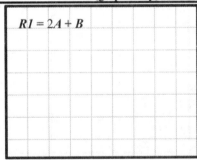

R1 = 2A + B

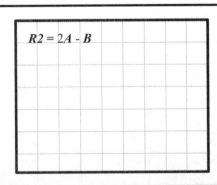

R2 = 2A - B

R3 = A - 2B

Name: _____

Problem 3

Resolve the following vectors

$F_x =$ _____ lb

$F_y =$ _____ lb

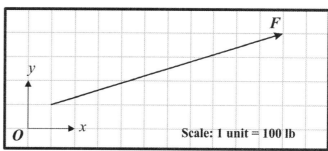

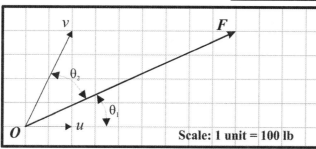

$F_u =$ _____ lb

$F_v =$ _____ lb

$F_u =$ _____ kN

$F_v =$ _____ kN

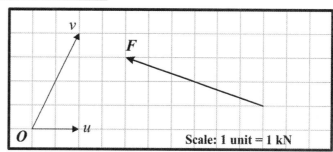

Problem 4

Perform the following vector operation and then, resolve the resulting vectors along u and v directions.

$$R = A - 2B$$

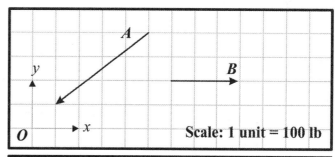

$R_x =$ _____ lb

$R_y =$ _____ lb

Name: _____

Problem 5

Perform the following vector operations and then, resolve the resulting vectors along u and v directions.

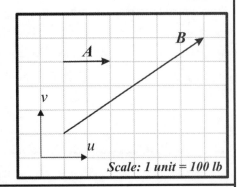

Scale: 1 unit = 100 lb

R = A + B

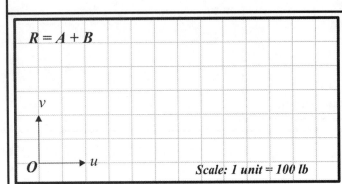

Scale: 1 unit = 100 lb

$F_u =$ _____ lb

$F_v =$ _____ lb

R = B - A

Scale: 1 unit = 100 lb

$F_u =$ _____ lb

$F_v =$ _____ lb

Problem 6

Determine the resultant force due to three forces acting on a ring.

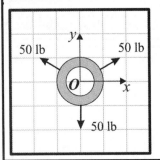

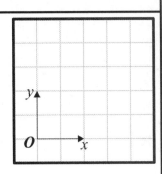

Resultant force vector: _____   Direction: _____ degrees to the x-axis

Name: _____

Problem 7
Determine the resultant of three forces acting on a ring.

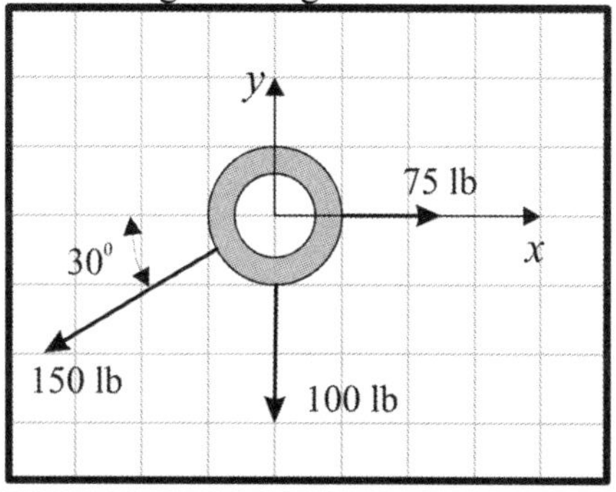

Step I: Determine the resultant of two forces (100 lb and 150 lb forces) using the parallelogram law.

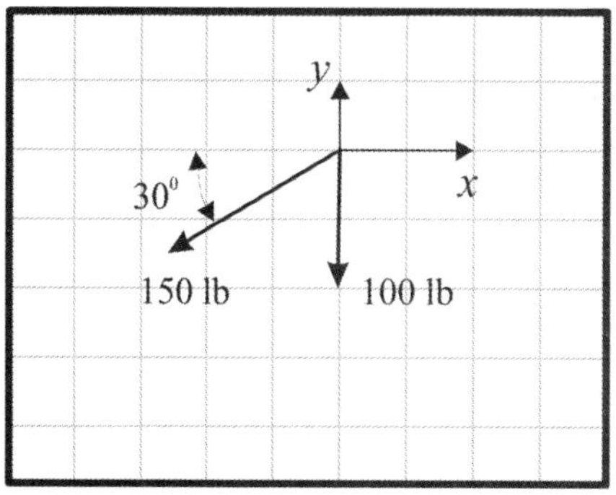

Resultant force vector: _____ Direction: _____ degrees to the x-axis

Step II: Add the third force to the resultant vector.

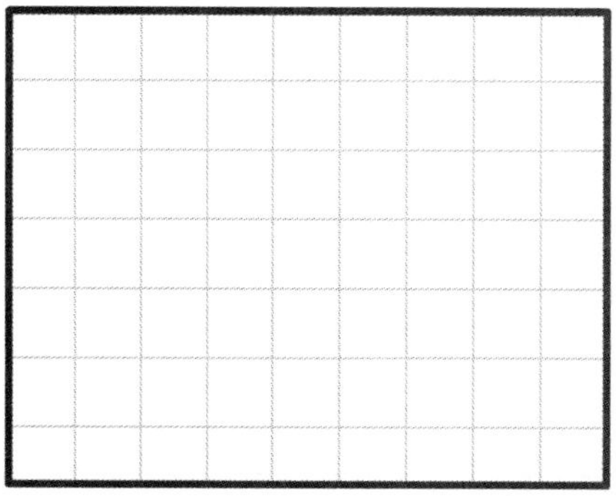

Resultant force vector: _____
Direction: _____ degrees to the x-axis

Problem 8
Determine the resultant due to four forces acting on the ring. (Look at the forces carefully.)

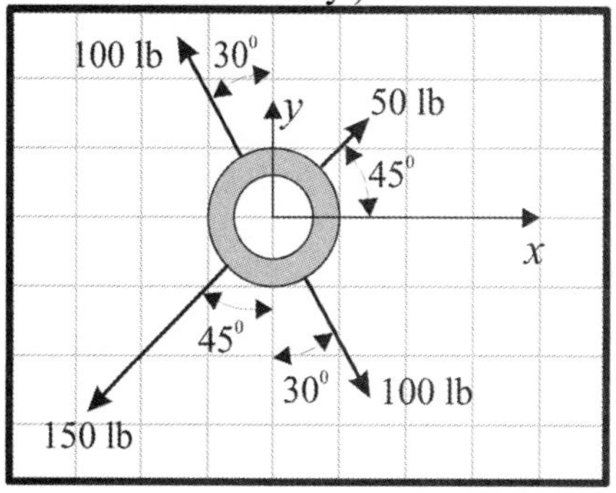

Resultant force vector: _____

Direction: _____ degrees to the x-axis

Name: _____

Problem 9

A rear-wheel drive car is taking a turn. The front steering wheels are at an angle. The two rear wheels are applying a net force of 1500 lb. Determine the force component that is pushing the car off its path.

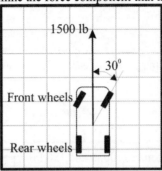

Step I: Establish a convenient coordinate system.

In this particular case, the coordinate system is established to easily resolve the force vector moving the car in the required direction (force component along x-axis) and the component pushing the car off its path (force component along y-axis).

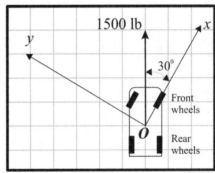

Step II: Resolve the force vector along the coordinate directions.

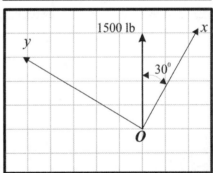

Problem 10

If the y-component of force vector ***F*** is 300 lb, determine the x-component of the force vector and also, the magnitude of the force vector.

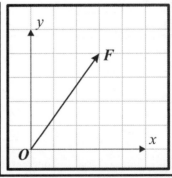

2.4. Two-Dimensional Cartesian Vectors

a. Two-dimensional Cartesian vector notation

In the previous section, we learned the graphical method for manipulating vectors. This method is useful in visualizing and understanding the components of a force vector and for determining the resultant of a system of forces. However, its application is limited to two-dimensional applications as it is impractical to graphically construct and reason about three-dimensional vectors on a two-dimensional paper. The Cartesian vector notation becomes a useful analysis tool in such situations.

Let us consider a vector in a two-dimensional Cartesian coordinate system xy. In this system, axes x and y are orthogonal i.e., perpendicular to each other. To aid in defining vectors, we introduce two dimensionless unit vectors i and j, whose magnitude is one unit and direction is that of positive x- and y-axes respectively. Now, consider vector A as shown in Fig. 14. We can resolve vector A into two components, $A_x i$ and $A_y j$, parallel to the x- and y-axes respectively. Then, we can write vector A as

$$A = A_x i + A_y j \qquad\qquad 3$$

The terms A_x and A_y are scalar quantities and they represent the magnitude of the components. The Cartesian components (A_x and A_y) represent the effectiveness of the force vector along x- and y-directions.

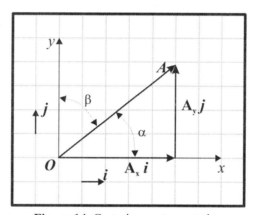

Figure 14. Cartesian vector notation

Selecting an Appropriate Coordinate System

Let us solve the problem of a flight plan: An airplane travels 1,000 miles north, 1,000 miles east, 1,000 miles south and then, 500 miles west. Determine the distance of the plane from the starting point. The first step involves establishing a coordinate system (North-South and East-West) and then, determining the resultant vector by aligning the heads to the tails. Fig. 15a shows the Cartesian coordinate system and Fig. 15b shows the vector addition.

According to the vector addition, the plane should arrive 500 miles off the starting location. But in practice, the plane would be off from the calculated destination. The disparity is due to the vector representation. We assumed a Cartesian coordinate system and the vectors to be Cartesian vectors. But in reality, the Cartesian coordinate system is inappropriate for this application because 1,000 miles east and west are traveled at different latitudes with different diameters. The example illustrates the importance of choosing an appropriate coordinate system.

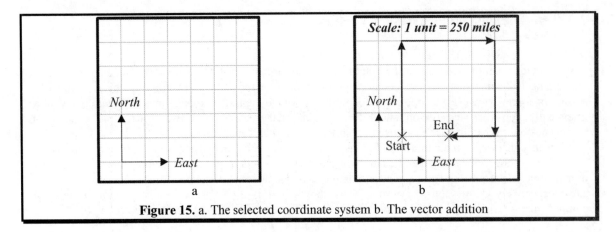

Figure 15. a. The selected coordinate system b. The vector addition

b. Direction cosines

The direction of vector A is defined by angles α and β, which, of course, are not independent. These angles are measured between the vector and the positive coordinate axes. The magnitude of these angles always lies between 0^0 and 180^0. Using these angles, we can resolve the vector into components:

$$\mathbf{A_x} = |A|\cos\alpha$$
$$\mathbf{A_y} = |A|\cos\beta$$

4

$\cos\alpha$ and $\cos\beta$ are called the direction cosines of vector A. The magnitude of vector A is

$$|A| = \sqrt{\mathbf{A_x}^2 + \mathbf{A_y}^2}$$

5

By substituting the values of $\mathbf{A_x}$ and $\mathbf{A_y}$, we can notice that the direction cosines of a vector in two-dimensional space conform to the following relationship:

$$\cos^2\alpha + \cos^2\beta = 1$$

6

c. Vector operations

In the Cartesian vector notation, the addition of two vectors A and B is equal to the algebraic sum of their corresponding components (refer to Fig. 16).

$$R = A + B = (\mathbf{A_x}i + \mathbf{A_y}j) + (\mathbf{B_x}i + \mathbf{B_y}j)$$
$$= (\mathbf{A_x} + \mathbf{B_x})i + (\mathbf{A_y} + \mathbf{B_y})j$$
$$= \mathbf{R_x}i + \mathbf{R_y}j$$

Using trigonometry, the magnitude and the direction of the resultant can be identified as

$$|R| = \sqrt{\mathbf{R_x}^2 + \mathbf{R_y}^2}$$
$$\theta = \tan^{-1}\left|\frac{\mathbf{R_y}}{\mathbf{R_x}}\right|$$

7

Vector scaling involves multiplying each component of the vector by the scale factor. Scaling vector A by scale factor a (a real number) is

$$\mathbf{a}A = \mathbf{aA_x}i + \mathbf{aA_y}j$$

8

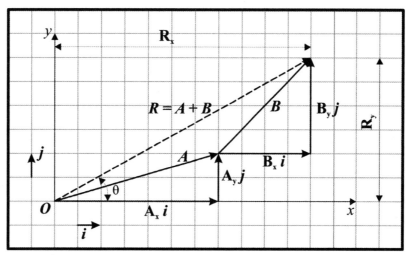

Figure 16. Vector addition as algebraic sum of its components

d. Unit vector

Unit vector is often used to conveniently represent the direction of the vector. We have seen unit vectors i, and j – vectors with one unit magnitude directed along x- and y-directions. We can obtain unit vector u_A of vector A by dividing the vector by its magnitude. As the units of the vector and the magnitude are same, they cancel each other out and result in a **dimensionless** unit vector.

$$u_A = \frac{A}{|A|}$$

$$= \frac{A_x}{|A|} i + \frac{A_y}{|A|} j$$

$$u_A = \cos\alpha\, i + \cos\beta\, j \qquad\qquad 9$$

Thus, we can articulate vector A by defining its magnitude $\left(|A| - \text{a scalar quantity}\right)$ and direction using unit vector $\left(u_A - \text{a dimensionless vector quantity}\right)$. Mathematically, vector A is expressed as $A = |A|\, u_A$.

e. Position vectors

We can represent the position of point A, whose spatial coordinates are (x_A, y_A) as $\left(r_A = x_A i + y_A j\right)$ using the Cartesian notation. Vector r_A specifies the position of point A in absolute terms with respect to Origin. On the other hand, a relative position is defined by a vector between the two points. For instance, Fig. 17 shows two absolute position vectors r_A and r_B. Now, the relative position vector r_{AB} defines the vector from point A to point B. Mathematically, we can identify the relationship

$$r_B = r_A + r_{AB} \qquad\qquad 10$$

Rearranging the terms, we get

$$r_{AB} = r_B - r_A$$

$$r_{AB} = \left(x_B - x_A\right)i + \left(y_B - y_A\right)j \qquad\qquad 11$$

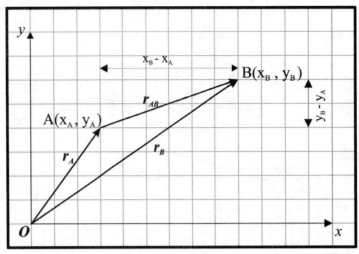

Figure 17. Absolute and relative position vectors r_A, r_B, and r_{AB}

f. Force vectors

To work with forces in the vector form, we need to represent a physical force using the Cartesian vector notation. In the real world, we usually know the magnitude of the force applied and its direction in terms of the angle or the two points through which it is applied. For instance, we may pull a cable with force F (refer to Fig. 18). We may know the magnitude of the force as $|F|$. We can write the force vector as

$$F = |F| . u_{AB} \qquad\qquad 12$$

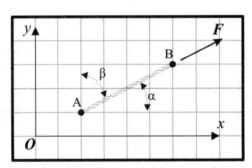

Figure 18. A force acting along a cable

Now to complete the force representation, we are faced with the task of finding its unit vector. If we know the angle $(\alpha \text{ or } \beta)$, then we can write the unit vector as:

$$u_{AB} = \cos\alpha\, i + \cos\beta\, j$$

Some times, instead of the angle, we know the coordinates of points A and B. In such cases, we can determine the unit vector u_{AB} using the equation:

$$u_{AB} = \frac{r_{AB}}{|r_{AB}|}$$

While the representation can sometimes be a tedious process, it simplifies vector manipulation. For instance, to add a number of Cartesian vectors, we can simply take the algebraic sums of the individual components of each force vector.

$$R = \sum F_x\, i + \sum F_y\, j$$

Spreadsheet "Force Analysis.xls" is available on CD to help solve two- and three-dimensional problems.

Example 4
Let us revisit the pulley problem in example 1. In this problem, a cable on a pulley is under tension of 100 lb. We need to determine the net force applied by this tension at the pivot. We assumed the weight of the pulley to be negligible. In the previous procedure, we added the two vectors using the parallelogram rule. Now, let us add the vectors using the Cartesian vector notation.

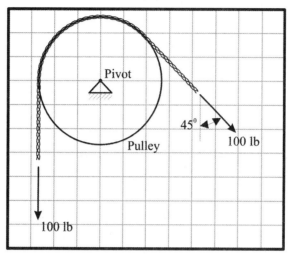

Figure 19. A pulley system with two forces

Step 1: Represent the forces using the Cartesian vector notation.

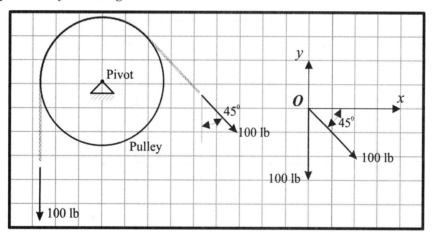

Figure 20. Cartesian vector representation

Vector A:

X component = 0 lb

Y component = -100 lb

Cartesian representation:

$$A = -100\,j \text{ lb}$$

Vector B:

X component = $100 \times \cos 45 = 70.71$ lb

Y component = $100 \times \cos 135 = -70.71$ lb [*]

Cartesian representation

$$B = 70.71\,i - 70.71\,j \text{ lb}$$

[*] Always measure the angle for direction between the vector and the positive coordinate axis.

Step 2: Determine the resultant force by taking the algebraic sum of the force components.

$$R = A + B$$
$$= (-100\,j) + (70.71i - 70.71\,j)\ \text{lb}$$
$$= (70.71)\,i + (-100 - 70.71)\,j\ \text{lb}$$
$$= 70.71\,i - 170.71\,j\ \text{lb}$$

Step 3: Determine the magnitude and direction of the resultant vector.
We can determine the magnitude of the resultant vector.

$$|R| = \sqrt{70.71^2 + 170.71^2}$$
$$\boxed{|R| = 185\ \text{lb}}$$

The solution is consistent with that of example 1. Also, notice that the solution (185 lb) is greater than the individual components.

Now let us compute the direction.

$$\theta = \tan^{-1}\left|\frac{R_y}{R_x}\right|$$
$$= \tan^{-1}\frac{170.71}{70.71}$$
$$\boxed{\theta = 67.5^0}$$

Note that θ refers to the angle between the resultant force vector and the x-axis.

Example 5
A known force F_1 (= 1000 lb) and an unknown force F_2 act on a hook. If the resultant of the two forces acts along the x-direction, determine the magnitude of F_2 and that of the resultant.

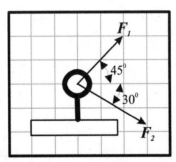

Figure 21. Two forces acting on a hook

Let us begin by establishing a Cartesian coordinate system and drawing the force vectors (see Fig. 22).

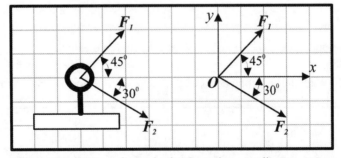

Figure 22. The two forces in the Cartesian coordinate system

Let us represent F_1 and F_2 using the vector notation:

$$F_1 = \mathbf{F_{1x}}\, i + \mathbf{F_{1y}}\, j$$

$$F = 1000 \times \sin 45\, i + 1000 \times \cos 45\, j$$

$$F_1 = 707.1\, i + 707.1\, j \text{ lb}$$

$$F_2 = \mathbf{F_{2x}}\, i + \mathbf{F_{2y}}\, j$$

$$F_2 = |F_2| \times \cos 30\, i - |F_2| \times \sin 30\, j$$

Now, the sum of the two vectors is:

$$R = \left(\mathbf{F_{1x}} + \mathbf{F_{2x}}\right) i + \left(\mathbf{F_{1y}} + \mathbf{F_{2y}}\right) j$$

$$R = \left(707.1 + |F_2| \times \cos 30\right) i + \left(707.1 - |F_2| \times \sin 30\right) j$$

The y-component of the resultant vector must be zero for the resultant to be horizontal. Therefore,

$$707.1 - |F_2| \times \sin 30 = 0$$

$$\boxed{|F_2| = 1414 \text{ lb}}$$

By substituting the value of F_2, we get

$$R = \left(707.1 + 1414.2 \times \cos 30\right) i$$

$$\boxed{R = 1932\, i \text{ lb}}$$

Example 6

Two ropes are pulling a boat with 2000 N each. Determine the net force on the ship.

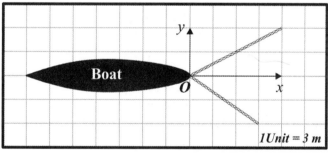

Figure 23. A boat pulled by two ropes

1. Represent each force in the Cartesian coordinate notation.
a. Set up a coordinate system and determine the position vectors.
The two position vectors are

$$r_A = 12\, i + 6\, j \text{ m}$$

$$r_B = 9\, i - 6\, j \text{ m}$$

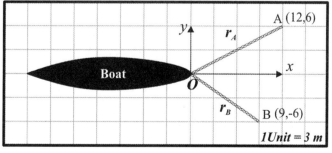

Figure 24. Position vectors along the two ropes

b. Find the unit vectors.
The magnitudes of the vectors are

$$|r_A| = \sqrt{12^2 + 6^2} = 13.42 \text{ m}$$

$$|r_B| = \sqrt{9^2 + 6^2} = 10.82 \text{ m}$$

Unit vectors are

$$u_A = \frac{r_A}{|r_A|} = 0.894\,i + 0.447\,j$$

$$u_B = \frac{r_B}{|r_B|} = 0.832\,i - 0.5545\,j$$

c. Represent the two forces.

$$F_A = 2000\,\text{N} \times (0.894\,i + 0.447\,j)$$
$$= 1788\,i + 894\,j \text{ N}$$
$$F_B = 2000\,\text{N} \times (0.832\,i - 0.5545\,j)$$
$$= 1664\,i - 1109\,j \text{ N}$$

2. Determine the resultant.
a. Add the two vectors.

$$R = F_A + F_B = (1788 + 1664)i + (894 - 1109)j \text{ N}$$
$$= 3452\,i - 215\,j \text{ N}$$

b. Determine the magnitude and angle of the resultant.
Magnitude:

$$R = \sqrt{3452^2 + 215^2}$$
$$\boxed{|R| = 3459\,N}$$

Direction:

$$\theta = \tan^{-1}\left(\frac{215}{3452}\right)$$

$$\boxed{\theta = 3.56^0}$$

Because the y-component is negative (-215), the angle is measured in a clockwise direction from the positive x-axis.

Example 7

Three forces, F_1, F_2, and F_3, act on a bracket. The magnitude of the resultant force should not exceed 50 kN. Determine the possible range of values for F_3.

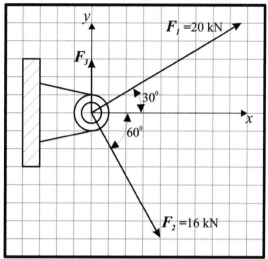

Figure 25. Three force vectors acting on a bracket

First let us represent the three vectors using the Cartesian notation.

$$F_1 = 20\cos30^0 \ i + 20\sin30^0 \ j \text{ kN} \Rightarrow F_1 = 17.32 \ i + 10 \ j \text{ kN}$$

$$F_2 = 16\cos60^0 \ i - 16\sin60^0 \ j \text{ kN} \Rightarrow F_2 = 8 \ i - 13.856 \ j \text{ kN}$$

$$F_3 = \mathbf{F_3} \ j \text{ kN}$$

The resultant vector R can be computed by adding the corresponding x- and y-components.

$$R = 25.32 \ i + \left(-3.856 + \mathbf{F_3}\right) i \text{ kN}$$

Now, the limiting magnitude for the resultant vector is 50 kN. Therefore,

$$\left(25.32\right)^2 + \left(-3.856 + \mathbf{F_3}\right)^2 = 50^2$$

$$\left(-3.856 + \mathbf{F_3}\right) = \pm 43.115 \text{ kN}$$

Solving the equation, we get the two extreme values for force vector F_3.

$$F_3 = 46.97 \ j \text{ kN (extreme value 1)}$$

$$F_3 = -39.26 \ j \text{ kN (extreme value 2)}$$

The range for force vector F_3 is

$$\boxed{-39.26 \ j \text{ kN} \le F_3 \le 46.97 \ j \text{ kN}}$$

Notes:

Concept Questions

Name: _____

1. TRUE/FALSE: A unit vector is a dimensionless quantity.

2. What is the difference between absolute and relative position vectors?

3. TRUE/FALSE: If the magnitude of a force is equal to zero, then each component of the force vector should be equal to zero.

4. TRUE/FALSE: The component of a force is always less than or equal to the magnitude of the force.

5. Vector A can be written as:
   A. $B + C + D + E$
   B. $B + C - D - E$
   C. $B + C - D + E$
   D. $-E + D - C - B$

6. The magnitude of the resultant of two vectors whose magnitudes are 5 lb and 12 lb can not be:
   A. greater than 17 lb
   B. greater than 13 lb
   C. greater than 12 lb
   D. greater than 5 lb

7. The resultant of three vectors whose magnitudes are equal (and nonzero) is zero. The following statement is false:
   A. The three vectors lie in the same plane
   B. The angle between any two vectors is 60^0 or 120^0
   C. The vectors can be arranged to form an equilateral triangle
   D. The angle between any two vectors is 90^0

8. A block is in equilibrium on an inclined plane. The component of weight along the inclined plane is:
   A. $W \sin\theta$
   B. $W \cos\theta$
   C. $W \tan\theta$
   D. W

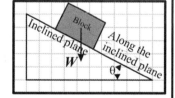

9. A known force $\left(F_1 = 100\sqrt{2} \text{ lb}\right)$ and an unknown force $\left(F_2\right)$ act on a hook. Determine the magnitude of unknown force if the resultant is 200 lb along the x-direction.
   A. 0 lb
   B. 100 lb
   C. $100\sqrt{2}$ lb
   D. None of the above

10. The unit vector for the force vector $F = 100i + 100j$ lb is:
   A. $i + j$
   B. $i + j$ lb
   C. $0.5i + 0.5j$
   D. $\dfrac{1}{\sqrt{2}}i + \dfrac{1}{\sqrt{2}}j$

Name: _____

Problem 1

Resolve the force vectors along x and y directions. Write each force vector using the Cartesian vector notation.

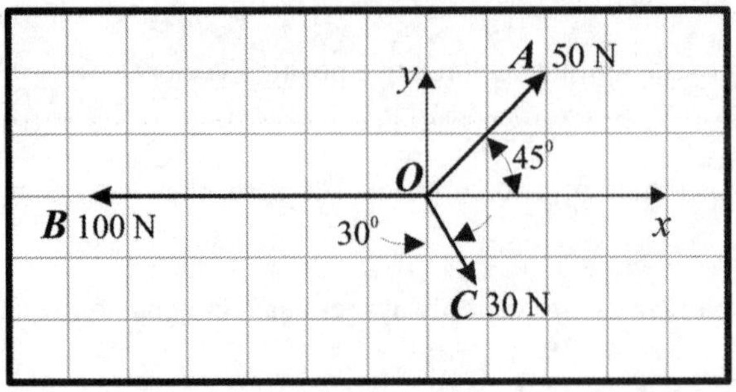

Vector *A*	Vector *B*	Vector *C*
X component: _____ N	X component: _____ N	X component: _____ N
Y component: _____ N	Y component: _____ N	Y component: _____ N
Cartesian representation:	Cartesian representation:	Cartesian representation:
_____	_____	_____

Problem 2

Resolve the force vectors along x and y directions. Write each force vector using the Cartesian vector notation.

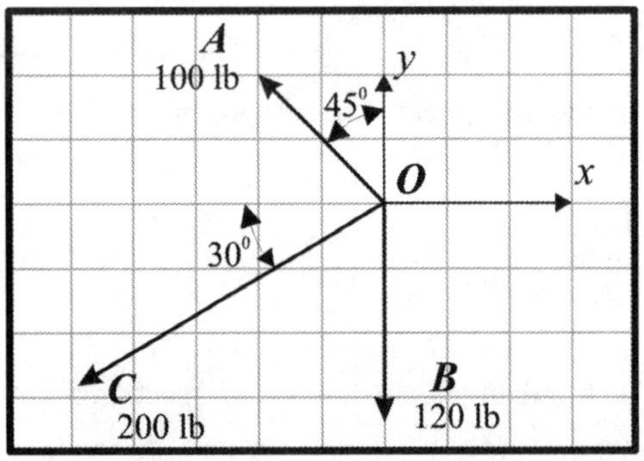

Vector *A*	Vector *B*	Vector *C*
X component: _____ lb	X component: _____ lb	X component: _____ lb
Y component: _____ lb	Y component: _____ lb	Y component: _____ lb
Cartesian representation:	Cartesian representation:	Cartesian representation:
_____	_____	_____

Name: _____

Problem 3

Sketch the following force vectors and determine their directions (the angle between the vector and the positive x-axis)

Vector A $200i + 300j$ lb	Vector B $300i - 300j$ lb	Vector C $-250i - 200j$ lb	Vector D $100i + 100j$ lb
Vector A Direction	Vector B Direction	Vector C Direction	Vector D Direction

Problem 4

Determine the resultant of the following force vectors using the Cartesian vector notation. Compute the magnitude and the direction of the resultant.

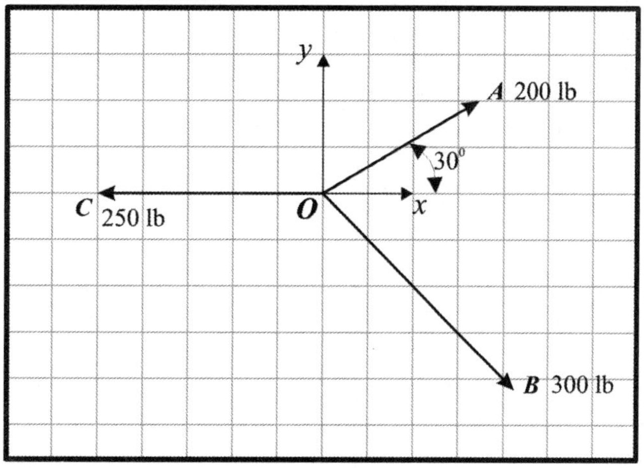

Cartesian representation of:

$A =$ _____

$B =$ _____

$C =$ _____

$R =$ _____

Magnitude of the resultant vector = _____

Direction: _____ to the positive x-axis
(measured in the counter-clockwise direction)

Name: _____

Problem 5

Three forces, F_1, F_2, and F_3, act on a bracket. The magnitude of F_3 is 10 kN. If the resultant force acts along the x-direction (horizontal), determine the direction of force vector F_3. Also, determine the magnitude of the resultant. Also, sketch force vector F_3.

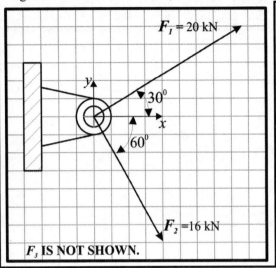

Problem 6

Three forces, F_1, F_2, and F_3, act on a bracket. Determine the magnitude and direction of force vector F_3 so as to minimize the magnitude of the resultant. (Hint: To minimize the resultant of F_1 and F_2, apply a force whose magnitude is equal to the resultant of F_1 and F_2 in the opposite direction.)

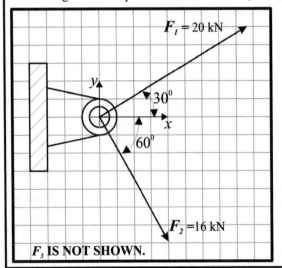

Name: _____

Problem 7

Three forces, F_1, F_2, and F_3, act on a bracket. The magnitude of the resultant force should not exceed 75 kN. Determine the possible range of values for F_3.

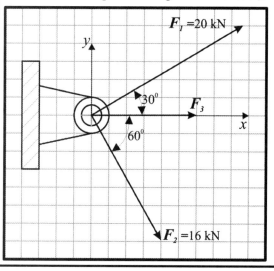

Problem 8

Three forces, F_1, F_2, and F_3, act on a bracket. The magnitude of the resultant force should not exceed 75 kN. Determine the possible values for F_3 .

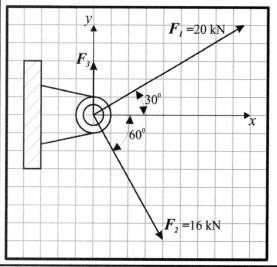

Name: _____

Problem 9

Represent each vector using the Cartesian vector notation. Also, determine the unknown angle.

	Magnitude	Angles		Vector representation
		$\propto$	β	
A	1000 lb		45^0	
B	200 N	120^0		
C	4500 lb		135^0	
D	3 kN	150^0		
E	75 kN	75^0		
F	130 lb		15^0	

Problem 10

Determine magnitude and the direction of each vector. Also, write the unit vectors.

	Vector	Magnitude	Unit vector	Angles	
				$\propto$	β
A	$200\,i + 210\,j$ lb				
B	$3\,i - 4\,j$ kN				
C	$-50i + 60j$ lb				
D	$90\,i + 40\,j$ lb				
E	$-16\,i - 63\,j$ kN				
F	$-110\,i - 600\,j$ lb				

Name: _____

Problem 11

Represent each position vector r_{AB} using the Cartesian vector notation. Also, find their lengths.

	Point A		Point B		Vector representation	Length
	x	**y**	**x**	**y**		
A	0	0	40	30		
B	40	30	0	0		
C	10	-2	5	10		
D	-3	10	5	-5		
E	-3	-22	4	2		
F	9	40	0	0		

Problem 12

Determine the unit and force vectors if a force with a given magnitude is acting along the position vector.

	Position vector (m)	Force magnitude (N)	Unit vector	Force vector (N)
A	$39i + 80j$	100		
B	$33i - 56j$	5		
C	$9i + 40j$	50		
D	$-65i + 72j$	5		
E	$28i + 45j$	1000		
F	$-12i + 35j$	75		

A Side Note

The numerical combinations in problems 10, 11, and 12 use Pythagorean triples. A Pythagorean triple is a set of three positive integers such that the sum of the squares of two integers is equal to the square of the third integer. An easy method for finding the triples is if a and b are integers, then the number set (a^2-b^2, $2ab$, a^2+b^2) form a Pythagorean triple.

Name: _____

Problem 13

A, *B*, *C*, *D*, *E*, and *F* are six position vectors. If a constant force of 1000 lb is acting along each of these position vectors, represent the force vectors F_A, F_B, F_C, F_D, F_E, and F_F using the Cartesian vector notation.

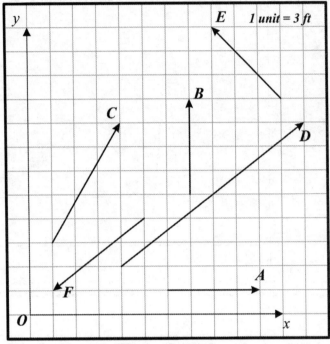

Name: _____

Problem 14

A pole is stabilized in a plane using four cables. The tension in each cable is shown in the figure. Determine the force on the pole due to these four cables. Note that 1 unit = 3 ft.

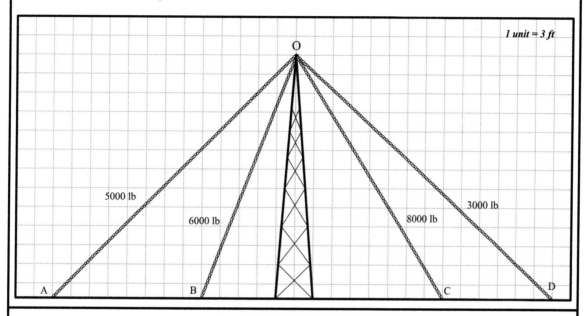

Name: _____

Problem 15

According to Coulomb's law, the magnitude of force exerted between two electric charges q_1 and q_2 is given by $k\dfrac{q_1 q_2}{r^2}$ where r is the distance between the charges and k is Coulomb's constant $\left(k = 9 \text{X} 10^9 \ \text{Nm}^2\text{C}^{-2}\right)$. The force acts along the line connecting the two charges, and is repulsive when both charges are of same sign and attractive when the charges are of opposite signs. Now, four charges are arranged in the form of a square whose side is 1 cm. Determine the force on charge A due to other three electric charges.

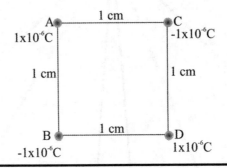

Problem 16

According to Coulomb's law, the magnitude of force exerted between two electric charges q_1 and q_2 is given by $k\dfrac{q_1 q_2}{r^2}$ where r is the distance between the charges and k is Coulomb's constant $\left(k = 9 \times 10^9 \ \text{Nm}^2\text{C}^{-2}\right)$. The force acts along the line connecting the two charges, and is repulsive when both charges are of same sign and attractive when the charges are of opposite signs. Now, three charges are arranged in the form of an equilateral triangle whose side is 1 cm. Determine the force on charge A due to other two electric charges.

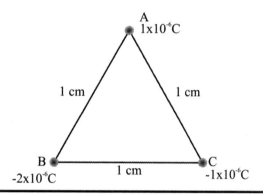

Notes:

2.5. Three-Dimensional Cartesian Vectors

a. Three-dimensional Cartesian vector notation

While two-dimensional sketches, drawings, and vectors usefully simplify problems for analysis, engineers must have the ability to create and work with three-dimensional forms. To show the force interactions in three dimensions, we use a three-dimensional Cartesian coordinate system *xyz* shown in Fig. 26 where the three axes are perpendicular to each other. If you align the fingers of your right hand along x-axis as shown in Fig. 26 and bend them towards y-axis, the thumb points in the direction of the positive z-axis. Orthogonal triad *i, j*, and *k* designate the dimensionless unit vectors along the positive x-, y- and z-axes respectively. A coordinate system that satisfies this criterion is known as a right-handed coordinate system. The relationships in this book are valid for a right-handed coordinate system.

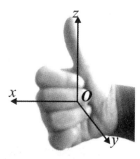

Figure 26. Three-dimensional Cartesian coordinate system and the use of the right hand for identifying the right handed coordinate system

Vector *A* shown in Fig. 27 can be resolved into components $A_x i$, $A_y j$, and $A_z k$ along x-, y- and z-axes. Therefore, we can represent vector *A* as:

$$A = A_x i + A_y j + A_z k \qquad 13$$

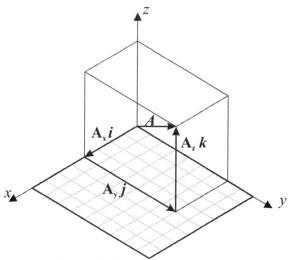

Figure 27. Components of vector *A*

The terms A_x, A_y, and A_z are scalar quantities, and they represent the magnitude of the components. The magnitude of vector *A* is

$$|A| = \sqrt{A_x^2 + A_y^2 + A_z^2} \qquad 14$$

b. Direction cosines

The direction of vector A is defined by angles α, β, and γ as shown in Fig. 28. These angles are measured between the vector and the positive coordinate axes. The magnitude of these angles always lies between 0^0 and 180^0. Using these angles, we can resolve the vector into components:

$$\mathbf{A_x} = |A|\cos\alpha$$
$$\mathbf{A_y} = |A|\cos\beta \qquad\qquad 15$$
$$\mathbf{A_z} = |A|\cos\gamma$$

$\cos\alpha$, $\cos\beta$, and $\cos\gamma$ are known as the direction cosines of vector A. Substituting the components $\mathbf{A_x}$, $\mathbf{A_y}$, and $\mathbf{A_z}$ into $|A| = \sqrt{\mathbf{A_x}^2 + \mathbf{A_y}^2 + \mathbf{A_z}^2}$, we get

$$\cos^2\alpha + \cos^2\beta + \cos^2\gamma = 1 \qquad\qquad 16$$

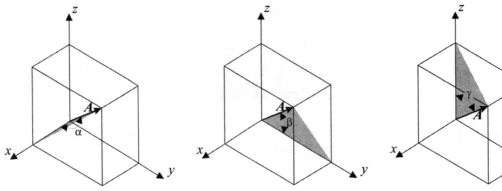

Figure 28. Angles α, β, and γ

c. Vector operations

The Cartesian representation simplifies vector manipulation operations i.e., addition, subtraction, and scaling. The sum $(\boldsymbol{R_1})$ or difference $(\boldsymbol{R_2})$ of two vectors $\boldsymbol{A}\left(=\mathbf{A_x}i + \mathbf{A_y}j + \mathbf{A_z}k\right)$ and $\boldsymbol{B}\left(=\mathbf{B_x}i + \mathbf{B_y}j + \mathbf{B_z}k\right)$ can be found by adding or subtracting the components of the individual vectors.

$$\boldsymbol{R_1} = \left(\mathbf{A_x} + \mathbf{B_x}\right)i + \left(\mathbf{A_y} + \mathbf{B_y}\right)j + \left(\mathbf{A_z} + \mathbf{B_z}\right)k \qquad\qquad 17$$
$$\boldsymbol{R_2} = \left(\mathbf{A_x} - \mathbf{B_x}\right)i + \left(\mathbf{A_y} - \mathbf{B_y}\right)j + \left(\mathbf{A_z} - \mathbf{B_z}\right)k \qquad\qquad 18$$

Vector scaling involves the multiplication of each component of the vector by the scale factor. Scaling vector A by scale factor a (a real number) is

$$a\boldsymbol{A} = a\mathbf{A_x}i + a\mathbf{A_y}j + a\mathbf{A_z}k \qquad\qquad 19$$

d. Unit vector

Unit vector is often used to conveniently represent the direction of the vector. We have seen unit vectors $\boldsymbol{i}$, $\boldsymbol{j}$, and $\boldsymbol{k}$ – vectors with one unit magnitude directed along x-, y-, and z-directions. To obtain unit vector $\boldsymbol{u_A}$ of vector $\boldsymbol{A}$, we divide the vector by its magnitude. As the units of the vector and its magnitude are same, in the division process, they cancel each other out and result in a ***dimensionless*** unit vector.

$$u_A = \frac{A}{|A|}$$
$$= \frac{\mathbf{A_x}}{|A|}i + \frac{\mathbf{A_y}}{|A|}j + \frac{\mathbf{A_z}}{|A|}k$$

$$u_A = \cos\alpha\, i + \cos\beta\, j + \cos\gamma\, k \qquad\qquad 20$$

Thus, we can articulate vector A by defining its magnitude $\left(|A| - \text{a scalar quantity}\right)$ and direction using unit vector $\left(u_A - \text{a dimension less vector quantity}\right)$. Mathematically, vector A is expressed as $A = |A|\,u_A$.

e. Position vector

Using the Cartesian notation, we can represent the position of point A, whose spatial coordinates are (x, y, z), as $\left(r_A = xi + yj + zk\right)$. Vector r_A specifies the position of point A in absolute terms with respect to the origin. If r_A and r_B are two position vectors, then the relative position vector r_{AB} defines the vector from point A to point B (shown in Fig. 29).

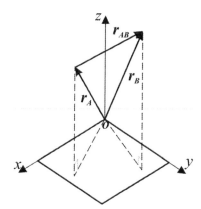

Figure 29. Relative position vector r_{AB}

Mathematically, we can identify the relationship
$$r_B = r_A + r_{AB}$$
Rearranging the terms, we get
$$r_{AB} = r_B - r_A$$
$$r_{AB} = \left(x_B - x_A\right)i + \left(y_B - y_A\right)j + \left(z_B - z_A\right)k \qquad\qquad 21$$

f. Force vectors

To represent three-dimensional forces, we must extend our understanding of two-dimensional Cartesian vector notation. In practice, we often denote the magnitude of the forces as $|F|$. We can write the force vector as
$$F = |F|\,.\,u_{AB} \qquad\qquad 22$$
Now, to represent the force, we are faced with the task of finding its direction i.e., unit vector u_{AB}. If we know angles α, β, and γ, then we can write the unit vector as
$$u_{AB} = \cos\alpha\, i + \cos\beta\, j + \cos\gamma\, k \qquad\qquad 23$$
However, in most situations, it is not practical to directly measure or determine these three angles.

Instead of the angle, in many situations, we know the coordinates of points A and B. In such cases, we can determine the unit vector u_{AB} using the equation
$$u_{AB} = \frac{r_{AB}}{|r_{AB}|} \qquad\qquad 24$$

where $r_{AB} = \left(x_B - x_A\right)i + \left(y_B - y_A\right)j + \left(z_B - z_A\right)k$.

In another common situation, we know angles θ and ϕ. Angle θ locates the plane containing the force vector and the z-axis with respect to the x-axis (refer to Fig. 30). θ is the angle between the force vector and the x-axis in the top view. On the other hand, ϕ is the angle between the force vector and the xy-plane. We can measure ϕ in the plane containing the force vector and the z-axis.

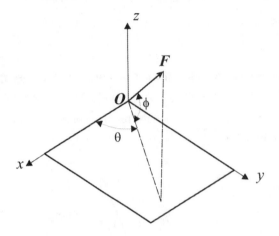

Figure 30. Determining the force vector when angles θ and ϕ are known

A good example of such a situation occurs in the operation of a telescopic boom crane. If we assume the ground to be the xy plane, then the swing cab can rotate the boom in this plane. θ is the angle of boom rotation in the xy plane. The operator can also rotate the boom about its pivot. ϕ is the rotational angle of the boom about the pivot.

Figure 31. Angles θ and ϕ (An animation file "crane.avi" is available on the CD)

In such situations, from geometry, we can determine the force components as

$$\mathbf{F}_x = |F| \cos\phi \cos\theta$$
$$\mathbf{F}_y = |F| \cos\phi \sin\theta \qquad\qquad 25$$
$$\mathbf{F}_z = |F| \sin\phi$$

We can add a number of Cartesian vectors by taking algebraic sums of the individual components of each force vector.

$$R = \sum \mathbf{F}_x\, i + \sum \mathbf{F}_y\, j + \sum \mathbf{F}_z\, k \qquad\qquad 26$$

Spreadsheet "Force Analysis.xls" is available on CD to help solve two- and three-dimensional problems.

Example 8

Using the Cartesian vector notation, represent force vector F. Given force component F_x is whose magnitude is 10 kN. Also, determine the magnitude of force vector F.

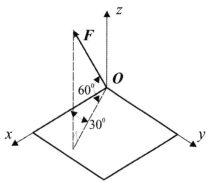

Figure 32. Force vector F whose x-component is 10 kN

From the geometry, we know that

$$F_x = |F| \cos \phi \cos \theta$$

Substituting the values of θ and ϕ, we get

$$F_x = |F| \cos 60. \cos 30 = 10 \text{kN}$$

$$\boxed{|F| = 23.09 \text{ kN}}$$

Now, we can compute the magnitudes of F_y and F_z as

$$F_y = |F| \cos \phi \sin \theta$$

$$F_y = 23.09 \cos 60. \sin 30 \text{ kN}$$

$$F_y = 5.772 \text{ kN}$$

$$F_z = |F| \sin \phi$$

$$F_z = 23.09 \sin 60 \text{ kN}$$

$$F_z = 20 \text{ kN}$$

Force vector F can be represented as

$$\boxed{F = 10\, i + 5.8\, j + 20\, k \text{ kN}}$$

Example 9

A 100 ft tall tower is stabilized in a plane using four cables. The tension in each cable is 1,000 lb. Determine the net force on the pole due to these four cables.

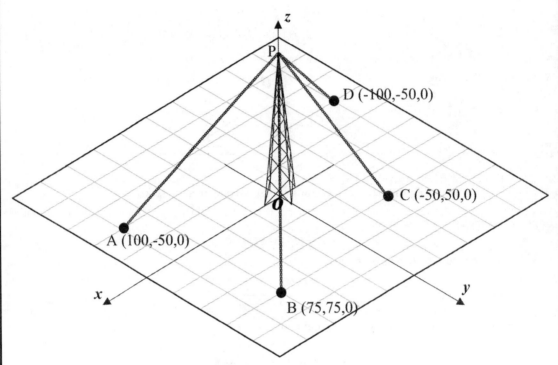

Figure 33. A tower stabilized by four cables

Step I: Determine the unit vectors along PA, PB, PC, and PD directions

Now, we will use the following table to systematically determine the unit vectors along PA, PB, PC, and PD. All four position vectors originate at point P, whose coordinates are (0, 0, 100). The position vector can be determined by using the equation

$$r_{SE} = (x_E - x_S)i + (y_E - y_S)j + (z_E - z_S)k$$

where suffix S is the start point and E is the end point. We can compute the magnitude (distance between the two points in this particular case) using

$$|r| = \sqrt{r_x^2 + r_y^2 + r_z^2}$$

Once we know the position vector and its magnitude, we can find the unit vector (the last column in the table) using

$$u = \frac{r}{|r|}$$

	Start point (P)			End Point			Position vector r	Distance (ft)	Unit vector u
	x	y	z	x	y	z			
PA	0	0	100	100	-50	0	100 i - 50 j - 100 k	150	0.667 i - 0.333 j - 0.667 k
PB	0	0	100	75	75	0	75 i + 75 j - 100 k	145.8	0.514 i + 0.514 j - 0.686 k
PC	0	0	100	-50	50	0	- 50 i + 50 j - 100 k	122.5	-0.408 i + 0.408 j - 0.816 k
PD	0	0	100	-100	-50	0	- 100 i - 50 j - 100 k	150	-0.667 i - 0.33 j - 0.667 k

We can find the force vectors by multiplying the magnitude of the force with the unit vector. The force vectors are

$$F_{PA} = |F_{PA}| \times u_{PA} = 667\,i - 333\,j - 667\,k \text{ lb}$$

$$F_{PA} = |F_{PB}| \times u_{PB} = 514\,i + 514\,j - 686\,k \text{ lb}$$

$$F_{PA} = |F_{PC}| \times u_{PC} = -408\,i + 408\,j - 816\,k \text{ lb}$$

$$F_{PA} = |F_{PD}| \times u_{PD} = -667\,i - 333\,j - 667\,k \text{ lb}$$

We can find the resultant vector by taking algebraic sums of the individual components of the force vectors.

$$R = \sum F_x\, i + \sum F_y\, j + \sum F_z\, k$$

$$\boxed{R = 106\,i + 256\,j - 2836\,k \text{ lb}}$$

2.6. Dot Product or Scalar Product

The dot product or scalar product of two vectors is the product of their magnitudes and the cosine of the angle between them. Note that the angle takes values between 0 and 180^0. For instance,

$$A.B = |A||B|\cos\theta \qquad\qquad 27$$

As all the three multipliers in the product are scalars, this vector operation is known as the scalar product. We can find the dot product between the Cartesian unit vectors (i, j, and k). Because the magnitude of these vectors is one unit, the dot product is equal to the cosine of the angle between the unit vectors of our interest. As $\cos 0^0 = 1 \; and \cos 90^0 = 0$, we get the following important relationships:

$$i.i = j.j = k.k = 1$$
$$i.j = i.k = j.k = 0 \qquad\qquad 28$$

The scalar product follows the commutative and distributive laws. In other words,

$$A.B = B.A$$
$$A.(B+C) = A.B + A.C \qquad\qquad 29$$

The dot product of vectors A and B is

$$A.B = \left(A_x\,i + A_y\,j + A_z\,k\right).\left(B_x\,i + B_y\,j + B_z\,k\right)$$
$$= A_x B_x\,(i.i) + A_x B_y\,(i.j) + A_x B_z\,(i.k)$$
$$+ A_y B_x\,(j.i) + A_y B_y\,(j.j) + A_y B_z\,(j.k)$$
$$+ A_z B_x\,(k.i) + A_z B_y\,(k.j) + A_z B_z\,(k.k)$$
$$A.B = A_x B_x + A_y B_y + A_z B_z \qquad\qquad 30$$

In Statics, the scalar product serves two important functions: (1) computing the angle between two vectors, and (2) determining the component of a vector along a specified direction. The angle between two vectors is given by

$$\cos\theta = \frac{A.B}{|A||B|}$$
$$= \frac{A_x B_x + A_y B_y + A_z B_z}{|A||B|} \qquad\qquad 31$$

Conceptually, *a component is the effectiveness of a given vector along a particular direction*. For instance, Fig. 34 shows the component of vector P along line AA. Component P_{AA} determines the effectiveness of the force along this direction. Note that when the force vector is aligned with line AA $\left(\theta = 0^0\right)$, the component takes the full magnitude of the force vector. At the other extreme, when the force vector is normal to line AA $\left(\theta = 90^0\right)$, the component is zero. Thus, the component of a force is always less than or equal to the magnitude of the force.

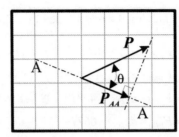

Figure 34. Componet of force vector *P* along line AA

Looking at the geometry, we can find

$$\mathbf{P_{AA}} = |P|\cos\theta \qquad\qquad 32$$

Spreadsheet "Force Analysis.xls" is available on CD to determine the dot product and find the angle between two vectors.

Example 10

Determine the angle between position vector *r* and force vector *F*. Also, find the components of the force along and perpendicular to the position vector.

$$r = i + 2j + 2k \text{ ft}$$
$$F = 200i + 300j + 600k \text{ lb}$$

Before we can find the angle, we must find the magnitudes of the position and force vectors.

$$|r| = \sqrt{r_x^2 + r_y^2 + r_z^2}$$
$$= 3\,\text{ft}$$

$$|F| = \sqrt{F_x^2 + F_y^2 + F_z^2}$$
$$= 700\,\text{lb}$$

Let us now find the angle (θ).

$$\cos\theta = \frac{r.P}{|r||P|}$$
$$= \frac{r_x P_x + r_y P_y + r_z P_z}{|r||P|}$$
$$= \frac{1\times200 + 2\times300 + 2\times600}{3\times700}$$
$$= 0.9524$$
$$\boxed{\theta = 17.75^0}$$

The component along position vector *r* is

$$F_{along\ vector\ r} = |F|\cos\theta$$
$$\boxed{\left|F_{along\ vector\ r}\right| = 666.68\,\text{lb}}$$

We can determine the component perpendicular to the position vector as

$$F_{normal\ to\ vector\ r} = |F|\sin\theta$$
$$\boxed{\left|F_{normal\ to\ r}\right| = 213.4\,\text{lb}}$$

We can represent the component in the vector form as

$$F_{along\ vector\ r} = \left| F_{along\ vector\ r} \right| u_r$$

$$= \left| F_{along\ vector\ r} \right| \frac{r}{|r|}$$

$$= 666.68\ \text{lb} \frac{(i + 2j + 2k)}{3}$$

$$\boxed{F_{along\ vector\ r} = 222.22\,i + 444.44\,j + 444.44\,k\ \text{lb}}$$

The sum of the horizontal and vertical components must be equal to the force vector. We can compute the component normal to the position vector by

$$F_{normal\ to\ vector\ r} = F - F_{along\ vector\ r}$$

$$= \left(200\,i + 300\,j + 600\,k \right)\text{lb} - \left(222.22\,i + 444.44\,j + 444.44\,k \right)\text{lb}$$

$$\boxed{F_{normal\ to\ vector\ r} = -22.22\,i - 144.44\,j + 155.56\,k\ \text{lb}}$$

Notes:

Concept Questions

Name: _____

1. TRUE/FALSE: Angles α, β, and γ that define the direction of a vector are independent of one another.

2. TRUE/FALSE: The coordinate system in the figure is a right-handed coordinate system.

3. The vector shown in the figure is _____ (r_{AB} or r_{BA})

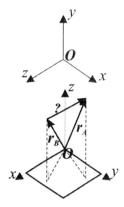

4. The dot product of a vector with itself is equal to _____.

5. The dot product of two vectors is a _____ (scalar/vector).

6. TRUE/FALSE: The dot product of two nonzero vectors can be zero.

7. $(10i \text{ ft}) \bullet (80j \text{ lb}) =$
    A. 0
    B. 800 ft.lb
    C. 800k ft.lb
    D. $-800k$ ft.lb

8. The direction of a vector is $\alpha = 90^0$, $\beta = 0^0$, and $\gamma =$
    A. 0^0
    B. 45^0
    C. 90^0
    D. 180^0

9. The unit vector for the force vector $F = 100i + 100j - 100k$ *lb* is:
    E. $i + j + k$
    F. $i + j - k$
    G. $\frac{1}{\sqrt{2}}i + \frac{1}{\sqrt{2}}j - \frac{1}{\sqrt{2}}k$
    H. $\frac{1}{\sqrt{3}}i + \frac{1}{\sqrt{3}}j - \frac{1}{\sqrt{3}}k$

10. A 1000 lb force is acting from point A (1, 1, 1) to B (4, 1, 5). The vector representation of the force is:
    A. $1000(3i + 4k)$ lb
    B. $1000(-3i - 4k)$ lb
    C. $200(3i + 4k)$ lb
    D. $200(-3i - 4k)$ lb

Name: _____

Problem 1

Represent each vector using the Cartesian vector notation. Also, determine the unknown angle.

	Magnitude	Angles			Vector representation
		$\propto$	β	γ	
A	1000 lb	45^0	45^0		
B	200 N	120^0		60^0	
C	4500 lb		135^0	60^0	
D	3 kN	150^0	60^0		
E	75 kN	75^0		150^0	
F [*]	130 lb		15^0	120^0	[*] Can you pick two of the three angles arbitrarily?

Problem 2

Determine magnitude and the direction of each vector. Also, write the unit vectors.

	Vector	Magnitude	Unit vector	Angles		
				$\propto$	β	γ
A	$100\,i + 200\,j - 200\,k$ lb					
B	$6\,i - 2\,j + 9\,k$ kN					
C	$-20\,i + 30\,j - 60\,k$ lb					
D	$600i + 700j - 600\,k$ lb					
E	$-70\,i - 40\,j - 40\,k$ kN					
F	$-100\,i - 400\,j - 800\,k$ lb					

Name: _____

Problem 3

Represent each position vector r_{AB} using the Cartesian vector notation. Also, find their lengths.

	Point A			Point B			Vector representation	Length
	x	**y**	**z**	**x**	**y**	**z**		
A	0	0	0	2	–1	2		
B	200	100	-200	0	-200	400		
C	400	-500	-200	0	200	200		
D	0	200	600	100	-200	-200		
E	30	50	–30	–30	–20	30		
F	4	5	5	2	–1	–4		

Problem 4

Determine the unit and force vectors if a force with a given magnitude is acting along the position vector.

	Position vector (m)	Force magnitude (N)	Unit vector	Force vector (N)
A	$60\,i + 70\,j + 60\,k$	750		
B	$i - 2\,j + 2\,k$	400		
C	$9\,i + 2\,j + 6\,k$	1,250		
D	$-8\,i + 4\,j + 1\,k$	5		
E	$8\,i + 36\,j + 3\,k$	100		
F	$-40\,i + 70\,j + 40\,k$	10,000		

A Side Note

The numerical combinations in problems 2, 3, and 4 use Pythagorean quadruples. A Pythagorean quadruple is a set of four positive integers such that the sum of the squares of three integers is equal to the square of the fourth integer.

Name: _____

Problem 5

Using the Cartesian vector notation, represent the position vector r_A whose magnitude is 4 ft.

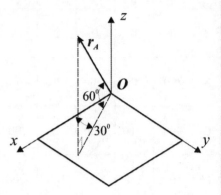

Problem 6

Using the Cartesian vector notation, represent the force vector F whose magnitude is 10 kN.

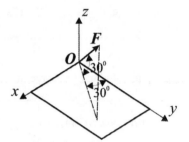

Problem 7

Using the Cartesian vector notation, represent the force vector F. Given force component F_z is whose magnitude is 10 kN.

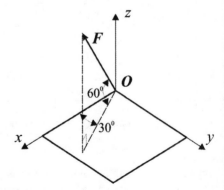

Name: _____

Problem 8

A 15 m tall tower is stabilized in a plane using four cables. The tension in each cable is 10 kN. Determine the net force on the pole due to these four cables.

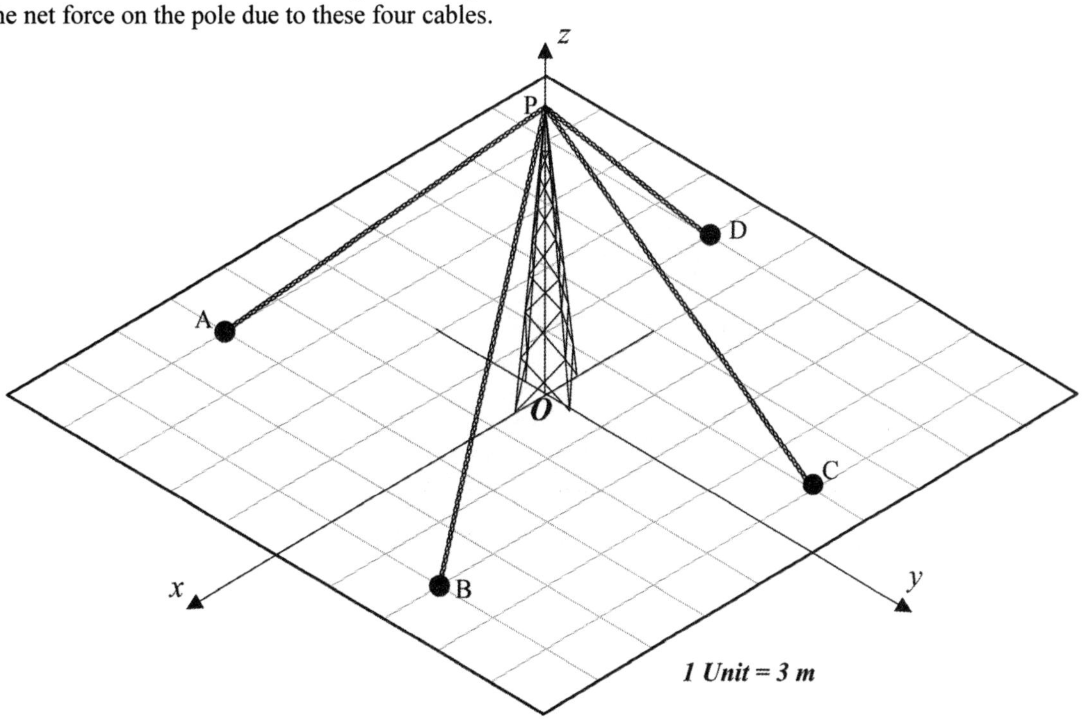

1 Unit = 3 m

Name: _____

Problem 9

A trapdoor hinged on one side is held by two cables as shown. The tension in each cable is 70 lb. Determine the net force applied at the hook.

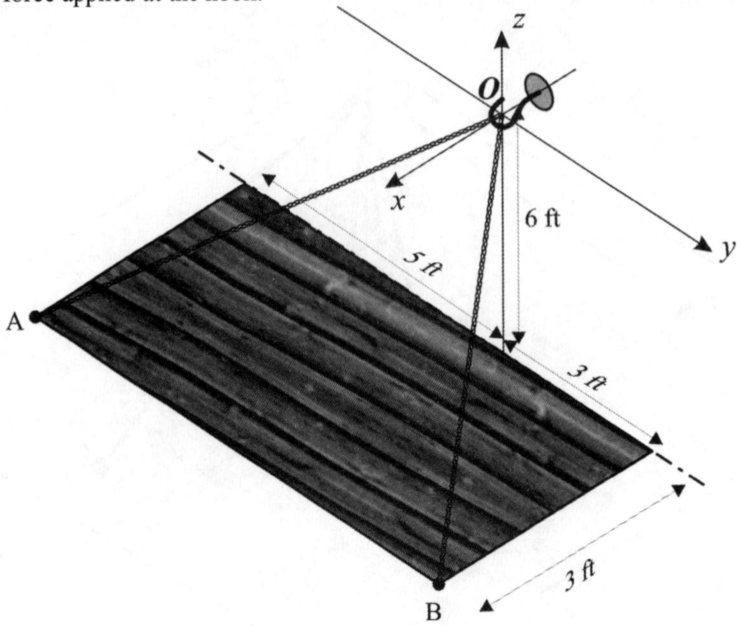

Name: _____

Problem 10

The tension in each tether is 200 lb. Determine the total force applied on the ring. Assume that points A, B, and C are equally spaced.

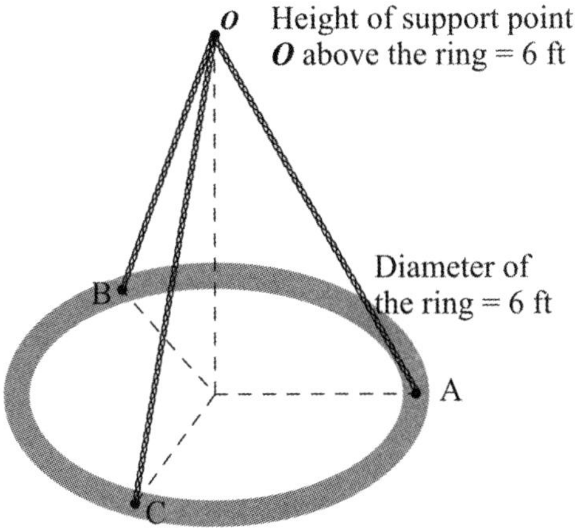

O   Height of support point
O above the ring = 6 ft

Diameter of
the ring = 6 ft

B

A

C

Name: _____

Problem 11

According to Coulomb's law, the force exerted between two electric charges q_1 and q_2 is given by $k\dfrac{q_1 q_2}{r^2}$ where r is the distance between the charges and k is Coulomb's constant $\left(k = 9\text{X}10^9 \ \text{Nm}^2\text{C}^{-2}\right)$. The force acts along the line connecting the two charges, and is repulsive when both charges are of same sign and attractive when the charges are of opposite signs. Now, eight charges are arranged in the form of a cube whose side is 1 cm. Determine the force on charge A due to other seven electric charges.

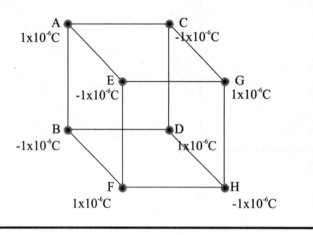

Name: _____

Problem 12

Draw force vector F and position vector r. Determine the angle between the two vectors and the components of the force along and perpendicular to the position vector using the dot product or the scalar product concept. Verify the result from the graph.

$$F = 100\,i + 50\,j \text{ lb}$$

$$r = 3\,i + 9\,j \text{ ft}$$

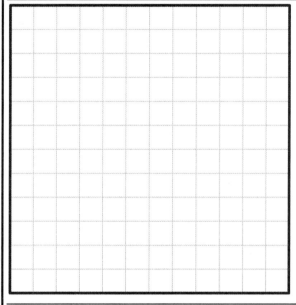

Problem 13

Draw force vector F and position vector r. Determine the angle between the two vectors and the components of the force along and perpendicular to the position vector using the dot product or the scalar product concept. Verify the result from the graph.

$$F = 3\,i + 10\,j \text{ kN}$$

$$r = 50\,i + 50\,j \text{ m}$$

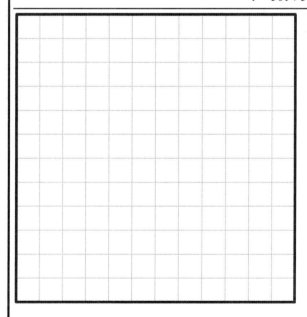

Name:_____

Problem 14

Determine the angle between the two vectors and the component of the force along the position vector using the dot product concept.

$$F = 3i + 10j - 10k \text{ kN}$$
$$r = 50i + 50j - 100k \text{ m}$$

Problem 15

A plane is ascending in a direction given by 40^0 to the x-axis, 70^0 to the y-axis. The thrust vector is given by $2500\,i + 3000\,j + 6000\,k$ lb. Determine the component of the thrust vector along the direction of ascent. Also, determine the angle between the thrust vector and the heading direction of the plane.

1. Determine the unit vector that describes the direction of the plane.

2. Determine the component of the thrust vector along the direction of ascent by taking a dot product.

3. Determine the angle between the thrust vector and the ascent direction.

Name: _____

Problem 16

Find the components of force **F** along and perpendicular to structural member OA.

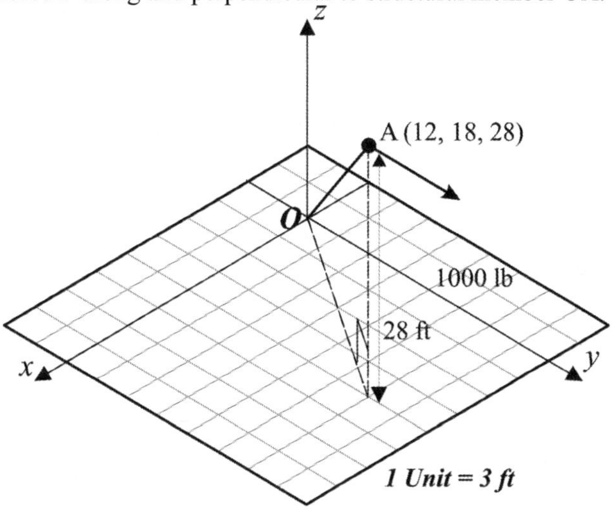

Name: _____

Problem 17

Compute the component of force *F* along to structural member AB, AC and AD.

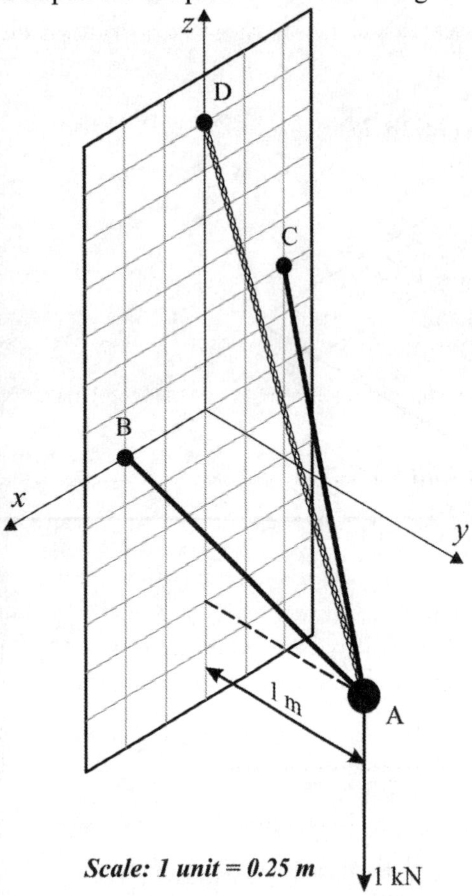

Scale: 1 unit = 0.25 m

1 m

1 kN

CHAPTER III
EQUILIBRIUM OF A PARTICLE

Learning Objectives:

The material presented in this chapter will enable you to accomplish the following:
1. Distinguish series from parallel spring arrangements.
2. Compute the effective spring rate.
3. Distinguish equilibrium from static equilibrium.
4. Determine the magnitude and direction of frictional forces.
5. Draw free-body diagrams of particles and rigid bodies subjected to pure translation.
6. Identify statically determinate and indeterminate systems.
7. Apply the equilibrium equations to analyze one-, two-, and three-dimensional systems.

Undersea Remotely Operated Vehicles

Remotely operated vehicles (ROVs) are used extensively in deep-water applications in which maintaining a human diver for any length of time is cost prohibitive. A typical ROV (shown in Fig. 1) is controlled and powered from the surface through a tether. The design of the tether is an interesting challenge because the teams working on other subsystems raise conflicting demands upon the tether designers.

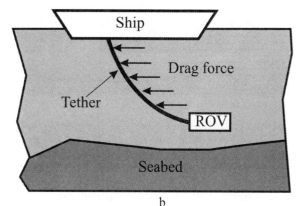

a   b

Figure 1. a. Remotely operated vehicle system, Photo courtesy - Santa Clara University
b. Schematic of the ROV system

The tether is the lifeline of the ROV: it transfers energy for navigation and control signals to the vehicle, and transmits visual information to the mother ship. This information and energy transfer is crucial for successful operation. The tether is neutrally buoyant to reduce the gravitational forces on the ROV. However, the drag force acting on the tether due to ocean currents could be significant, requiring the ROV to continuously resist it. As a result, the tether is not only a lifeline, but also a burden on the ROV's limited resources. These considerations result in three functions in the tether design task: "transfer energy," "transfer information" and "reduce drag force."

To satisfy these functions, the tether design team can modify several key variables; for example, the cable diameter and length. A short cable with a large diameter is preferred for effective power transmission because it reduces power losses and voltage drop. Such a cable also increases the communication bandwidth and rate. The initial task requirements usually establish a lower bound for the length, leaving the designer with more freedom to change the diameter. However, an increase in diameter affects the drag force, which in turn increases the power requirement. Thus, this system design is limited to applications where the drag force is low.

An innovation system layout uses an additional weight in the form of a cage (launcher) to the tether. The ROV is lifted and lowered using the cage. The cage acts as an anchor or a stabilizer. As a consequence, the ROV does not experience the high drag force on the tether. Therefore, the cable diameter between the ship and the cage has no impact on the ROV. The length of the cable from the cage to the ROV is short and therefore, imposes very little drag force.

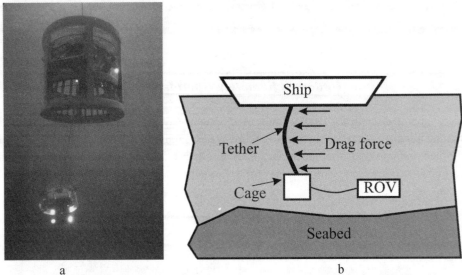

a

b

Figure 2. a. Remotely operated vehicle system with a cage, Photo courtesy: NOAA
b. Schematic of the ROV system with a cage

In this system design, the ROV can be viewed as a particle. The load on the ROV without the cage due to ocean currents is eliminated by reconfiguring the system. Such an intelligent system design requires a fundamental under of the equilibrium of particle.

3.1. Equilibrium and Static Equilibrium

A *particle* idealizes a body by placing its mass at its center and neglecting its physical size. In other words, a particle has mass, but negligible size. *A particle is in equilibrium when the resultant force acting on the particle is equal to zero.* In other words, the sum of all forces acting on the particle must be equal to zero. Thus, the *equilibrium equation* for a particle is given by

$$\sum F = 0 \qquad\qquad 1$$

According to Newton's second law $\left(F = \mathbf{m}a\right)$, when there is no net force acting on a particle, its acceleration will be zero. This condition ensures that the body continues to be in a state-of-rest or constant velocity.

Forces on an Airplane

Four forces – thrust, drag, lift, and weight – act on an airplane in a straight flight. Thrust generated from the engine is designed to overcome the drag caused by wind resistance. The lift created by the wings counteracts the weight incurred by gravity. When thrust is equal to drag, the airplane will continue at a constant velocity and does not experience any acceleration or deceleration. Similarly, when the lift-weight pairing is in balance (lift = weight), the airplane experiences a level flight. The airplane can be viewed as a particle in equilibrium.

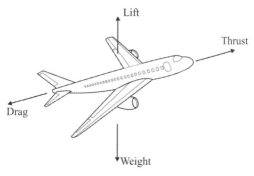

Figure 3. Forces acting on an airplane

Often, in Statics we use the term *static equilibrium* to describe an object that is at rest. For such a body, the forces acting on it satisfy the equilibrium equation. The term *static* simply means at rest or stationary. Thus, the airplane discussed is in equilibrium and not static equilibrium because it is not in a state of rest. On the other hand, we consider most structures such as bridges to be in static equilibrium. Before discussing the equilibrium of a particle, let us first review the fundamental concepts of springs, which are very useful in structural analysis.

3.2. Springs

A spring is an elastic element which deforms under the action of forces. Springs come in various shapes and sizes. Even seemingly rigid structural elements (such as columns and beams) can be considered springs as they deform (to a much lesser extent) under the action of forces. For the ease of sketching, the schematic shown in Fig. 4 is commonly used to denote a spring.

Figure 4. A schematic of a spring

When a tensile (pulling) force is applied, a spring stretches or extends. On the other hand, a compressive (squeezing) force decreases the length. When the spring is unloaded, it returns to its original length (see Fig. 5). This property of returning to its original shape is known as elasticity. A spring that returns to its original shape is an elastic spring.

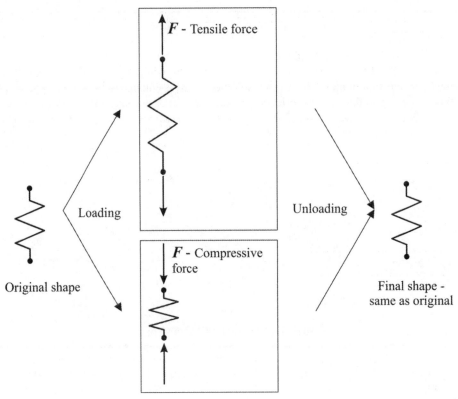

Figure 5. The process of loading and unloading a spring

The spring rate or spring constant defines the stiffness of a spring. It is the slope of the force versus the deflection curve. A linear spring has a constant slope. For example, the force vs. deflection diagram shown in Fig. 6 is a straight line. Force F is linearly proportional to deflection δ and therefore, it characterizes a linear spring.

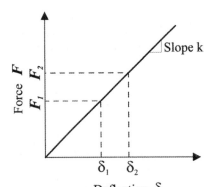

Deflection δ
Figure 6. Force versus deflection curve for a linear spring

The slope of the force-deflection diagram provides the stiffness of the spring. For extension and compression springs, obtain the spring rate (k) by dividing the applied force (ΔF) by the deflection ($\Delta \delta$).

$$k = \frac{\Delta F}{\Delta \delta} = \frac{F_2 - F_1}{\delta_2 - \delta_1} \qquad 2$$

The spring rate uses the units N/m or lb/in. A stiff spring has a high spring constant and requires larger force per unit deflection compared to a flexible spring.

Springs can be arranged in a series or in parallel or in a combination of series and parallel arrangements. In a parallel arrangement, the force is shared between the springs. For instance, the two springs in Fig 7 share force F. In the parallel arrangement, the deflections are the same for all the springs. The effective spring constant for a parallel arrangement is given by

$$k_{eff} = k_1 + k_2 + \cdots \qquad\qquad 3$$

When springs act in parallel, the assembly becomes stiffer and, therefore, the effective spring constant is larger than the individual spring constants. One can use this property to qualitatively verify the numerical calculations.

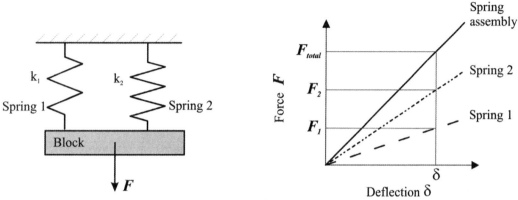

Figure 7. A parallel spring assembly

In a series arrangement, the individual springs experience the same force. Both springs in the spring assembly (see Fig. 8) experience the same force F. The total deflection (δ) is equal to the sum of individual spring deflections.

$$\delta = \delta_1 + \delta_2 + \cdots \qquad\qquad 4$$

The effective or equivalent spring constant $\left(k_{eff}\right)$ for the spring assembly can be computed using

$$\frac{1}{k_{eff}} = \frac{1}{k_1} + \frac{1}{k_2} + \cdots \qquad\qquad 5$$

As a quick qualitative check, the numerical calculations are correct if the effective spring constant k_{eff} is smaller than the spring constants of the individual springs.

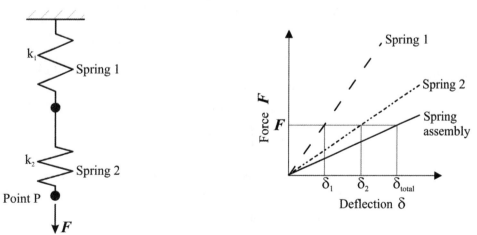

Figure 8. A series spring assembly

3.3. The Free Body Diagram

The free body diagram is a very powerful, yet simple, tool to show the forces acting on a body and allow for the application of the equilibrium equation. It is a sketch showing only the body of our interest, isolated from its surroundings, while capturing all the forces acting on it. Drawing a free body diagram takes four steps:

1. *Sketch the overall shape:* Draw the object removed or isolated from its surroundings. When analyzing the equilibrium of a particle, the overall shape is not important. However, this chapter also deals with rigid bodies (which do not change shape under the action of forces) that experience only translation. All particles in a rigid body subjected to pure translation undergo the same displacement. The equilibrium concepts of a particle extend to such rigid bodies. When dealing with rigid bodies, try to capture the overall shape without focusing on details.
2. *Show ALL forces:* Pencil in all the forces acting on the body. Represent the body forces at its center. Remember that the supports or constraints that prevent motion offer resisting forces at the interface. Use the proper direction if the direction of the force is given or known by physical reasoning.
3. *Label each force:* Identify each known force with its magnitude and unknown forces with a consistent lettering scheme.
4. *Specify characteristic dimensions:* Specify the dimensions that aid in the resolution of force vectors.

This technique for sketching a free body diagram focuses the attention on forces and important geometric information while removing superficial issues from consideration. It is useful in the analysis of one-, two-, and three-dimensional systems of forces.

Example 1
Draw the free-body diagrams for the block and knot A.

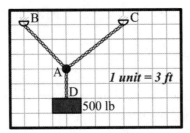

Figure 9. A load supported by two cables

    Two forces act on the block: the weight of the block which pulls it down and the force exerted by the cable, which holds the block up. Fig. 10 shows the free-body diagram for the block. The weight is applied at the center and F_{DA} is applied at the point where the cable attaches to the block. In this one-dimensional case, the dimensions are not important.

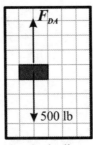

Figure 10. The free-body diagram for the block

Three forces act on the knot: F_{AB}, F_{AC}, and F_{AD} as shown in the free-diagram. F_{AD} tries to pull the knot down. F_{AB} and F_{AC} also try to pull the knot to keep it in its position. Therefore, all the three forces are pointed away from the knot. From the geometry, we can calculate the characteristic dimensions $\left(\tan^{-1}(1) = 45^0 \text{ and } \tan^{-1}\left(\frac{3}{4}\right) = 36.87^0 \right)$.

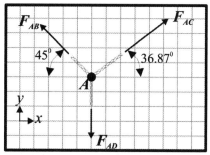

Figure 11. The free-body diagram for knot A

3.4. One-Dimensional Systems in Equilibrium

Let us suppose that a particle is subjected to a set of forces along a single direction. By orienting the x-axis along this direction, we can write the force equilibrium equation as

$$\sum F = \left(\sum F_x \right) i = 0 \qquad 6$$

or simply in its scalar form

$$\sum F_x = 0 \qquad 7$$

Systems in equilibrium can be classified into statically determinate and statically indeterminate structures. To analyze a statically determinate system, we draw the free-body diagram and then apply the equilibrium equation $\left(\sum F_x = 0 \text{ in this particular case} \right)$. Statically determinate structures are easier to design and analyze. For instance, consider the spring assembly shown in Fig. 12a. By drawing the free-body of the assembly (refer to Fig. 12b) and applying the equilibrium equation, we can determine that the reaction at the fixed end (R) is equal to the applied force and acts in the opposite direction. By applying the equilibrium equations to the free-body diagrams of springs 1 and 2 (see Fig. 12c and d), we can determine the internal force acting between the two springs. Note that force F_{12} acts in the opposite direction on springs 1 and 2, in accordance with Newton's third law. Because one can solve for the unknown forces using the equilibrium equation alone, this assembly is a statically determinate structure.

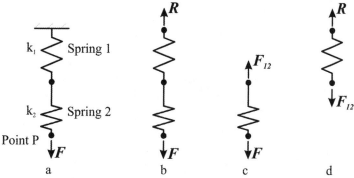

Figure 12. A series spring assembly – an example of statically determinate structure

Example 2

Determine the tension in each cable.

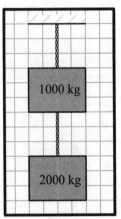

Figure 13. Two masses connected by cables

To determine the tension, we must draw the free-body diagrams. One possible solution is to draw free-body diagrams for the individual masses. Note that 1000 kg = 9.81 kN.

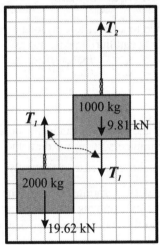

Figure 14. The free-body diagrams for blocks 1 and 2

Now, let us write the equilibrium equation for the 2000 kg mass, as the equation has only one unknown quantity. We get

$$\sum F = T_1 - 19.62\,\text{kN} = 0$$

$$T_1 = 19.62\,\text{kN}$$

Note that the same T_1 appears on the second mass, but acts in the opposite direction. Physically, the cable pulls 1000 kg mass down and therefore, the vector is pointed in the downward direction. It is also consistent with Newton's third law regarding equal and opposite action-reaction pairs. We can find the tension in the second cable by writing the equilibrium equation for the 1000 kg mass.

$$\sum F = T_2 - T_1 - 9.81\,\text{kN} = 0$$

$$T_2 = T_1 + 9.81\,\text{kN} = 29.43\,\text{kN}$$

Alternatively, we can determine the tension in the cable by drawing the free-body diagram for the two masses together and applying the equilibrium equation.

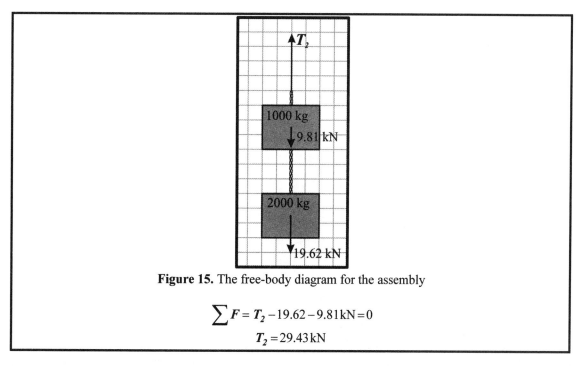

Figure 15. The free-body diagram for the assembly

$$\sum F = T_2 - 19.62 - 9.81\,\text{kN} = 0$$
$$T_2 = 29.43\,\text{kN}$$

Statically indeterminate structures require the consideration of both the equilibrium equation and the deformations to determine the internal forces and reactions. A good example is a parallel spring assembly (see Fig. 16). If the block is guided so that it moves vertically down under the action of applied force, the displacement of the two springs will be equal. The equilibrium equation yields $F_1 + F_2 = F$ with two unknown forces. To solve for the unknown forces, we need to know the stiffness of the springs.

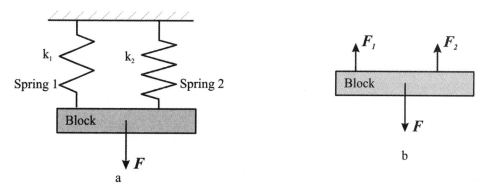

Figure 16. A parallel spring assembly – an example of statically indeterminate structure

Solving a statically indeterminate structure takes four steps:
1. Apply the equilibrium equations;
2. Establish geometric compatibility;
3. Relate forces and deformations; and
4. Solve for the unknown forces.
The following example illustrates these steps in detail.

Example 3

Force F is applied on a spring assembly at node A. The spring constants $k_1 = 1$ kN/m and $k_2 = 1.5$ kN/m. If the magnitude of F is 500 N, determine the force in each spring and the deflection of node A.

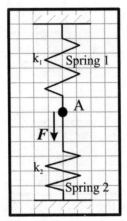

Figure 17. Spring assembly

Step I: *Apply the equilibrium equations*

First, let us draw a free body diagram of node A where the known force F and two unknown spring forces are applied. Force F tends to displace node A in the downward direction. Therefore, spring 1 pulls node A up, whereas spring 2 pushes node A in the same upward direction (see Fig. 18). Now, applying the equilibrium equation, we get

$$F_1 + F_2 - F = 0$$
$$F = F_1 + F_2$$

With two unknown quantities and only one equation, we cannot solve the unknown internal forces. Therefore, the spring assembly is a statically indeterminate structure.

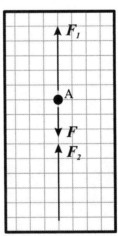

Figure 18. The free-body diagram of node A

Step II: *Establish geometric compatibility*

In this step, we look at the required geometric compatibility at node A. One can easily notice that the extension or stretch of spring 1 (δ_1) is equal to the compression of spring 2 (δ_2). Therefore, we can write the geometric compatibility as

$$\delta_1 = \delta_2$$

Step III: *Relate forces and deformations*

The two force deformation equations are

$$F_1 = k_1\delta_1$$
$$F_2 = k_2\delta_2$$

Step IV: *Solve for the unknown forces*
Substituting $\delta_1 = \delta_2$ into the force-deformation relationships, we get

$$F_1 = k_1\delta_1$$
$$F_2 = k_2\delta_1$$

Substituting this result into the equilibrium equation $\left(F = F_1 + F_2\right)$ (step 1), we get

$$F = F_1 + F_2$$
$$F = k_1\delta_1 + k_2\delta_1$$
$$F = \left(k_1 + k_2\right)\delta_1$$

Substituting the values of F, k_1, and k_2, we get

$$\boxed{\delta_1 = 0.2\,m}$$

$$\boxed{\begin{aligned}F_1 &= k_1\delta_1 = 200\,\text{N} \\ F_2 &= k_2\delta_1 = 300\,\text{N}\end{aligned}}$$

The results make sense because the sum of the two forces is equal to the applied force, and the stiffer spring is carrying more load (because its deflection is the same as that of the weaker spring).

Notes:

Notes:

Concept Questions

Name: _____

1. TRUE/FALSE: An airplane flying at constant speed at a certain altitude is in a state of static equilibrium.

2. TRUE/FALSE: The units of spring rate are N/m or lb/in.

3. TRUE/FALSE: A stiff spring requires less force to deflect than a flexible spring does.

4. TRUE/FALSE: Objects that return to their original shapes when unloaded are referred to as elastic.

5. TRUE/FALSE: In a series spring arrangement, the forces experienced by the individual springs are the same.

6. TRUE/FALSE: In a series spring arrangement, the displacements experienced by the individual springs are the same.

7. Two springs with spring rates 10 kN/m and 20 kN/m are arranged in parallel. The effective spring rate is
    a. less than 10 kN/m
    b. greater than 20 kN/m
    c. between 10 and 20 kN/m

8. Two springs with spring rates 10 kN/m and 20 kN/m are arranged in series. The effective spring rate is
    a. less than 10 kN/m
    b. greater than 20 kN/m
    c. between 10 and 20 kN/m

9. What is a particle?

10. What is a linear spring?

11. Determine the magnitude of force pairs acting between the blocks.

$F_1 =$ _____

$F_2 =$ _____

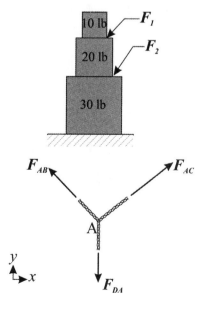

12. Identify two mistakes in the following free-body diagram.

13. For a parallel spring arrangement, write the effective spring constant in terms of the individual spring constants, k_1, k_2, k_3,....

14. The effective spring constant for the spring assembly is given by

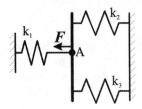

A. $k_1 + \dfrac{k_2 k_3}{k_2 + k_3}$

B. $\dfrac{k_1(k_2 + k_3)}{k_1 + k_2 + k_3}$

C. $k_1 + k_2 + k_3$

D. None of the above

15. Assume that the vertical link moves in the horizontal direction without rotation. The spring assembly in is:

a. a series spring assembly
b. a parallel spring assembly
c. a combination of series and parallel arrangement
d. none of the above

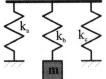

16. TRUE/FALSE: Statically determinate structures require the consideration of both the equilibrium equations and the deformation to determine the internal forces and reactions.

17. TRUE/FALSE: Assume that the horizontal link moves in the vertical direction without rotation. The springs in the spring assembly are in parallel.

18. TRUE/FALSE: The spring assembly is a statically determinate structure.

19. Draw the free body diagram for the two blocks. **W1** and **W2** are the weights of the blocks.

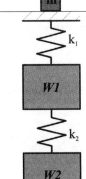

20. For the spring whose force vs. deflection diagram is shown in the adjacent figure, the spring constant is:

    a. zero
    b. can't be determined
    c. 50 kN/cm
    d. infinite

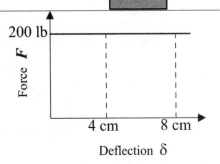

Name: _____

Problem 1

In the stunt act of a human pyramid, circus artists form a pyramid. Each person stands on two others and distributes one-half of the weight to the people below. If w is the weight of each artist, identify the person carrying the maximum weight and determine the amount of that weight. (Hint: Start drawing the free-body diagram for each person.)

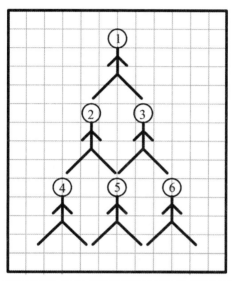

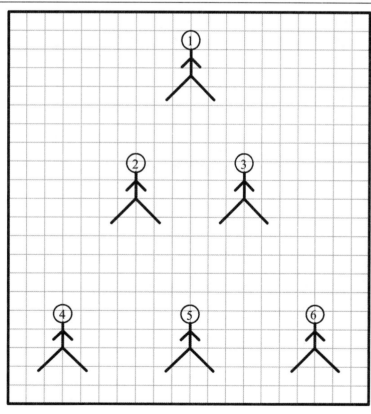

Problem 2

Determine the load carried by the nut in case A and case B. Assume the weight of the support rod is negligible when compared to the weights.

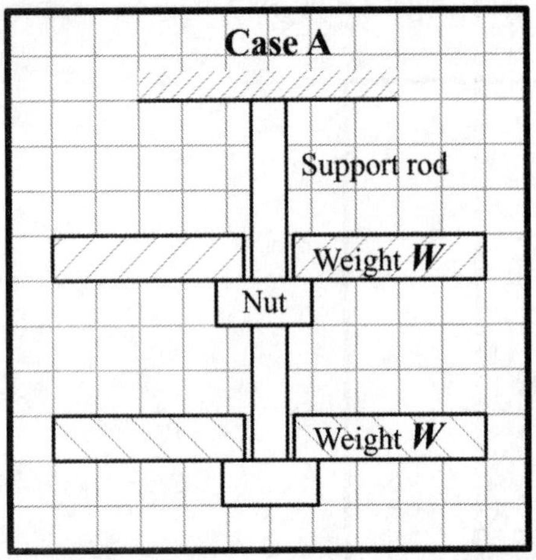

Case A

Support rod

Weight *W*

Nut

Weight *W*

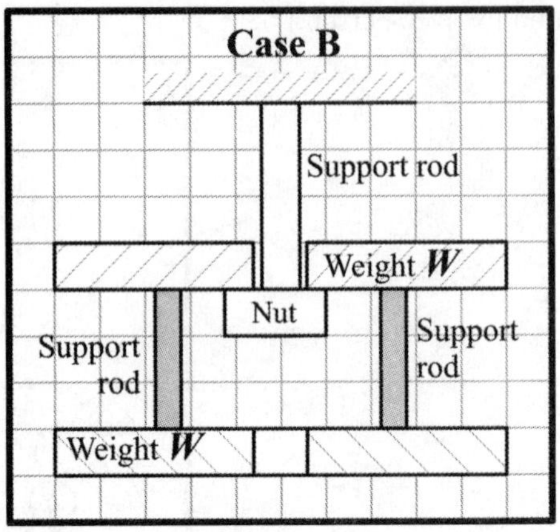

Case B

Support rod

Weight *W*

Nut

Support rod

Support rod

Weight *W*

Name: _____

Problem 3

Determine the deflection of each spring and the total deflection if the spring constants k_1 = 100 lb/in and k_2 = 200 lb/in.

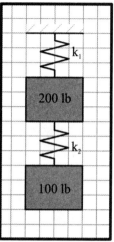

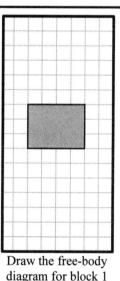

Draw the free-body diagram for block 1 (100lb block)

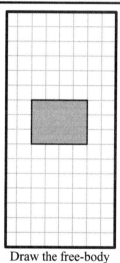

Draw the free-body diagram for block 2 (200lb block)

Name: _____

Problem 4

A mass is suspended by four springs with spring constants $k_a = 100$ lb/in, $k_b = 150$ lb/in, $k_c = 150$ lb/in, and $k_d = 100$ lb/in. The original (unstretched) lengths of springs are equal. The mass remains horizontal due to symmetry of loading. Determine the force in each spring.

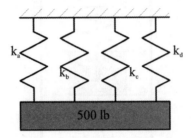

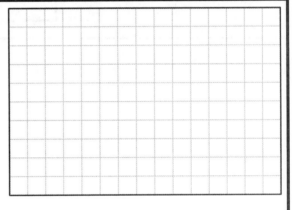

Hint: Due to symmetry, the force in springs A and D are equal, and the forces in spring B and C are equal. The equilibrium equation has two unknown forces. To solve these two unknowns, use the spring equation $F = kx$, where x is same for all the springs.

The results make sense only if the force carried by the stiffer springs is greater.

Name: _____

Problem 5

A mass is suspended by a spring assembly. If spring constants $k_a = 1$ kN/cm, $k_b = 2$kN/cm, $k_c = 1$ kN/cm, $m = 1000$ kg, determine the force in each spring. The rigid rod remains horizontal due to symmetry of loading. Also determine the deflection of mass **m**.

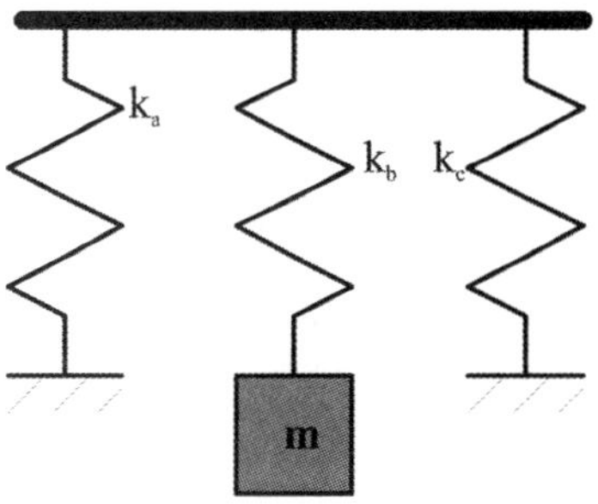

Name: _____

Problem 6

Force F = 550 lb is applied on a spring assembly at node A. The spring constants k_1 = 1000 lb/in, k_2 = 2000 lb/in, and k_3 = 3000 lb/in. Determine the force in each spring and the deflections of nodes A and B.

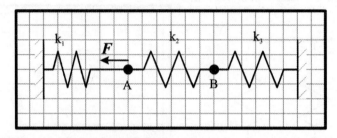

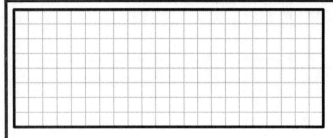

Name:

Problem 7

Determine the force in each spring and the deflection of node A.

F = 2.2 kN, k_1 = 1 kN/cm, k_2 = 2 kN/cm, and k_3 = 3 kN/cm.

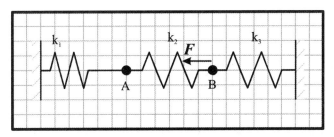

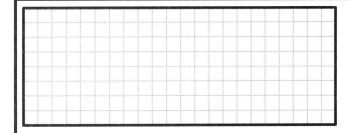

Name: _____

Problem 8

Determine the force in each spring and the deflection of node A.

F = 10,000 lb, k_1 = 5000 lb/in, k_2 = 10,000 lb/in, and k_3 = 10,000 lb/in.

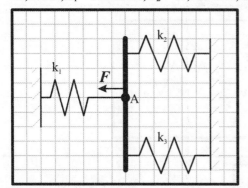 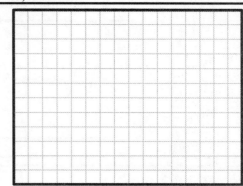

Problem 9

Two concentric springs are nested to form a spring assembly. Force F is applied to the top plate, while the bottom plate is fixed. Determine the deflection of the individual springs if F = 4000 lb, k_1 = 3000 lb/in, k_2 = 2000 lb/in, l_1 = 4.5 in, and l_2 = 4 in.

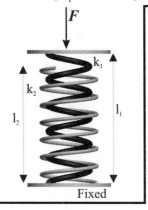

Fixed

Name: _____

Problem 10

Draw the force vs deflection diagram for the spring assembly.

$k_1 = 1\,\text{kN/m}$, $k_2 = 0.5\,\text{kN/m}$, $l_1 = 2$ m, and $l_2 = 1.75$ m.

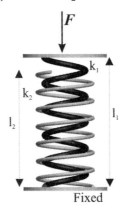

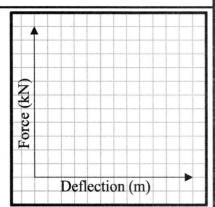

Notes:

The Collapse of the Kansas City Hyatt Regency Walkway

The collapse of the Kansas City Hyatt Regency Walkway illustrates the impact of a simple mistake in determining the forces in a one-dimensional system. The walkway that collapsed connected the second and the fourth floors across a multistoried atrium. In the original design, the second and fourth floor walkways were suspended with a set of steel tie-rods, as shown in Fig. 19a. A major design change was introduced during construction. Due to this change, the second floor was suspended from the fourth floor, as shown in Fig. 19b. The nut that was originally designed to take the load of one floor then had to carry the load of two floors (similar to Problem 2). On July 17, 1981, during a tea dance contest, the two walkways collapsed (refer to Fig. 20), killing more than one hundred people.

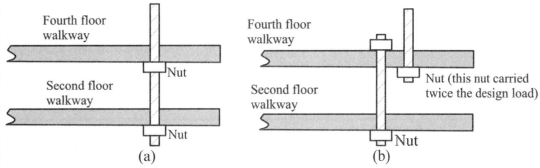

Figure 19. (a) Original design (b) modified design

Figure 20. Images of the collapsed Kansas City Hyatt Regency Walkways
Photo Courtesy - Dr. Lee Lowery, Jr., P.E.

3.5. Two-Dimensional Systems in Equilibrium

We can extend the concept of equilibrium from one- to two-dimensional systems. Suppose a particle is subjected to a set of forces in a single plane. We can orient the xy-plane in such a way that the forces lie on it. Using the Cartesian notion, we can represent each force. Then, we can write the equilibrium equation as

$$\sum F = \left(\sum F_x\right) i + \left(\sum F_y\right) j = 0 \quad . \qquad 8$$

or simply in its scalar form:

$$\sum F_x = 0$$
$$\sum F_y = 0$$

9

To analyze such a system, we need to do the following:

1. **Draw the free-body diagram**. This step involves isolating an appropriate part of or the entire system from the surrounding environment. The goal while selecting the part is to capture the forces that need to be determined. Determining an appropriate part to isolate for drawing a free-body diagram is a skill that you will develop as you practice solving different types of problems. Then, we must establish the coordinate system. While establishing the coordinate system is often trivial, an intelligent choice of the coordinate system in complex problems can greatly simplify the solution procedure. We must identify and label all known and unknown forces. The direction for the unknown forces is assumed. Finally, we must specify characteristic dimensions to aid in the resolution of force vectors.

2. **Apply the equilibrium equations** $\left(\sum F_x = 0 \text{ and } \sum F_y = 0 \text{ in this particular case} \right)$. Solve for unknown forces. When we solve the equations, if the unknown force comes out to be negative, then the assumed direction is reversed to identify the proper direction.

Example 4

A weight is suspended using three cables. Determine the tension in each cable.

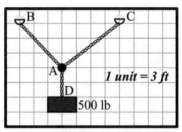

Figure 21. A weight suspended by three cables

Step 1: Draw the free-body diagram

If we draw a free-body diagram for node A where the three cables join, we can determine the tension in each cable. We can establish the x-axis along the horizontal direction and y-axis along the vertical direction. Then, we identify the three forces (tensions in the three cables) as F_{AB}, F_{AC}, and F_{AD}. The directions are assumed to point away from the joint as the tension will pull the joint away and along the cable. Finally, we specify two angular dimensions $\left(\tan^{-1}(1) = 45^0 \text{ and } \tan^{-1}\left(\frac{3}{4}\right) = 36.87^0 \right)$ to aid the resolution of force vectors.

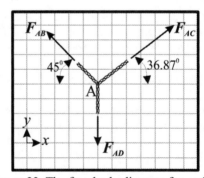

Figure 22. The free-body diagram for node A

Step II: Apply the equilibrium equations

From our intuition as well as previous knowledge (Example 1), we know that

$$F_{AD} = 1000\,\text{lb}$$

Now, the equilibrium equations are

$$\sum F_x = F_{AC}\cos\left(36.87^0\right) - F_{AB}\cos\left(45^0\right) = 0$$

$$F_{AC} = 0.8839\,F_{AB}$$

$$\sum F_y = F_{AC}\sin\left(36.87^0\right) + F_{AB}\sin\left(45^0\right) - 1000\,\text{lb} = 0$$

$$0.6 \times F_{AC} + 0.7071 \times F_{AB} = 1000\,\text{lb}$$

Substituting the value of F_{AC} into the final equation, we get

$$F_{AB} = 808\,\text{lb}$$
$$F_{AC} = 714\,\text{lb}$$

As the x-components of F_{AB} and F_{AC} should cancel each other, F_{AB} (acting at 45^0 to x-axis) should be greater than F_{AC}.

Example 5

A particle is in equilibrium acted on by three forces. Determine the force magnitudes for F_1 and F_2.

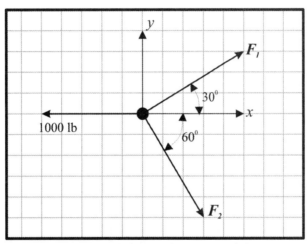

Figure 23. Forces acting on a particle

Step 1: Draw the free-body diagram

In this particular problem, Fig. 23 represents the free-body diagram. In this figure, the particle is isolated from the surrounding environment. Also, it shows the forces acting on it along with the coordinate system. The two characteristic dimensions are specified.

Step II: Apply the equilibrium equations

The equilibrium equations are

$$\sum \mathbf{F}_x = F_1\cos 30^0 + F_2\cos 60^0 - 1000 = 0\,\text{lb}$$

$$\therefore F_1\cos 30^0 + F_2\cos 60^0 = 1000\,\text{lb}$$

$$\sum \mathbf{F}_y = F_1\sin 30^0 - F_2\sin 60^0 = 0\,\text{lb}$$

$$\therefore F_1\sin 30^0 = F_2\sin 60^0$$

$$F_1 = \frac{\sin 60^0}{\sin 30^0} F_2$$

Substituting the value of F_1 into the $\mathbf{F}_x$ equilibrium equation, we get

$$\frac{\sin 60^0}{\sin 30^0} F_2 \cos 30^0 + F_2 \cos 60^0 = 1000 \text{ lb}$$

$$\boxed{\begin{array}{l} F_1 = 866 \text{ lb} \\ F_2 = 500 \text{ lb} \end{array}}$$

Alternative Approach

Step 1: Draw the free-body diagram

A careful examination of Fig. 24 reveals that the two unknown forces (F_1 and F_2) are perpendicular to each other. An intelligent choice would be to orient the coordinate system along these two force vectors (refer to Fig. 24).

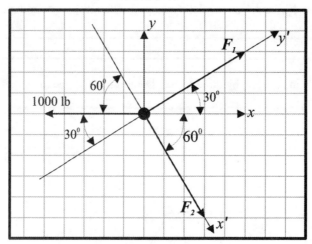

Figure 24. The free-body diagram of the particle

Step II: Apply the equilibrium equations

The equilibrium equations are

$$\sum \mathbf{F}_{x'} = F_2 - (1000 \text{ lb}) \cos 60^0 = 0$$
$$F_2 = 500 \text{ lb}$$
$$\sum \mathbf{F}_{y'} = F_1 - (1000 \text{ lb}) \cos 30^0 = 0$$
$$F_1 = 866 \text{ lb}$$

Note that the intelligent choice of the coordinate system resulted in a simple, yet elegant, solution procedure. The unknown forces are

$$\boxed{\begin{array}{l} F_1 = 866 \text{ lb} \\ F_2 = 500 \text{ lb} \end{array}}$$

Example 6
Force F is applied on a spring assembly. The spring constants $k_1 = k_2 = 500$ lb/in. Determine the force in each spring and the deflection of node A if the magnitude of force F is 500 lb.

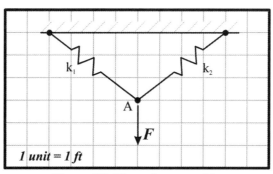

Figure 25. The spring assembly

Step I: *Apply the equilibrium equations*
Let us assume that node A displaces in the downward direction by δ. The free-body diagram (Fig. 26) of node A has the known force F and two unknown spring forces. Now, applying the equilibrium equation, we get

$$F_1 \cos\theta_1 = F_2 \cos\theta_2$$
$$F_1 \sin\theta_1 + F_2 \sin\theta_2 = 500\,\text{lb}$$

With four unknown quantities and two equations, the spring assembly is a statically indeterminate structure.

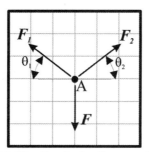

Figure 26. The free-body diagram of node A

Step II: *Establish geometric compatibility*
To solve the unknown internal forces, we must establish the geometric compatibility relationships. From symmetry, we can deduce that $\theta_1 = \theta_2$. If we assume that node A moves down by distance δ (refer to Fig. 27), then the equation for the geometric compatibility becomes

$$\delta_1 = \sqrt{x^2 + (y+\delta)^2} - \sqrt{x^2 + y^2}$$
$$\delta_2 = \delta_1$$

where δ_1 and δ_2 are the deflections of the spring.

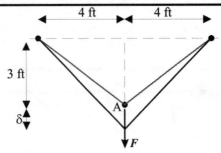

Figure 27. Deformed spring assembly over laid on the original undeformed assembly

Step III: *Relate forces and deformations*
The two force deformation equations are

$$F_1 = k_1\delta_1$$
$$F_2 = k_2\delta_2$$

Step IV: *Solve for the unknown forces*
Substituting $\delta_1 = \delta_2$ and $k_1 = k_2$ into the force-deformation relationships, we get

$$F_1 = F_2 = k_1\delta_1$$

Substituting this result into the equilibrium equation (step 1), we get

$$2F_1 \sin\theta_1 = 500$$

Substituting the values of F and θ_1, we get

$$2k_1\delta_1\sin\theta_1 = 2k_1\left(\sqrt{x^2+(y+\delta)^2}-\sqrt{x^2+y^2}\right)\frac{(y+\delta)}{\sqrt{x^2+(y+\delta)^2}} = 500$$

In this equation, the only unknown quantity is δ. Because the equation does not yield a closed-form solution, we solve this equation iteratively by guessing the value of δ until the equation is satisfied. Before we start the iterative process, let us rearrange the equation and substitute the value of k_1.

$$R = \left(\sqrt{x^2+(y+\delta)^2}-\sqrt{x^2+y^2}\right)\frac{(y+\delta)}{\sqrt{x^2+(y+\delta)^2}} - 0.5 = 0$$

In this equation, parameter R stands for the residual. We continually vary δ until the residual becomes zero (or extremely small), i.e, the equation is satisfied. Our initial guess $(\delta = 0\,\text{in})$ provides a base-line value for the residual. Looking at the order of magnitude of k_1 (500 lb/in) and F (500 lb), we made our second guess $(\delta = 1\,\text{in})$, and then, we continue our educated guesses.

Guess	Residual
0	-0.5
1	-0.03553
1.1	+0.02109

Because the residual changes sign between our last two guesses, the value of δ must lie between 1 and 1.1. By making a few more guesses, we can arrive at 1.0631, for which the value of the residual is very small 6.21×10^{-6}. Therefore, the deflection of node A is

$$\boxed{\delta = 1.0631\,\text{in}}$$

The force in each spring is

$$F_1 = F_2 = k_1\delta_1 = k\sqrt{x^2+(y+\delta)^2}-\sqrt{x^2+y^2}$$
$$\boxed{F_1 = F_2 = k_1\delta_1 = 350.82\,\text{lb}}$$

Name: _____

Problem 1

A particle is in equilibrium acted on by three forces. Determine the force magnitudes for F_1 and F_2.

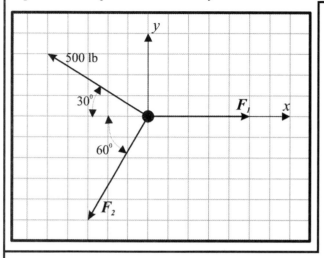

Problem 2

A particle is in equilibrium acted on by four forces. Determine the force magnitudes for F_1 and F_2.

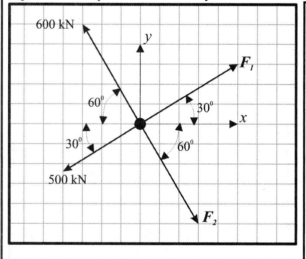

Name: _____

Problem 3

Particle A is in equilibrium. Compute the magnitude and direction of the unknown force *F*.

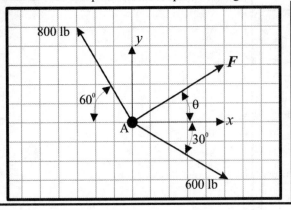

Problem 4

If the system is in equilibrium, determine mass M. Assume negligible frictional forces.

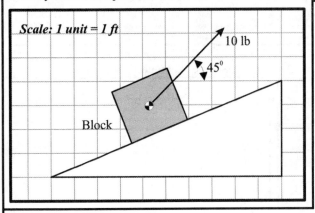

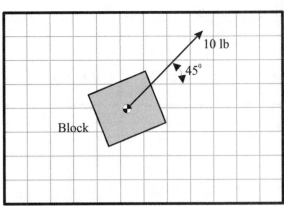

Name: _____

Problem 5

If the system is in equilibrium, determine the magnitude of force *F*. Assume negligible frictional forces.

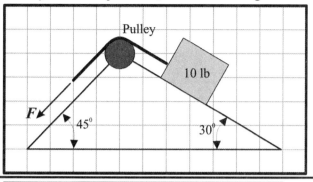

The free-body diagram for the 10 lb block

Problem 6

If the system is in equilibrium, determine weight *W*. Assume negligible frictional forces.

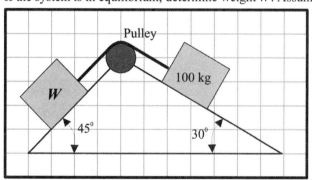

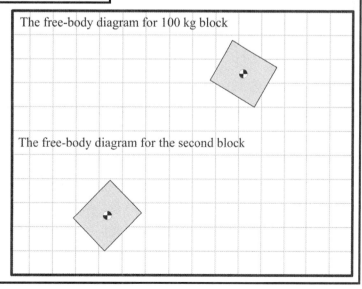

The free-body diagram for 100 kg block

The free-body diagram for the second block

Name: _____

Problem 7

Determine the tensions in the cables if $|F| = 500\,\text{kN}$.

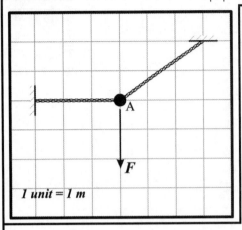

1 unit = 1 m

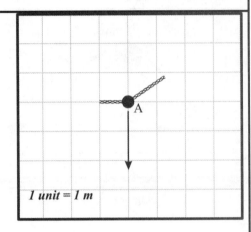

1 unit = 1 m

Problem 8

The spring assembly is in equilibrium. If $|F| = 1000\,\text{lb}$ and k = 1000 lb/in, determine the tension in the cable as well as the unstreched length of the spring.

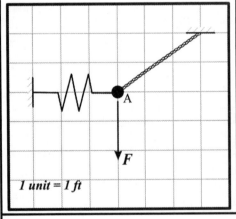

1 unit = 1 ft

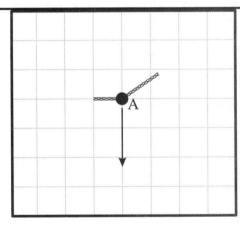

Name: _____

Problem 9

Determine the tensions in the cables if weight *W* is 200 lb.

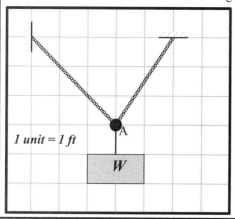

1 unit = 1 ft

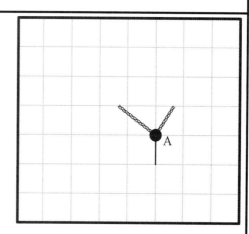

Problem 10

What is the maximum mass **m** that can be supported if the cables can support a tension of 10 kN?

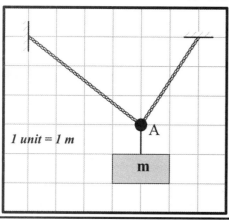

1 unit = 1 m

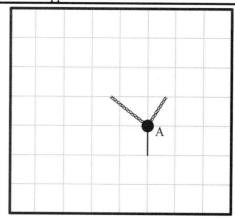

Name: _____

Problem 11

A shipping container weighing 1 ton needs to be supported by a cable that is 30 ft long. The figure below shows the possible cable attachment points. Determine which pair of attachment points produces the least tension in the cable. Also, determine the tension in the cable.

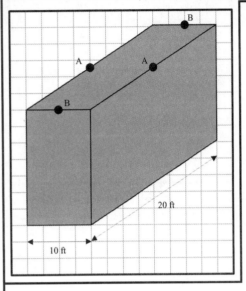

Problem 12

A force is applied to node A. Determine the unstretched lengths of the springs if $F = 1000$ lb, and the spring constants $k_1 = 250$ lb/in and $k_2 = 500$ lb/in.

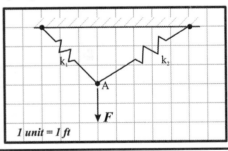

Name: _____

Problem 13

Determine mass *m* if the system is in equilibrium. Assume the diameter of the pulley to be negligible.

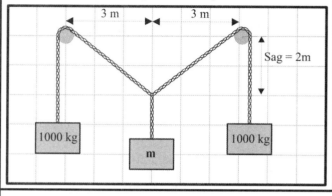

Problem 14

Determine the sag and the unknown weight *W* if the system is in equilibrium. Assume the diameter of the pulley to be negligible.

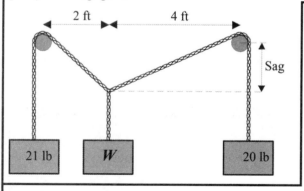

Name: _____

Problem 15

Determine the force in each spring and the deflection of node A if $|F|$ =1kN and the spring constants k_1 = k_2 = 10 kN/m. The spring assembly is shown in the initial position.

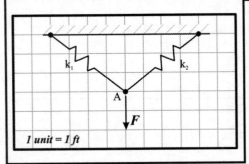

3.6. Friction

An in-depth understanding of the concept of friction is the key for solving many engineering problems. Friction always exists between two contacting objects and manifests as a force pair acting tangentially at the contact surfaces. The magnitude of this tangential force depends on the contacting surfaces. Some times, the friction force is essential for the functioning. For example, the traction at the road-tire interface is the key for the motion of any vehicle. In other instances, designers try to minimize friction to improve efficiency and reduce wear. For instance, bearings reduce friction and improve the efficiency of vehicles.

The friction force on each object acts in the direction that would resist the relative motion between the two bodies. The following examples expand on the thought process for determining the direction of the friction force.

The Frictional Force Between the Latch and the Strike Plate

Let us consider the friction between the latch and a strike plate during the closing of a door (see the schematic in Fig. 28). As the door closes, the latch hits the strike plate and, due to contact, a normal force comes into play and acts perpendicular to the contact surface. The frictional force should act along the surface, which leads in two possible directions. Because friction opposes the inward motion of the latch, it acts in the direction shown in Fig. 29.

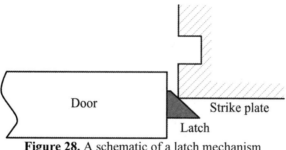

Figure 28. A schematic of a latch mechanism

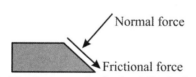

Figure 29. The forces on the latch while closing the door

The Frictional Force between the Wheels of the Car and the Road

A friction force pair exists between the wheels of a car and the road at the contact interface. When the car accelerates, the front drive wheels spin in a clockwise direction (see Fig 30). Because the friction force opposes this spinning motion, it acts in the forward direction (same direction as the motion of the car), which is sometimes counter-intuitive. The rear wheels follow the motion of the car, and the friction force opposes this forward motion. Therefore, it acts in the direction opposite to the motion of the car and spins the rear wheels.

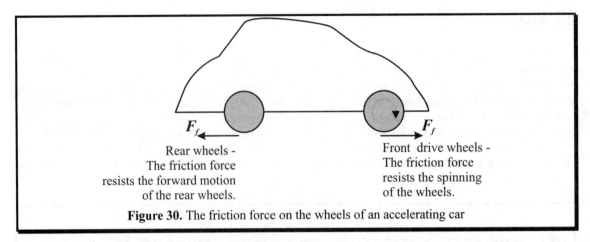

Figure 30. The friction force on the wheels of an accelerating car

The friction force at an interface is characterized by the coefficient of friction, denoted by μ. It is *independent* of the surface roughness and the area of the two contact surfaces. The coefficient of friction μ is the ratio of the maximum friction force and normal force N acting on the surfaces, and therefore, is a dimensionless scalar quantity. Friction force F_f at the interface is given by

$$F_f \leq \mu N \qquad\qquad 10$$

Let us consider a block with a negligible weight resting on a flat surface as shown in Fig. 31a. When normal force N but no horizontal force is applied to the block, the frictional force at the interface is zero (see Fig. 31b for the free body diagram of the block). The frictional force starts acting only when we start applying the horizontal force. As we increase the horizontal force, the frictional force increases to match the applied horizontal force until it reaches a limiting value. When the applied force exceeds this limiting value, the block starts sliding. The limiting value of the friction force at the point of impending motion is equal to μN .

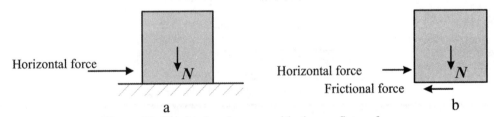

Figure 31. The friction force on a block on a flat surface

Example 7

A block rests on an inclined plane. The mass of the block is 100 kg. Determine the friction force at the interface. The angle of the incline plane is 30^0.

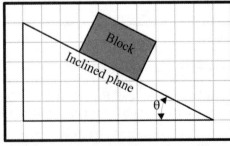

Figure 32. A block on an inclined plane

In this section, we will formally approach this problem using the equilibrium equations.

Step I: Draw the free-body diagram
The three forces that act on the block are: **mg** – gravitational force, F_{normal} – normal reaction force from the inclined plane, and $F_{friction}$ – friction force. By aligning the coordinate axes as shown in the free-body diagram, the force resolution becomes simple. The free-body diagram also shows the characteristic dimension θ .

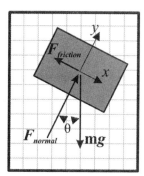

Figure 33. The free-body diagram of the block

Step 2: Apply the equilibrium equations

$$\sum F_x = mg \sin \theta - F_{friction} = 0$$

$$F_{friction} = mg \sin \theta$$

$$\boxed{F_{friction} = 490\,\text{N}}$$

The direction assumed for the friction force is correct (as the result is positive) and its magnitude is 490 N.

Example 8
A block rests on an inclined plane. The weight of the block is 10 lb. If the coefficient of friction is 0.4, determine the range of values for force F. The angle of the incline plane is 30^0.

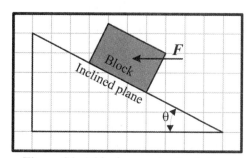

Figure 34. A block on an inclined plane

Step I: Draw the free-body diagram
When force **F** is applied, the block will be in equilibrium if the force is large enough to prevent the block from slipping down the incline plane and small enough not to push the block up the incline. Analyzing these two extreme conditions helps to determine the limiting values for force **F**. Now, in both these cases, the four forces that act on the block are: **F** – applied force **W** – gravitational force, F_{normal} – normal reaction force from the inclined plane, and $F_{friction}$ – friction force. Note that the direction of friction fore $F_{friction}$ depends on the direction of the impending motion. The two free-body diagrams are shown in Fig. 35.

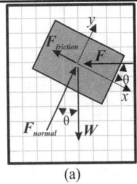 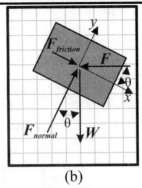

(a)   (b)

Figure 35. The free-body diagram of the block when the impending motion is to
(a) slide down (b) slide up

Step 2: Apply the equilibrium equations
Let us start with writing the equilibrium equations for the free-body diagram in Fig. 35(a) where the impending motion is sliding down and force F keeps the block in equilibrium. The equilibrium equations are:

$$\sum \mathbf{F_x} = W \sin \theta - F_{friction} - F \cos \theta = 0$$

$$\sum \mathbf{F_y} = F_{normal} - W \cos \theta - F \sin \theta = 0$$

Note that these equations are coupled. Rearrganging the terms of $\sum \mathbf{F_y}$ equation, we get

$$F_{normal} = W \cos \theta + F \sin \theta$$

Also, at the point of impending motion,

$$F_{friction} = \mu \times F_{normal}$$

Substituting these relationships in $\sum \mathbf{F_x}$ equation, we get

$$\sum \mathbf{F_x} = W \sin \theta - \mu (W \cos \theta + F \sin \theta) - F \cos \theta = 0$$

Rearranging the terms, we get

$$-F (\mu \sin \theta + \cos \theta) + W (\sin \theta - \mu \cos \theta) = 0$$

$$F = \frac{W (\sin \theta - \mu \cos \theta)}{(\mu \sin \theta + \cos \theta)}$$

Substituting the values of μ, θ, and W, we get the minimum force required to keep the block in equilibrium as

$$F = 1.44 \text{ lb}$$

Now, Let us write the equilibrium equations for the free-body diagram in Fig. 35(b) - the impending motion is upwards and force F keeps the block in equilibrium. The equilibrium equations are:

$$\sum \mathbf{F_x} = W \sin \theta + F_{friction} - F \cos \theta = 0$$

$$\sum \mathbf{F_y} = F_{normal} - W \cos \theta - F \sin \theta = 0$$

Note that these equations are coupled. Rearrganging the terms of $\sum \mathbf{F_y}$ equation, we get

$$F_{normal} = W \cos \theta + F \sin \theta$$

Also, at the point of impending motion,

$$F_{friction} = \mu \times F_{normal}$$

Substituting these relationships in $\sum \mathbf{F_x}$ equation, we get

$$\sum F_x = W \sin\theta + \mu\left(W \cos\theta + F \sin\theta\right) - F \cos\theta = 0$$

Rearranging the terms, we get

$$F\left(\mu\sin\theta - \cos\theta\right) + W\left(\sin\theta + \mu\cos\theta\right) = 0$$

$$F = \frac{W\left(\sin\theta + \mu\cos\theta\right)}{\left(\cos\theta - \mu\sin\theta\right)}$$

Substituting the values of μ, θ, and W, we get the maximum force that can be applied on the block while keeping it in equilibrium

$$F = 12.71 \text{ lb}$$

Therefore, the acceptable range of values for force F is

$$\boxed{1.44 \text{ lb} \le F \le 12.71 \text{ lb}}$$

Note that a different coordinate system with axes along the horizontal and vertical directions will simplify the solution procedure.

Notes:

Concept Questions

Name: _____

1. A car has rear-wheel drive. If the car is accelerating, the direction of the friction force on the wheels:
  A. Front wheels in the forward direction, Rear wheels in the forward direction
  B. Front wheels in the forward direction, Rear wheels in the reverse direction
  C. Front wheels in the reverse direction, Rear wheels in the forward direction
  D. Front wheels in the reverse direction, Rear wheels in the reverse direction

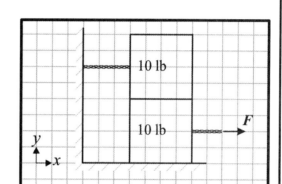

2. Determine the force *F* required to pull the block if the coefficient of friction is 1:
  A. 0 lb
  B. 10 lb
  C. 20 lb
  D. 30 lb

3. TRUE/FALSE: The friction force acts normal to the contacting surfaces.

4. TRUE/FALSE: The coefficient of friction is independent of surface roughness.

5. A 10 lb block is on a flat table. The coefficient of friction is 0.1. What is the magnitude of the friction force if there are no other external forces (except gravity) are acting on the block?

6. TRUE/FALSE: The coefficient of friction is dimensionless.

A block is resting on an inclined plane (see the adjacent figure).

7. TRUE/FALSE: The frictional force increases with the increase in angle θ - Assume that the block does not slide down.

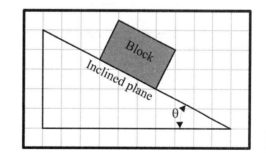

8. TRUE/FALSE: The angle at which the block slides down is dependent on the weight of the block.

9. Give two applications where high coefficient of friction is beneficial.

10. Give two applications where low coefficient of friction is desirable.

Name: _____

Problem 1

Force **F** (30 N) pulls a 10 kg block at a constant velocity. Determine the coefficient of friction.

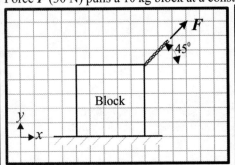 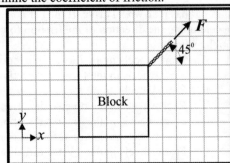

Problem 2

Determine force **F** required to move block B from an assembly of two blocks. The weight of each block is 10 lb. The coefficient of friction between the blocks is 0.3 and the coefficient of friction between the block and the ground is 0.6.

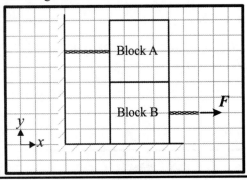 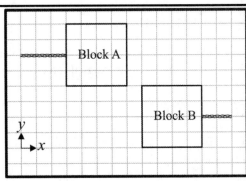

Name: _____

Problem 3

A 10 lb block is in equilibrium on an inclined plane. Assume the coefficient of friction to be 1.1. Determine the friction force at the interface.

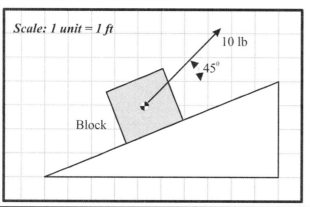

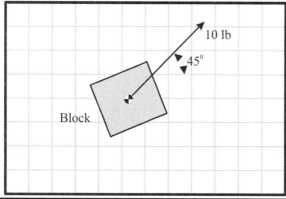

Problem 4

A block of weight W is on an inclined plane. Assume the coefficient of friction to be 0.5. Determine angle θ when the block begins to slide.

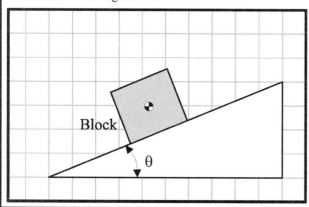 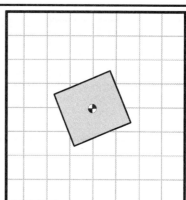

Is the angle independent of the weight?   YES/NO

Name: _____

Problem 5

A block is resting on an incline. Assume the coefficient of friction to be 0.1.

a. Determine the force required for moving the block up the incline.

b. Determine the force required to keep the block from slipping down.

Hint – Think about the direction of the frictional force in each situation.

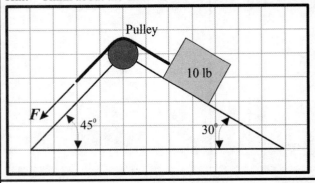

a.

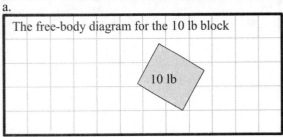

The free-body diagram for the 10 lb block

10 lb

b.

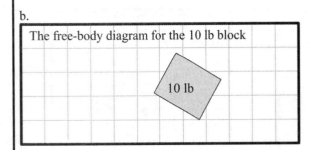

The free-body diagram for the 10 lb block

10 lb

Name: _____

Problem 6

If the system is in equilibrium, determine the range of possible values for weight *W*. The coefficient of friction is 0.1.

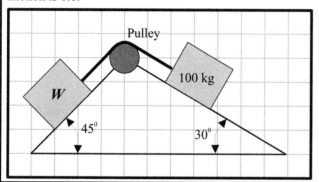

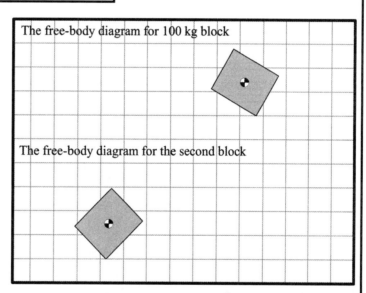

The free-body diagram for 100 kg block

The free-body diagram for the second block

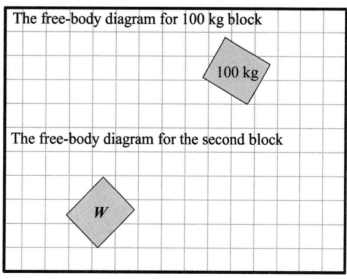

The free-body diagram for 100 kg block

The free-body diagram for the second block

Notes:

3.7. Three-Dimensional Systems in Equilibrium

A natural extension of the concept of equilibrium of one- to two-dimensional systems is three-dimensional systems. It provides the generic case where the forces are not restricted to a single plane. Using the Cartesian notion, we can represent each force and then write the equilibrium equation as

$$\sum F = \left(\sum F_x\right)i + \left(\sum F_y\right)j + \left(\sum F_z\right)k = 0 \qquad 11$$

or simply in its scalar form:

$$\sum F_x = 0$$
$$\sum F_y = 0 \qquad 12$$
$$\sum F_z = 0$$

To analyze such a system, we need to take the following steps:

1. **Draw the free-body diagram**. This step involves isolating an appropriate part of or the entire system from the surrounding environment. The goal while selecting the part is to capture the forces that needs to be determined. Then, we must establish the coordinate system. Remember that an intelligent choice of the coordinate system can greatly simplify the solution procedure. We must identify and label all known and unknown forces. The direction for the unknown forces is assumed. Finally, we must specify characteristic dimensions to aid in the resolution of force vectors.

2. **Apply the equilibrium equations**. Use scalar notation only if the forces can easily be resolved into x-, y- and z-components. Otherwise, use the vector formulation and add the vectors. Solve for unknown forces. When we solve the equations, if the unknown force comes out to be negative, then the assumed direction is reversed to identify the proper direction.

Example 9

A 200 lb ring is hoisted by three chains. Determine the tension in the chains.

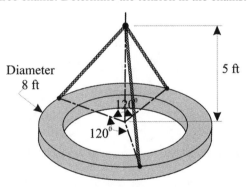

Figure 36. A ring hoisted by three chains

Solution using scalar formulation:

We can draw the free-body diagram as shown. It captures the unknown forces (tension in the cables). By symmetry, we can infer that the tension is same in all three cables.

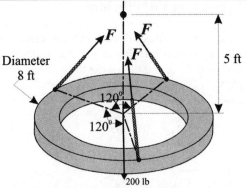

Figure 37. The free-body diagram of the ring

Now, we examine any cable and draw the tension in a two-dimensional plane containing the chain. The tension in the chain can be resolved into two components: horizontal and vertical (see fig. 38).

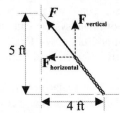

Figure 38. Resolving the forces of one chain

Now, the horizontal components from each chain, which are equal in magnitude and 120^0 apart, cancel each other.

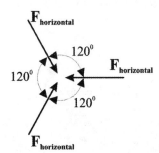

Figure 39. The three horizontal force components

Now, the three vertical components counter the weight of the ring. We can write the equilibrium equation in the vertical direction as

$$\sum \mathbf{F_z} = 3 \times \mathbf{F_{vertical}} - 200\,\text{lb} = 0$$

Rearranging the terms and solving for $\mathbf{F_{vertical}}$, we get

$$\mathbf{F_{vertical}} = 66.67\,\text{lb}$$

Now, we can compute F using the geometry as

$$F = \mathbf{F_{vertical}}\, \frac{\sqrt{5^2 + 4^2}}{5}\,\text{lb}$$

$$\boxed{F = 85.38\,\text{lb}}$$

Example 10

A boom is supporting a 2000 lb weight at its end. The projection of its end A on an xy plane is shown in the figure. The boom is supported by two cables, AB and AC. The cables can only exert tensile load, whereas the boom can take loads along its axis in both directions. Determine the tension in the cables and the force carried by the boom.

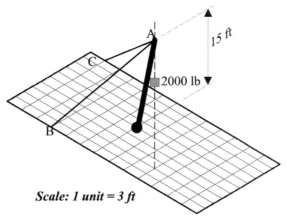

Scale: 1 unit = 3 ft

Figure 40. A boom supporting a weight

The free-body diagram for joint A (Fig. 41) shows three unknown forces (two tensions in the cable and one force in the boom). The tensions in the cable pull the joint along their length. Therefore, the arrows point toward joint B and C. On the other hand, we assumed that the boom will be in compression and, therefore, will push on joint A.

Let us find the unit vectors for OA, AB, and AC. Note that unit vector $u_A = \dfrac{A}{|A|}$.

$$u_{OA} = \frac{9i + 9j + 15k}{\sqrt{9^2 + 9^2 + 15^2}}$$
$$= 0.4575i + 0.4575j + 0.7625k$$

$$u_{AB} = \frac{6i - 18j - 15k}{\sqrt{6^2 + 18^2 + 15^2}}$$
$$= 0.2481i - 0.7442j - 0.6201k$$

$$u_{AC} = \frac{-24i - 24j - 15k}{\sqrt{24^2 + 24^2 + 15^2}}$$
$$= -0.6468i - 0.6468j - 0.4042k$$

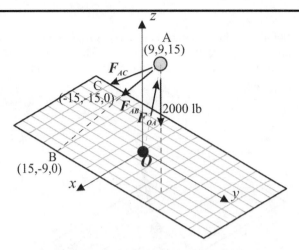

Figure 41. The free-body diagram of joint A

Now, the four force vectors are

$$W = -2000k$$

$$F_{OA} = (0.4575i + 0.4575j + 0.7625k)|F_{OA}|$$

$$F_{AB} = (0.2481i - 0.7442j - 0.6202k)|F_{AB}|$$

$$F_{AC} = (-0.6468i - 0.6468j - 0.4042k)|F_{AC}|$$

Applying the equilibrium equations and equating the components along x-, y-, and z-directions, we get

$$\sum F_x = 0.4575|F_{OA}| + 0.2481|F_{AB}| - 0.6468|F_{AC}| = 0$$

$$\sum F_y = 0.4575|F_{OA}| - 0.7442|F_{AB}| - 0.6468|F_{AC}| = 0$$

$$\sum F_z = 0.7625|F_{OA}| - 0.6202|F_{AB}| - 0.4042|F_{AC}| - 2000 = 0$$

The solution of these equations yields

$$|F_{OA}| = 4196\,lb$$
$$|F_{AB}| = 0$$
$$|F_{AC}| = 2968\,lb$$

Now, let us look at the solution carefully. The tension in the cable AB is zero. This is due to the fact that rest of the forces lie in a single plane (refer to Fig. 42). F_{AB} is the only out-of-the-plane force acting on joint A. For the out-of-plane component to be zero, this force must be equal to zero. If we pick a proper coordinate system as shown in Fig. 42, we could have worked this problem as a two-dimensional system.

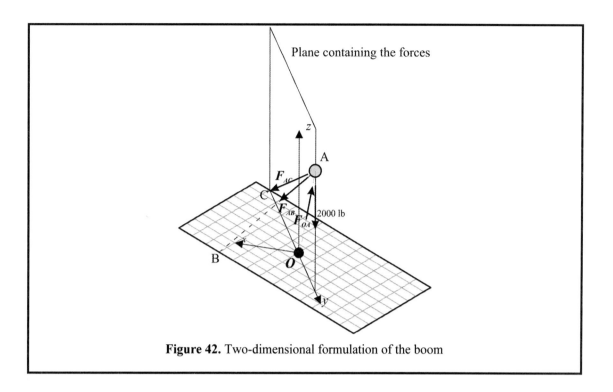

Figure 42. Two-dimensional formulation of the boom

Notes:

Name: _____

Problem 1

Three forces F_1, F_2, and F_3 (F_3 is not shown in the figure) act on a joint. The joint is in equilibrium under the action of these three forces. F_1, whose magnitude is 600 lb, is acting along the negative z-direction. If force F_3 is in the xy plane, determine the magnitude of F_2 and F_3. Also, sketch force F_3.

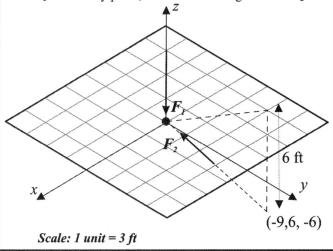

Scale: 1 unit = 3 ft

Problem 2

Four forces F_1, F_2, F_3, and F_4 (F_4 is not shown in the figure) act on joint A. The joint is in equilibrium under the action of these four forces. F_1, whose magnitude is 50 kN, is acting along the negative z-direction. F_2, whose magnitude is 25 kN, is acting along the positive y-direction. If force F_4 is in the xy plane, determine the magnitude of F_3 and F_4. Also, sketch force F_4.

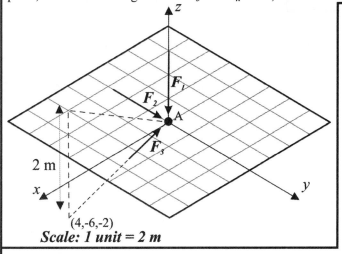

Scale: 1 unit = 2 m

Name: _____

Problem 3

A container is hanging from two supports that are pivoted at joints B and C. Frame BAC support is held by cable AD. Determine the forces in the support structure and, in the cable. Use symmetry to deduce relationships.

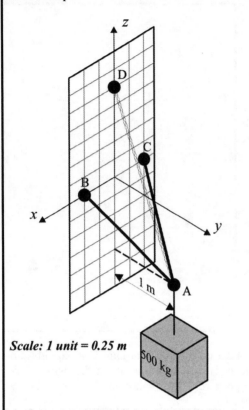

Scale: 1 unit = 0.25 m

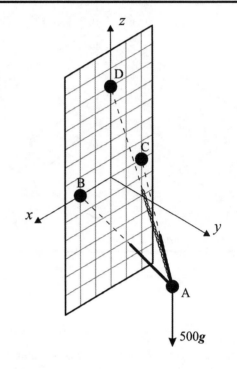

Name: _____

Problem 4

A rectangular plate is hoisted by a crane. If the weight of the plate is 500 lb, determine the tension in each cable.

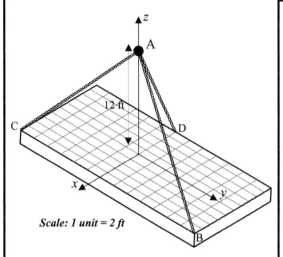

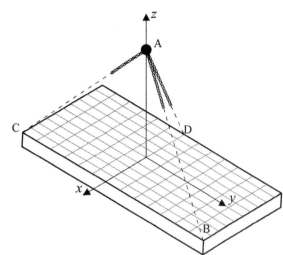

Name: _____

Problem 5

Rigid pole OA is supported by two cables. At joint A, a 1000 lb force acts along the positive y-axis, and a 500 lb force acts along the negative z-axis. Determine the tension in the two cables if points B and C lie in the xy plane.

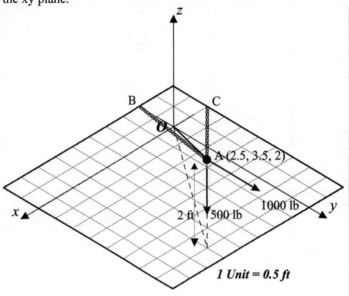

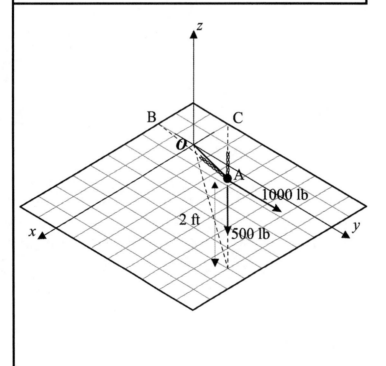

Name: _____

Problem 6

A 15 ft tall pole is supported by three cables. The pole is subjected only to vertical loading due to the tension in the cables. If the tension in cable PA is 500 lb, determine the tension in the other two cables. Also, determine the force exerted by the pole on joint P.

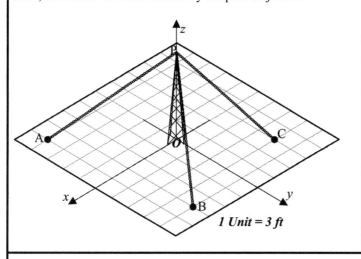

1 Unit = 3 ft

Name:_____

Problem 7

If the maximum allowable tension in cables is 1 kN, determine the maximum allowable weight *W* for the block.

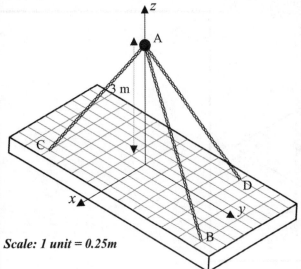

Scale: 1 unit = 0.25m

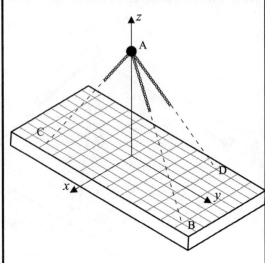

Is the block stable?

Name: _____

Problem 8

Cables AB and AC are 6 ft long and force **F** = 750 lb. If the maximum allowable tension in cables AB and AC is 750 lb, determine the maximum allowable weight for **W**. Also, find the values of a and b. Note that point A lies in the *yz* plane.

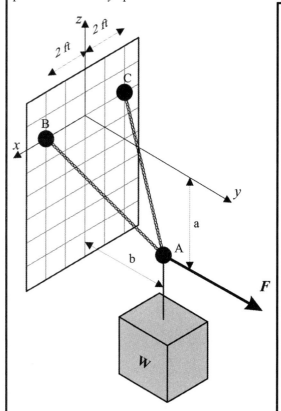
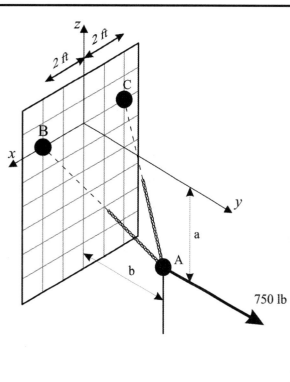

Name: _____

Problem 9

A 200 lb ring is hoisted by three chains. Determine the tension in the chains.

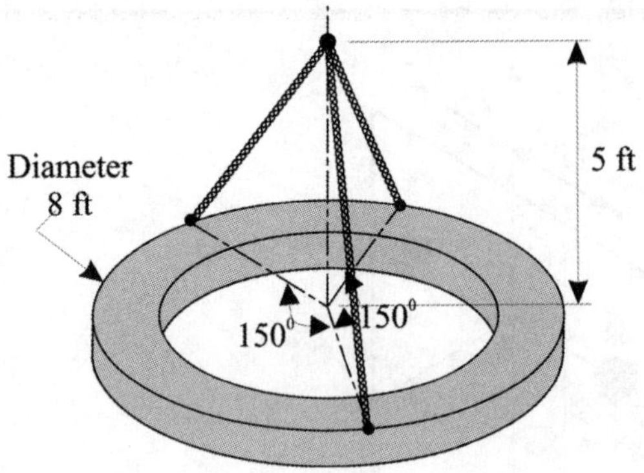

Name: _____

Problem 10

A 5 lb weight is supported by three (w = 3 lb) weights. The pulleys (are in a horizontal plane) form an equilateral triangle with each side 4 ft in length. Determine the sag in the central weight. Assume that the dimensions of the pulleys to be negligible.

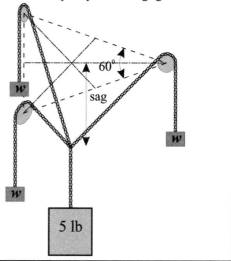

Name: _____

Problem 11

A force **F** is applied on node A. The support points B, C, and D form an equilateral triangle. Node A is 6 ft below the xy plane. If the magnitude of force **F** is 1000 lb., determine the force in each cable.

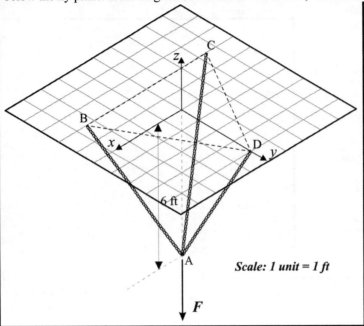

6 ft

Scale: 1 unit = 1 ft

F

Name: _____

Problem 12

A force *F* is applied on node A. The support points B, C, and D form an equilateral triangle. The cables can be viewed as springs whose spring constant is 50 kN/m. After the application of the force, the system is in equilibrium with node A 4 m below the xy plane. If the magnitude of force *F* is 5 kN, determine the stretch of the cables as well as the force in each cable.

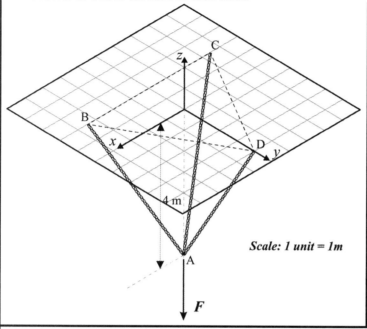

Scale: 1 unit = 1m

Name: _____

Problem 13

A force F is applied on node A. The support points B, C, and D form an equilateral triangle. Initially, before the application of the force, node A is 6 ft below the xy plane. The cables can be viewed as springs whose spring constant is 5000 lb/ft. If the magnitude of force F is 1000 lb., determine the sag of node A as well as the force in each cable.

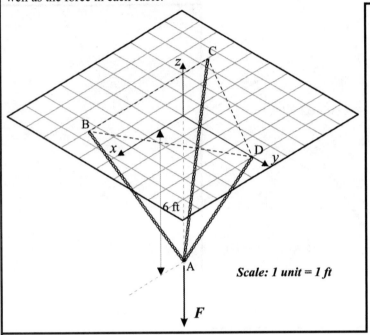

Scale: 1 unit = 1 ft

Name: _____

Problem 14 (Challenge problem)

A cardboard sheet is folded to create a trihedral cavity. A golf ball is placed in the cavity. The diameter of the golf ball is 40 mm. Its mass is 45 g. Determine the reaction forces at the three points of contact.

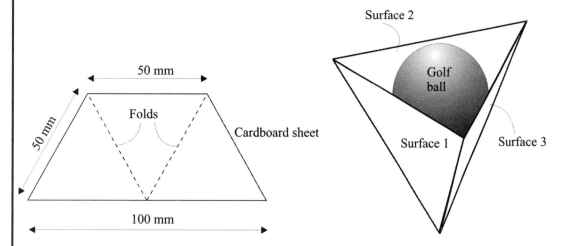

Think about the location of the golf ball's center with respect to an equilateral triangle. Also, decide on the angle between one of the surfaces and the ball. Use symmetry to solve the problem.

Notes:

CHAPTER IV
THE MOMENT VECTOR

Learning Objectives

The material presented in this chapter will enable you to accomplish the following objectives:
1. Develop an overview of moment vectors.
2. Understand and distinguish twisting and bending moments.
3. Calculate the moment about a point using both scalar and vector formulations.
4. Apply the mixed triple product to compute the moment about an axis.
5. Determine the moment of a couple.
6. Evaluate the equivalency of two systems.
7. Simplify coplanar system of forces and couples.

VayuWind – A Vertical Axis Wind Turbine

The energy crisis is one of the major problems that the world is facing today. On the supply side, fossil fuel supplies are depleting quickly. At the same time, in both industrialized and developing countries, the demand for energy is growing exponentially. Many countries are seriously developing renewable and nonpolluting technologies, such as wind energy, to solve their energy needs. However, harvesting of wind energy often occurs far away from the areas in need of power. An inexpensive method of tapping wind energy in cities and industrial centers and rural communities in both developed and developing countries is very much needed at this time.

One possible solution to this problem is a VayuWind turbine that can be used effectively both in urban and rural environments and that would be considered an attractive architectural feature, as well. VayuWind turbine deploys airfoils parallel to the rotational axis in such a way that, unlike other windmills, it rotates around a ring frame, leaving the central portion open for other uses. This enables VayuWind to extract wind power using existing structures such as commercial buildings and skywalks with minimal noise pollution.

Figure 1. VayuWind (for animation – see VayuWind folder on the CD)

In an urban environment, VayuWind offers several marketing points apart from the price:
- The windmill provides a green corporate image.
- Vertical axis windmills are silent when compared to their counter parts, horizontal axis windmills.
- Bird hits, which are a common problem for traditional windmills, are eliminated.
- It adds an interesting and appealing aesthetic element to city skylines.

To design or analyze any such windmill, we must understand how aerodynamic forces create the moment vector about the axis of the windmill and must be able to compute the moment.

4.1. Formulation of the Moment Vector about a Point

The moment of a force is a vector that strives to rotate a body. To understand moment vectors, think about force vector F acting on a body which is pivoted at point P (see Fig. 2). This force tends to rotate the body around the pivot axis. To increase the rotational effect, one can increase either force F or distance d. The moment of a force about a point which causes the rotation is defined as the product of force F and the perpendicular distance from the point to the line of action of the force d. Distance d is often referred to as *moment arm*. Mathematically, we can compute the magnitude of the moment vector M_P (M for moment and subscript P for point P) as

$$M_P = Fd \qquad\qquad 1$$

Because the moment vector is the product of force and distance, its units take the form of N.m, kN.m, lb.ft, or lb.in. It is important to recognize that when the force's line of action coincides with point P, the moment arm (d) becomes zero and hence the net moment also reduces to zero.

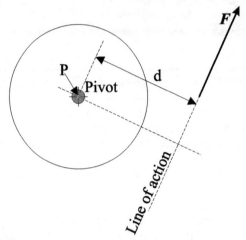

Figure 2. Moment formulation due to force vector F

We can identify the direction of the moment vector by using the right-hand rule: curl the right hand fingers in the direction of possible rotation and the thumb points to the direction of the moment vector. For the body in Fig. 3, the force vector tries to rotate the body in a counter-clockwise direction. If we align our right-hand fingers along this counter-clockwise direction, the thumb points out of the paper – the direction of the moment vector. Fig. 3 shows the moment vector caused by force F. Based on the right-hand rule, the direction of the moment vector is along the negative or positive z-direction. Also, note that the curl on the moment vector is sometimes used to denote the direction of the moment.

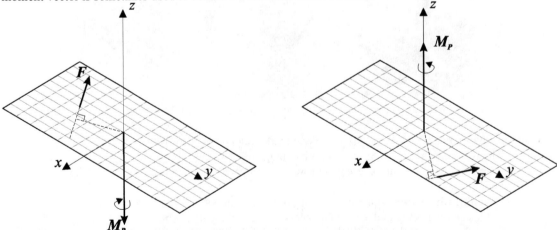

Figure 3. Direction of the moment due to force vector F

Let us consider the moment vector in more detail. In Fig. 4, position vector r goes from point P to any point on the line of action. Often, it is the position vector from point P to the point of force application. Angle θ specifies the angle between the position vector and the direction of force application. Now, we write the moment equation as

$$M_P = |F||r|\sin\theta = Fd \qquad\qquad 2$$

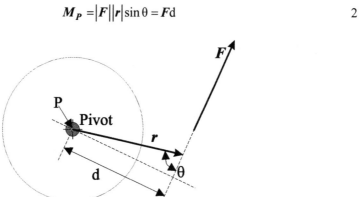

Figure 4. Moment formulation in terms of force vector F and position vector r

As the distance $|r|\sin\theta$ represents the moment arm d, it is independent of r as long as r goes from point P to any point on the line of action. Sliding the force along the line of action does not change d, so the moment at point P remains constant. This property is referred to as the *principle of transmissibility*. This principle allows us to choose any convenient point on the line of action of the force to define the position vector r.

All forces acting in a plane i.e., coplanar forces, create collinear moment vectors. To compute the moment that results from a set of coplanar forces, we can algebraically add the individual moments caused by each force (refer to Fig. 5). Note that a moment vector along the positive z-axis is considered positive.

$$M_R = \sum Fd \qquad\qquad 3$$

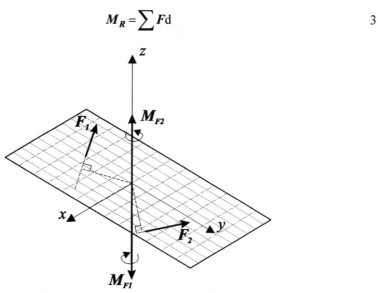

Figure 5. Resultant moment due to two force vectors

According to the *principle of moments* or *Varignon's theorem, the sum of moments about point O due to a set of concurrent forces whose lines of action intersect at point P is equal to the moment about the same point due to the resultant force (vector sum of the forces) acting at point P.* In other words, the moment about point P due to three concurrent forces F_1, F_2, and F_3 is equal to the moment caused by the resultant force F_R acting along the intersection of the lines of action of F_1, F_2, and F_3, as shown in Fig. 6.

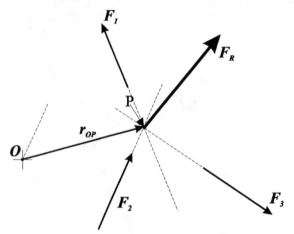

Figure 6. The moment due to concurrent force vectors

This theorem is useful in calculating the moments of a force by allowing us (a) to compute the moment due to force components and (b) to find the moment of the force by combining them. The following example uses the principle of moments to find the moment due to a force.

Example 1
Determine the moment due to 5 kN force at point P.

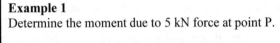

Figure 7. A beam under the action of a force

First, let us resolve the force vector into horizontal and vertical components.

$$\mathbf{F_{horizontal}} = 5\,kN \times \cos 45$$
$$= 3.536\,kN$$

$$\mathbf{F_{vertical}} = 5\,kN \times \sin 45$$
$$= 3.536\,kN$$

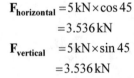
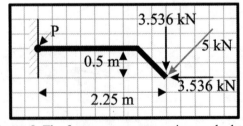

Figure 8. The force components acting on the beam

Now, we can compute the moment about point P:
$$M_P = -\mathbf{F}_{horizontal} \times 0.5\,m - \mathbf{F}_{vertical} \times 2.25\,m$$
$$\boxed{M_P = -9.723\,kN.m}$$
Both force components tend to rotate the rod in a clockwise direction, resulting in the negative sign.

Example 2
Determine the resultant moment due to three coplanar force vectors.

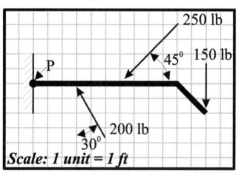

Figure 9. A beam under the action of three coplanar forces

Moment due to 150 lb force:
$$M_{150} = -150\,lb \times 12\,ft$$
$$= -1800\,lb.ft$$
Note that 12 ft refers to the moment arm. The sense of the moment is clockwise i.e., considered negative.

Moment due to 250 lb force:
$$M_{250} = -250\,lb \times 6\,ft \times \sin 45$$
$$= -1061\,lb.ft$$
6 ft refers to the distance from point P to the point of force application. 45^0 is the angle between position vector r and the force's line of action. The sense of the moment is clockwise i.e., negative. Note that we could arrive at the same solution by resolving the 250 lb force into x- and y-components.

Moment due to 200 lb force:
$$M_{200} = 200\,lb \times 3\,ft \times \cos 30$$
$$= 520\,lb.ft$$
60^0 is the angle between position vector r and the force's line of action. The sense of the moment is counter-clockwise i.e., positive.

Now, the resultant moment is
$$M_R = (-1800 - 1061 + 520)\,lb.ft$$
$$\boxed{M_R = -2341\,lb.ft}$$

The negative sign indicates that the sense of the resultant vector is clockwise.

Example 3

If the total moment about point P is zero, determine angle θ.

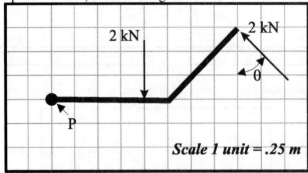

Figure 10. A beam under the action of two forces

Moment at point P

$$M_P = -(2 \text{ kN})(1 \text{ m}) + (2 \text{ kN})(0.75 \text{ m})\sin\theta + (2 \text{ kN})(2 \text{ m})\cos\theta = 0 \text{ kN.m}$$

Solving this equation iteratively, we get

$$\theta = 82.6^0$$

Concept Questions

Name: _____

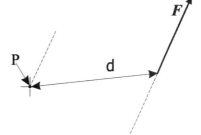

1.   TRUE/FALSE: The moment due to force *F* (see the adjacent figure) is equal to *F*d.

2.   TRUE/FALSE: Sliding the force away from point P along the line of action increases the moment.

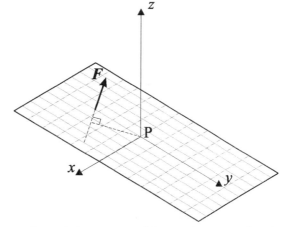

3.   TRUE/FALSE: The force vector creates a positive moment about point P.

4.   TRUE/FALSE: To determine the moment due to a force, it is an acceptable practice to resolve the force and algebraically add individual moments due to each force component.

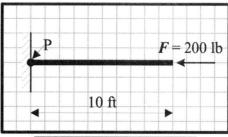

5.   The moment due to force F is equal to .

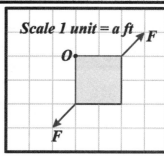

6. The moment at point O is
   A. $2Fa$
   B. $2\sqrt{2}Fa$
   C. $-2\sqrt{2}Fa$
   D. 0

Name: _____

Problem 1

Determine the moment at point P.

Scale 1 unit = 1 ft   ↓150 lb

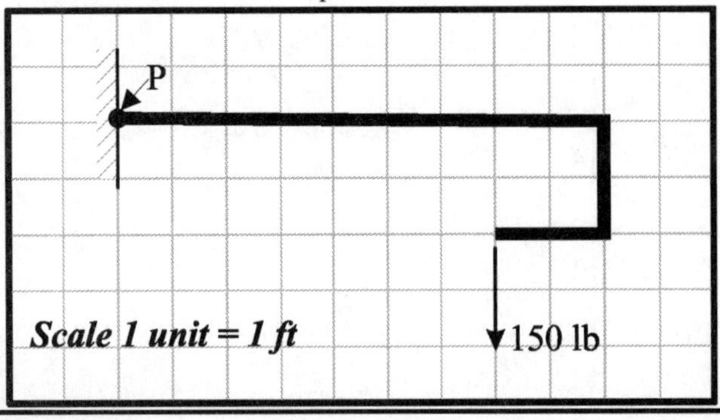

Problem 2

Determine the moment at point P.

P   1.5 kN   45°

Scale 1 unit = 0.5 m

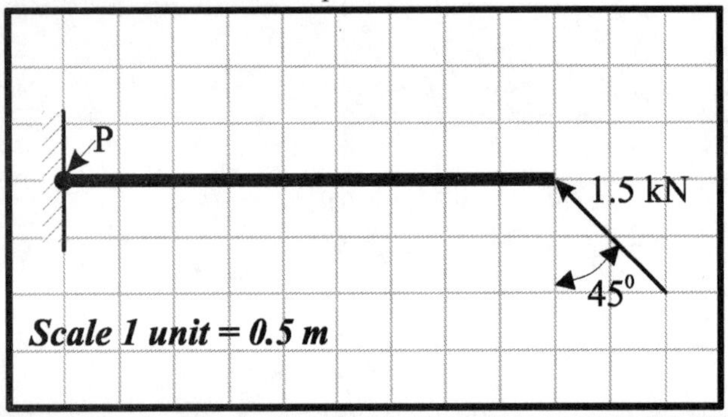

Problem 3

Determine the moment at point P.

50 lb   50 lb   45°

P

50 lb   45°   Scale 1 unit = 1 ft

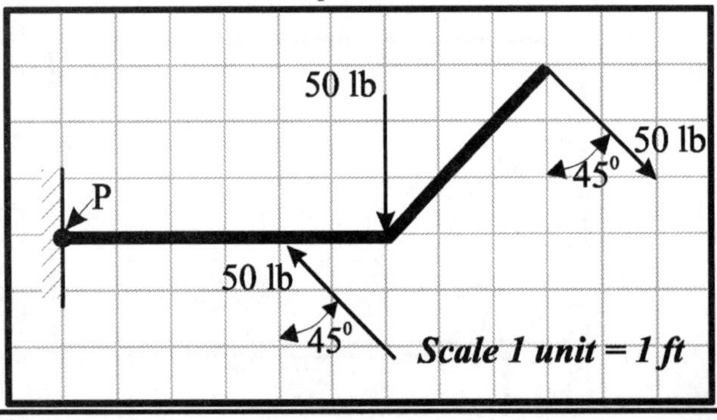

Problem 4

Determine the moment at point P.

2 kN   1 kN   45°

1 kN   P

45°   Scale 1 unit = .25 m

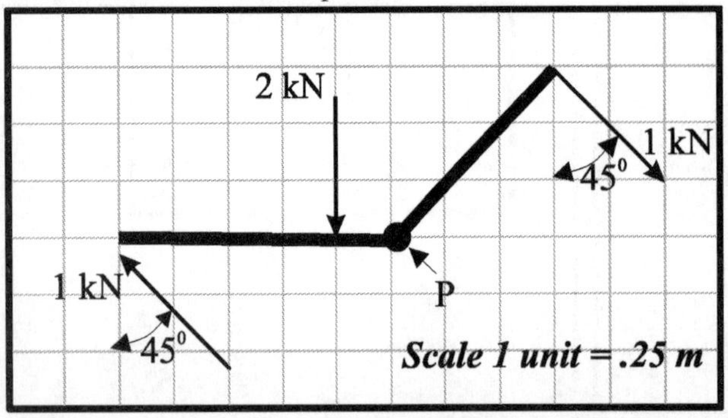

Name: _____

Problem 5

Determine the moment at point O due to three forces.

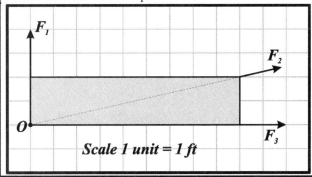

Problem 6

The moment at point P due to force *F* is 1 kN.m. Determine the magnitude of force *F*.

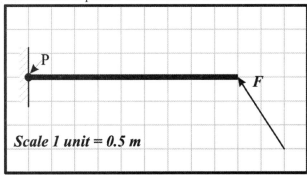

Problem 7

Determine the moment at point P.

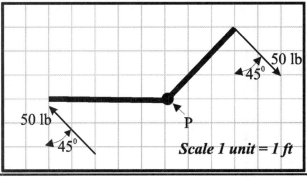

Problem 8

Determine the moment at point P.

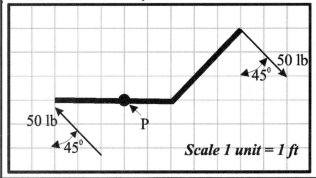

Name: _____

Problem 9

Determine the magnitude of minimum force *F* that must be applied to create a counterclockwise moment about P.

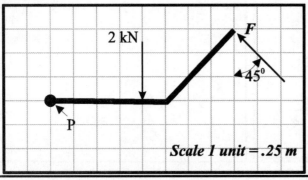

Problem 10

If the total moment about point P is 2 kN.m in the counter-clockwise direction, determine angle θ.

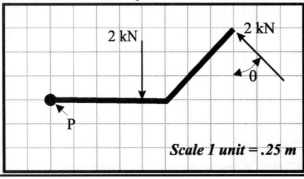

4.2. Twisting and Bending Moments

The moment of a force manifests as either a twisting or a bending moment load. To analyze structures, it is important to understand and distinguish between the two types of moments. In engineering, the *twisting moment* refers to the moment applied along the axis of a structural member. For instance, if we take an eraser and twist it holding its ends, the moment acts along the length (or axis) of the eraser. In Fig. 11, symbol *T* refers to the twisting moment. *Torsion* and *torque* are other commonly used terms to refer to the twisting moment. Another example involves the tightening of the lug nuts of a car wheel. The force applied to the wrench creates a moment along the axis of the nut. The torsion (the moment about the axis) tends to turn the nut. Torsion rotates a drill bit, the wheels of a car, a screw, a computer hard disk, and the main rotor of a helicopter. In each of these cases, torsion tends to twist the structural element.

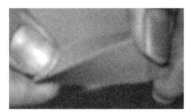

Figure 11. An eraser subjected to torsion

As opposed to torsion, a *bending moment* acts normal to the axis of the structural element and tends to bend the structural element. If we hold an eraser (see Fig. 12) at its ends and bend it, the moment acts perpendicular to the axis (or the length) of the eraser. The bending moment is a common form of structural loading. High-rise buildings acted on by the wind loads, the wings of an airplane subjected to lift, and the diving board supporting a diver are some examples of structural members in bending.

Figure 12. Bending moment

Example 4

Determine the twisting moment and bending moment at the bottom of the sign post. The wind load on the sign post is 5 kN. The weight of the sign post is 3 kN. Assume the weight of the structure is negligible.

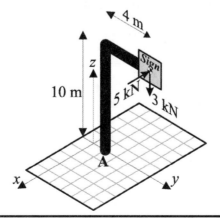

Figure 13. Wind and gravity loads on the sign post

If the sign post is pivoted at the bottom, it will rotate about the vertical axis (see Fig. 14a). Now, the twisting moment is given by

$$T = F \times d$$

In this equation, the wind is causing the sign post to rotate about the vertical axis. The distance (d) is the moment arm (shortest distance), which is equal to 4 m.

$$T = 5 \text{ kN} \times 4 \text{ m}$$

$$\boxed{T = 20 \text{ kN.m}}$$

The two forces cause two bending moments about two different axes. The gravitational load causes the structure to bend about the x-axis (see Fig. 14b). The wind force bends the structure about the y-axis (see Fig. 14c).

$$M_{about\ x\text{-}axis} = 3 \text{ kN} \times 4 \text{ m}$$

$$\boxed{M_{about\ x\text{-}axis} = 12 \text{ kN.m}}$$

$$M_{about\ y\text{-}axis} = 5 \text{ kN} \times 10 \text{ m}$$

$$\boxed{M_{about\ y\text{-}axis} = 50 \text{ kN.m}}$$

We can find the total bending moment by the vector addition of these two bending moments.

$$M = \sqrt{50^2 + 12^2}$$

$$\boxed{M = 51.42 \text{ kN.m}}$$

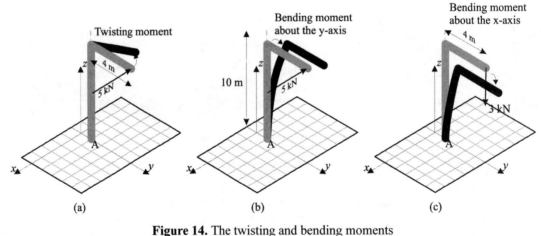

Figure 14. The twisting and bending moments

4.3. Vector Formulation of Moment

The vector formulation of moment involves the cross product of the position and force vectors. Before discussing the vector formulation, let us briefly review the properties of a cross product. The *cross product* or *vector product* of two vectors A and B is defined as

$$A \times B = |A||B| \sin \theta \, u_C \qquad\qquad 4$$

where θ is the angle between the two vectors. Vector u_C is a unit vector that defines the direction of the resulting vector. This direction is always perpendicular to the direction of vectors A and B and is defined by the right-hand rule (align the fingers along vector **A** and bend them towards vector **B** to make the thumb point in the direction of vector u_C) discussed in the previous section. From the equation, we can see that when θ is equal to zero i.e., when the two vectors are parallel to each other, the cross-product will be a null vector. Due to the right-hand rule, the order of vectors in a cross product plays an important role.

Therefore, the **cross product is *not* commutative**. In other words, $A \times B \neq B \times A$, but $A \times B = -B \times A$. The cross product satisfies the distributive law i.e., $A \times (B + C) = A \times B + A \times C$. The distributive relationship is very useful in computing the cross product of two vectors. It also satisfies the associative law with respect to multiplication by a scalar $\left(\mathbf{a}(A \times B) = (\mathbf{a}A) \times B = A \times (\mathbf{a}B) \text{ where } \mathbf{a} \text{ is a scalar} \right)$.

To compute the cross product of two vectors using their components, we need to determine the cross product of unit vectors i, j, and k. The cross product of any vector with itself is zero as they are parallel (i.e. $\theta = 0$).

$$i \times i = j \times j = k \times k = 0 \qquad\qquad 5$$

As the Cartesian unit vectors i, j, and k are orthogonal to each other, the cross product of any two of these vectors is unity because the magnitude of unit vectors is 1 and $\sin\theta$ is equal to 1. The sense or u_C can be obtained by the right-hand rule. Applying the right hand rule, we get

$$
\begin{aligned}
i \times j &= k & j \times i &= -k \\
j \times k &= i & k \times j &= -i \\
k \times i &= j & i \times k &= j
\end{aligned}
\qquad 6
$$

We can remember these relationships using Fig. 15. If we move in a counter-clockwise direction, the cross product of any two consequent unit vectors is equal to the third unit vector. For instance, $j \times k = i$. If the direction is reversed, the cross product of two unit vectors is equal to the negative of the third unit vector (for example, $k \times j = -i$).

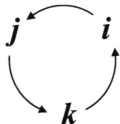

Figure 15. Use of circular arrangement to determine the cross product of Cartesian unit vectors

Now, we can write the cross-product of two vectors A and B as

$$
\begin{aligned}
A \times B &= \left(A_x i + A_y j + A_z k \right) \times \left(B_x i + B_y j + B_z k \right) \\
&= A_x B_x (i \times i) + A_x B_y (i \times j) + A_x B_z (i \times k) + \\
&\quad A_y B_x (j \times i) + A_y B_y (j \times j) + A_y B_z (j \times k) + \\
&\quad A_z B_x (k \times i) + A_z B_y (k \times j) + A_z B_z (k \times k)
\end{aligned}
$$

$$A \times B = \left(A_y B_z - A_z B_y \right) i - \left(A_x B_z - A_z B_x \right) j + \left(A_x B_y - A_y B_x \right) k$$

We can express the result of this cross product in a compact manner using the determinant as

$$
A \times B = \begin{vmatrix} i & j & k \\ A_x & A_y & A_z \\ B_x & B_y & B_z \end{vmatrix}
\qquad 7
$$

We can expand this cross product as

$$
A \times B = \begin{vmatrix} i & j & k \\ A_x & A_y & A_z \\ B_x & B_y & B_z \end{vmatrix}
\qquad
\begin{array}{l}\textbf{Remember:} \text{ Sign of the} \\ \text{second minor is negative}\end{array}
$$

$$
= i \begin{vmatrix} A_y & A_z \\ B_y & B_z \end{vmatrix} - j \begin{vmatrix} A_x & A_z \\ B_x & B_z \end{vmatrix} + k \begin{vmatrix} A_x & A_y \\ B_x & B_y \end{vmatrix}
$$

$$A \times B = \left(A_y B_z - A_z B_y \right) i - \left(A_x B_z - A_z B_x \right) j + \left(A_x B_y - A_y B_x \right) k \qquad 8$$

We arrive at the same solution if we expand the determinant. Also, it is important to assign a negative sign to the second minor (in front of j).

The moment of a force about point P can be defined as the cross product of position vector r and force vector F. Mathematically, we can write

$$M_P = r \times F \qquad 9$$

$$M_P = \begin{vmatrix} i & j & k \\ r_x & r_y & r_z \\ F_x & F_y & F_z \end{vmatrix}$$

$$M_P = \left(r_y F_z - r_z F_y \right) i - \left(r_x F_z - r_z F_x \right) j + \left(r_x F_y - r_y F_x \right) k \qquad 10$$

To understand the last equations, let us closely examine Fig. 16. It shows vector r and its components r_x, r_y, and r_z; and vector F and its components F_x, F_y, and F_z. Now, let us find out which force components will produce a moment around the x-axis. F_x is parallel to the x-axis and therefore does not produce any moment. On the other hand, F_y and F_z produce moments $r_z F_y$ and $r_y F_z$, respectively. Because moment $r_z F_y$ is clockwise, we find the net moment by subtracting $r_z F_y$ from $r_y F_z$. Hence, the moment around the x-axis is given by $\left(r_y F_z - r_z F_y \right) i$. A similar approach works for calculating the other two moment components around the y- and z-axes.

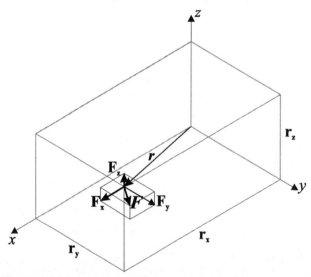

Figure 16. Moment caused by components of force vector F

According to the *principle of moments* or *Varignon's theorem, the sum of moments about point O due to a set of concurrent forces whose lines of action intersect at point P is equal to the moment about the same point due to the resultant force (vector sum of the forces) acting at point P*. Mathematically, we can express the principle of moments as

$$\sum \left(r_{OP} \times F_i \right) = r_{OP} \times \left(\sum F_i \right) = \left(r_{OP} \times F_R \right) \qquad 11$$

In other words, the moment about point P due to three concurrent forces F_1, F_2, and F_3 is equal to the moment caused by the resultant force F_R acting along the intersection of the lines of action of F_1, F_2, and F_3.

$$\left(r_{OP} \times F_1 \right) + \left(r_{OP} \times F_2 \right) + \left(r_{OP} \times F_3 \right) = r_{OP} \times \left(F_1 + F_2 + F_3 \right) = \left(r_{OP} \times F_R \right)$$

Example 5
Determine the moment caused by the 1000 lb force at the origin.

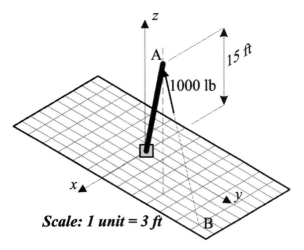

Figure 17. A force acting on a rigid rod

To find the moment, we need to define position vector r_A and the force vector. The position vector is
$$r_A = 9i + 9j + 15k \text{ ft}$$
The unit vector along BA is given by
$$u_{BA} = \frac{-3i - 9j + 15k}{\sqrt{3^2 + 9^2 + 15^2}}$$
$$= -0.1690\,i - 0.5070\,j + 0.8452\,k$$
Now, the force vector will be
$$F = 1000 \times u_{BA} = -169i - 507j + 845.2k \text{ lb}$$
The moment vector is
$$M_P = \begin{vmatrix} i & j & k \\ 9 & 9 & 15 \\ -169 & -507 & 845.2 \end{vmatrix}$$
$$= i\begin{vmatrix} 9 & 15 \\ -507 & 845.2 \end{vmatrix} - j\begin{vmatrix} 9 & 15 \\ -169 & 845.2 \end{vmatrix} + k\begin{vmatrix} 9 & 9 \\ -169 & -507 \end{vmatrix}$$
$$\boxed{M_P = 15212\,i - 10142\,j - 3042\,k \text{ lb.ft}}$$

As the line of action passes through point B, *we get the identical solution* even *if we calculate the cross product between r_B and F* as shown below:
$$M_P = \begin{vmatrix} i & j & k \\ 12 & 18 & 0 \\ -169 & -507 & 845 \end{vmatrix}$$
$$= i\begin{vmatrix} 18 & 0 \\ -507 & 845.2 \end{vmatrix} - j\begin{vmatrix} 12 & 0 \\ -169 & 845.2 \end{vmatrix} + k\begin{vmatrix} 12 & 18 \\ -169 & -507 \end{vmatrix}$$
$$\boxed{M_P = 15212\,i - 10142\,j - 3042\,k \text{ lb.ft}}$$

Further, the cross product of r_B and F is easier to calculate.

"Moment Analysis.xls" on the CD can help to determine the moment due to several force vectors.

Notes:

Concept Questions

Name: _____

1. TRUE/FALSE: The bending moment acts along the axis of a structural element.

2. Give two examples of structural elements subjected to torsion.

3. Give two examples of structural elements subjected to a bending moment.

4. The twisting moment at the base of the structure is:
    A. 50 kN.m
    B. 30 kN.m
    C. 20 kN.m
    D. 12 kN.m

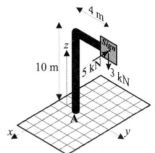

5. What is the principle of moments or Varignon's theorem?

6. The tension in the cable AB is *T*. The moment of this tension about point O is:
    A. $T \times r_{OA}$
    B. $r_{AB} \times T$
    C. $r_{OB} \times T$
    D. None of the above

7. Write the equation for the moment about the x-axis (Refer to the adjacent figure).

8. Write the equation for the moment about the y-axis (Refer to the adjacent figure).

9. Write the equation for the moment about the z-axis (Refer to the adjacent figure).

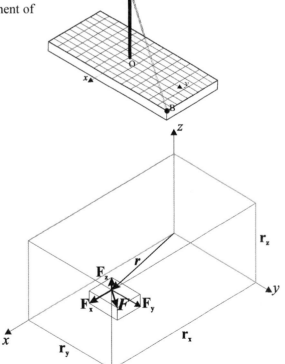

10. TRUE/FALSE: The moment of a force about point P can be defined as the cross product of force vector *F* and position vector *r*. Mathematically, we can write it as
$$M_P = F \times r$$

Name: _____

Problem 1

Determine the twisting and bending moments for the structure at the base.

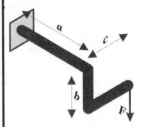

Problem 2

Determine the twisting and bending moments for the structure at the base due to each force.

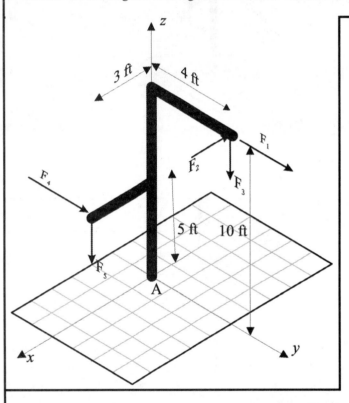

Force	Torque T	Bending moment about the x-axis $M_{about\ x\text{-}axis}$	Bending moment about the y-axis $M_{about\ y\text{-}axis}$	Total bending moment M
$F_1 = 100$ lb				
$F_2 = 150$ lb				
$F_3 = 200$ lb				
$F_4 = 300$ lb				
$F_5 = 400$ lb				

(A partial solution using the vector representation is given in "Moment Analysis.xls" on the CD)

Name: _____

Problem 3

Determine the twisting and bending moments for the structure at the base.

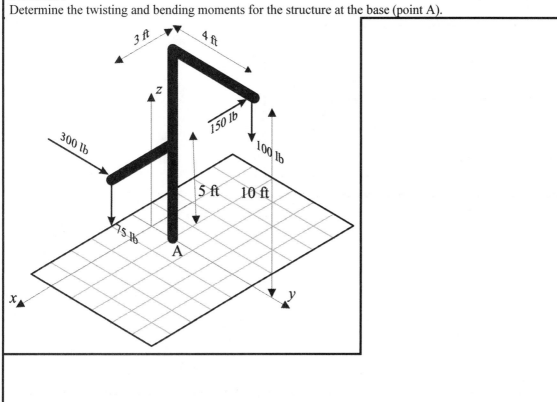

Problem 4

Determine the twisting and bending moments for the structure at the base (point A).

Name: _____

Problem 5

Determine the moment at point P using the vector formulation (the cross product method).

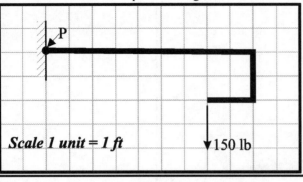

Scale 1 unit = 1 ft

150 lb

Problem 6

Determine the moment at point P using the vector formulation (the cross product method).

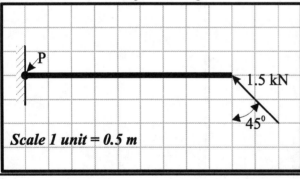

Scale 1 unit = 0.5 m

1.5 kN

45⁰

Name: _____

Problem 7

Determine the moment at point P using the vector formulation (the cross product method).

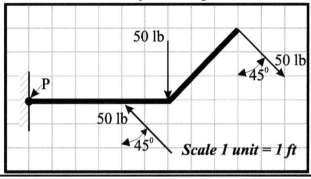

Problem 8

Determine the moment at point P using the vector formulation (the cross product method).

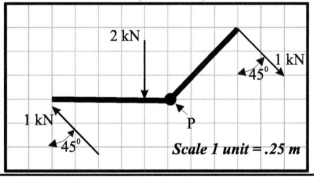

Name: _____

Problem 9

Determine the moment caused by the three forces at point P (use the principle of moments).

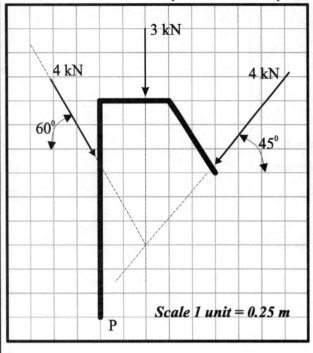

Scale 1 unit = 0.25 m

Problem 10

A pole is pulled by a cable. If the tension in the cable is 200 lb, determine the moment at point P using the vector formulation (the cross product method).

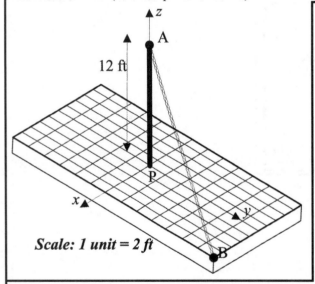

Scale: 1 unit = 2 ft

Name: _____

Problem 11

A 40 ft tall tower is stabilized in a plane using four cables. The tension in each cable is 800 lb. Determine the net bending moment at point O using the vector formulation (the cross product method).

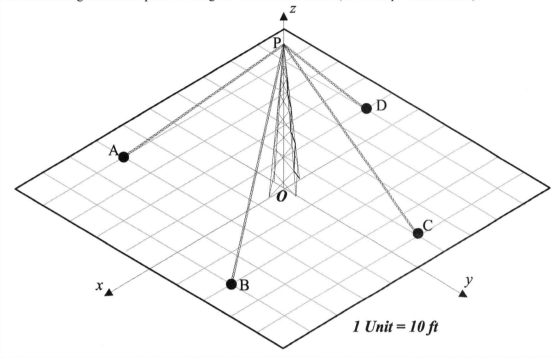

1 Unit = 10 ft

Notes:

4.4. Moment of a Force about an Axis

Drawbridges of Chicago

Drawbridges are known as bascule bridges in the technical jargon. The French word "Bascule" means seesaw. While many types of bascule bridges exist, the Chicago bascule bridge is a common type which originated, extensively used, and perfected in the city of Chicago (Refer to Fig. 18).

Figure 18. A Chicago bascule bridge

A Chicago Bascule bridge consists of the bridge span (called a leaf), an axle about which the bridge rotates (called a trunnion), and a counterweight. While the weight of the bridge span produces a clockwise moment, the counterweight produces moment in the opposite direction. These moments cancel each other, and the net moment about the axis through the trunnion is equal to zero. Thus, the counterweight minimizes the energy loss in lifting unnecessary weight. The task of the drive motor is reduced to overcoming only the inertial and frictional forces. This clever principle of balancing is used in all bascule bridges and can also be noticed in many designs such as elevators.

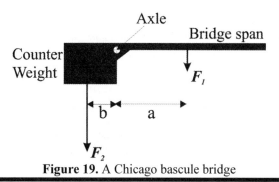

Figure 19. A Chicago bascule bridge

Often, determining the moment of a force about an axis involves an operation known as the *mixed triple product*. The mixed triple product of three vectors A, B, and C is

$$A \cdot (B \times C) = \left(A_x i + A_y j + A_z k \right) \cdot \begin{vmatrix} i & j & k \\ B_x & B_y & B_z \\ C_x & C_y & C_z \end{vmatrix}$$

$$A \cdot (B \times C) = \left(A_x i + A_y j + A_z k \right) \cdot \left(B_y C_z - B_z C_y \right) i - \left(B_x C_z - B_z C_x \right) j + \left(B_x C_y - B_y C_x \right) k$$

$$A \cdot (B \times C) = A_x \left(B_y C_z - B_z C_y \right) - A_y \left(B_x C_z - B_z C_x \right) + A_z \left(B_x C_y - B_y C_x \right)$$

The result can be concisely expressed as

$$A \cdot (B \times C) = \begin{vmatrix} A_x & A_y & A_z \\ B_x & B_y & B_z \\ C_x & C_y & C_z \end{vmatrix}$$

12

Now, let us try to qualitatively understand the mixed triple product operation. The cross product $B \times C$ results in a vector. If A is a unit vector, the dot product between A and $B \times C$ will determine the component of the resultant cross product vector along vector A – a scalar quantity.

In the previous section, we discussed the procedure for finding the moment of a force about a point. The moment of force F about point P is

$$M_P = r \times F$$

13

The direction of moment M_P is defined by the normal to the plane containing force F and position vector r. However sometimes, we need to compute the moment about a specific axis passing through point P. If we resolve moment M_P along the axis, we get the moment about the axis - M_A. We can compute the magnitude of moment M_A by taking a dot product between u_A (a unit vector along the axis about which we need to determine the moment), and moment M_P. The direction of moment M_A is defined by unit vector u_A. Mathematically, we can write

$$M_A = (u_A . M_P) u_A$$

14

This equation can be expanded to form a mixed triple product operation:

$$M_A = (u_A \cdot (r \times F)) u_A$$

$$M_A = \begin{vmatrix} u_{Ax} & u_{Ay} & u_{Az} \\ r_x & r_y & r_z \\ F_x & F_y & F_z \end{vmatrix} u_A$$

15

Let us review the equation once again to understand each term. The term $u_A \cdot (r \times F)$ is a scalar and defines the magnitude of the moment. Because the moment about an axis is a vector whose direction is specified by the axis itself, the moment is the product of the triple cross product $(u_A \cdot (r \times F)$ - a scalar$)$ and the unit vector defining the axis $(u_A$ - a vector$)$.

Example 6
A door lying in the xy plane is pivoted along one edge. A cable is holding the door in position. Determine the moment created by the cable about the pivot axis if the tension in the cable is 100 lb.

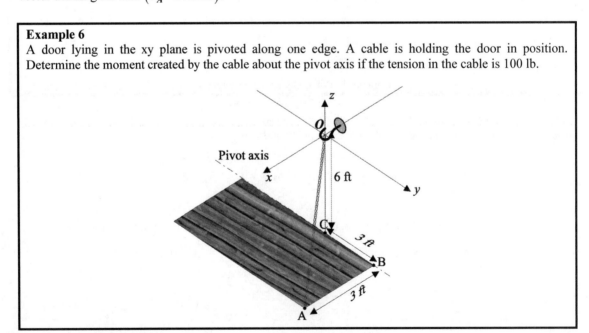

Figure 20. A door supported by a cable

We can use two solution procedures to solve this problem.

Solution Procedure I:

The moment about an axis is given by

$$M_A = \left(u_A \cdot \left(r \times F \right) \right) u_A$$

To compute the moment, we need to write u_A, r, and F.

The pivot axis is parallel to the y axis. Therefore, we can write

$$u_A = j$$

Now, we can write vector r from C to A.

$$r_{CA} = 3i + 3j \text{ ft}$$

To express the force vector using the Cartesian vector notation, we need to find the unit vector along the AO direction.

$$u_{AO} = \frac{-3i - 3j + 6k}{\sqrt{3^2 + 3^2 + 6^2}}$$

$$= -0.408i - 0.408j + 0.816k$$

The force vector is given by

$$F_{AO} = -40.8i - 40.8j + 81.6k \text{ lb}$$

Now, the moment vector about the pivot axis M_A is

$$M_A = \left(u_A \cdot \left(r \times F \right) \right) u_A$$

$$M_A = \begin{vmatrix} u_{Ax} & u_{Ay} & u_{Az} \\ r_x & r_y & r_z \\ F_x & F_y & F_z \end{vmatrix} u_A$$

$$M_A = \begin{vmatrix} 0 & 1 & 0 \\ 3 & 3 & 0 \\ -40.8 & -40.8 & 81.6 \end{vmatrix} j$$

$$\boxed{M_A = -244.8 \, j \text{ lb. ft}}$$

As vector r goes from the any point on the axis to a point on the force's line of action, we can use r_{BA} or r_{CO} and come up with the same result. Needless to say, an intelligent choice of the position vector can reduce the complexity of calculations needed.

Solution Procedure II

The second procedure involves the resolution of the force vector into its components and the computing of the moment caused by these individual components along the pivot axis.

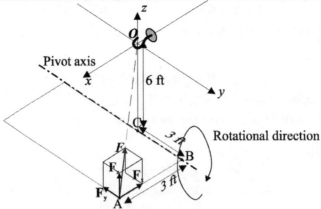

Figure 21. Force components acting on the door

To determine the force vector using the Cartesian vector notation, we must find the unit vector along the AO direction.

$$u_{AO} = \frac{-3i - 3j + 6k}{\sqrt{3^2 + 3^2 + 6^2}}$$

$$= -0.408i - 0.408j + 0.816k$$

The force vector is given by

$$F_{AO} = -40.8i - 40.8j + 81.6k \text{ lb}$$

The force components are

$$\mathbf{F_x} = -40.8 \text{ lb}; \quad \mathbf{F_y} = -40.8 \text{ lb}; \quad \mathbf{F_z} = 81.6 \text{ lb}$$

Because the x-component of the force passes through the pivot axis, it does not produce any moment about the pivot axis. Similarly, the moment about the pivot axis due to the y-component is zero because the force is parallel to the pivot axis. Now, only the z-component produces a moment. The moment is given by

$$M_A = \mathbf{F_z} d$$

where d is the moment arm (= 3 ft).
Substituting the values for $\mathbf{F_z}$ and d, we get

$$\boxed{M_A = 244.8 \text{ lb.ft}}$$

The force vector has the tendency to rotate the door in a clockwise direction around the pivot axis (see Fig. 21). Therefore, using the right-hand rule, we can determine the direction of M_A as $-j$. vc 676

Name: _____

Problem 1 (Use solution procedure II – example 6)

Determine the moment due to force vector $2i + 3j + 4k$ lb acting at P(6,8,12) about each coordinate axis.

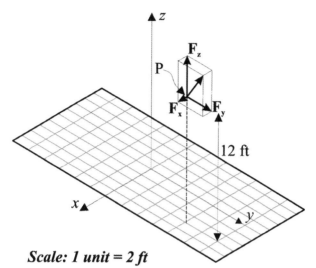

Scale: 1 unit = 2 ft

	Moment about					
	x-axis		y-axis		z-axis	
F^* components	F_y	F_z				
d						
Magnitude of M_A						
Direction of M_A						
Total Moment Vector M_A						

* Component of the force vector causing moment about the specified axis.

Problem 2

Determine the moment due to force vector $2i + 3j - 4k$ kN acting at P(-2,-3,-4) about each coordinate axis.

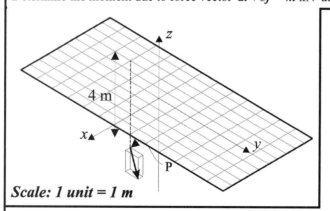

Scale: 1 unit = 1 m

Name: _____

Problem 3

Determine the moment due to force vector $2i + 3j + 4k$ lb acting at P(6,6,12) about axis A.

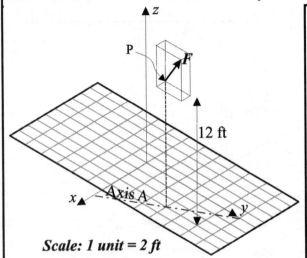

Scale: 1 unit = 2 ft

Determine unit vector along axis A - u_A.

Determine the position vector r (make an intelligence choice).

Determine the moment about axis A using the mixed triple product.

Problem 4

Determine the moment due to force vector $2i + 3j + 4k$ lb acting at P(6,6,12) about axis A.

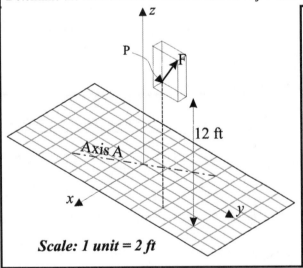

Scale: 1 unit = 2 ft

Name: _____

Problem 5

Determine the moment due to force vector $60i + 30j - 50k$ kN acting at D about axis AB using both solution procedures.

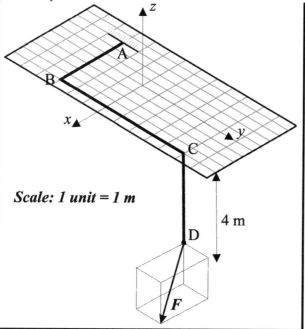

Scale: 1 unit = 1 m

4 m

Name: _____

Problem 6

Determine the torque and bending moment about the x- and y-axes for the structure at the base due to each force (using solution procedure I). $F_1 = 100$ lb, $F_2 = 150$ lb, $F_3 = 200$ lb, $F_4 = 300$ lb, $F_5 = 400$ lb. Compare the results with those for Problem 2 in Exercise Set II.

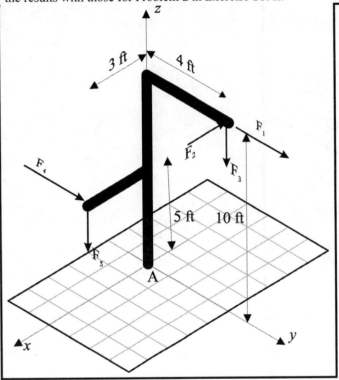

4.5. Moment of a Couple

A *couple* is defined as two equal and opposite forces offset by a distance. Fig. 22(a) shows two collinear (same line of action) forces whose magnitude is equal but whose direction is opposite to one another. The resultant force due to these two force vectors is equal to zero. The moment about point P is also equal to zero as these two forces pass through point P. Fig. 22(b) shows these two forces offset by distance d (*the perpendicular distance between the lines of action of the two forces*). The resultant force remains at zero. However, the moment due to these forces is not equal to zero, and is termed as a couple.

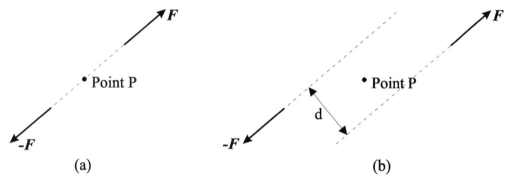

Figure 22. Two equal and opposite forces with (a) no offset, and (b) offset d

Let us find the moment due to these two forces about points P_1 and P_2 (see Fig. 23). About point P_1, force F produces a counterclockwise moment whose magnitude is $F.d_2$. Force $-F$ also produces a counterclockwise moment, whose magnitude is $F.d_1$. Therefore, the net moment about point P_1 is

$$M_{P1} = Fd_1 + Fd_2$$
$$= F(d_1 + d_2)$$
$$M_{P1} = F\,d \qquad\qquad 16$$

The moment about point P_2 is caused only by force F as force $-F$ passes through point P_2. About point P_2, force F produces a counterclockwise moment whose magnitude is Fd. It is important to note that *the moment of a couple is the same irrespective of where the moment is calculated*. Therefore, we often calculate the moment about a point on the line of action of one of the forces. In the vector form, we can compute the moment using the formula

$$M = r \times F \qquad\qquad 17$$

where r is the position vector from the line of action of one force to a point on the other. We apply force couples all the time to wrenches and the handles of screwdrivers.

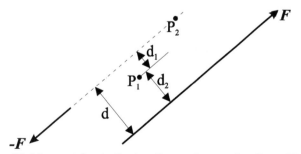

Figure 23. Moment due to the two forces about points P_1 and P_2

Design of Casters for an Office Chair

An intelligent application of a couple is the design of casters for office chairs. In the caster design, the axis of rotation of the caster is offset from the rotational axis of the wheel. As a result, when a user pushes the chair, the moment of the force couple rotates the wheel and aligns it along the direction of the motion. This self-aligning design can be found in various applications, such as shopping carts.

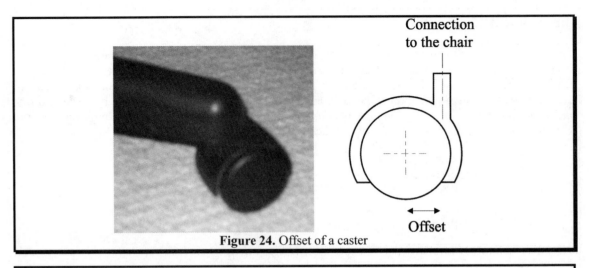

Figure 24. Offset of a caster

Example 7

Determine the couple moment. Force F is given by $60i + 30j - 50k$ lb.

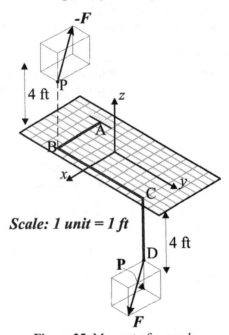

Figure 25. Moment of a couple

This particular problem involves the forces acting in three-dimensional space. To determine the moment, first we need to find the position vector from a point on the line of action of $-F$ force to the second force. One such position vector is r_{PD}.

$$r_{PD} = 8j - 8k \text{ ft}$$

Now, the moment due to the couple is

$$M = r_{PD} \times F$$

$$M = \begin{vmatrix} i & j & k \\ 0 & 8 & -8 \\ 60 & 30 & -50 \end{vmatrix}$$

$$\boxed{M = -160i + 480j - 480k \text{ lb.ft}}$$

Name: _____

Problem 1

Determine the moment of the couple (use equation 16).

1 kN

1 kN

Scale 1 unit = .25 m

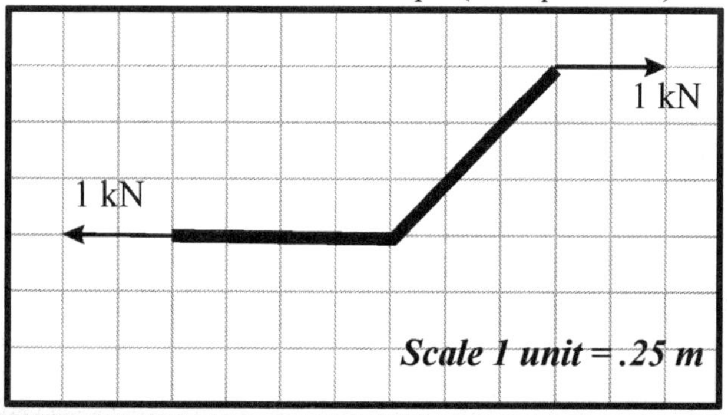

Problem 2

Determine the moment of the couple (use equation 16).

1 kN

1 kN

Scale 1 unit = .25 m

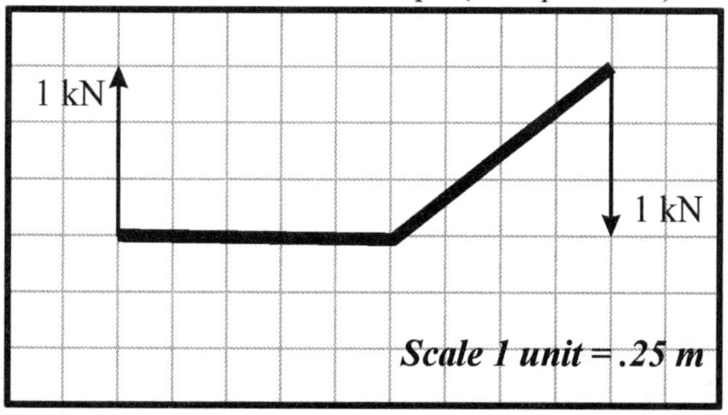

Problem 3

Determine the moment of the couple (use equation 16).

1 kN

45°

1 kN

45°

Scale 1 unit = .25 m

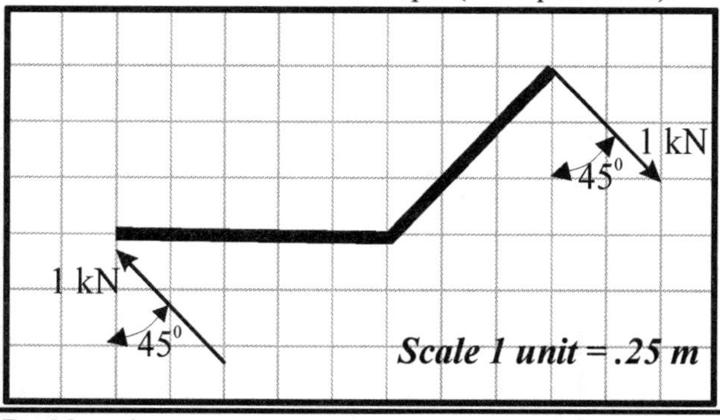

Problem 4

Determine the moment of the couple (use equation 16).

1 kN

45°

2 kN

45°

1 kN

45°

Scale 1 unit = .25 m

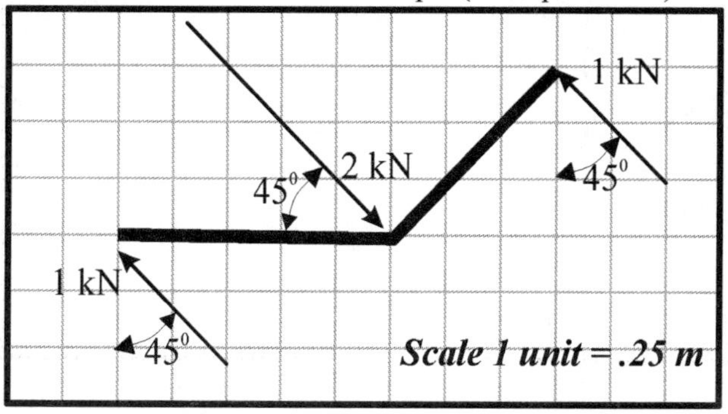

Name: _____

Problem 5

Determine the moment of the couple (use equation 17). Compare the results with problem 3.

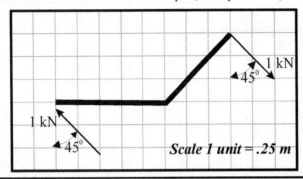

Scale 1 unit = .25 m

Problem 6

Determine the moment of the couple (use equation 17).

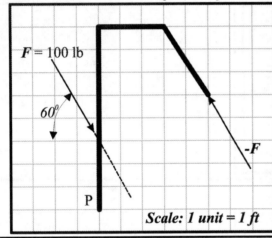

Scale: 1 unit = 1 ft

Problem 7

Determine the moment of the couple. Force F is $2i + 3j + 4k$ kN. The coordinates of point P_1 are $(6,6,12)$. The coordinates of point P_2 are $(-6,-8,-12)$.

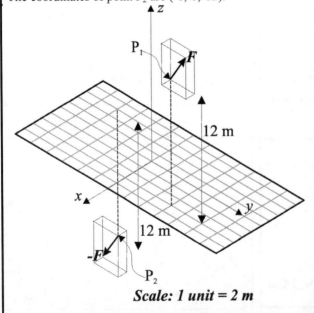

Scale: 1 unit = 2 m

4.6. Equivalent Systems

Analysis often calls for the simplification of real world problems into idealized systems. For instance, the gravitational pull (or weight) is a body force that acts on the entire volume of a rigid body. In the analysis methods covered in earlier chapters, we simplified this distributed force with a concentrated force that acts at the center of gravity of the rigid body. Intuitively, we understand that these two systems (real world and idealized) are equivalent or alike. While the concentrated force due to weight creates a different internal force distribution, the external behavior (reactions, and translational and rotational motion) remains unchanged.

Two systems of forces and moments are equivalent if the resultant force and the resultant moment about any point of the first system are identical to those of the second system. Mathematically, if two systems are equivalent, then

$$\left(\sum F\right)_{\text{system 1}} = \left(\sum F\right)_{\text{system 2}}$$

$$\left(\sum M\right)_{\text{about point P - system 1}} = \left(\sum F\right)_{\text{about point P - system 2}}$$

18

For instance, consider the two systems summarized in Table 1. The resultant force as well as the moment about any point are the same for the two systems. Therefore, they are equivalent systems.

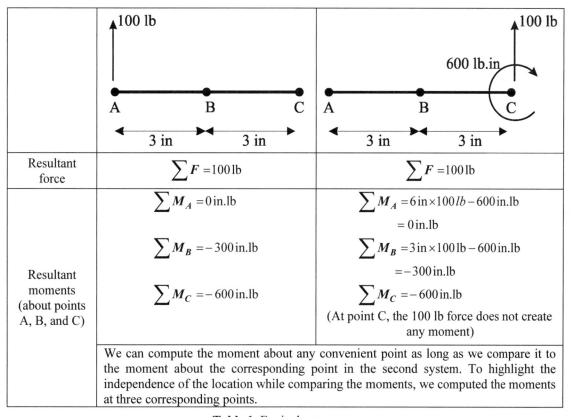

Resultant force	$\sum F = 100\,\text{lb}$	$\sum F = 100\,\text{lb}$
Resultant moments (about points A, B, and C)	$\sum M_A = 0\,\text{in.lb}$ $\sum M_B = -300\,\text{in.lb}$ $\sum M_C = -600\,\text{in.lb}$	$\sum M_A = 6\,\text{in} \times 100\,lb - 600\,\text{in.lb}$ $= 0\,\text{in.lb}$ $\sum M_B = 3\,\text{in} \times 100\,\text{lb} - 600\,\text{in.lb}$ $= -300\,\text{in.lb}$ $\sum M_C = -600\,\text{in.lb}$ (At point C, the 100 lb force does not create any moment)
	We can compute the moment about any convenient point as long as we compare it to the moment about the corresponding point in the second system. To highlight the independence of the location while comparing the moments, we computed the moments at three corresponding points.	

Table 1. Equivalent systems

Example 8

Determine whether the two systems of forces and moments are equivalent.

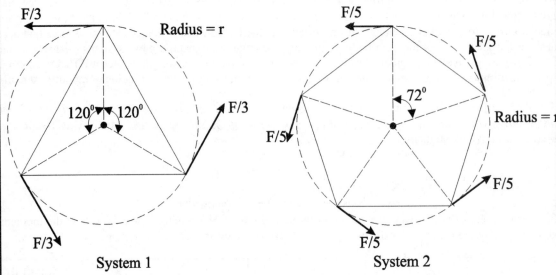

Figure 26. Two systems with different loading

To establish the equivalency of two systems, we must compare the resultant force and the resultant moment about any arbitrary point.

Now, the resultant force in both systems is zero. In both systems, we can align the heads to tails (as shown in Fig. 27) and determine the resultant force to be zero.

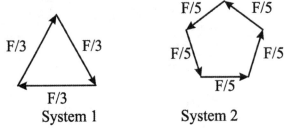

Figure 27. The resultant force

The resultant force equivalency leads to the second condition, the moment equivalency. The resultant moment for system I about the center of the circle is

$$M_{System\,I} = \sum F.d$$
$$= 3 \times \left(\frac{F}{3} \times r \right)$$
$$= Fr$$

The resultant moment for system II about the center of the circle is

$$M_{System\,II} = \sum F.d$$
$$= 5 \times \left(\frac{F}{5} \times r \right)$$
$$= Fr$$

By comparing the resultant force and the resultant moment, we can conclude that the two systems are equivalent.

Let us first consider the method for simplifying a coplanar system of forces and couples that act perpendicular to the plane. Fig. 28(a) shows three forces acting in a single plane and three couples that are perpendicular to the plane, i.e., rotating about the z-axis. This force system is equivalent to the resultant force F_R and the resultant moment M_{R_O} at point O as shown in Fig. 28(b), where

$$F_R = \sum F_i$$

$$M_{R\_O} = \sum M_i + \sum r \times F$$

We can now move the force vector F_R away from point O to create the resultant moment M_{R_O} at point O. For this condition to occur, $F \times d = M_{R\_O}$. This simplified system with a single force, shown in Fig. 28(c), is equivalent to the earlier systems. This method can be applied only if the resultant force is non-zero. If the resultant force is zero, then the system can be reduced to a system with concentrated moment.

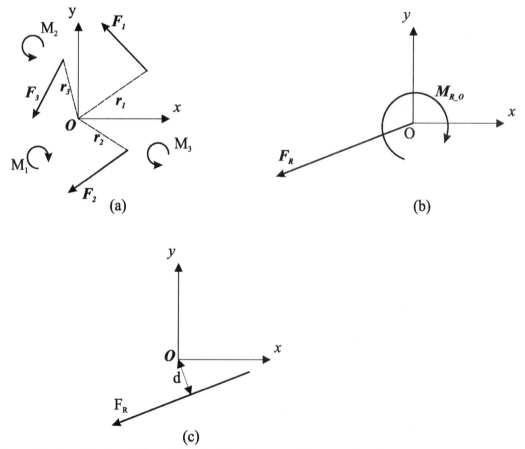

Figure 28. Simplification of a system of coplanar forces with moments acting perpendicular to the plane

Example 9
Create a simplified force system for the beam.

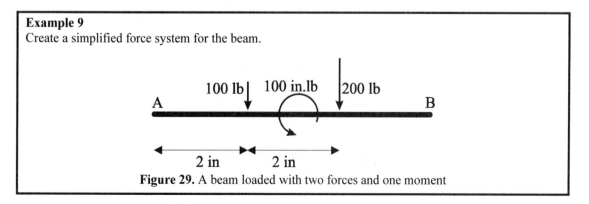

Figure 29. A beam loaded with two forces and one moment

The solution calls for the determination of the resultant force and the resultant moment about an arbitrary point and then relocating or offsetting the resultant force vector to eliminate the resultant moment.

In the first step, we can determine the resultant force and the resultant moment about point A as

$$F_R = \sum F_i$$

$$\boxed{F_R = -300\,\text{lb}}$$

$$M_{R\_A} = \sum M_i + \sum r \times F$$

$$= +100\,\text{in.lb} - 200\,\text{in.lb} - 800\,\text{in.lb}$$

$$= -900\,\text{in.lb}$$

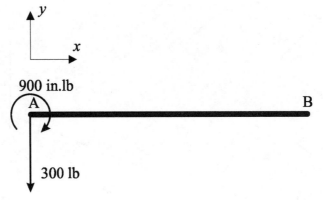

Figure 30. Equivalent system with force and moment at point A

The negative signs for the resultant force and the resultant moment are dropped from the numerical values and are incorporated by an appropriate use of arrowheads.

The second step involves repositioning the force vector to create the result moment of 900 in.lb.

$$F \times d = M_{R\_A}$$

$$-300\,\text{lb} \times d = -900\,\text{in.lb}$$

$$\boxed{d = 3\,\text{in}}$$

Figure 31. Simplified system

Example 10

Create a simplified force system for the plate.

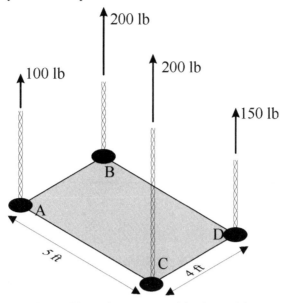

Figure 32. A plate supported by four cables

The resultant force of the four force vectors is

$$F_R = \sum F_i$$

$$\boxed{F_R = 650\,\text{lb}}$$

Now, let us establish a coordinate system and locate the resultant force in terms of two unknown quantities (refer to Fig. 33).

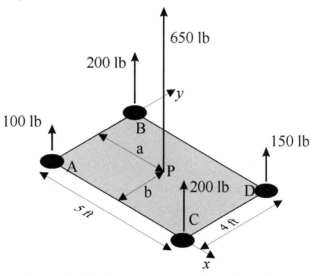

Figure 33. The force vectors and the resultant force

Now, the coordinates of the points are A (0,0,0), B (0,4,0), C (5,0,0), and D (5,4,0). Let the coordinates of point P be (a,b,0).

$$M_{R\_A} = \begin{vmatrix} i & j & k \\ 0 & 0 & 0 \\ 0 & 0 & 100 \end{vmatrix} + \begin{vmatrix} i & j & k \\ 0 & 4 & 0 \\ 0 & 0 & 200 \end{vmatrix} + \begin{vmatrix} i & j & k \\ 5 & 0 & 0 \\ 0 & 0 & 200 \end{vmatrix} + \begin{vmatrix} i & j & k \\ 5 & 4 & 0 \\ 0 & 0 & 150 \end{vmatrix}$$

$$M_{R\_A} = \left(800 + 600\right)i + \left(-1000 - 750\right)j + 0k$$

$$M_{R\_A} = 1400i - 1750j + 0k$$

Now, equating M_{R_O} with $r \times F$, we get

$$r \times F = M_{R\_A}$$

$$\begin{vmatrix} i & j & k \\ a & b & 0 \\ 0 & 0 & 650 \end{vmatrix} = 1400i - 1750j + 0k$$

$$650\,b\,i - 650\,a\,j + 0k = 1400i - 1750j + 0k$$

$$\boxed{\begin{array}{l} a = 2.692\,\text{ft} \\ b = 2.154\,\text{ft} \end{array}}$$

Name: _____

Problem 1

Determine whether the two systems of forces and moments are equivalent.

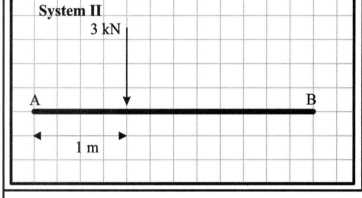

Problem 2

Determine whether the two systems of forces and moments are equivalent.

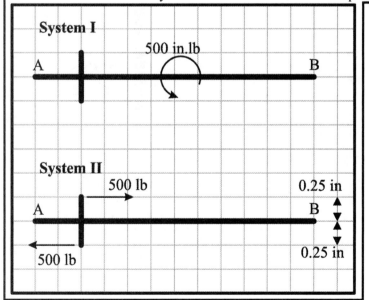

Name: _____

Problem 3
Determine whether the two systems of forces and moments are equivalent.

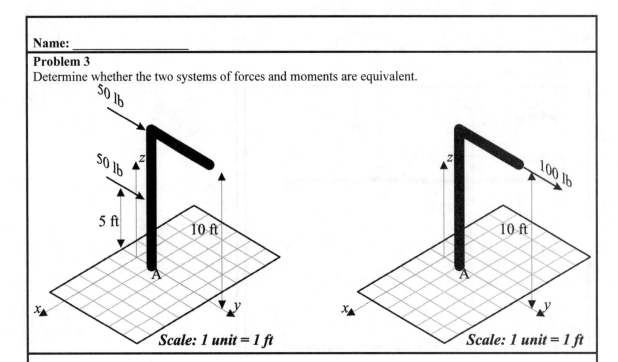

Scale: 1 unit = 1 ft   *Scale: 1 unit = 1 ft*

Problem 4
Determine whether the two systems of forces and moments are equivalent.

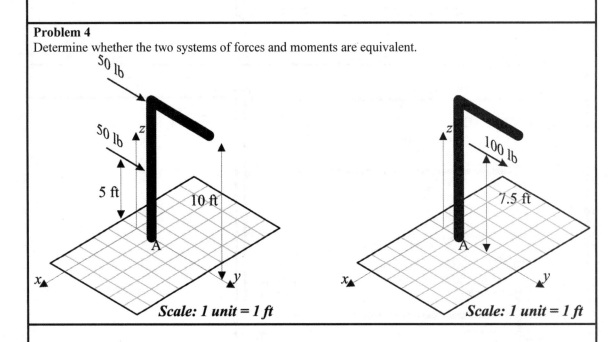

Scale: 1 unit = 1 ft   *Scale: 1 unit = 1 ft*

Name: _____

Problem 5
Create a simplified force system for the beam.

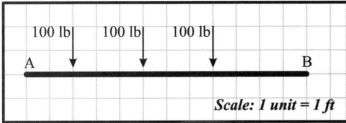

Problem 6
Create a simplified force system for the beam.

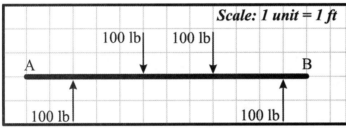

Problem 7
Create a simplified force system for the beam.

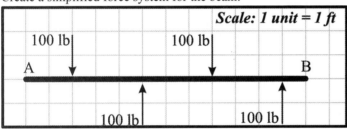

Problem 8
Create a simplified force system for the beam.

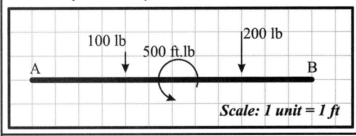

Problem 9
Create a simplified force system for the beam.

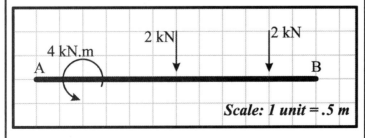

Name: _____

Problem 10

Create a simplified force system for the plate. Use the three-dimensional vector formulation $\left(M_{R\_O} = r \times F\right)$ to locate the resultant force vector.

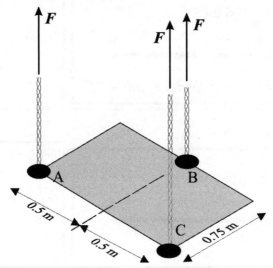

CHAPTER V
EQUILIBRIUM OF A RIGID BODY

Learning Objectives

The material presented in this chapter will enable you to accomplish the following:
1. Define a rigid body.
2. Understand different types of supports and the reactions that they offer.
3. Identify two- and three-force systems.
4. Convert distributed forces into concentrated forces.
5. Analyze two- and three-dimensional force systems.
6. Evaluate the conditions for the tipping of a rigid body.

The Front-Wheel Suspension System

In a traditional fork design for a motorcycle suspension system (refer to Fig. 1a), when the driver applies the brake, brake force F can be resolved into two components: one along the steering column (F_A) and the second normal or transverse to the steering column (F_T) (refer to Fig. 1a). Force component F_A compresses the steering column and physically manifests as the brake dive. The second component (F_T) bends the telescopic mechanism of the suspension system. A hard braking causes a significant brake dive and a temporary loss of suspension due to the binding of the telescopic mechanism. This interaction is critical in the design of suspension systems with Anti-lock Braking Systems (ABS). In this design layout, a designer can vary the angle of the steering column and change the magnitude of these two components.

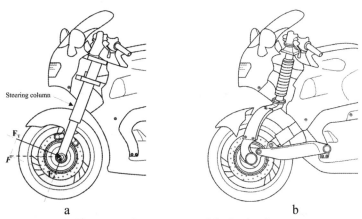

a   b

Figure 1. Components of the brake force

To address this interaction, Parker created an innovative suspension known as Rationally ADvanced Design (RADD) (see figure 1b). It was first commercially incorporated into the Yamaha GTS 1000A motorcycle. In this design, the brake force is transmitted from the front wheel to the body through a short and direct transmission path using a lower control arm. Because the lower arm is in-line with the braking force, it is a two-force member and avoids bending loads. This innovation reduced the steered mass and the brake dive by fifty and seventy-five percent, respectively. The system is light with a lower center of gravity and a reduced polar moment of inertia.

The concepts in this chapter help to evaluate the loads experienced by various structural members and synthesize alternative designs that minimize the loads.

5.1. Equilibrium of a Rigid Body

A rigid body is an idealization of a real object whose geometry (shape and dimensions) remains the same when a set of forces and moments is applied. Because all objects deform to a smaller or greater extent under the application of load, there is no rigid body in the real world. However, it serves as a useful idealization in solving equilibrium problems and can be applied to situations where the deformation under the action of forces and moments is negligible in comparison to the overall dimensions of the body and when the deformation does not affect the force and moment calculations.

When dealing with the equilibrium of particles, we were concerned with the force equilibrium equation $\left(\sum F = 0\right)$ alone. The equilibrium of rigid bodies, on the other hand, requires two equations:

The force equilibrium equation – The sum of the forces should be equal to zero.

$$\sum F = 0 \qquad\qquad 1$$

The moment equilibrium equation – The sum of the moments should be equal to zero.

$$\sum M_{about\ any\ point} = 0 \qquad\qquad 2$$

The two equilibrium equations (force and moment equilibrium equations) form the necessary and sufficient conditions for the equilibrium of rigid objects. If the moment about one point is zero, the moment about any other point will also be zero because the moment is a free vector. Therefore, in the moment equation, the moment can be computed about any point in the rigid body.

The analysis of rigid bodies acted on by a system of forces and moments requires the same procedure as that of a particle. Before understanding the steps, which include drawing the free body diagram and applying the equilibrium equations, we must first understand the reactions offered at the supports.

5.2. Support Reactions for a Coplanar Force System

In a two-dimensional space, a rigid body has three degrees of freedom. It can translate along the x- and y-directions, and can rotate about the z-axis (see Fig. 2). A support restricts translations and/or rotations of the body of our interest. For instance, the rigid body in Fig. 3 has a slot and is connected to the xy-plane with a pin. The rigid body is free to move along the y-direction and can rotate about the z-axis. However, a horizontal motion is constrained by the slot-pin mechanism. To restrict the translation in a certain direction, the support exerts a reaction force in the opposite direction. In other words, if we try to push the rigid body (refer to Fig. 3) in the positive x-direction, the pin exerts a force reaction along the negative x-direction. Thus, the body experiences a force in the opposite direction. Similarly, a support prevents the rotations by providing a moment reaction.

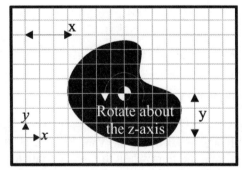

Figure 2. A rigid body in the xy plane

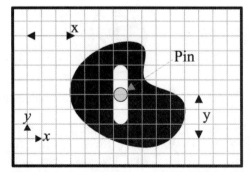

Figure 3. A rigid body constrained in the x-direction.

For a coplanar force system, Table 1 provides common supports and the reactions that they incur.

	Schematic	Reactions
Pin or hinge support: Prevents the translations, but allows the rotation about the pin axis.		
Roller support: A pinned support mounted on rollers. Prevents translation perpendicular to the surface. Offers no resistance to motion along the surface. Allows rotation about the pin axis.		
Rocker support: Prevents translation perpendicular to the surface. Offers no resistance to motion along the surface. Allows rotation about the pin axis.		
Cable support: Provides a pulling force along the cable.		
Spring support: Provides a force along the spring.		
Smooth contacting surface support: Prevents translation normal to the surface.		
Constrained sliding pin support: Prevents motion normal to the sliding axis.		
Slider connection: Prevents translation and rotation normal to the sliding axis.		
Fixed or built-in support: Prevents both translations and rotations.		

Table 1. Supports, schematic representation, and reactions offered by different supports

5.3. Analysis Procedure

Analysis involves two steps: (1) drawing the free-body diagram and (2) applying the equilibrium equations. We have already learned how to create free-body diagrams. It call for a sketch showing only the body of our interest, isolated from its surroundings, while capturing all the forces acting on it. To review, drawing a free body diagram takes four steps:

1. *Sketch the overall shape:* Draw the object removed or isolated from its surroundings at the locations where they act. Try to capture the overall shape without focusing on details.
2. *Show ALL forces:* Pencil in all the forces acting on the body. Represent the body forces at its center. Remember that the supports or constraints that prevent motion offer resisting forces at the interface. Use the proper direction if the direction of the force is given or known by physical reasoning.

3. *Label each force:* Identify each known force with its magnitude and unknown forces with a consistent lettering scheme.

4. *Specify characteristic dimensions:* Specify the dimensions that aid in the resolution of force vectors.

After sketching the free-body diagram, the second step involves the application of the force and moment equilibrium equations. The equilibrium equations in the vector form can be written as

$$\sum F = 0 \qquad\qquad 3$$

$$\sum M_{about\ any\ point} = 0 \qquad\qquad 4$$

The force equilibrium equation can be expanded as

$$\sum F = \sum \mathbf{F}_x i + \sum \mathbf{F}_y k + \sum \mathbf{F}_z k = 0$$

As each component should be zero to satisfy equilibrium, we get the scalar form

$$\sum \mathbf{F}_x = 0$$
$$\sum \mathbf{F}_y = 0 \qquad\qquad 5$$
$$\sum \mathbf{F}_z = 0$$

Similar to the force equilibrium equation, the moment equilibrium can be expanded as

$$\sum M = \sum \mathbf{M}_x i + \sum \mathbf{M}_y k + \sum \mathbf{M}_z k = 0$$

As each component should be zero to satisfy equilibrium, we get the scalar form

$$\sum \mathbf{M}_x = 0$$
$$\sum \mathbf{M}_y = 0 \qquad\qquad 6$$
$$\sum \mathbf{M}_z = 0$$

Depending on whether it is a one-, two-, or three-dimensional problem, we apply one, two, or three of these scalar force and moment equilibrium equations.

5.4. Two- and Three-Force Members in Equilibrium

a. Two-force members

In structural analysis, we often deal with members acted on by two and three forces. This section discusses strategies that support a qualitative check of the free body diagram of two- and three-force members. While the concepts are simple, they are quite powerful.

Let us suppose that there are only two forces acting on a rigid body (shown in Fig. 4). For the rigid body to be in equilibrium, they should satisfy the force equilibrium equation.

$$\sum F = F_1 + F_2 = 0$$
$$F_1 = -F_2$$

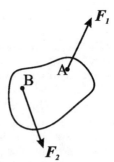

Figure 4. Two forces acting on a rigid body

Therefore, the two forces must be equal and opposite, as shown in Fig. 5.

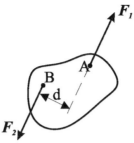

Figure 5. To satisfy the force equilibrium equation, the two forces are made equal and opposite in direction

To satisfy the moment equilibrium equation,

$$\sum M = F_1 \mathrm{d} = 0$$

$$\mathrm{d} = 0$$

The lines of action should coincide, as shown in Fig. 6. Therefore, *when only two forces are acting on any structural member, make sure that (a) the forces are equal and opposite, and (b) the two forces are collinear.*

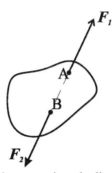

Figure 6. To satisfy the moment equilibrium equation, the lines of action of the two forces must aligned

---

Locating the Center of Gravity of a Two-Dimensional Plate

The center of a two-dimensional irregular plate can be located using the property of two-force members. When the plate is supported at a point, two forces act on the plate - the weight of the plate and the support reaction. These two forces must lineup to satisfy the moment equilibrium equation. These forces must be vertical as one of the forces (the weight) acts vertically. Further, this line must pass through the support and the center of gravity where the forces act. Thus, by supporting the plate at a single point, one can identify the vertical line that contains the center of gravity (refer to Fig. 7a).

Repeating this process by supporting the plate at another point, we can identify a second vertical line. As the center of gravity must lie on both lines, the intersection of these lines locates the center of gravity (refer to Fig. 7b). A third non-collinear support can be used to verify its location (refer to Fig. 7c).

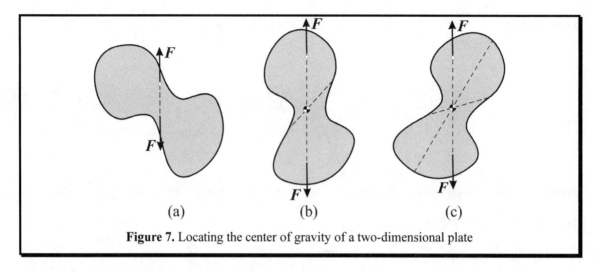

Figure 7. Locating the center of gravity of a two-dimensional plate

b. Three-force members

Let us suppose that three forces are acting on a rigid body, as shown in Fig. 8. If we align a plane such that two of the three forces (F_1 and F_2) are parallel to the plane, then the system will contain only one out-of-the-plane force. To satisfy the force equilibrium equation $\sum F = 0$, the out-of-the-plane force must be equal to zero. In other words, equilibrium of a three-force system requires that *all three forces be coplanar*.

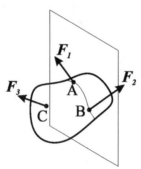

Figure 8. Three forces acting on a rigid body

With this insight that the three forces must be coplanar, let us consider a rigid body, as shown in Fig. 9. For equilibrium, the system must satisfy the moment equilibrium equation. If we take the moment about point D, forces F_1 and F_2 do not produce any moment because their lines of action pass through the point. On the other hand, force F_3 creates a moment. To satisfy, the force equilibrium equation, force F_3 must also pass through point D. Therefore, *when three forces are acting on any structural member, (a) the forces must be coplanar, and (b) the forces must intersect at a common point* (refer to Fig. 10).

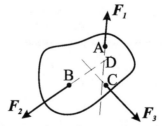

Figure 9. Three coplanar forces acting on a rigid body

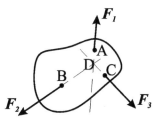

Figure 10. For equilibrium, the lines of action of the three forces must intersect at a common point

A special case of equilibrium under the action of three forces is shown in Fig. 11. In this case, the point of intersection can be viewed to be at an infinite distance away. In other words, three coplanar parallel forces can satisfy both force and moment equilibrium equations.

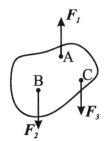

Figure 11. A special case of equilibrium of a rigid body acted on by three forces

---

Example 1
A 6 kN force is supported away from the wall. Determine the reactions at the supports.

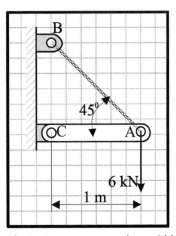

Figure 12. A structure supporting a 6 kN force

Step I: Draw the free-body diagram for the structure
The free-body diagram is shown below. Because AB is a cable, the force is applied along the cable. Given that the structure is a three-force system, the third force should apply along AC to intersect the other two forces at a common point A. Also, note that the system identified is not stable by itself. This is an acceptable practice in drawing free-body diagrams.

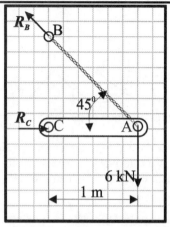

Figure 13. The free-body diagram

Step II: Apply the equilibrium equations
We can write the vertical force equilibrium equation to find R_B.

$$\sum F_{vertical} = R_B \sin 45 - 6\,\text{kN} = 0$$

$$\boxed{R_B = 8.485\,\text{kN}}$$

Then, the horizontal force equilibrium equation gives us

$$\sum F_{horizontal} = R_B \cos 45 - R_C = 0$$

$$\boxed{R_C = 6\,\text{kN}}$$

Example 2
Determine the weight on front and rear wheels of a van. The wheelbase (the distance between the front and rear wheels) is 10 ft. The weight of the van is 5000 lb. Assume that the center of gravity is close to the front tires and at a distance of one-third of the wheelbase from the front wheels.

Step I: Draw the free-body diagram of the van
The free-body diagram shows two reactions (R_{rear} and R_{front}) along with the weight of the van. The weight of the van is placed at its center of gravity. The distances between the forces are marked in terms of wheel base L. From the free-body diagram, it is clear that this is a three-force system.

 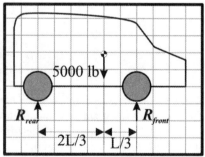

Figure 14. The free-body diagram of the van

Step II: Apply the equilibrium equations
The force equilibrium equation can be written as

$$\sum F = 5000\,\text{lb} - R_{rear} - R_{front} = 0$$

$$R_{rear} + R_{front} = 5000\,\text{lb}$$

If we take the moment about the rear wheel, the reactions at the rear wheels (R_{rear}) do not create any moment. We get

$$\sum M = R_{front}L - 5000\,\text{lb} \times \frac{2L}{3} = 0$$

$$\boxed{R_{front} = 3,333\,\text{lb}}$$

Substituting the value of R_{rear} in the force equilibrium equation, we get

$$\boxed{R_{rear} = 1,667\,\text{lb}}$$

Each front wheel carries 1667 lb (half of R_{front}), and each rear wheel carries 834 lb. The results make sense because the front wheels, which are close to the load application, carry more weight than the rear wheels.

A side note: Auto designers arrange the subsystems in such a way that the center of gravity is closer to the drive wheels. As a result, the drive wheels carry more weight and, therefore, have increased traction (frictional force). Typically, the drive wheels carry about 55% of the total weight.

Example 3
Determine the reactions at points A and C if P = 1000 lb.

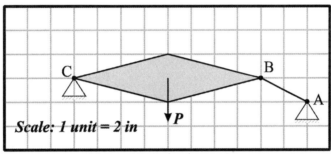

Figure 15. A simple structure

AB is a two-force member. Now, Fig. 16 shows the free-body diagram for the structure. In the free-body diagram, force F_{AB} is aligned with member AB. As three forces are acting on the structure, to satisfy the property of a three-force member, force F_C is oriented to pass through a common point.

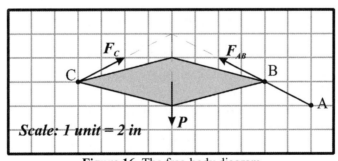

Figure 16. The free-body diagram

Now, from symmetry we know that

$$\left| F_{AB} \right| = \left| F_C \right|$$

Applying the equilibrium equation along the vertical direction,

$$\sum F_y = 2F_{AB} \frac{1}{\sqrt{1^2 + 2^2}} - P = 0$$

$$\boxed{F_{AB} = P\frac{\sqrt{5}}{2} = 1118\,\text{lb}}$$

Notes:

Concept Questions

Name: _____

1. In a two-dimensional space, a rigid body has _____ (one/two/three) degrees of freedom.

2. What are the conditions for equilibrium for a two-force member?

3. TRUE/FALSE: The rigid body (adjacent figure) can be in a state of equilibrium under the application of three non-zero forces.

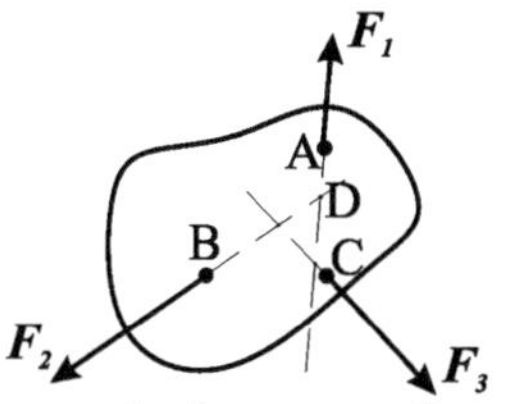

4. TRUE/FALSE: Three non-coplanar non-zero forces can be in a state of equilibrium.

5. Draw the support reactions offered by pinned support.

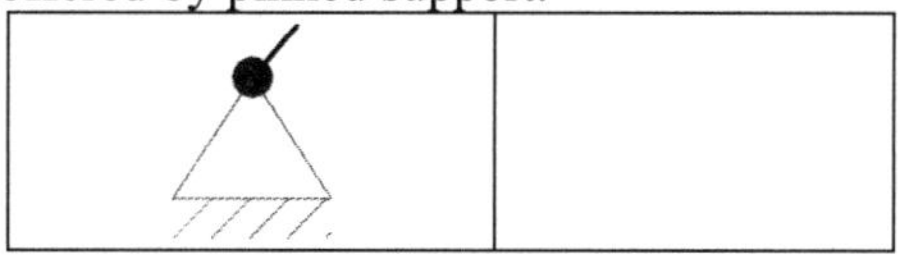

6. Draw the support reactions offered by roller support.

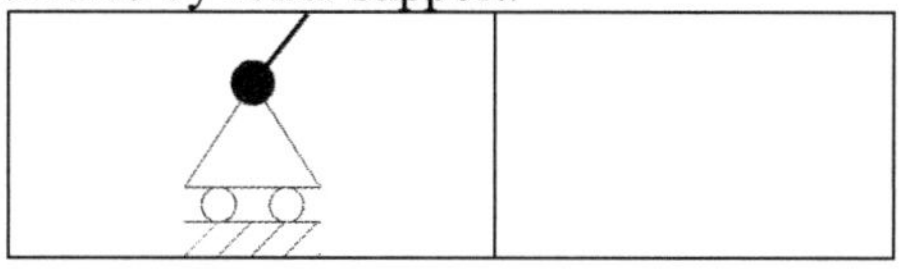

7. Draw the support reactions offered by rocker support.

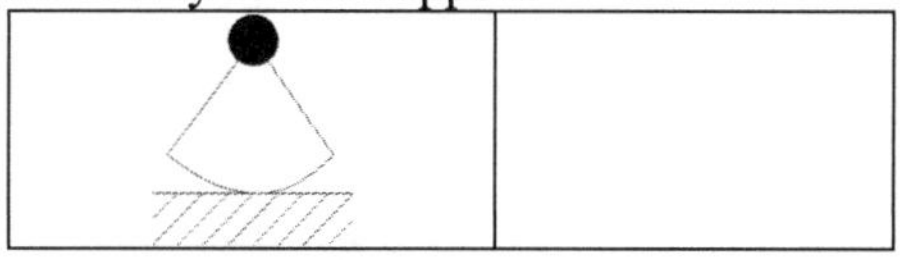

8. Draw the support reactions offered by fixed support.

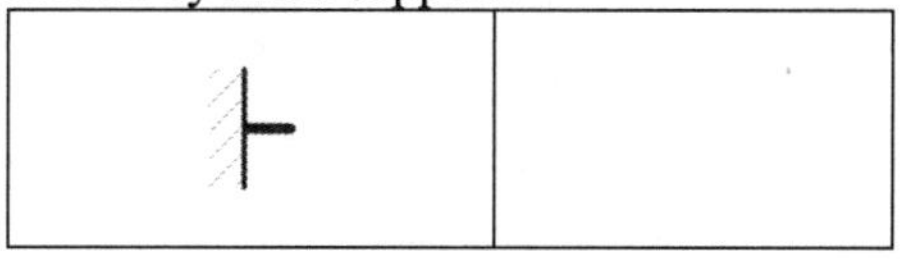

9. Draw the support reactions offered by smooth contact support.

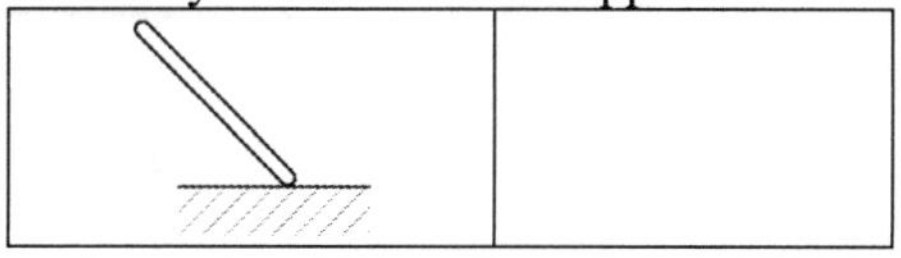

10. Identify the two force member in the structure.
    A. Link 1
    B. Link 2
    C. Both link 1 and 2
    D. None of the above

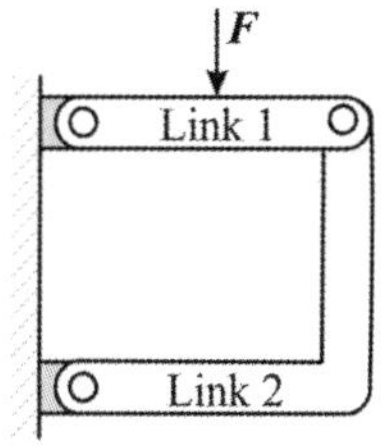

Name: _____

Problem 1

Determine the reactions at the supports if $P = 1$ kN and L = 4 m.

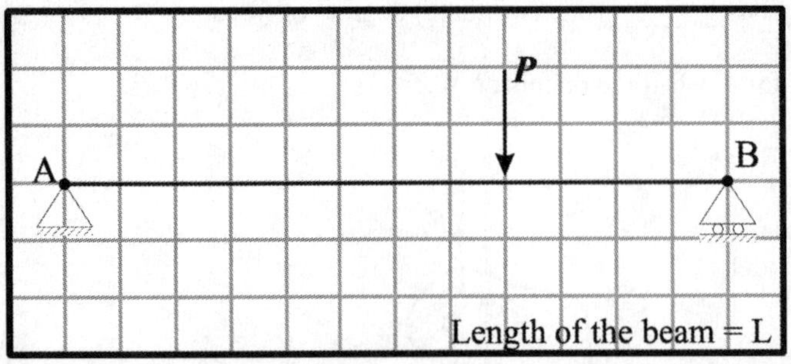

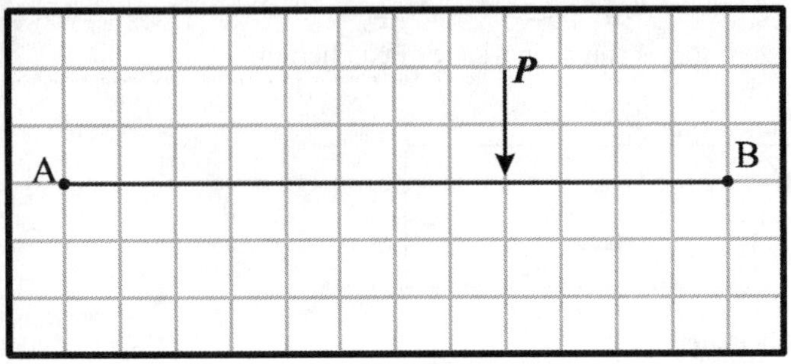

A
B
P
Length of the beam = L

A
B
P

Problem 2

The rigid link pinned at point A is in equilibrium. Determine the magnitude of P_2 and the reactions at point A if $P_1 = 500$ lb and L = 12 ft.

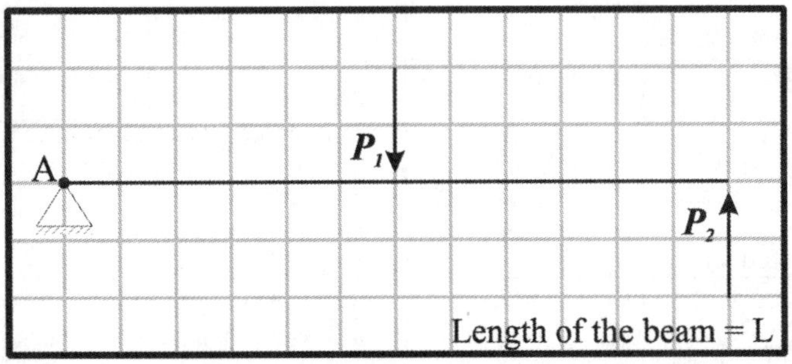

A
P_1
P_2
Length of the beam = L

Name: _____

Problem 3

A car wheel hits a curb. Determine the reaction at points A and B. The radius of the wheel is 15 in.

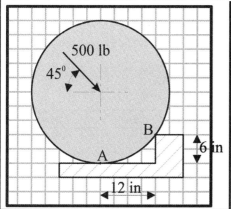

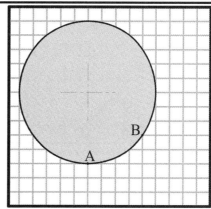

Problem 4

A 200 lb force is applied on ladder AB. Assume that the self-weight of the ladder is negligible and that no frictional forces are in play at point A. Determine the reaction at point A and B. Use the property of three force members.

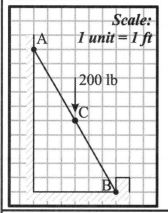

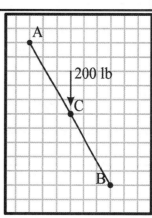

Name: _____

Problem 5

Determine the reactions at points B and C. Use the property of three force members.

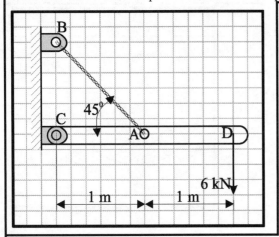
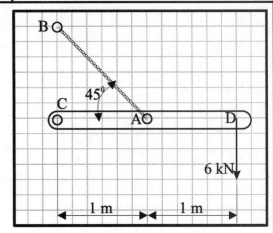

Problem 6

Determine the reactions at points A and B.

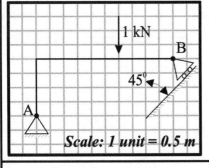
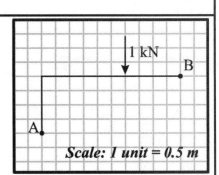

Name: _____

Problem 7

The rod shown is in equilibrium. The reaction at the ground is unknown and includes friction. Use the property of three force elements. Determine the reaction at ground and the tension in the cable if the weight of the rod is 1 lb.

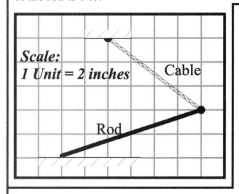

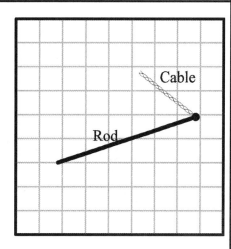

Name: _____

Problem 8

Three cylinders rest in a rectangular well. The diameter of each cylinder is 4 ft. The width of the well is 9 ft. If the weight of each cylinder is 500 lb, determine the contact forces. Use symmetry.

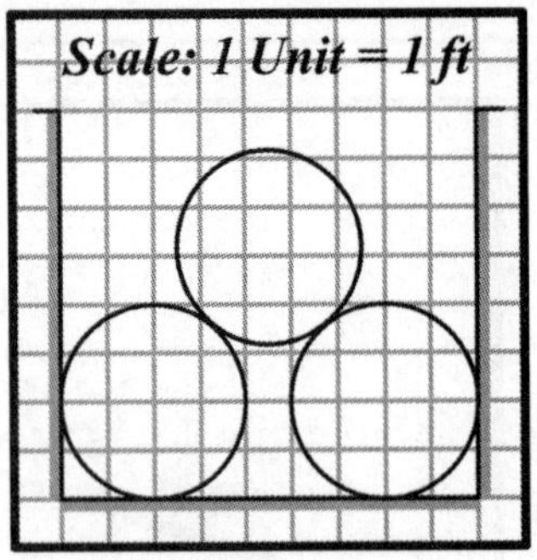

Scale: 1 Unit = 1 ft

5.5. Distributed Force Systems

While concentrated forces often serve as useful idealizations, distributed forces are a part of engineering reality. All forces in the real world are distributed over an area/volume. For instance, the pressure on the wings of an airplane is a distributed load on the wing surface. Similarly, the gravitational pull is distributed over the entire volume of an object. To find reactions, it is useful to convert this distributed load into an equivalent concentrated load. To achieve this objective, we are faced with two tasks:
1. Determining the equivalent force from a force distribution.
2. Finding the location where the equivalent force must be placed.

In this section, we will learn to perform these two tasks in the two common arrangements of distributed loads that we encounter in statics.

a. Distributed force along a line

A distributed load along a line, which can be an idealization of a physical geometry such as a beam (refer to Fig. 17), is often characterized by a load intensity diagram. The load intensity diagram shows the magnitude of load per unit length at different locations on the line. The units of the load intensity w take the form of force over length: $\dfrac{lb}{in}$, $\dfrac{lb}{ft}$, $\dfrac{N}{m}$, and $\dfrac{kN}{m}$. To find the equivalent load, let us consider a differential element whose length is dx at distance x. The force exerted on this element is $w\,dx$. Now, we can find the total force exerted on the line by integrating this elemental load along the line. We get

$$F_R = \int_L w(x)\,dx \qquad\qquad 7$$

Note that the equivalent force is equal to the area under the load intensity diagram.

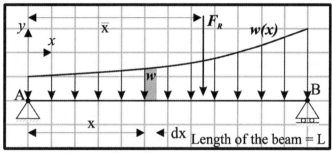

Figure 17. Distributed force along a line

The equivalent load F_R should be located such that it causes the same moment as that of the distributed load distribution about any point. If we equate the moments about point A, we get

$$\overline{x}\, F_R = \int_L x\, w(x)\,dx$$

$$\overline{x} = \frac{\displaystyle\int_L x\, w(x)\,dx}{F_R} \qquad\qquad 8$$

b. Distributed force on a surface

Pressure p is a distributed load on a surface. It is the force per unit area and its units take the form of $\dfrac{lb}{in^2}$ (or psi), $\dfrac{lb}{ft^2}$, $\dfrac{N}{m^2}$, and $\dfrac{kN}{m^2}$. The equation for calculating the net force due to a pressure distribution on a two-dimensional surface is similar to equation 7, but the integration is performed over the area.

$$F_R = \int_A p(x, y)\, dA \qquad\qquad 9$$

Now, we need to determine the location for the equivalent load. By equating the moments about the x- and y-axes, we can find the coordinates $(\bar{x}, \bar{y})$ as

$$\bar{x} = \frac{\int_A x p\, dA}{F_R} \qquad\qquad \bar{y} = \frac{\int_A y p\, dA}{F_R} \qquad\qquad 10$$

Example 4

Determine the equivalent force and its location for the load intensity diagram.

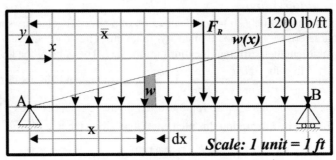

Figure 18. A distributed load

Before we can apply equation 7 to determine the equivalent load, we need to write the load intensity w as a function of x. As w varies from 0 to 1200 lb/ft over 12 ft, we can write w as

$$w(x) = 100\, x\, \frac{lb}{ft}$$

Substituting the value of w in equation 7, we get

$$F_R = \int_L w(x)\, dx$$

$$F_R = \int_0^{12} 100\, x\, dx = \left[50 x^2 \right]_0^{12}$$

$$\boxed{F_R = 7200\, lb}$$

Now, we could have arrived at the same result by taking the area of the load intensity triangle.

To find $\bar{x}$, let us apply equation 8:

$$\bar{x} = \frac{\int_L x\, w(x)\, dx}{F_R}$$

$$\bar{x} = \frac{\int_0^{12} 100\, x^2\, dx}{F_R} = \frac{\left[\dfrac{100}{3} x^3 \right]_0^{12}}{7200\, lb}$$

$$\boxed{\bar{x} = 8\, ft}$$

Example 5

Determine the equivalent force and its location for the load intensity diagram.

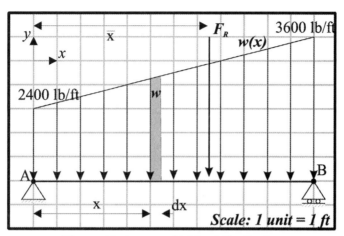

Figure 19. A trapezoidal load distribution

We can approach this problem in two ways. The method involves writing w as a function of x and then integrating the function to find the value of F_R similar to the earlier example. Alternatively, we can divide the load intensity diagram into two parts (see Fig. 20).

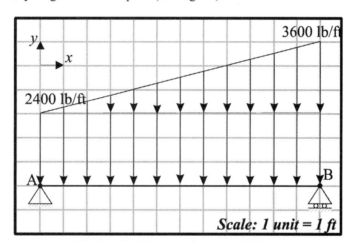

Figure 20. Division of trapezoidal load

In the previous problem, we know that for the triangular,

$$F_{R1} = 7,200\,\text{lb}$$

$$\overline{x}_1 = 8\,\text{ft}$$

For the rectangular distribution, we can find the equivalent load F_{R2} by computing the area. The equivalent load acts at the center. Therefore,

$$F_{R2} = 28,800\,\text{lb}$$

$$\overline{x}_1 = 6\,\text{ft}$$

Now the two load distributions can be replaced by the equivalent loads as shown in Fig. 21.

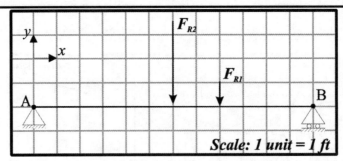

Figure 21. Equivalent loads from the two constituent load distributions

The equivalent force should be the sum of the equivalent loads.
$$F_R = F_{R1} + F_{R2}$$
$$\boxed{F_R = 36,000\,\text{lb}}$$

We can find the location of the equivalent load by taking moments.
$$F_R \bar{x} = F_{R1}\bar{x}_1 + F_{R2}\bar{x}_2$$
$$\bar{x} = \frac{F_{R1}\bar{x}_1 + F_{R2}\bar{x}_2}{F_R}$$
$$\boxed{\bar{x} = 6.4\,\text{ft}}$$

The result makes sense because the equivalent load is closer to F_{R2}, whose magnitude is significantly higher.

Name: _____

Problem 1

Determine the equivalent load and its location for the load distribution. Use the differential element method.

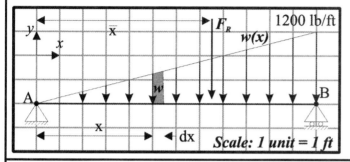

Problem 2

Determine the equivalent load and its location for the load distribution. Use the differential element method. The load intensity is given by $w(x)=x^2$.

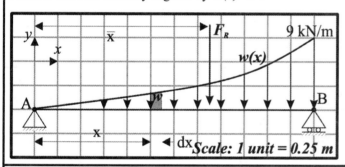

Problem 3

Determine the equivalent load and its location for the load distribution. The load intensity follows the equation $\dfrac{x^2}{6^2}+\dfrac{w(x)}{100}=1$, where the units of $w(x)$ are lb/ft. Note the location of the coordinate system.

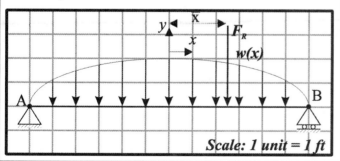

Name: _____

Problem 4

Determine the equivalent load and its location for the load distribution. Use the differential element method. Compare the results with those of example 5.

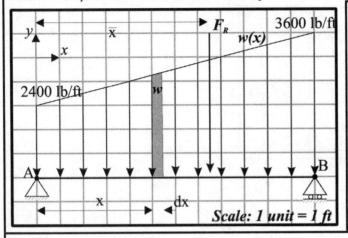

Problem 5

Determine the equivalent load and its location for the load distribution.

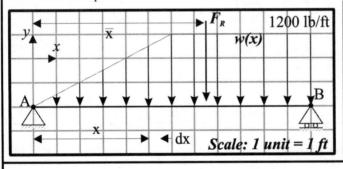

Name: _____

Problem 6

Determine the equivalent load and its location for the load distribution.

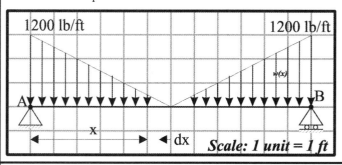

Problem 7

Determine the equivalent load and its location for the load distribution. What is an appropriate location for the equivalent force of a symmetric load distribution?

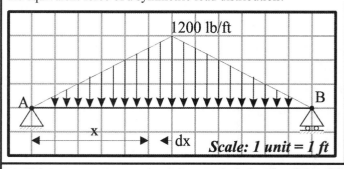

Name: _____

Problem 8

Determine the equivalent load and its location for the load distribution.

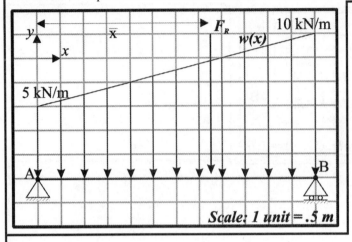

Problem 9

Determine the equivalent load and its location for the load distribution. The distribution combines a uniformly distributed load of 15 kN and a non-uniform load which is given by $w(x)=x^2$. Use the results of problem 2.

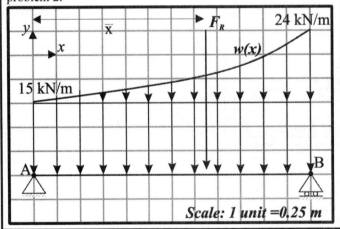

5.6. Equilibrium of a Two-Dimensional System

Two- and three-force systems are special cases of two-dimensional systems. The analysis of a two-dimensional system involves our familiar two steps: drawing the free-body diagram and applying the equilibrium equations. The equilibrium equations take the form of

$$\sum \mathbf{F_x} = 0$$
$$\sum \mathbf{F_y} = 0 \qquad\qquad 11$$
$$\sum M_{about\ any\ point} = 0$$

Because we can take the moment about any point, we can sometimes simplify the analysis either by computing the moment about a point where several forces intersect or by applying the moment equation at several points in the rigid body.

Self-help – The Design of Drum Brakes

Before disc brakes became popular, most automobiles used drum brakes. Even today, most cars use drum brakes for the rear-wheels and for the hand brakes. The primary advantage of drum brakes is the "self-help" or "self-energizing" or "self-servo" characteristic. We can understand this characteristic by deriving the relationship between the actuation force and the braking torque for the drum brake configuration shown in Fig. 22.

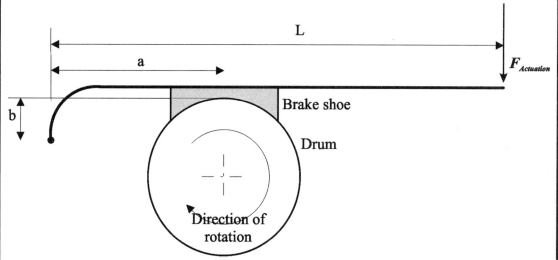

Figure 22. Schematic of a drum brake

As a first step to understanding the working of the drum brake, let us draw the free-body diagram for the drum and the brake mechanism (refer to Fig. 23). Now, the frictional force on the drum opposes the motion as shown in Fig. 23. Also, the brake shoe pushes the drum, and hence, the normal force is towards the center of the drum. The forces on the brake shoe are reversed in accordance with the Newton's third law. Now, the torque resisting the motion is

$$T_{Resisting} = F_{Friction}R$$
$$T_{Resisting} = \mu N R$$

where μ is the coefficient of friction and N is the normal force. Let us now concentrate on the brake mechanism to find the relationship between $F_{Actuation}$ and N. Let us take the moment about the pivot point.

$$M_{Pivot} = F_{Actuation} \times L + F_{Friction} \times b - N \times a = 0$$

Rearranging the terms and substituting the value for $F_{Friction}$ $\left(F_{Friction} = \mu N \right)$, we get

---

$$F_{Actuation} \times L + F_{Friction} \times b - N \times a = 0$$

$$N = \frac{F_{Actuation} \times L}{(a - \mu b)}$$

Now, let us examine the elements of the normal force equation carefully. If the pivot was inline with the friction force $(b = 0)$, then the normal force is proportional to the actuation force $\left(N = \frac{F_{Actuation} \times L}{a} \right)$.

Due to offset b, the friction force creates a moment about the pivot in the same direction as that of the actuation force. Therefore, it creates a higher normal force and higher braking torque for the same actuation force. The parameters a and b can be varied to create a large advantage using this self-help characteristic.

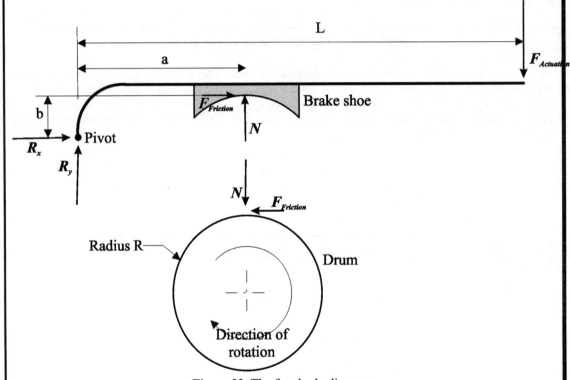

Figure 23. The free-body diagrams

The self-help characteristic reduces the force required from the driver. Note that for the brake shown in Figs. 22 and 23, reversing the direction of drum rotation negatively affects the normal force. The "self-help" advantage, which is the cornerstone of the drum brake, became one of its major problems. It creates a non-linear relationship between the actuation force and resisting torque on the drum. Because the coefficient of friction can vary significantly, it becomes difficult for drivers to predict the required actuation force to safely decelerate an automobile. Note that disc brakes do not have the self-help characteristic.

Example 6
Determine the reactions at the supports. The length of the beam is L.

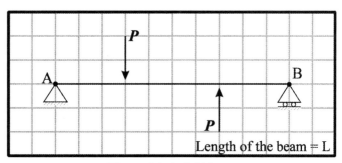

Figure 24. A rigid beam

We follow our two-step procedure for solving this problem.
Step I: Draw the free-body diagram
While drawing the free-body diagram, the pin support provides both horizontal and vertical reaction. On the other hand, the roller provides a vertical reaction. The free-body diagram is shown in Fig. 25.

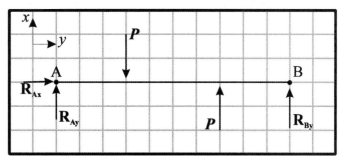

Figure 25. The free-body diagram of the beam

Step II: Apply the equilibrium equations

If we take the force equilibrium equation along the x-axis, we get

$$\sum \mathbf{F_x} = 0$$

$$\mathbf{R_{Ax}} = 0$$

Now we can apply the moment equation at points A and B to find the reactions. The moment equilibrium equation at point A yields

$$\sum M_A = \mathbf{R_{By}}L + P \times 0.7L - P \times 0.3L = 0$$

$$\boxed{\mathbf{R_{By}} = -0.4P}$$

Similarly, the moment at point B gives us

$$\sum M_B = -\mathbf{R_{Ay}}L + P \times 0.7L - P \times 0.3L = 0$$

$$\boxed{\mathbf{R_{Ay}} = 0.4P}$$

An alternative procedure for solving this problem involves writing the force equilibrium equation in the vertical direction and substituting the result of the moment equilibrium equation about point A in the force equilibrium equation.

5.7. The Principle of Superposition

The principle of superposition is a generic principle. It helps to decompose a complex problem into smaller problems that are easy to solve and combine these solutions to formulate the solution to the overall problem. In fact, the superposition principle was used several times in the previous sections. The superposition principle was the basis for finding the resultant force by adding individual forces acting on a particle. To determine the equivalent load in example 5 (refer to Fig. 26), this principle was used to divide the trapezoidal force distribution into two simple force distributions.

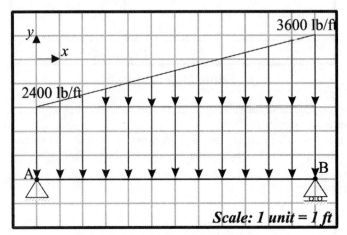

Figure 26. Division of trapezoidal load

For our purpose in Statics, the superposition principle can be stated as

The reaction at any point due to a system of forces and moments is same as the algebraic sum of the reactions due to individual forces and moments acting at their respective location.

According to the principle, the order in which forces and moments are applied is not important. The systems which obey the superposition principle are known as *linear systems*. The systems in Statics are linear systems and the superposition principle can be applied to them. It provides an easier way to solve problems. To understand the power of superposition theorem, let us examine the following problem.

Example 7
Determine the reactions at the supports. The length of the beam is L.

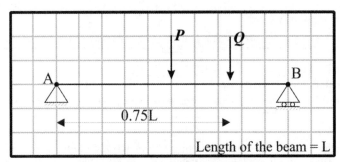

Figure 27. A rigid beam

Let us decompose the problem into two problems – the beam with concentrated force *P* and the beam with concentrated force *Q*. The two free-body diagrams are shown in Fig. 28.

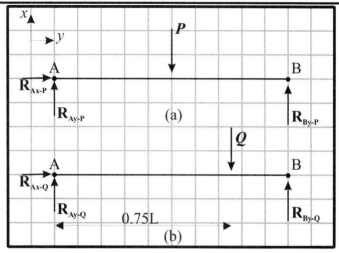

Figure 28. The free-body diagram of the beam under the action of
(a) force P only and (b) force Q only

Now, looking at the free-body diagram of the beam under the action of force P, the following observation can be made

$$\mathbf{R}_{Ax\text{-}P} = 0 \text{ (from the equilibrium equations along the horizontal direction)}$$

$$\mathbf{R}_{Ay\text{-}P} = \mathbf{R}_{By\text{-}P} = \frac{P}{2} \text{ (from symmetry)}$$

Examining the free-body diagram of the beam under the action of force Q, we know that

$$\mathbf{R}_{Ax\text{-}Q} = 0 \text{ (from the equilibrium equations along the horizontal direction)}$$

Now, we also learned from the previous section that the support that is close to the load carries more load and the load is carried by a support is inversely proportional to the distance of the support from the applied load. Therefore,

$$\mathbf{R}_{Ay\text{-}Q} = 0.25Q$$

$$\mathbf{R}_{By\text{-}Q} = 0.75Q$$

Now, to determine the reaction forces due to these two force (P and Q), we use the superposition principle. The reactions are

$$\boxed{\begin{aligned} \mathbf{R}_{Ax} &= \mathbf{R}_{Ax\text{-}P} + \mathbf{R}_{Ax\text{-}Q} = 0 \\ \mathbf{R}_{Ay} &= \mathbf{R}_{Ay\text{-}P} + \mathbf{R}_{Ay\text{-}Q} = 0.5P + 0.25Q \\ \mathbf{R}_{By} &= \mathbf{R}_{By\text{-}P} + \mathbf{R}_{By\text{-}Q} = 0.5P + 0.75Q \end{aligned}}$$

5.8. Tipping and Foot Print

Tail Tipping

Tail tipping is a phenomenon where an airplane tips over the rear wheels due to an increased load in the aft section. Fig. 29 shows a small airplane before and after tipping due to weight of a person sitting on its tail. Note that the tail tipping occurs about the rear wheels. It can occur even in large cargo airplanes, particularly while loading. When the airplane is approaching the tipping condition, the normal force acting on the nose wheel is greatly reduced. As a result, an airplane close to tail tipping looses the traction force needed for steering during the take-off or landing.

a

b

Figure 29. Tail tipping

To understand the concept of tipping, let us consider a table shown in Fig. 30. The weight of the table (W) and the force applied by a person leaning on the table (F) are the two forces acting on the table. If we assume the loading to be in the xy plane, then the front view captures these two applied forces and the reactions. The principle of superposition can be used to analyze this situation.

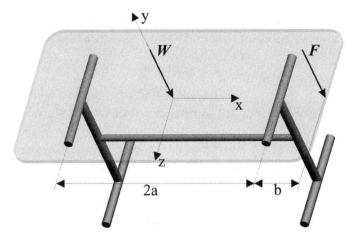

Figure 30. A glass table with a concentrated force at the end

If the weight distribution is uniform, the weight the table (W) can be applied at the center of gravity (refer to Fig. 31a). The reactions at the supports will be

$$R_{A-W} = 0.5W$$

$$R_{B-W} = 0.5W$$

Now, consider only force F acting at the end of the table. For this situation (refer to Fig. 31b), the equilibrium equations are

$$\sum F = R_{A\text{-}F} + R_{B\text{-}F} = F$$

$$\sum M_{about\ point\ B} = R_{A\text{-}F} \times 2a + F \times b = 0$$

$$R_{A\text{-}F} = -\frac{Fb}{2a}$$

$$R_{B\text{-}F} = F\left(1 + \frac{b}{2a}\right)$$

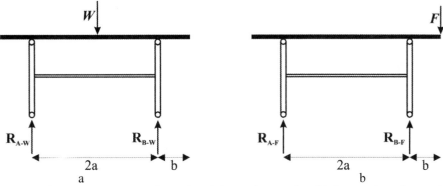

Figure 31. The free-body diagram when (a) weight W alone acting (b) force F is acting on the table

Using the principle of superposition, the reactions when both forces (W and F) are considered will be

$$R_A = R_{A\text{-}W} + R_{A\text{-}F} = 0.5W - \frac{Fb}{2a}$$

$$R_B = R_{B\text{-}W} + R_{B\text{-}F} = 0.5W + F\left(1 + \frac{b}{2a}\right)$$

Increasing the magnitude of force F reduces the reaction at support A and increases the reaction at support B. At a certain magnitude of force F, support A is about to loose contact with the ground which indicates the possible tipping condition.

$$R_A = 0 \quad \rightarrow \quad W = \frac{Fb}{a}$$

Thus, at the point of impending tipping, the reaction at one of the supports reduces to zero. This property is useful to experimentally determine the impending tipping condition by measuring the reaction force at the supports by sensors.

Another method for determining the impending tipping condition uses the equilibrium equation. The equilibrium equations for the free-body diagram (refer to Fig. 32)

$$\sum M_{about\ point\ B} = R_A \times 2a - W \times a + F \times b = 0$$

At tipping the magnitude of R_A is equal to zero. Substituting the magnitude of R_A, we get

$$W = \frac{Fb}{a}$$

This method is often used to calculate the magnitude of the force required for tipping.

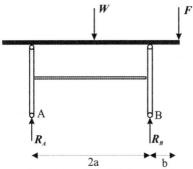

Figure 32. The free-body diagram when (a) weight W alone acting on the table (b) force F is acting

A third method for determining the tipping condition is the use of footprint. Footprint is *the minimum area by a closed curve with nonnegative (positive or zero) curvature at any point on the curve encompassing the base.* While the definition seems to be complex, the method for determining the footprint is quite simple. Imagine an elastic band stretched to encompass the object at its base. The area encompassed by the band indicates the footprint. Therefore, Fig. 33 shows the footprint for the table.

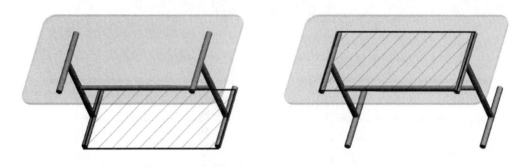

a   b

Figure 33. The footprint assuming (a) the whole table is tipping (b) the glass top is tipping

---

Example 8

Draw a rough sketch of the footprint of the glass table. Assume that the glass top tips when loaded.

Figure 34. The free-body diagram

If we consider the tipping of the glass top, the footprint should be drawn at the top of the base. The shape is shown in Fig. 35. Note that the curve encompasses the base. The curvature at any point on the curve is positive or zero.

Figure 35. The free-body diagram

Let us create a simplified force system for the table. The equivalent load is equal to $W + F$. The location at which the equivalent load acts depends on the magnitude of the two loads (W and F). Mathematically, we can write distance x (refer to Fig. 36) as

$$(W + F)x = F(a + b)$$

$$x = \frac{F(a+b)}{(W+F)}$$

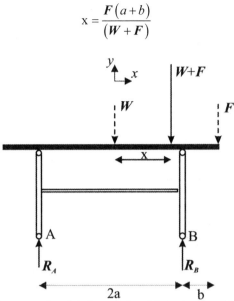

Figure 36. The footprint assuming (a) the whole table is tipping (b) the glass top is tipping

According to this method, tipping occurs when the line of action of the resultant applied force vector passes outside the footprint. Now, as force **F** increased, distance x increases and reaches a critical value where the equivalent applied force is at the edge of footprint signifying impending tipping. For this condition to occur,

$$x = a$$

$$a = \frac{F(a+b)}{(W+F)}$$

Rearranging the terms, we get

$$W = \frac{Fb}{a}$$

This method is useful to qualitatively determine the tipping condition from the geometric information.
  While the final results are the same, the three methods for determining impending tipping are:
- *One or more support reactions reduce to zero.*
- *The moment about the tipping axis is equal to zero.*
- *The line of action of the resultant applied force passes outside the footprint.*

The Leaning Tower of Pisa

The Tower of Pisa is the tallest self-supporting bell tower (refer to Fig. 37). With a diameter of 15.5 m and height of 56 m, the tower weighs 15,000 metric tons. Due to the foundation problems, the tower started leaning, and this design failure resulted in one of the Seven Wonders of the World. Now, the tower leans at an angle of 5.5^0. If we want to find the critical angle at which it will become unstable (from the rigid-body point of view), we need to make an assumption. The Tower is approximated as a cylinder with uniform density. The tower will tip-over when the weight passes outside the footprint as shown in the Fig. 38. The critical angle can be calculated as

$$\tan\theta = \frac{7.75 \text{ m}}{28 \text{ m}}$$

$$\theta = 15.47^0$$

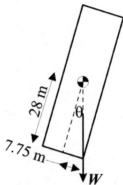

Figure 37. The Leaning Tower of Pisa   **Figure 38.** The position of the tower
at the tipping point

The assumption of approximating the tower as a cylinder is conservative one as the top level has smaller diameter and thinner walls. As this section weighs less, the true center of gravity is lower than that of the idealization. Therefore, the tower will be more stable or can tilt more than this critical angle (θ).

Example 9
The crane (refer to Fig. 39) weighs 10,000 lb and its boom weighs 1000 lb. The centers of gravity of the crane and the boom are known. Determine the maximum load the crane can carry at a boom angle of 45^0.

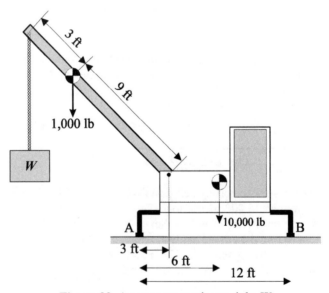

Figure 39. A crane supporting weight W

For tipping, the moment caused by the load W and the boom weight overcomes the moment caused by the weight of the crane. At the point of tipping, the reaction at the support B is zero. The free-body diagram is shown in Fig. 40. Taking the moments about A, we get

$$W \times (12\cos 45 - 3) + 1000 \times (9\cos 45 - 3) = 10000 \times 6$$

$$\boxed{W = 10,325\,\text{lb}}$$

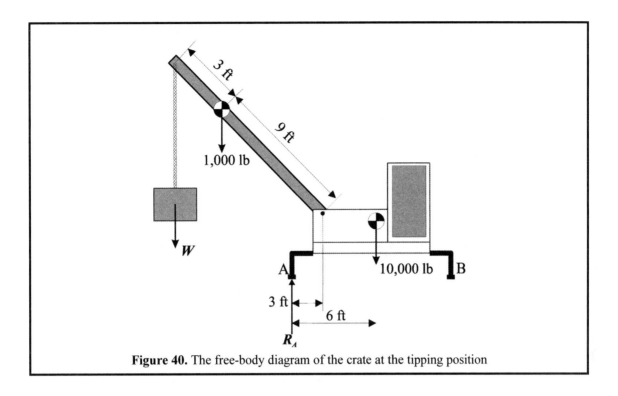

Figure 40. The free-body diagram of the crate at the tipping position

Notes:

Concept Questions

Name: _____

1. Angle θ is equal to 30^0 and the coefficient of friction is 1. If the dimensions of the block are $a = 1''$ and $b = 1''$, the block will:
   - A. remain in equilibrium
   - B. tip
   - C. slip down
   - D. slide up.

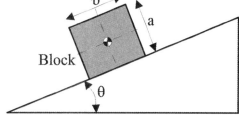

Block

2. At tipping, the magnitude of the reaction forces:
   - A. R_A and R_B are equal
   - B. R_A is zero and R_B is equal to $P+F$
   - C. R_B is zero and R_A is equal to $P+F$
   - D. R_A is P and R_B is equal to F

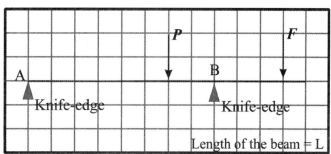

3. A force F is applied to the block. Determine the necessary condition for the block to tip.
   - E. $F \geq \mu W$ and $F \geq 2W$
   - F. $F \leq \mu W$ and $F \geq 0.5W$
   - G. $F \geq \mu W$ and $F \geq 0.5W$
   - H. $F \leq \mu W$ and $F \leq 2W$

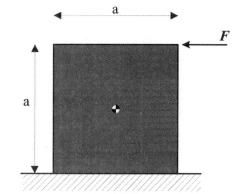

4. The equivalent load and its location for the overall load distribution is:

   - A. 28,800 lb and $x = 6'$
   - B. 14,400 lb and $x = 6'$
   - C. 7,200 lb and $x = 6'$
   - D. 7,200 lb and $x = 4'$

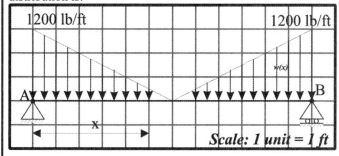

5. A 12 kN force is supported away from the wall. The magnitude of force reaction at point C, R_C =

  A. 8.485 kN
  B. 16.97 kN
  C. 6 kN
  D. 12 kN

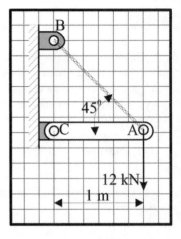

6. The range of angle for θ at which force F must be applied for the wheel to go over the curb. The radius of the car wheel is 15 inches.

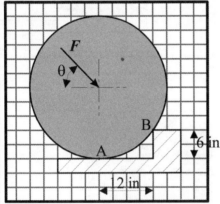

             Range of θ = _____

7. The footprint for the glass table top is resting on two supports is

 A.

 B.

 C.

 D.

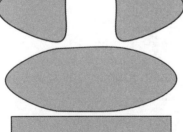

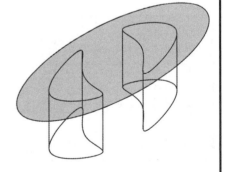

Concept Questions

Name: _____

8. A glass table top is supported by a star-shaped base. Overlay the footprint on the table top.

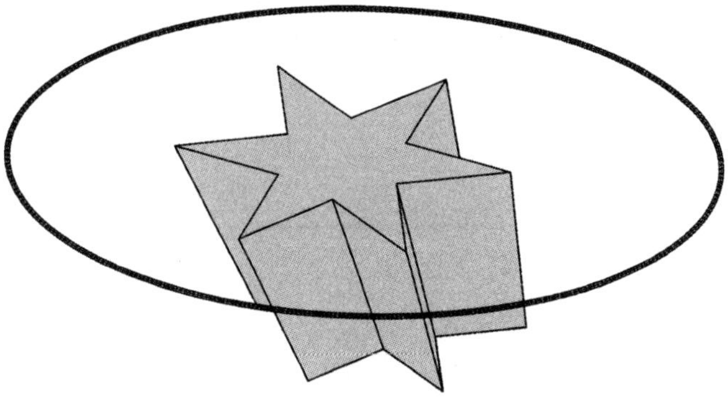

9. In a three-dimensional space, a rigid body has _____ degrees of freedom.
   A. One
   B. Three
   C. Four
   D. Six

10. What is the principle of superposition?

Name: _____

Problem 1

Determine the reactions at the supports if *P* = 750 lb and L = 12 ft..

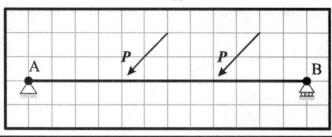

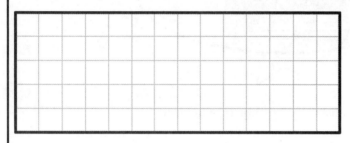

Problem 2

Determine the reactions at the supports. Use symmetry to determine whether the results make sense.

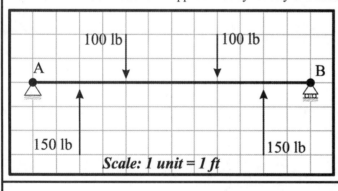

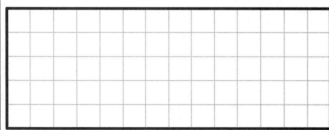

Name: _____

Problem 3

Determine the reactions at the supports. Use symmetry to determine whether the results make sense.

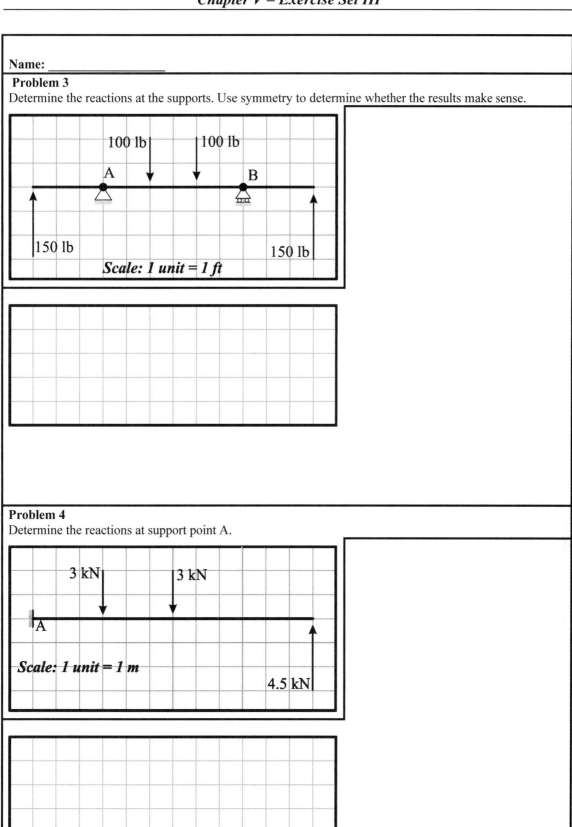

Problem 4

Determine the reactions at support point A.

Name: _____

Problem 5

Determine the reactions at the supports.

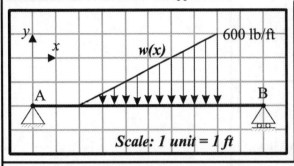

Problem 6

Determine the reactions at the support.

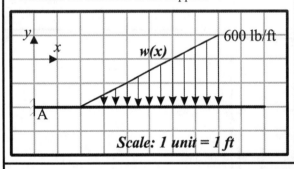

Name: _____

Problem 7

Determine the reactions at the supports (use the principle of superposition).

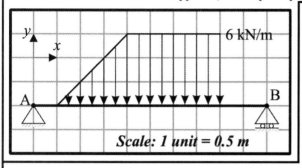

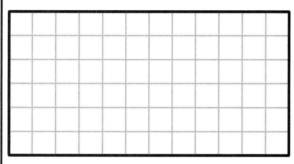

Problem 8

Determine the reactions at the support.

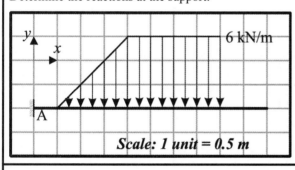

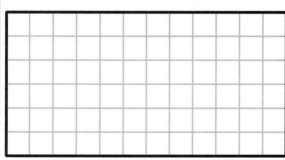

Name: _____

Problem 9

Determine the reactions at the support.

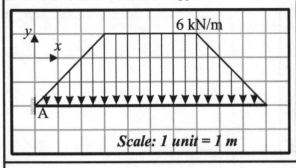

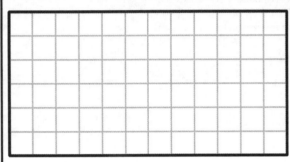

Problem 10

Determine the reactions at the supports (use the principle of superposition).

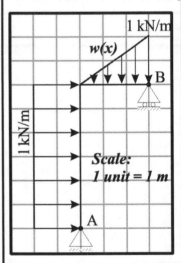

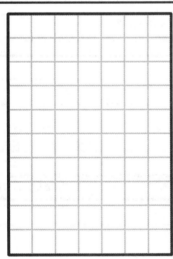

Name: _____

Problem 11

Determine the force required for tipping if the weight of the block is 10 lb. Note that at the tipping point, the reaction comes only from the corner of the fixed support.

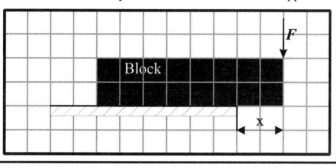

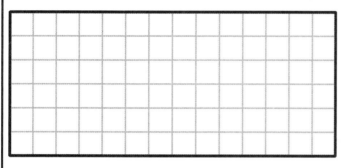

Problem 12

Determine the value of x at which a pencil will tip over the edge of a desk. The weight of a pencil is 10 grams and its length is 10 cm. The eraser at the end weighs 1 gram and is 1 cm long.

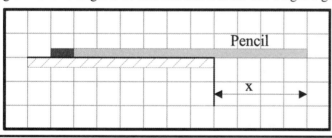

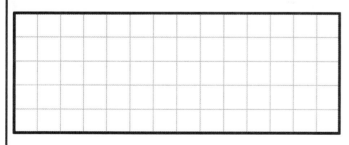

Name: _____

Problem 13

Determine the value of x at which a pencil will tip over the edge of a desk. The weight of a pencil is 15 grams and its length is 10 cm. The eraser at the end weighs 1 gram and is 1 cm long.

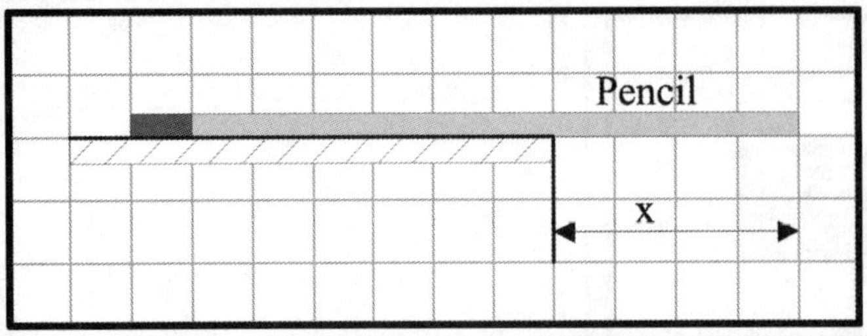

Problem 14

Determine the value of x at which a pencil will tip over the edge of a desk. The weight of a pencil is 10 grams and its length is 10 cm. The eraser at the end weighs 2 gram and is 1 cm long.

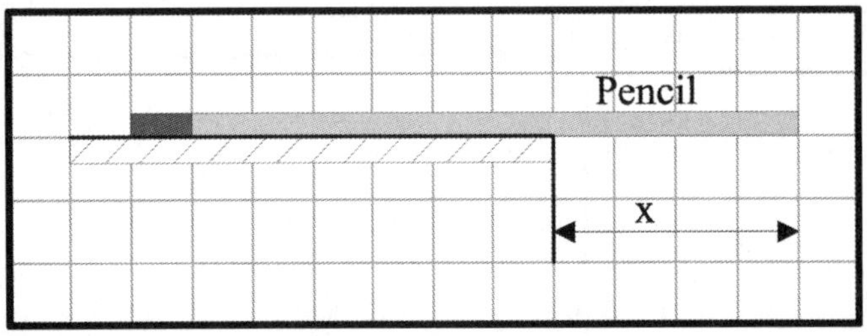

Compare the tipping points for the three pencil problems and see whether they make sense.

Name: _____

Problem 15

A car wheel hits a curb. The radius of the wheel is 15″. Determine reaction forces at points A and B.

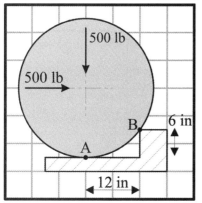
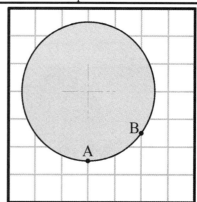

Problem 16

A car wheel hits a curb. The radius of the wheel is 15″. Determine force *F* required to go over the curb. Hint: While drawing the free-body diagram, think about the reaction force at point A.

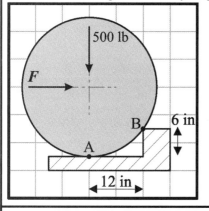
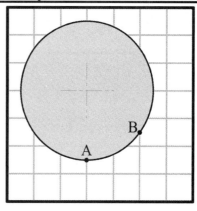

Name: _____

Problem 17

Two golf balls are placed in a cylinder with an open top and bottom. The diameter of a golf ball is 40 mm. Its mass is 45 gm. The mass of the cylinder is 50 gm and its diameter is 68.28 mm. Draw the free-body diagrams for individual balls and the cylinder. Determine whether the cylinder will tip.

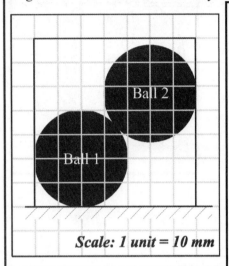

Scale: 1 unit = 10 mm

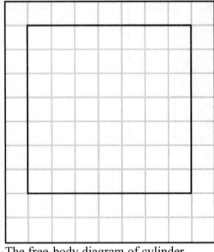

The free-body diagram of cylinder

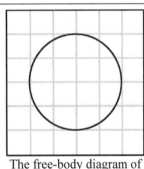

The free-body diagram of ball 1

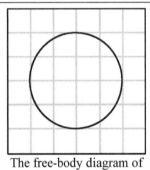

The free-body diagram of ball 2

Name: _____

Problem 18

Two golf balls are placed in a cylinder with an open top and bottom. The diameter of a golf ball is 40 mm. Its mass is 45 gm. The mass of the cylinder is 50 gm and its diameter is 50 mm. Draw the free-body diagrams for individual balls and the cylinder. Determine whether the cylinder will tip.

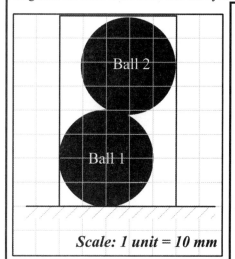

Scale: 1 unit = 10 mm

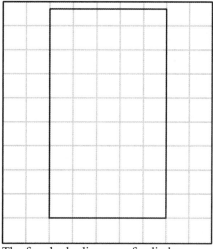

The free-body diagram of cylinder

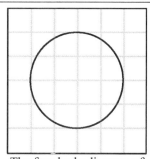

The free-body diagram of ball 1

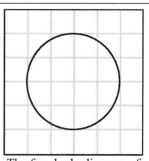

The free-body diagram of ball 2

Name: _____

Problem 19

Determine the force exerted by the hydraulic cylinder on the dumpster.

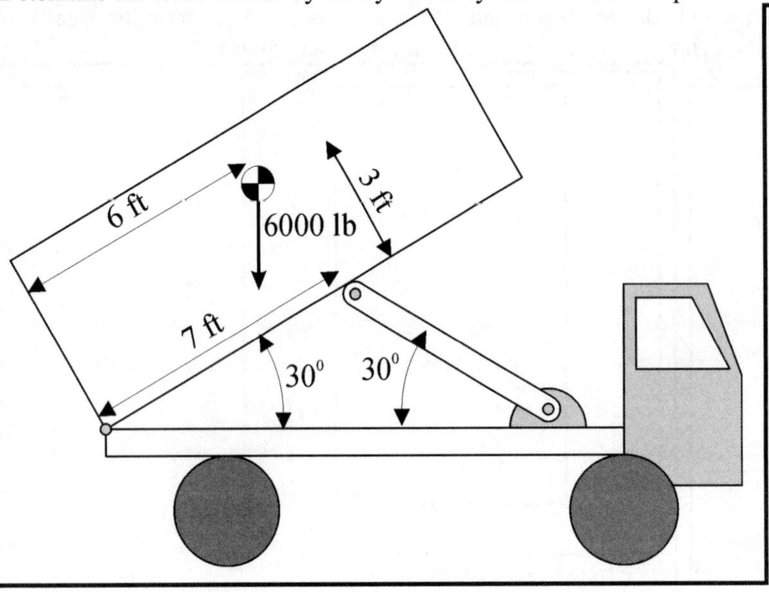

6 ft

3 ft

6000 lb

7 ft

30° 30°

5.9. Equilibrium of a Three-Dimensional System

This analysis also involves our two steps: drawing the free-body diagram and applying the equilibrium equations. The equilibrium equations take the form

$$\sum F_x = 0$$
$$\sum F_y = 0$$
$$\sum F_z = 0$$
$$\sum M_{about\ any\ point} = 0$$

12

Sometimes, in three-dimensional problems it is advantageous to take the force equilibrium equation in the vector form. Before we proceed to solve problems, let us review supports in three-dimensional systems and the reactions that they incur. Table 2 summarizes the supports in three-dimensional systems.

	Supports	Schematic	Reactions
	Ball and socket support: Prevents translations, but allows all three rotations.		
	Roller support: A ball and socket supported mounted on rollers. Prevents translation perpendicular to the surface. Offers no resistance to motion along the surface. Allows the rotation about the three axes.		
	Bearing: Prevents motion normal to the shaft axis.		
	Hinge: Allows rotation only about the hinge axis. Prevents translations in all three directions.		
	Fixed or built-in support: Prevents both translations and rotations.		

Table 2. Supports, schematic representation, and reactions incurred by different supports

Example 10

A glass table is supported by three legs and a triangular frame. The weight of the table is W. Determine the minimum downward force that could tip the table. Also, identify the point where this force must be applied.

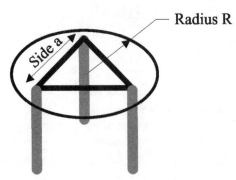

Figure 41. A glass table

One can tip the table by applying the force at points A or B. A force at point B creates the least moment about leg 2 while the countering moment caused by the weight of the table is far away from the leg.

A force at point A creates the maximum tipping moment about the line joining legs 1 and 2, and the counteracting moment caused by the weight is also closer to this line. Therefore, it is easier to tip by applying the force at point A.

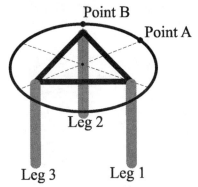

Figure 42. Potential load application points

Fig. 43 shows the tipping force (F) and the weight (W) along with the distance from the line connecting legs 1 and 2. Note that at tipping, leg 3 starts losing contact with the ground.dropping the force on leg 3 to zero.

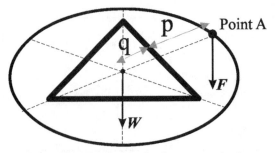

Figure 43. The free-body diagram at tipping

From geometry, we can compute

$$p = \left(R - \frac{a}{2\sqrt{3}} \right)$$

$$q = \frac{a}{2\sqrt{3}}$$

At tipping, there will be no reaction at leg 3. Taking the moments, we get

$$F \times p = W \times q$$

$$F = \frac{W \times q}{p}$$

$$F = \frac{Wa}{2\sqrt{3} \left(R - \dfrac{a}{2\sqrt{3}} \right)}$$

$$\boxed{F = \frac{Wa}{\left(2\sqrt{3}R - a \right)}}$$

Notes:

Name: _____

Problem 1

Determine the tension in each cable. The weight of the concrete slab is 100 kN. Assume that the center of gravity is at the geometric center.

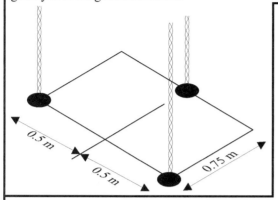

Problem 2

The weight of the concrete slab is 100 kN. Assume that the center of gravity is at the geometric center. Determine the required force (**F**) if the cable attached at point A does not carry any load.

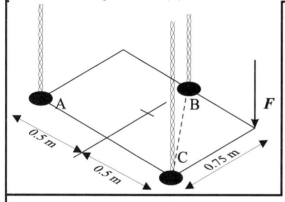

Problem 3

Determine the minimum load for tipping the table. The weight of the table is **W**.

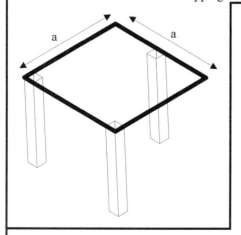

Name: _____

Problem 4

Determine the minimum load for tipping the table. The weight of the table is *W*.

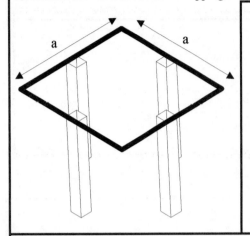

Problem 5

Determine the tension in each cable. Assume the weight of the quarter circle slab is negligible. The magnitude of force *F* is 10 kN.

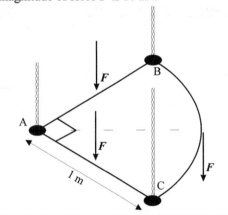

Problem 6

Determine the magnitude of force F if the tension in the cable at point A is zero.

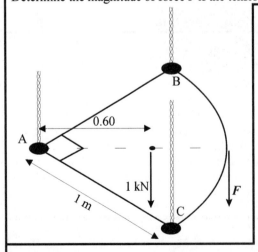

CHAPTER VI
STRUCTURAL DESIGN & ANALYSIS

Learning Objectives

The material presented in this chapter will enable you to accomplish the following:
1. Define a truss and identify its members.
2. Compute the internal forces in structural elements using the method of joints and the method of sections.
3. Identify zero-force members.
4. Analyze frames and machines.

Kickstart

Kickstart (formerly ApproTEC) was co-founded by Fisher and Moon to bring sustainable products to the developing world. The goal of Kickstart is to bring appropriate technologies which will have a lasting impact by addressing the fundamental problems of the people. The traditional approach of bring in advanced farming machinery and building dams and irrigation systems made an initial impact. But when the organization left, within a few years the system would be breaking down and no longer used. Therefore, there was no lasting impact. Kisckstart solved this problem by applying appropriate technologies and emphasizing sustainability.

The Action Pack Block Press (refer to Fig. 1) is the first technology created by Kickstart in 1991. This press compacts soil with a small amount of cement to create construction blocks. These highly pressurized blocks require less cement than the regular blocks and need not be kiln fired. Apart from the resulting savings in construction cost, each machine employs about six workers to make 600 blocks a day.

Figure 1. The Action Pack Block Press[*]

The Super MoneyMaker Pump (refer to Fig. 2) is a small irrigation pump that uses human power to pump water from as deep as 23ft. The pump weighs 45 pounds, and can water 2 acres in a 6 hour days at a rate of 1 liter/second. Two dual pistons are energized by two treadles that are actuated by the weight of the person. The operation of the treadles mimics the natural walking motion. Further, the treadles are designed to allow two kids to fit on it, but designed specifically NOT to allow two adults to fit so that actual loads don't exceed design loads. These simple machines can be designed and analyzed using the concepts in Statics.

Figure 2. Super MoneyMaker Pump[*]

[*]Courtesy: University of Detroit Mercy and Kickstart. This case study was developed by University of Detroit Mercy in collaboration with Kickstart through a grant from Kern Entrepreneurship Education Network. The complete case study is available on the CD in the "kickstart" folder.

6.1. What is Structural Design & Analysis?

A structure, often composed of several structural elements or members, is designed to withstand loads imposed on it. We divide structures into trusses (where individual members experience loads along their length), frames (where the members experience more complicated loads), and machines (which move and exercise forces). Structural design is the art of combining interesting new structural forms to meet emerging needs of society.

The Geodesic Dome

While a straight line is the shortest path between two points in a plane, a *geodesic* is the shortest path on a curved surface. For instance, geodesics are used in determining the flight path across the world. A lattice structure of geodesics intersects to form a triangular micro-structure which is very stable. This concept is used in the construction geodesic domes and spheres. The geodesic dome (shown in Fig. 2) combines structural and energy efficiency with rain-water harvesting to create an aesthetically appealing green building.

Figure 3. A geodesic dome
Photo Courtesy: Sri Siddartha Institute of Technology, India

For successful and safe design, engineers must estimate the forces and moments experienced by the entire structure as well as the individual members. Structural analysis helps us to determine the internal forces in a structure. With advances in high-performance computing, software tools and numerical techniques such as the finite-element method are extensively employed in the analysis of complex structures.

The Statue of Liberty and the Eiffel Tower

Gustave Eiffel designed the internal structure of the Statue of Liberty. The structure is a *frame* where internal members are subjected to both axial and transverse loads. Later, he designed the Eiffel Tower, which is a *truss* structure comprising more than 15,000 girders (pieces of iron) and 2,500,000 rivets. For its height of 1,063 feet, it uses a meager 7,300 tons of iron. To appreciate the power of trusses, let us compare the Eiffel Tower with the Washington Monument whose height is 555 feet and weight is 82,000 tons. Even though it is made of different materials and reaches to twice the height, the Eiffel Tower uses substantially less material – a full order of magnitude less material, in fact – than the Washington Monument does. This contrast shows the advantage in structural efficiency that a truss structure enjoys over a solid beam.

Figure 4. The Statue of Liberty

Figure 5. The Eiffel Tower

6.2. What is a Truss?

Often, we encounter the problem of supporting external loads from a distance. For instance, the bridge shown in Fig. 6 transfers the weight of cars/trucks, self-weight, and wind loads to the support structures and to the banks of the river.

Figure 6. A bridge

We can achieve the purpose of transferring load to the support structure in a number of different ways. One possible design is to join several slender structural elements using pinned connections. We refer to such a structure as a truss. The slender members known as *struts* intersect at *truss joints*. The struts forming the top and bottom of the truss are referred to as *chords*. The inclined and vertical elements connecting the upper and lower chords are known as the *web* of the truss. Typically, chords carry significantly higher loads than the web elements.

The struts are *two-force members* i.e. only two forces act on the strut. To satisfy the force equilibrium equation with only two forces acting, these forces must be equal and opposite in direction. To satisfy the moment equilibrium equation, the forces must be collinear. Depending on their direction, the forces subject the struts to compression or tension (pushing or pulling), as shown in Fig. 7.

(a) (b)

Figure 7. Struts in (a) compression and (b) tension

6.3. Development of a Truss

Definition: *A truss is a structure made of slender structural elements that take loads only in the form of compression or tension.*

At a fundamental level, a truss must support the load and remain stable. When the load is applied, the truss should not collapse, and its struts should not move. Most trusses build on the concept of a triangle, as the triangle is inherently the most stable geometric form. In other words, we cannot change the shape of a triangle without distorting one of its sides. In Fig. 8, load P acts on a triangular truss. The pin support provides force reactions in the horizontal and vertical directions. The roller support provides a vertical reaction. The truss cannot move in any direction. Similarly, tetrahedrons and octahedrons (see Fig. 9) are the most stable three-dimensional shapes, offering more stability than a cube. On closer inspection, one will notice that a tetrahedron and an octahedron are, in fact, an assemblage of triangles.

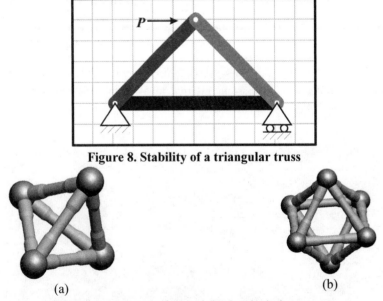

Figure 8. Stability of a triangular truss

(a) (b)

Figure 9. (a) Tetrahedral and (b) Octahedral structures

On the other hand, other geometric forms change their shapes when the load is applied. For instance, a rectangle transforms into a parallelogram (see Fig. 10) without its sides distorting. To prevent the collapse of this truss, we can add a diagonal strut as shown in Fig. 11. We can view the new truss as one that is made of two triangles, returning us, once again, to a truss made of triangles. Thus, we can synthesize planar trusses (ones that lie in a single plane) by putting triangular trusses together. A planar truss made of triangles is called a *simple truss*.

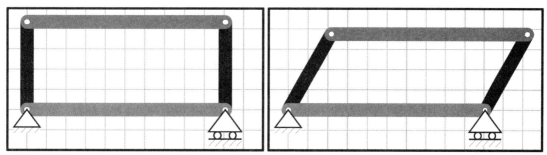

Figure 10. Instability of a rectangular truss

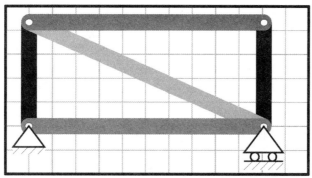

Figure 11. A stable configuration (made of two triangles)

6.4. Assumptions

Truss analysis is based on two major assumptions:
- *All loads are applied at the joints:* In the analysis, we assume that the loads are applied only at the joints. We neglect the self-weight of the struts. If the self- weight is significant in comparison to the external loads, then we apply half of the weight of each strut at its corresponding joint.
- *The joints do not transmit moment loads:* The struts in a truss comprise two force members which accept loads as compression or tension. Therefore, we must ensure that the joints do not to transmit moment loads. A smooth pin connection satisfies this assumption.

6.5. Method of Joints

The name for this method derives from its procedure: analyze one joint at a time by examining the forces that the struts exert on the joint. This procedure involves the following steps:
1. Solve unknown external reactions:
   a. Draw the free-body diagram for the entire structure.
   b. Write the equilibrium equations.
   c. Solve for the support reactions.
2. Analyze one-joint at a time:
   a. Choose a joint: Select a joint with <u>a maximum of two unknown forces</u> and <u>a minimum of one known force</u>.

    b. Draw the free-body diagram for the joint: While drawing the free-body diagram, <u>point the unknown forces away from the joint</u>. In other words, the strut is under tension and therefore pulls the joint.

    c. Write the force equilibrium equations: As all the forces pass through the joint, we only establish the force equilibrium equation. It is not useful to establish the moment equilibrium equation as it does not provide any insight.

    d. Solve for the forces exerted by the struts. If we get a positive value for the unknown force, then the strut is experiencing tension and the direction shown in the free body diagram is correct. A negative value indicates that the strut is experiencing compression. The direction of the vector should be switched.

An intelligent choice of the sequence of joints to be analyzed greatly simplifies the problem.

Example 1

The Warren truss is the most common truss for bridge construction (refer to Fig. 12). For this truss structure, determine the forces in the members of the truss.

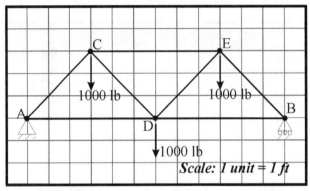

Figure 12. Warren bridge truss

Step 1: Solve unknown external reactions

a. Draw the free-body diagram for the entire structure

Fig. 13 shows the free-body diagram of the Warren truss. The pin support provides both horizontal and vertical reactions. The roller support at joint B provides only vertical support.

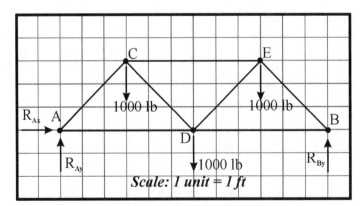

Figure 13. Free-body diagram of the Warren truss

---

b. Write the equilibrium equations
The equilibrium equations are

$$\sum \mathbf{F_x} = \mathbf{R_{Ax}} = 0$$

$$\sum \mathbf{F_y} = \mathbf{R_{Ay}} + \mathbf{R_{By}} - 1000 - 1000 - 1000 = 0$$

$$\sum M_A = \left(1000\,\mathrm{lb} \times 3\,\mathrm{ft}\right) + \left(1000\,\mathrm{lb} \times 6\,\mathrm{ft}\right) + \left(1000\ \mathrm{lb} \times 9\ \mathrm{ft}\right) - \mathbf{R_{By}} \times 12\,\mathrm{ft} = 0$$

c. Solve for the support reactions
Rearranging the moment equation, we get

$$\mathbf{R_{By}} = 1500 \text{ lb}$$

Substituting the value of R_{By} in the force equilibrium equation, we get

$$\mathbf{R_{Ay}} = 1500 \text{ lb}$$

The results make sense because the loading is symmetric and, therefore, equally distributed on joints A and B.

Step 2: Analyze one-joint at a time:
We start the analysis with joint A. At joint A, we have two unknown forces (the forces exerted by the struts) and one known force (reaction force). The direction of the unknown forces is assumed to be pointing away from the joint.

Choose a joint	Joint A	Joint B
Draw the free-body diagram		
Write the force equilibrium equations	$\sum \mathbf{F_x} = F_{AC} \cos 45 + F_{AD} = 0$ $\sum \mathbf{F_y} = F_{AC} \sin 45 + 1500 = 0$	$\sum \mathbf{F_x} = F_{BE} \cos 45 + F_{BD} = 0$ $\sum \mathbf{F_y} = F_{BE} \sin 45 + 1500 = 0$
Solve for the forces exerted by the struts	$F_{AC} = -\dfrac{1500}{\sin 45} = -2120 \text{ lb}$ $F_{AD} = 1500 \text{ lb}$	$F_{BE} = -\dfrac{1500}{\sin 45} = -2120 \text{ lb}$ $F_{BD} = 1500 \text{ lb}$

Points to consider:
1. The forces in the web members AC and BE are negative. In other words, the force in these members manifests as compression, not tension.
2. As we can see, the forces in struts AC and BE are equal, as are the forces in struts AD and BD. We could have reached the same conclusion without analyzing joint B by looking at the effect of symmetry. Now, we analyze joint C, solve for the force in strut CD, and then use the effect of symmetry to identify the forces in the rest of the structure.

Choose a joint	Joint C
Draw the free-body diagram	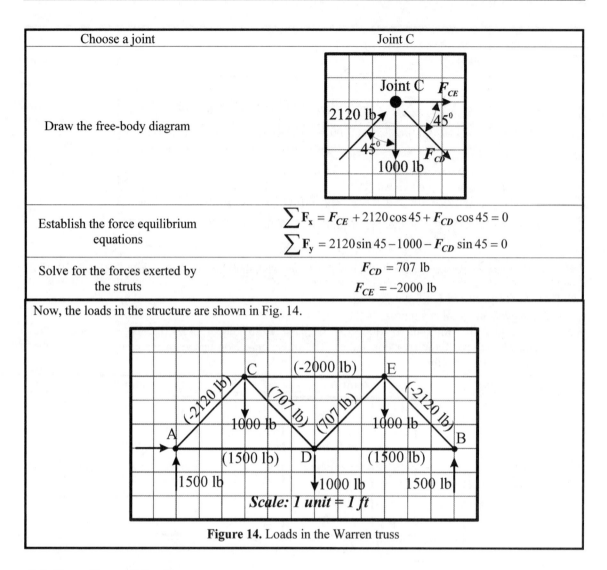
Establish the force equilibrium equations	$\sum \mathbf{F_x} = F_{CE} + 2120\cos 45 + F_{CD}\cos 45 = 0$ $\sum \mathbf{F_y} = 2120\sin 45 - 1000 - F_{CD}\sin 45 = 0$
Solve for the forces exerted by the struts	$F_{CD} = 707$ lb $F_{CE} = -2000$ lb

Now, the loads in the structure are shown in Fig. 14.

Figure 14. Loads in the Warren truss

6.6. Zero-Force Members

Definition: *A zero-force member is a strut that does not carry any load.*

In trusses, some members may not carry any loads, i.e. they are not subject to tension or compression. These zero-force members serve four purposes:
1. They prevent buckling in the long structural members by increasing the rigidity in the transverse direction.
2. They become redundant members and come into play when normally load-carrying structural elements fail. Thus, they provide a fail-safe future for a truss.
3. They support loads during construction.

To understand how to identify zero-force members, let us add three struts to the Warren truss discussed earlier. Fig. 15 highlights the additional struts in the truss.

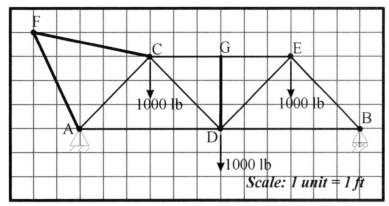

Figure 15. The Warren truss with three additional members

Let us draw the free-body diagram for the node G. As the free-body diagram shows (see Fig. 16), two forces F_{GC} and F_{GE} are collinear and oppose each other. Force F_{GD} remains unbalanced. To achieve equilibrium, this force must be equal to zero.

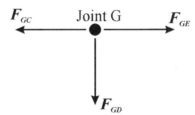

Figure 16. The free-body diagram of joint G

Now let us analyze joint F by drawing its free-body diagram (see Fig. 17). Once again, two non-collinear forces $\left(F_{FA} \text{ and } F_{FC} \right)$ are acting at this joint. These forces will satisfy the equilibrium equations only if the magnitude of both forces is equal to zero.

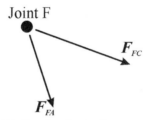

Figure 17. The free-body diagram of joint F

We can generalize these two observations and formulate our two rules to identify zero-force members:

1. *At a joint where three members meet, two of the members are collinear, and if there is no external load, the non-collinear member is a zero-force member.*
2. *At a joint where two members meet and there is no external load, the two members are zero-force members.*

Note that to identify zero-force members, we should look at the joints that bear no external load. By eliminating the zero-force members from consideration, we simplify the analysis of the truss.

Notes:

Concept Questions

Name: _____

1. What is a slender member?

2. What are the two basic assumptions made in the truss?

3. Label chord members as 1 and web elements as 2.

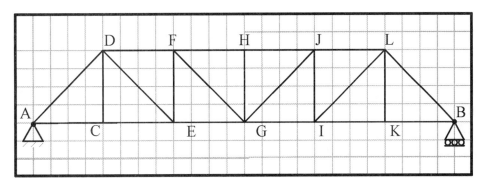

4. What are the two basic building blocks for a truss in three-dimensional geometry?

5. While analyzing a plane truss using the method of joints, for a joint you can write _____ (one/two/three/four) equilibrium equations.

6. The load carried by member GC is:
   A.   0 lb
   B.   300 lb
   C.   600 lb
   D.   None of the above

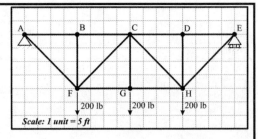

Scale: 1 unit = 5 ft

7. The number of zero-force members in this structure is:
   A.   4
   B.   5
   C.   6
   D.   None of the above

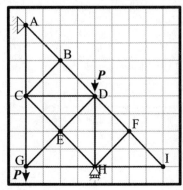

8. Determine the load in member BC.

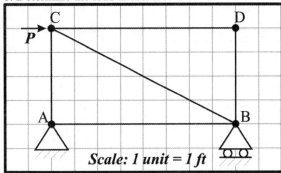

Scale: 1 unit = 1 ft

A. P (tension)

B. $-P$ (tension)

C. $\dfrac{\sqrt{80}}{8}\, P$ (tension)

D. $-\dfrac{\sqrt{80}}{8}\, P$ (compression)

9. Determine the load in member AC.

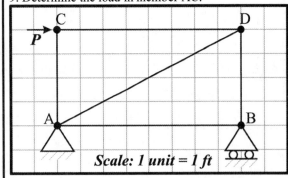

Scale: 1 unit = 1 ft

10. The triangle is inherently the most stable geometric form. The most stable three-dimensional shapes are:

_____ and _____

Name: _____

Problem 1

Determine the loads in each member if the magnitude of force **P** is 1000 lb.

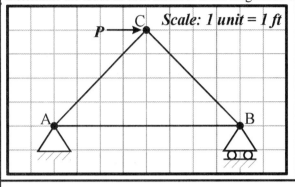

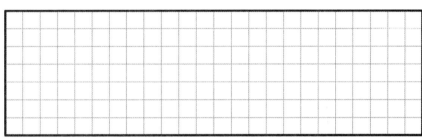

Problem 2

Determine the loads in each member if the magnitude of force **P** is 1000 lb.

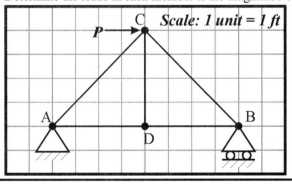

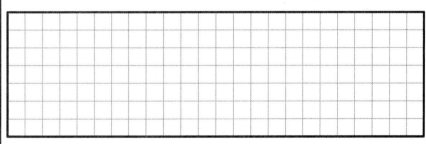

Name: _____

Problem 3

Determine the loads in each member if the magnitude of force *P* is 1000 lb.

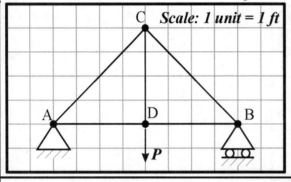

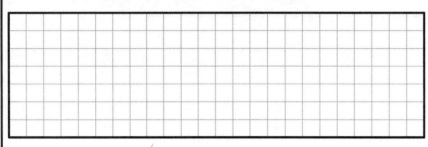

Problem 4

Determine the loads in each member if the magnitude of force *P* is 1000 lb.

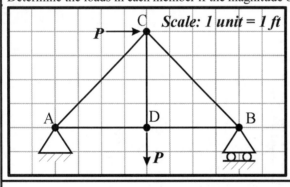

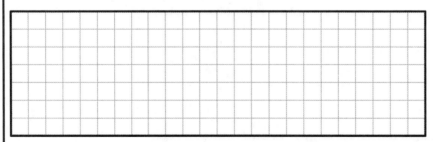

Name: _____

Problem 5

Determine the loads in each member if the magnitude of force *P* is 5 kN.

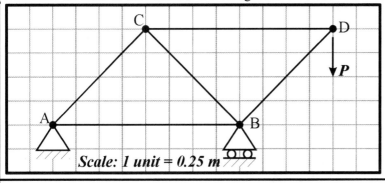

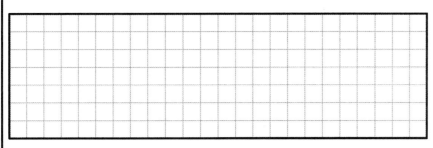

Problem 6

Determine the loads in each member if the magnitude of force *P* is 5 kN.

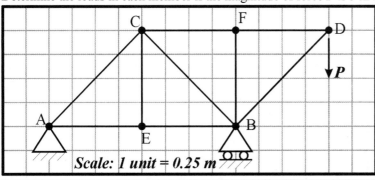

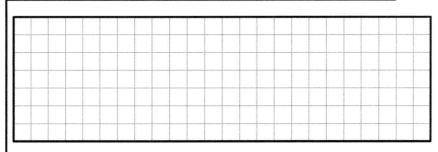

Name: _____

Problem7

Determine the loads in each member if the magnitude of force **P** is 5 kN.

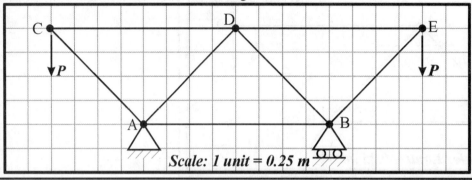

Scale: 1 unit = 0.25 m

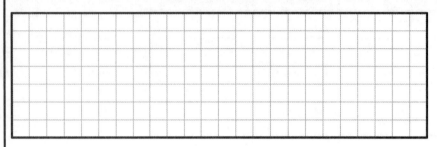

Problem 8

Determine the loads in each member.

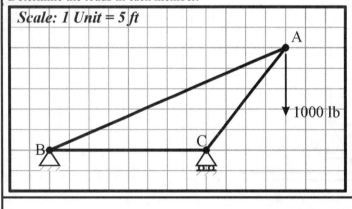

Scale: 1 Unit = 5 ft

1000 lb

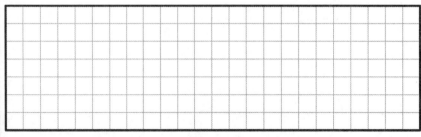

Name: _____

Problem 9

Determine the loads in each member.

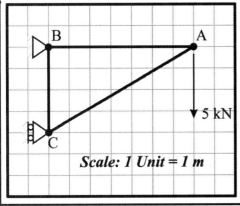

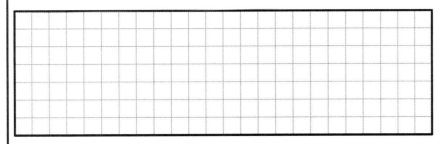

Problem 10

Determine the loads in each member.

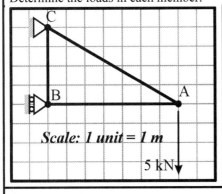

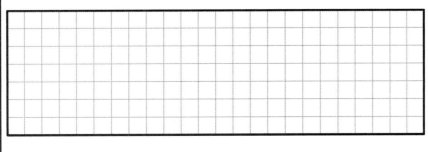

Name: _____

Problem 11

Determine the loads in each member.

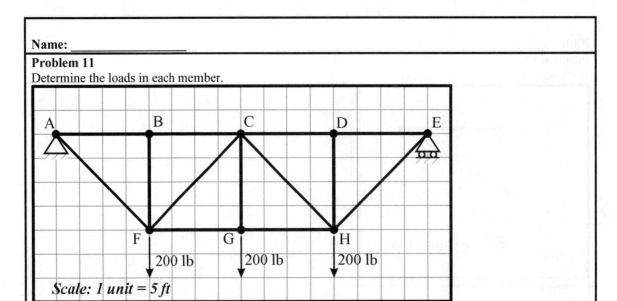

Scale: 1 unit = 5 ft

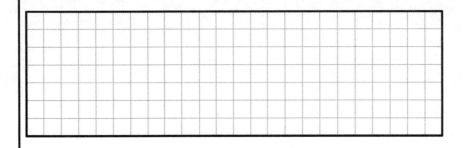

Name: _____

Problem 12

Determine the loads in each member.

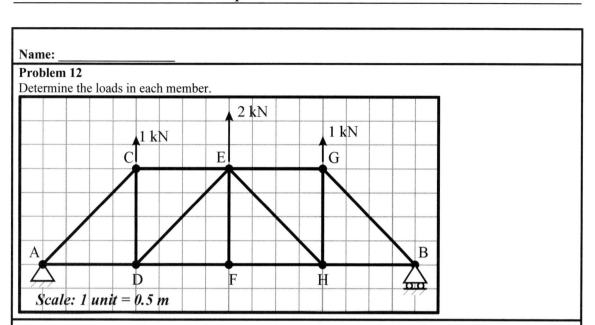

Scale: 1 unit = 0.5 m

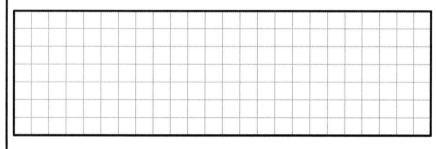

Name: _____

Problem 13

Determine the maximum allowable load **F** if the allowable load for each member is 10 kN.

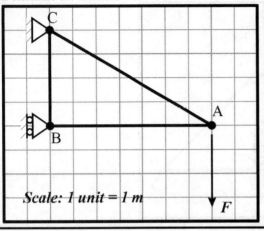

Scale: 1 unit = 1 m

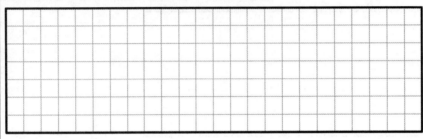

Problem 14

Determine the maximum allowable load **F** if the allowable load for each member is 10 kN in compression and 7.5 kN in tension.

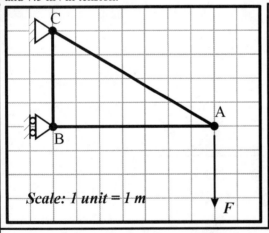

Scale: 1 unit = 1 m

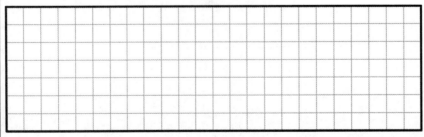

Name: _____

Problem 15

Determine the maximum allowable load *P* if the allowable load for each member is 1000 lb.

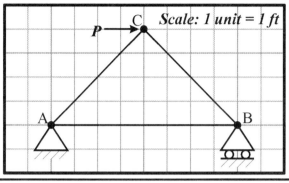

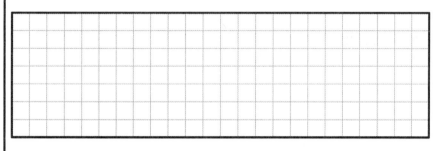

Problem 16

Determine the maximum allowable load *P* if the allowable load for each member is 1000 lb in compression and 1500 lb in tension.

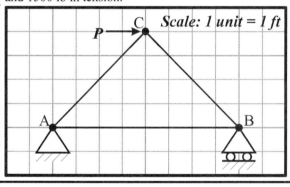

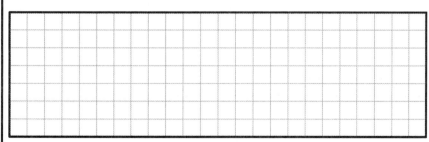

Notes:

6.7. Method of Sections

As the name implies, the method of sections uses an imaginary sectional plane to divide the truss into two parts. Because the entire truss is in equilibrium, each of its parts should also be in equilibrium. Therefore, we can draw the free-body diagram for one of the two parts of the truss and set the equilibrium equations. As we can establish three equilibrium equations $\left(\sum F_x, \sum F_y, \sum M_z\right)$ for a planar structure, we can solve for a maximum of three unknown forces. Therefore, it is important that the sectional plane not cut across more than three struts with unknown forces. This method is very useful in finding the forces in a certain member in a large truss without determining the forces in all the individual struts.

The procedure for the method of sections involves two basic steps:

1. Solve unknown external reactions: Note that by, depending on the type of structure, we may be able to solve the problem even by skipping this step.
    a. Draw the free-body diagram for the entire structure.
    b. Write the equilibrium equations.
    c. Solve for the support reactions.
2. Analyze a part of the truss:
    a. Choose a sectional plane: Create a sectional plane that cuts across a maximum of three struts with unknown forces.
    b. Draw the free-body diagram for a part of the truss: Pick a part of the truss which is easy to analyze. While drawing the free-body diagram, point out the unknown forces pulling the strut. In other words, the strut is experiencing tension.
    c. Write the equilibrium equations.
    d. Solve for the forces exerted by the struts. If we get a positive value for the unknown force, then the strut is in tension and the direction shown in the free body diagram is correct. A negative value indicates that the strut is in compression. The direction of the vector should be reversed.

Example 2
Determine the forces in struts EG, FG, and FH. This truss is known as the Pratt truss. In this truss, all the diagonal web elements except the end elements are slanted towards the center.

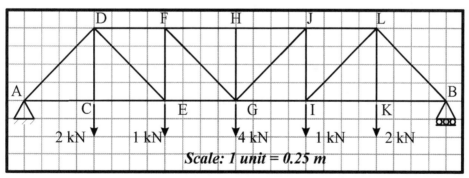

Figure 18. The Pratt Truss

STEP 1: Determine the support reactions.
The free-body diagram for the Pratt truss is shown in Fig. 19. By looking at the symmetry, we can write the support reactions as

$$\mathbf{R}_{Ax} = 0$$
$$\mathbf{R}_{Ay} = 5 \text{ kN}$$
$$\mathbf{R}_{By} = 5 \text{ kN}$$

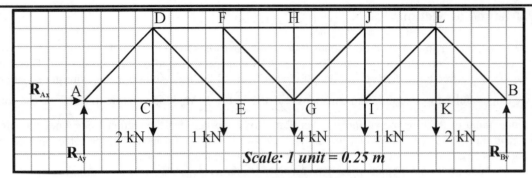

Figure 19. The free-body diagram of the Pratt truss

STEP 2: Analyze a part of the truss

a. *Choose a sectional plane*: The first step involves the creation of a sectional plane. In this particular case, we are interested in finding the forces in struts EG, FG, and FH. Therefore, we can draw a vertical section cutting these three struts as shown in Fig. 20.

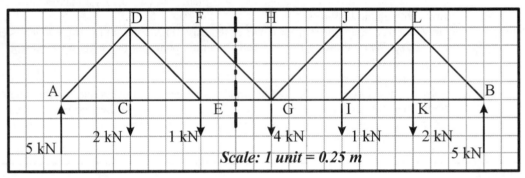

Figure 20. A vertical section cutting the three struts of our interest

b. *Draw the free-body diagram for a part of the truss*: In this particular problem, the left side is easier to solve because it involves fewer loads. As we do not know the sense of the forces in struts EG, FG, and FH, we can assume that they are pulling the struts. Fig. 21 shows the resulting free-body diagram.

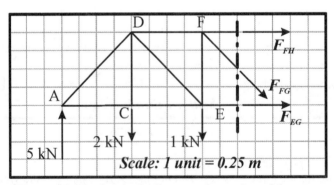

Figure 21. The free-body diagram of a portion of the truss

c. *Write the equilibrium equations*: Because the whole Pratt truss is in equilibrium, this part of the truss should also satisfy the equilibrium equations. While we can routinely write the force equilibrium equations, the appropriate choice of the point about which moments are taken can greatly simplify the problem. For instance, if we take the moments about point F, the moment equation will involve the force in strut EG only. The forces in struts FH and FG will not produce any moment about the point F.

$$\sum \mathbf{F_x} = F_{EG} + F_{FG} \sin 45 + F_{FH} = 0$$

$$\sum \mathbf{F_y} = 5 \text{ kN} - 2 \text{ kN} - 1 \text{ kN} - F_{FG} \cos 45 = 0$$

$$\sum M_F = -5 \text{ kN} \times 4 \text{ m} + 2 \text{ kN} \times 2 \text{ m} + F_{EG} \times 2 \text{ m} = 0$$

d.   *Solve for the forces exerted by the struts.*

$$F_{EG} = 8 \text{ kN}$$

$$F_{FG} = 2.83 \text{ kN}$$

$$F_{FH} = -10 \text{ kN}$$

Notes:

Name: _____

Problem 1

Determine the loads in BC, CF, and FG. Compare your solution with Problem 11.

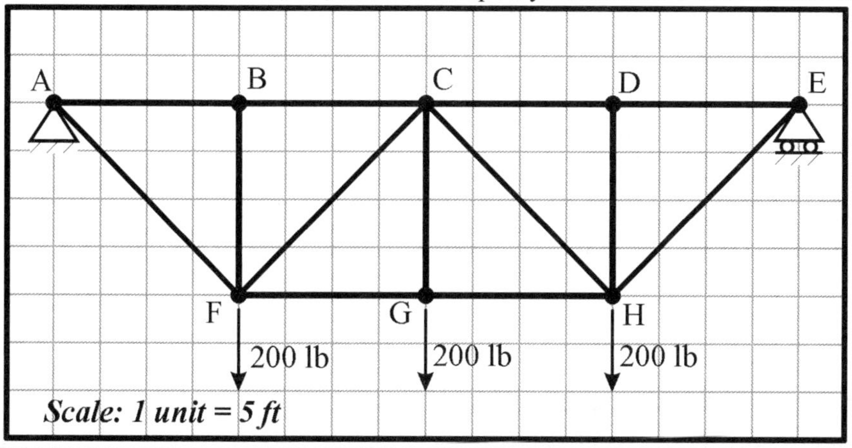

A   B   C   D   E

F   G   H

200 lb   200 lb   200 lb

Scale: 1 unit = 5 ft

Name: _____

Problem 2

Determine the loads in FH, FG, and EG in terms of *F* and L.

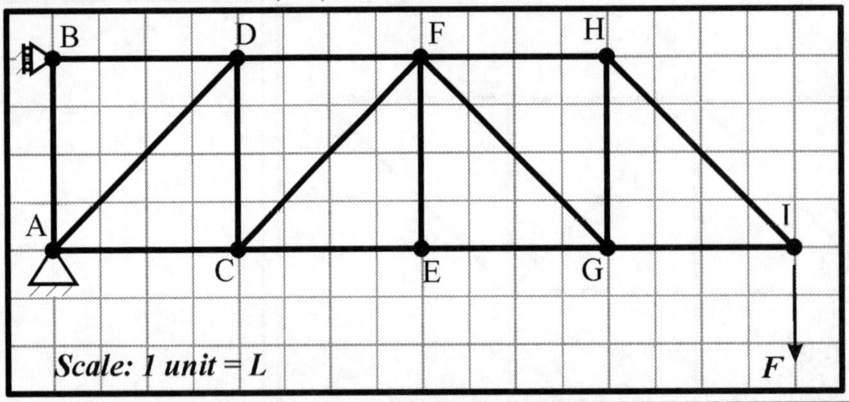

Scale: *1 unit = L*

Name: _____

Problem 3
Determine the loads in DF and EG.

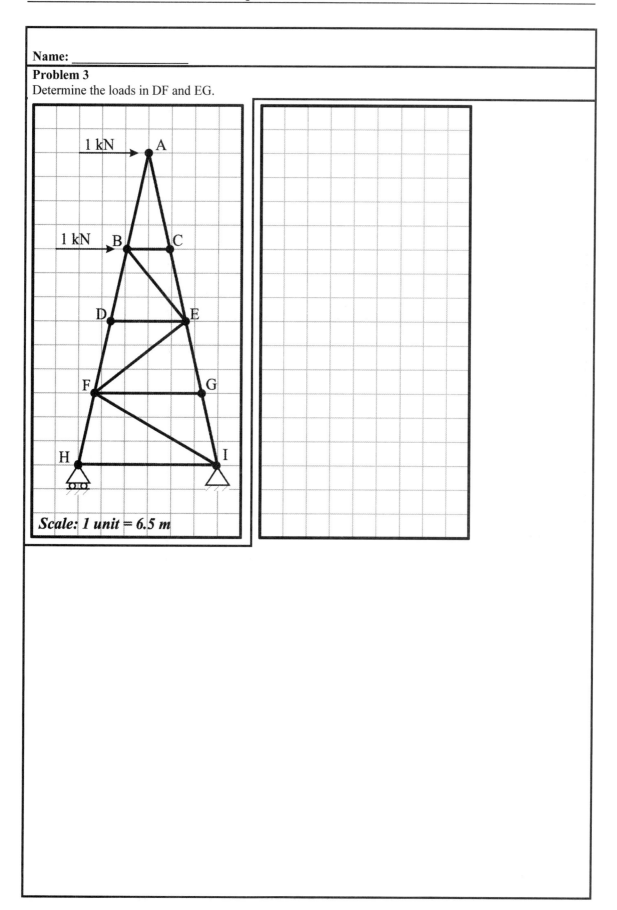

Scale: *1 unit = 6.5 m*

Name: _____

Problem 4

Determine the loads in CE, DE and DF.

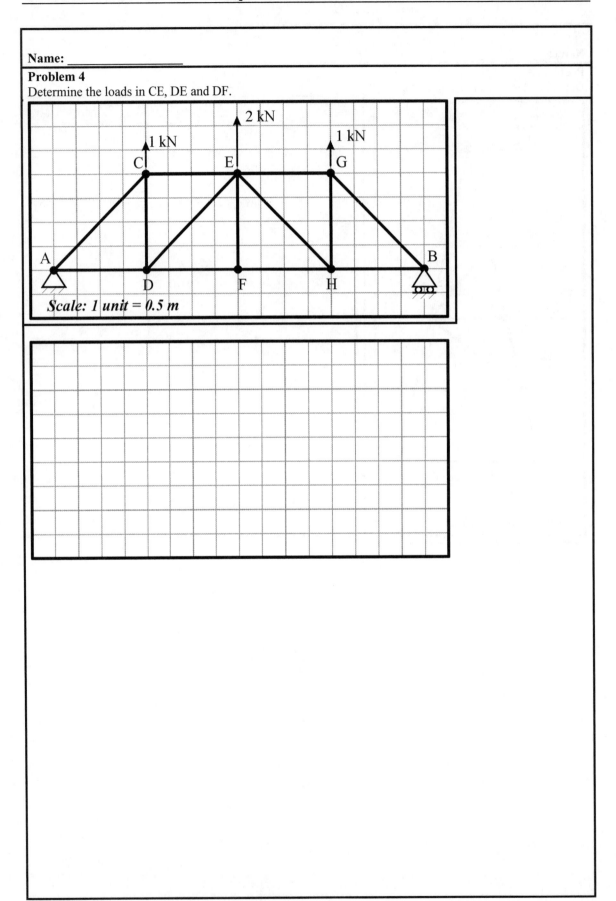

Scale: *1 unit = 0.5 m*

Name: ____________________

Problem 5

Determine the loads in DE and DB if the magnitude of force ***P*** is 5 kN.

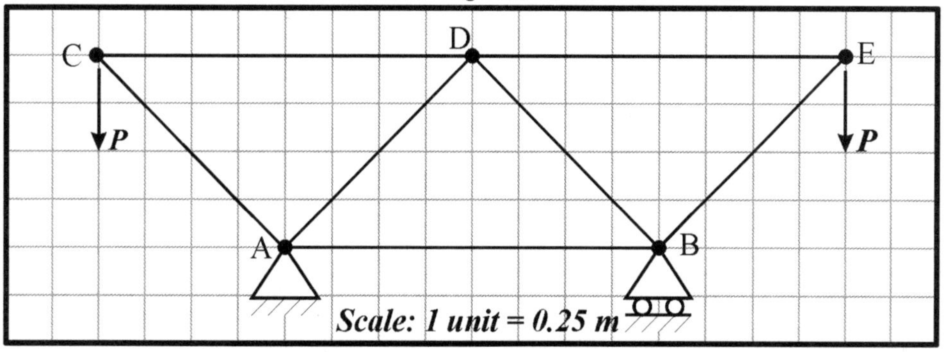
C
D
E
P
P
A
B
Scale: 1 unit = 0.25 m

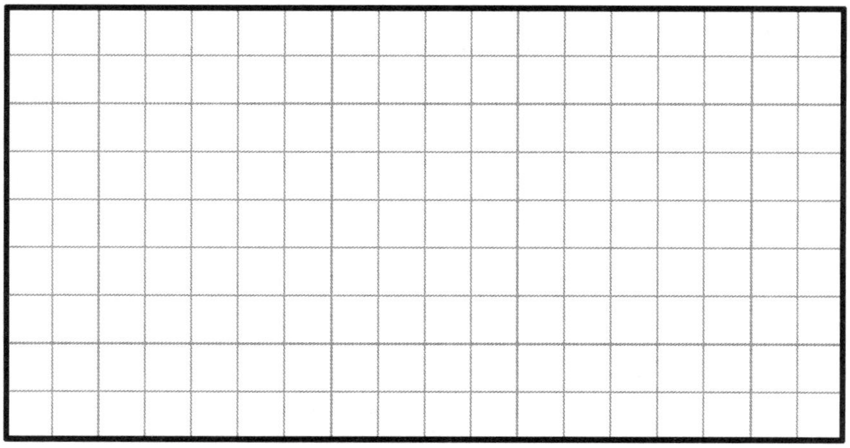

Name: _____

Problem 6

Determine the allowable load *F* if a strut can support 2 kN tensile load and 1 kN compressive load and if the length of the beam is 10 m

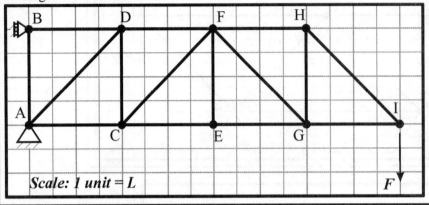

Scale: 1 unit = L

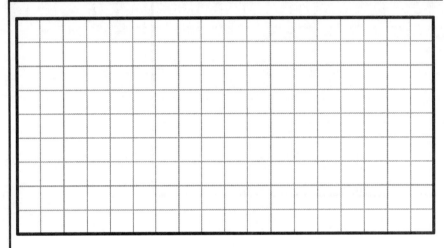

Name: _____

Problem 7

Determine the loads in BD, CD, and CE.

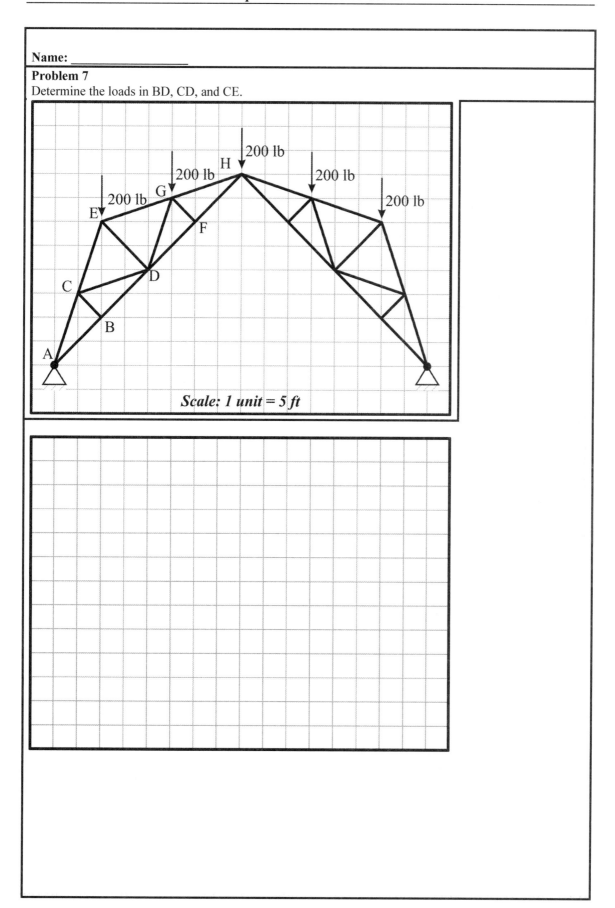

Scale: 1 unit = 5 ft

Name: _____

Problem 8
Determine the loads in BC, HC, and HG.

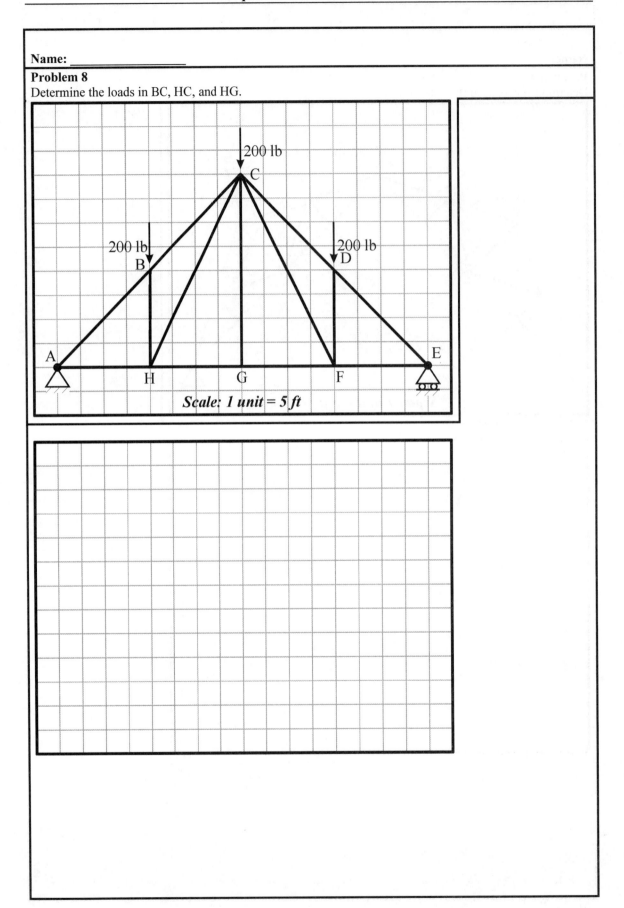

Scale: 1 unit = 5 ft

Name: _____

Problem 9
Determine the loads in BC, BG, and FG.

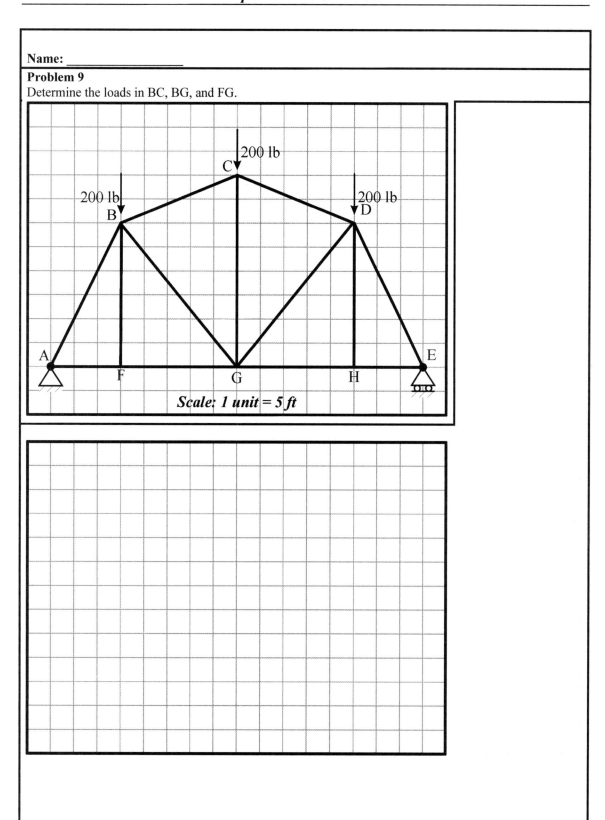

Scale: 1 unit = 5 ft

Name: _____

Problem 10
Determine the loads in CD, GD, GF, EF, and DE.

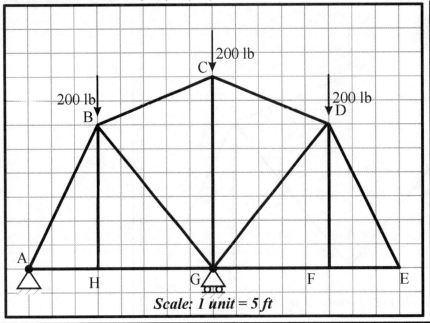

Scale: 1 unit = 5 ft

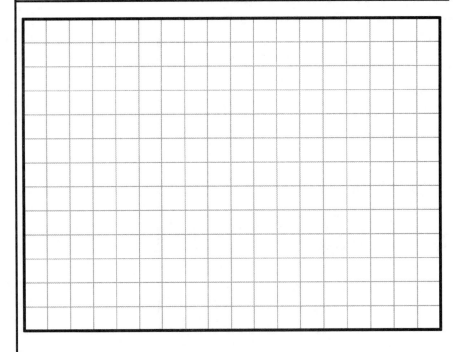

6.8. Frames and Machines

While trusses are composed of two-force members and do not transmit moments, frames are stationary structures that comprise pinned structural members carrying multiple forces and moments. Machines, on the other hand, contain moving parts along with stationary members. The analysis of frames and machines is more complex because the method for solving the problem is more flexible, requiring more thinking on our part to structure the solution. The general procedure for analyzing frames or machines involves two steps.

Step I - Apply the equilibrium equations to the entire structure: While we determined the reaction forces using the equilibrium equations in the case of trusses, often we may not be able to find the reaction forces in frames and machines using the equilibrium equations of the entire structure alone. Make an effort to determine as many reactions as possible.

Step II – Apply the equilibrium equations to individual members or groups of members: In this step, disassemble the structure into parts composed of individual members or groups of members. Draw the free-body diagrams for the parts. Represent only the external forces. In other words, if a part comprises two members, don't identify the forces acting between the components. On the other hand, when drawing a free-body diagram for individual components, identify the forces acting between components and make sure to label them to be equal and opposite. Assume the direction of unknown forces. Try to identify the two force members and represent the forces along the length of the member. Doing so simplifies the problem and reduces the number of unknown forces. Then, apply the equilibrium equations and try to solve from a member with the least number of unknowns. Sometimes, in complex problems, it becomes necessary to solve the equations simultaneously.

Example 3
Determine the loads in the structural members.

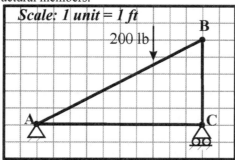

Figure 22. A simple frame with a concentrated load

Step I - Apply the equilibrium equations to the entire structure
The free-body diagram for the entire structure is shown in Fig. 23.

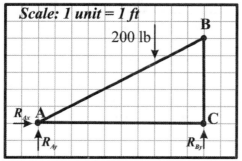

Figure 23. The free-body diagram for the entire structure

The equilibrium equations can be written as:

$$\sum F_x = R_{Ax} = 0$$
$$\sum M_A = -(200\ \text{lb}) \times (7\ \text{ft}) - R_{Cy} \times (10\ \text{ft}) = 0$$
$$\sum F_y = R_{Ay} + R_{By} - 200\ \text{lb} = 0$$

Solving the equilibrium equations, we get

$$R_{Cy} = 140\ \text{lb}$$
$$R_{Ay} = 60\ \text{lb}$$

Step II – Apply the equilibrium equations to individual members or groups of members.
The free-body diagrams are shown in Fig. 24.

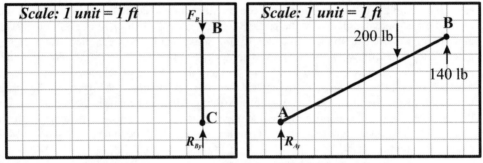

Figure 24. The free-body diagrams of the individual members

Note that member AC is a zero-force member. The forces experienced by the different members are shown in Fig. 27.

Example 4
Determine the loads carried by each member of the two-member frame.

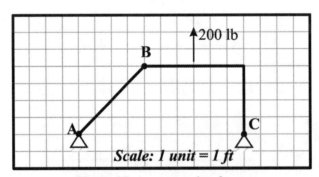

Figure 25. A two-member frame

Step I - Apply the equilibrium equations to the entire structure
In this step, we draw the free-body diagram for the entire structure. Support A provides reactions in the x- and y-directions, so we identify two forces, A_x and A_y. The fixed support C provides both force and moment reactions.

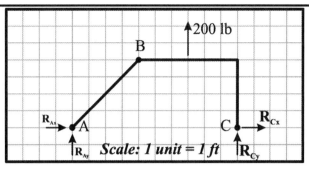

Figure 26. The free-body diagram of the frame

Now, we can write the equilibrium equations as

$$\sum F_x = R_{Ax} + R_{Cx} = 0$$

$$\sum F_y = R_{Ay} + R_{Cy} + 200\,\text{lb} = 0$$

$$\sum M_C = R_{Ay}\,(10\,\text{ft}) + (200\,\text{lb})(3\,\text{ft}) = 0$$

Solving these equations, we get

$$R_{Ax} = -R_{Cx} \qquad\qquad R_{Ay} = -60\,\text{lb} \qquad\qquad R_{Cy} = -140\,\text{lb}$$

Note that the equilibrium equations are not sufficient to solve all the unknown reactions.

Step II – Apply the equilibrium equations to individual members or groups of members.
From inspection, we know that AB is a two-force member. The free-body diagrams for the two individual members are shown in Fig. 27.

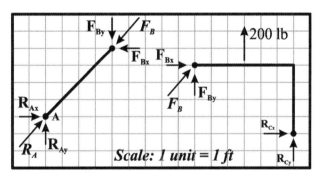

Figure 27. The free-body diagrams of individual elements

Now, as we know force R_{Ay}, we can compute force R_{Ax} and R_A.

$$R_{Ax} = -60\ \text{lb} \qquad\qquad R_A = -84.853\,\text{lb} \qquad\qquad R_{Cx} = 60\,\text{lb}$$

The negative sign for the magnitudes of R_{Ay}, R_A, and R_{Cy} indicate that the assumed direction must be reversed.

Example 5

Determine the loads in the structural members.

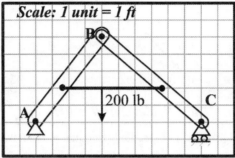

Figure 28. The frame

Step I - Apply the equilibrium equations to the entire structure
The free-body diagram for the entire structure is shown in Fig. 29.

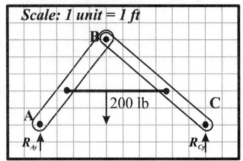

Figure 29. The free-body diagram of overall frame

The equilibrium equations are

$$\sum F_x = R_{Ax} = 0$$
$$\sum M_A = -(200 \text{ lb}) \times (4 \text{ ft}) - R_{Cy} \times (10 \text{ ft}) = 0$$
$$R_{Cy} = 80 \text{ lb}$$
$$\sum F_y = R_{Ay} + R_{By} - 200 \text{ lb} = 0$$
$$R_{Ay} = 120 \text{ lb}$$

Step II – Apply the equilibrium equations to individual members or groups of members.
The free-body diagrams for the individual members are shown in Fig. 30.

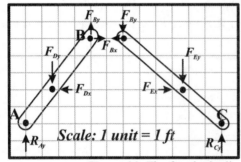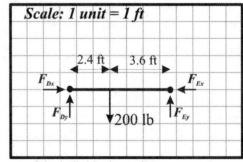

Figure 30. The free-body diagrams of the individual members

Applying the equilibrium equations to member DE, we get

$$\sum \mathbf{M_D} = -(200 \text{ lb}) \times (2.4 \text{ ft}) + F_{Ey}(6 \text{ ft}) = 0 \quad \rightarrow \quad F_{Ey} = 80 \text{ lb}$$

$$\sum \mathbf{F_y} = F_{Dy} + F_{Ey} - 200 \text{ lb} = 0 \quad \rightarrow \quad F_{Dy} = 120 \text{ lb}$$

$$\sum \mathbf{F_x} = F_{Dx} - F_{Ey} = 0 \quad \rightarrow \quad F_{Dx} = F_{Ex}$$

Applying the moment equilibrium equation to member AB,

$$\sum \mathbf{M_B} = F_{Dy} \times (2.4 \text{ ft}) - F_{Dx} \times (3 \text{ ft}) - R_{Ay} \times (4 \text{ ft}) = 0 \quad \rightarrow \quad F_{Dx} = -64 \text{ lb} = F_{Ex}$$

Now, using the force equilibrium equation in the x-direction, we get

$$F_{Bx} = 64 \text{ lb}$$

$$F_{By} = 0 \text{ lb}$$

Example 6

Determine the required weight W to keep the system in equilibrium.

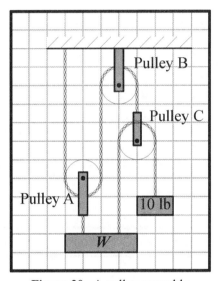

Figure 30. A pulley assembly

We can solve the problem by first drawing the free-body diagrams for the three pulleys and two weights (see Fig. 32). Note that initially, except for the 10 lb weight, all other forces are unknowns. The dotted lines show the action-reaction pairs acting between different objects. Now, we can solve by using the equilibrium equation for the 10 lb weight. We get

$$\sum F = T_2 - 10 \text{ lb} = 0$$

$$T_2 = 10 \text{ lb}$$

Next, applying the equilibrium equations for pulley C, we get

$$\sum F = T_1 - 2 \times T_2 = 0$$

$$T_1 = 2 \times T_2 = 20 \text{ lb}$$

Now, we can apply the equilibrium equations to pulley A. We get

$$\sum F = 2 \times T_1 - F_1 = 0$$

$$F_1 = 2 \times T_1 = 40 \text{ lb}$$

Finally, applying the equilibrium equation to the unknown weight, we get

$$\sum F = F_1 + T_2 - W = 0$$

$$W = F_1 + T_2 = 50 \text{ lb}$$

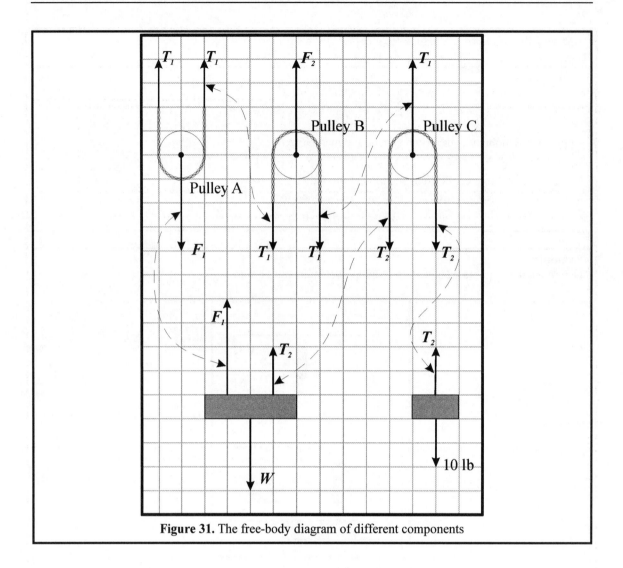

Figure 31. The free-body diagram of different components

Name: _____

Problem 1

Determine the loads in AB and BC of a compound beam.

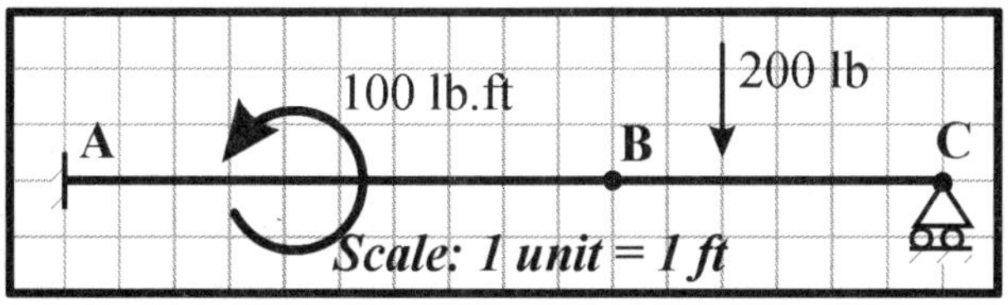

Problem 2

Determine the loads in the structural members.

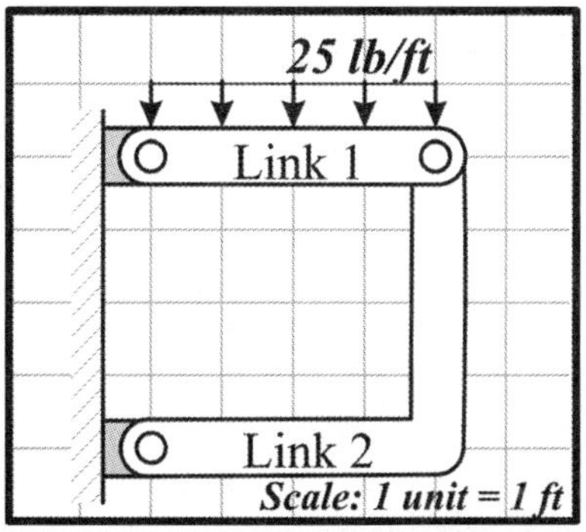

Name: _____

Problem 3
Determine the loads in AB and BC of a compound beam.

Problem 4
Determine the loads in the structural members.

Name: ___________________

Problem 5

Determine the loads in the structural members.

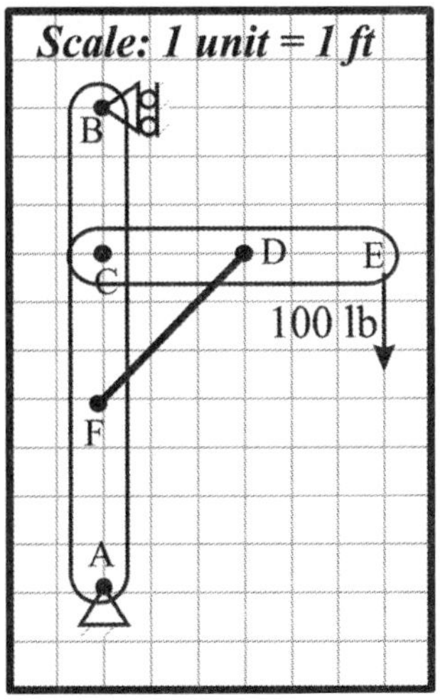
Scale: 1 unit = 1 ft
B
D
E
C
100 lb
F
A

Name: _____

Problem 6

Determine the force required by a person to lift himself up using the pulley arrangement. The mass of the person is 70 kg.

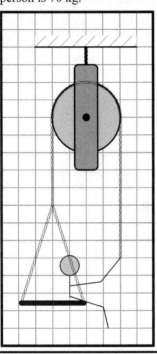

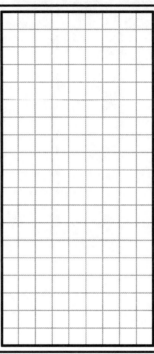

Problem 7

The block and tackle, invented by Archimedes, is a useful mechanism for hoisting heavy weights. It provides a significant mechanical advantage. In the block and tackle system shown, determine the force required to hoist 1000 lb.

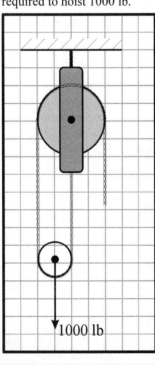

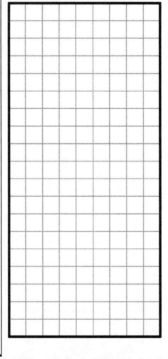

1000 lb

The mechanical advantage is equal to the number of lines going between the fixed and moving pulleys.

Name: _____

Problem 8

Determine the tension in the two cables. Also, determine the two unknown weights (W_1 and W_2).

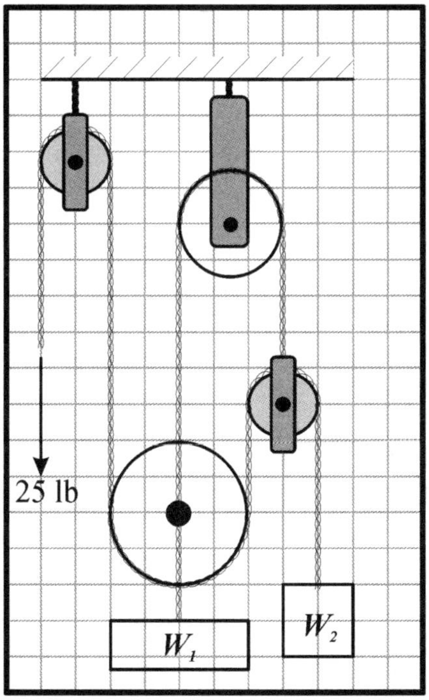

25 lb

W_1

W_2

Problem 9

Under what conditions can the system be in a state of equilibrium?

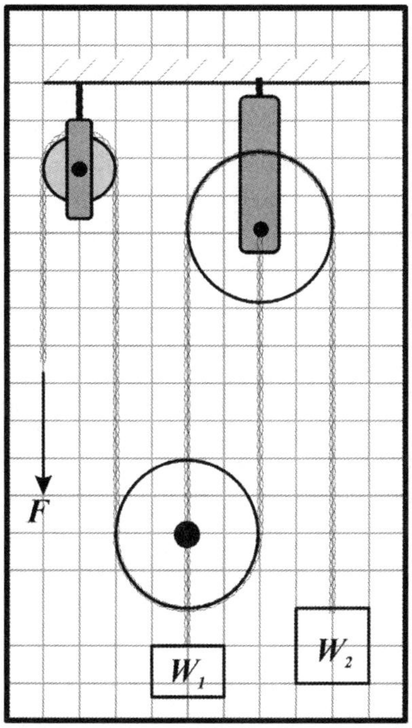

F

W_1

W_2

Name: _____

Problem 10
Determine weight **W**.

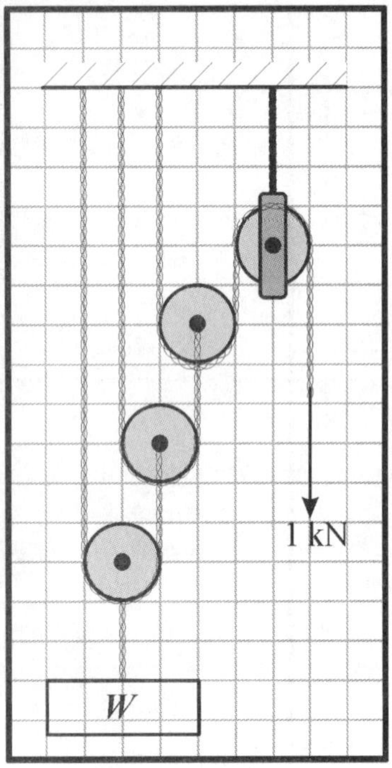

1 kN

W

Problem 11
Determine the force required to pulley weight **W**.

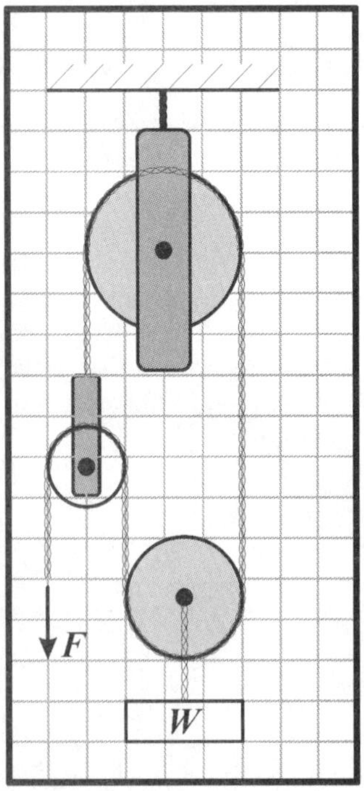

F

W

Carefully examine whether the pulley system will be in equilibrium. This system is known as a "fool's tackle."

CHAPTER VII
SHEAR FORCES & BENDING MOMENTS

Learning Objectives:

In this chapter, you will learn to perform four key tasks:
1. Define a beam.
2. Identify different types of beams and loading.
3. Calculate the shear force and bending moment at any point along a beam.
4. Draw the shear force and bending moment diagrams.

The Wings of an Airplane

On the ground, the gravitational force is the only force that acts on the wings of an airplane. The self-weight of the wing including the fuel is distributed along the wing span. On the other hand, the weight of the engine can be considered as a concentrated load because it acts on a small span. The loads change significantly in flight. The aerodynamic forces act on the surface of the wing in the upward direction.

Figure 1. Wings of aircrafts

The magnitude of the shear force and bending moment play an important role in the design of the wing. The maximum thickness of the wing is at the root of the wing where the bending moment is maximum. The wing tip is thin as the bending moment is zero.

7.1. What is a Beam?

Beams are the most common structural element. *A beam is a structural element subjected to lateral loading.* Typically, they are long members of a constant or varying cross-section that are subjected to bending loads. The term "lateral load" refers to the forces or moments that act upon the beam perpendicular to its axis. In Fig. 2a, for instance, the weight acts perpendicular to the length of the forearm. Similarly, the self-weight of a bridge and the weight of vehicles passing over it act normal to the length of the bridge. In addition to the lateral load, a beam may carry an axial load (forces and torques along its axis). Fig. 2 illustrates the difference between the axial and lateral loads.

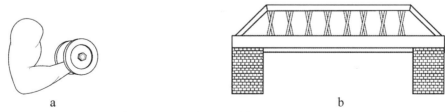

a   b

Figure 2. Examples of beams – (a) forearm lifting weight, and (b) bridge

---

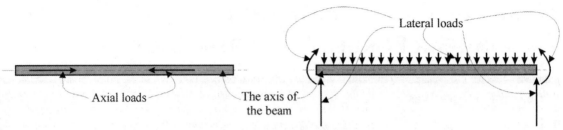

Figure 3. Axial and lateral loads

In this chapter, we will focus on straight beams loaded in a vertical plane passing through the axis of the beam.

7.2. Types of Loading

a. Concentrated Loads
A concentrated load is a force or a moment applied at a point on the beam. When the load acts on a very small portion of the beam, we can consider it to be a concentrated load. Consider a diver on a diving board (refer to Fig. 4), who lifts himself/herself upon the toes. Thus, the entire weight of the diver is applied on a very small area of the diving board. We can consider the diver's weight to be a concentrated load on the diving board as the dimensions of the applied load are quite small compared to the overall dimensions of the diving board.

Figure 4. Example of a concentrated load – Diver on a diving board

b. Distributed Load
A distributed load is a load that is applied over a certain length. A distributed load is described by the intensity of the force per unit length of the beam and is represented by the symbol q. It is also referred to as the *running load*. The units of q are lb/in, lb/ft, N/m and kN/m. Common sources of distributed forces include self-weight, magnetic forces, and pressure loading. For instance, the self-weight of a bridge (see Fig. 5) is considered to be a distributed load.

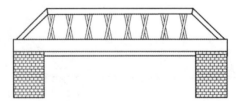

Figure 5. Example of a distributed load – Bridge

A distributed load with a constant intensity is called a *uniformly distributed load* or a *uniform load*. Another commonly encountered distribution is a linearly varying load where the intensity q varies linearly along the beam axis. Non-linear distributions exist and are often handled through numerical procedures.

7.3. Types of Beams

Beams are classified according to their supports. A beam with the minimum number of supports is known as a *statically determinate beam*. For a statically determinate beam, we can compute the reactions at the supports using the equilibrium equations alone. Additional supports make the beam *statically indeterminate*, where we need to consider the deformation of the beam along with the equilibrium equations to determine the reactions. The mechanics of solids course covers the topic of statically indeterminate structures. We can identify four types of statically determinate beams: simply supported, simply supported with an overhang, cantilever, and balancing beams.

a. Simply Supported Beams
A simply supported beam is a beam with a pin support at one end and a roller support at the other end. Fig. 6 shows a schematic representation of a simply supported beam. The distance between the supports is known as the *span*. The pinned support prevents translation in both horizontal and vertical directions, and therefore provides force reactions along these two directions. However, it does not resist the rotation of the beam and hence does not provide moment reaction. In the absence of an axial load, the horizontal reaction R_{Ax} at the pinned support is equal to zero. At the other end, the roller support provides only a vertical reaction.

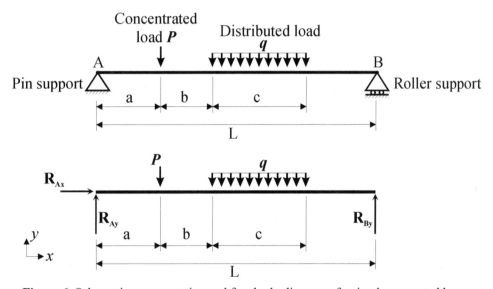

Figure 6. Schematic representation and free body diagram of a simply supported beam

b. Simply Supported Beams with an Overhang
A simply supported beam with an overhang is a beam that is supported by a pin and a roller support, but which hangs beyond the support(s). Fig. 7 shows an overhang beam with the beam extending beyond the roller support.

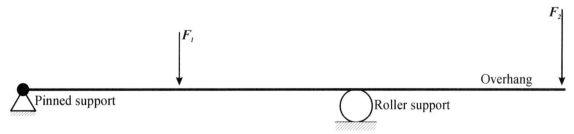

Figure 7. Schematic representation of an overhang beam

c. Cantilever Beams

A cantilever beam is a beam with only one support – a fixed support at one end. Two good examples of cantilever beams are the wings of an airplane, which experience distributed load, and a diving board with the concentrated load of a diver.

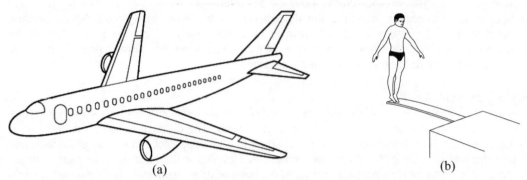

(a)   (b)

Figure 8. Examples of a cantilever beam – (a) Wings of an airplane, and (b) Diving board

Because it restricts both translations and rotations, the fixed support provides both force and moment reactions. Fig. 9 shows a representation of a cantilever beam and the corresponding free-body diagram.

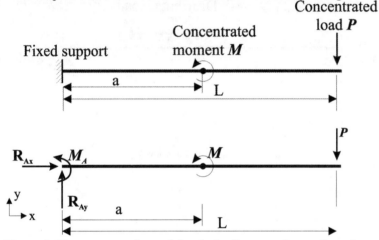

Figure 9. The representation and free body diagram of a cantilever beam

d. Balancing Beams

A balancing beam is a beam with only one pin connection. The pin support at the center cannot resist any moment. A scientific balance and a playground see-saw serve as two examples of balancing beams. Fig. 11 shows the corresponding free-body diagram. While the method of support is quite different, the free-body diagram for the balancing beam is identical to that of a simply supported beam. To appreciate the similarity, the reader is encouraged to compare Fig. 11 to Fig. 6.

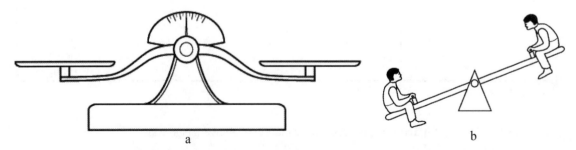

a   b

Figure 10. Examples of balancing beam – (a) Balance (b) see-saw

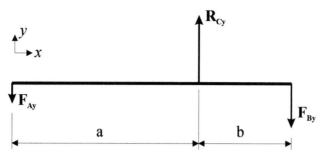

Figure 11. The free-body diagram of a balancing beam

Notes:

Concept Questions

Name: _____

1. A beam is a structural element subjected to _____ loading.
2. Imagine yourself jumping from the end of a diving board. When analyzing the diving board, we can approximate your weight as a _____ load.
3. The cantilever beam is not externally loaded. We can approximate the self-weight of the beam as a _____ load.
4. What is a statically determinate structure?

5. YES/NO: In the case of a statically indeterminate structure, can we compute the reactions at the supports using the equilibrium equations alone?
6. What is the difference between a pin and a fixed support?

7. What type of resistance can a roller support offer?

8. What does the term "span" refer to in the case of a simply supported beam?

9. Identify the type of beam for the following examples:

Aircraft wing		
Seesaw or teeter totter	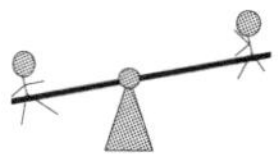	
Skateboard		
The plank of a bookshelf	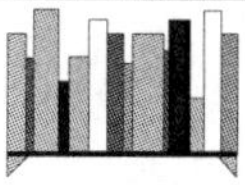	
The horizontal member of a traffic post	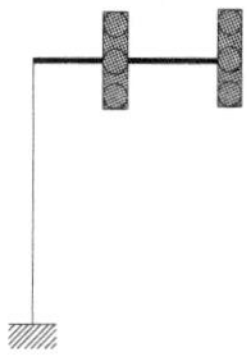	

10. TRUE/FALSE: The free body diagrams for the simply supported and balancing beams are the same.

Notes:

7.4. Shear Force & Bending Moment Determination at a Particular Section

To design and/or to analyze a beam, we must determine the internal forces and moments acting within the beam. We can calculate these internal forces and moments at any point along the beam using the method of *sections*. Let us say we want to find the shear force and bending moment at a point along the beam shown in Fig. 12a. Using the method of sections, we divide the beam into two parts at the point of interest (shown in Fig. 12b). Then, we can draw the free-body diagram for the two parts. To satisfy the equilibrium equations, we must apply internal forces and moments at the section, as shown in Fig. 12c. These internal forces and moments acting on the adjacent faces of the section are equal in magnitude, but opposite in direction.

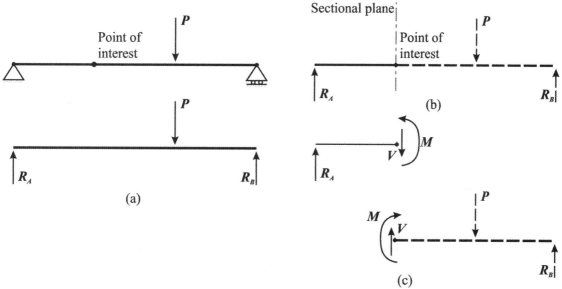

Figure 12. The method of sections

The internal force acting perpendicular to the beam axis at the section is called the *shear force* and is denoted by V. Similarly, the term *bending moment,* denoted by M, refers to the internal moment at the section. The procedure for finding the shear force and bending moment involves three steps:

Step I: Determine support reactions
    a. Draw a free-body diagram of the entire beam.
    b. Apply the equilibrium equations.
    c. Solve for the unknown reactions
Step II: Draw the free-body diagram of the selected portion of the beam
    a. Using a sectional plane, divide the beam into two parts at the location where the shear force and bending moment must be determined.
    b. Select the part of the beam that is easy to analyze. Typically the part of the beam that has the least number of forces, moments, and unknown reactions is the easiest to analyze.
    c. Draw the free-body diagram for the selected part of the beam showing the unknown section force, the moment components, and the applied loads.
Step III: Determine the values for the shear force and bending moment
    a. Apply the equilibrium equations.
    b. Solve for the unknown shear force and bending moment.

Example 1
Determine the shear force and bending moment at Point C.

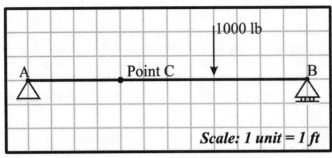

Figure 13. A simply supported beam with a concentrated load

Step I: Determine support reactions
a. Draw the free-body diagram of the entire beam.

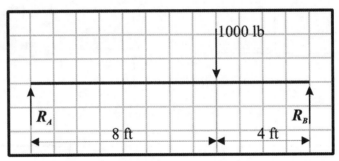

Figure 14. The free-body diagram of the entire beam

b. Apply the equilibrium equations.
The summation of forces in the vertical direction and the moment calculation around point A yield

$$\sum F_y = R_A + R_B - 1000 = 0$$

$$\sum M_A = -1000\,\text{lb} \times 8\,\text{ft} + R_B \times 12\,\text{ft} = 0$$

c. Solve for unknown reactions.
From the moment equation, we get

$$R_B = 667\,\text{lb}$$

Substituting the value of R_B in the force equilibrium equation, we get

$$R_A = 333\,\text{lb}$$

The results make sense because the support closest to the applied load carries a significant portion of the load.

Step II: Draw the free-body diagram for the selected portion of the beam.
a. Using a sectional plane, divide the beam into two parts at Point C, the point of interest.

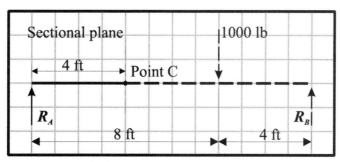

Figure 15. The beam is divided into two parts at Point C

b. Select the part of the beam that is easy to analyze. In this particular problem, the portion of the beam shown with a solid line is easier to analyze because the computation of the shear force and bending moment involve the reaction at the left end only.

c. Draw the free-body diagram for the selected part of the beam showing the applied loads as well as the unknown sectional force and moment components.
For the body shown in Fig. 16a to satisfy the force equilibrium, a vertical force must be acting at Point C. Now for the body with two forces separated by a distance to be in equilibrium, there must be a moment acting at C. In Fig. 16b, the directions of *V* and *M* are chosen to resist motion. Even if you choose a wrong direction, you will get a correct answer – a negative value indicates the opposite direction.

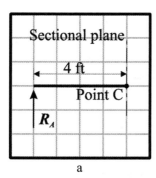
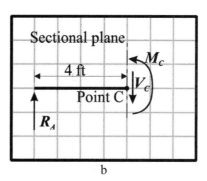

a   b

Figure 16. The free-body diagram for the selected portion of the beam

Step III: Determine the values of the shear force and bending moment
a. Apply equilibrium equations.

$$\sum F_y = R_A - V_C = 0$$
$$333\,\text{lb} - V_C = 0$$
$$\sum M_C = -R_A \times 4\,\text{ft} + M_C = 0$$
$$-333\,\text{lb} \times 4\,\text{ft} + M_C = 0$$

b. Solve for the unknown forces and moments.
From the force equilibrium equation, we get
$$\boxed{V_C = 333 \text{ lb}}$$
Substituting V_C into the moment equilibrium equation, we get
$$\boxed{M_C = 1332 \text{ ft.lb}}$$

Example 2
Determine the shear force and bending moment at Point B.

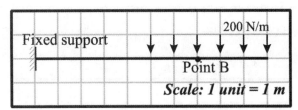

Figure 17. A cantilever beam with a uniform load

Step I: Determine support reactions
a. Draw the free-body diagram of the entire beam.

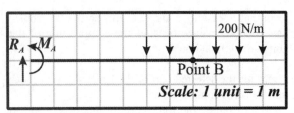

Figure 18. The free-body diagram of the entire beam

b. Apply the equilibrium equations.
The force equilibrium equations can be written as

$$\sum F_y = R_A - 200 \frac{\text{N}}{\text{m}} \times 5 \text{ m} = 0$$

For writing the moment equilibrium equation at A, we can substitute for the distributed load with a concentrated force acting at the center of the distribution, as shown in Fig. 19.

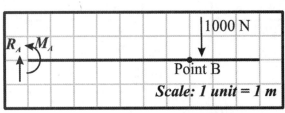

Figure 19. The free-body diagram with the uniform load replaced by a concentrated force

Then, the moment equation becomes

$$\sum M = M_A - 1000 \text{ N} \times 7.5 \text{ m} = 0$$

c. Solve for unknown reactions.
From the force equilibrium equation, we get

$$R_A = 1000 \text{ N}$$

From the moment equilibrium equation, we get

$$M_A = 750 \text{ N.m}$$

Step II: Draw the free-body diagram for the selected portion of the beam
a. Using a sectional plane, divide the beam into two parts at Point B, the point of interest.

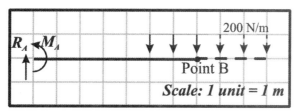

Figure 20. The beam is divided into two parts at Point B

b. Select the part of the beam that is easy to analyze. In this problem, the portion of the beam shown with a dotted line is easier to analyze because the computation of the shear force and bending moment involve only the distributed load.

c. Draw the free-body diagram for the selected part of the beam showing the unknown section force and moment components as well as the applied loads.

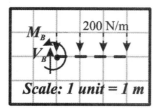

Figure 21. The free-body diagram for the selected portion of the beam

Step III: Determine the values for the shear force and bending moment
a. Apply equilibrium equations.

$$\sum F_y = V_B - \left(200 \ \frac{N}{m}\right)(3\,m) = 0$$

$$V_B - 600\,N = 0$$

$$\sum M_B = M_B - \left(200\frac{N}{m}\right)(3\,m)(1.5\,m) = 0$$

$$M_B - 900\,N.m = 0$$

Note that in the moment equilibrium equation, we substituted the uniformly distributed load with an equivalent load at the middle of the load distribution (1.5 m away from point B).

b. Solve for the unknown forces and moments.
From the force equilibrium equation, we get

$$\boxed{V_B = 600 \text{ N}}$$

Substituting V_B into the moment equilibrium equation, we get

$$\boxed{M_B = 900 \text{ N.m}}$$

Insight: *We could skip Step I and still solve this problem because we have used an element towards the free end where the reactions play no role in determining the shear force and bending moment. Note that this short-cut works only with cantilever beams.*

Example 3
Determine the shear force and bending moment at Point B.

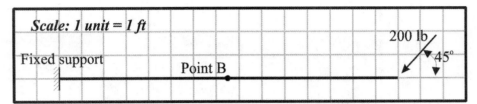

Figure 22. A cantilever beam with a uniform load

Step I: Determine the shear force and bending moment at Point B.
Based on the insight developed in the previous problems, we will skip step I.

Step II: Draw the free-body diagram for the selected portion of the beam.
a. Using a sectional plane, divide the beam into two parts at Point B. The 200 lb. load is resolved into horizontal and vertical components.

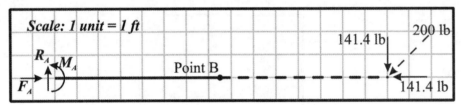

Figure 23. The beam is divided into two parts at Point B

b. Select the part of the beam that is easy to analyze. In this problem, the portion of the beam shown with a dotted line is easier to analyze because the computation of the shear force and bending moment involve only the concentrated load at the right end. We need not solve for the unknown reactions at the fixed end.

c. Draw the free-body diagram for the selected part of the beam showing the unknown section force and moment components as well as the applied loads. Note that we do not use V for axial loads.

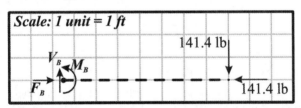

Figure 24. The free-body diagram for the selected portion of the beam

Step III: Determine the values for the shear force and bending moment
a. Apply equilibrium equations.

$$\sum F_x = F_B - 141.4 \text{ lb} = 0$$

$$\sum F_y = V_B - 141.4 \text{ lb} = 0$$

$$\sum M = M_B - V_B (7.5 \text{ ft}) = 0$$

b. Solve for the unknown forces and moments.
From the force equilibrium equation, we get

$$\boxed{F_B = 141.4 \text{ lb}} \qquad \boxed{V_B = 141.4 \text{ lb}}$$

Substituting V_B into the moment equilibrium equation, we get

$$\boxed{M_B = 1060 \text{ ft.lb}}$$

Name: _____

Problem 1

Determine the shear force and bending moment at Point P (midpoint).

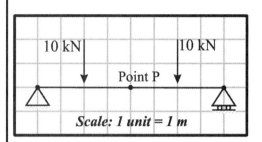

Step I: Determine the support reactions
a. Draw the free-body diagram

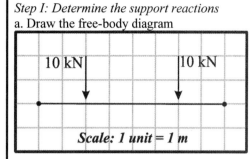

b. Apply the equilibrium equations

c. Solve for the unknown reactions

Do you think the results make sense?
By looking at the symmetry, we could have determined the reactions to be numerically equal to the assigned load. In many cases, the symmetry helps in solving the problems by inspection.

Step II: Draw the free body diagram for the selected portion of the beam
(Remember: In your mind, divide the beam at point P. Then, decide which portion is easy to analyze)

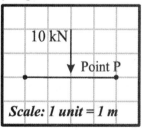

Step III: Determine the values of the shear force and bending moment
a. Apply the equilibrium equations

b. Solve for the shear force and bending moment

$V =$ _____ $M =$ _____

Does the value of the shear force make sense?

Name: _____

Problem 2

Determine the shear force and bending moment at point P.

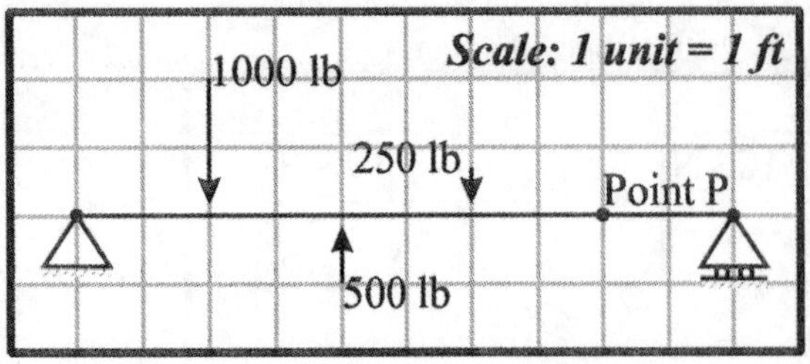

1000 lb   *Scale: 1 unit = 1 ft*

250 lb

Point P

500 lb

Step I: Determine the support reactions

a. Draw the free-body diagram

b. Apply the equilibrium equations

c. Solve for the unknown reactions

Step II: Draw the free body diagram for the selected portion of the beam

(Remember: In your mind, divide the beam at point P. Then, decide which portion is easy to analyze)

Step III: Determine the values of the shear force and bending moment

a. Apply the equilibrium equations

b. Solve for the shear force and bending moment

$V =$ _____ $M =$ _____

Does the value of the shear force make sense?

Name: _____

Problem 3

Determine the shear force and bending moment at point P.

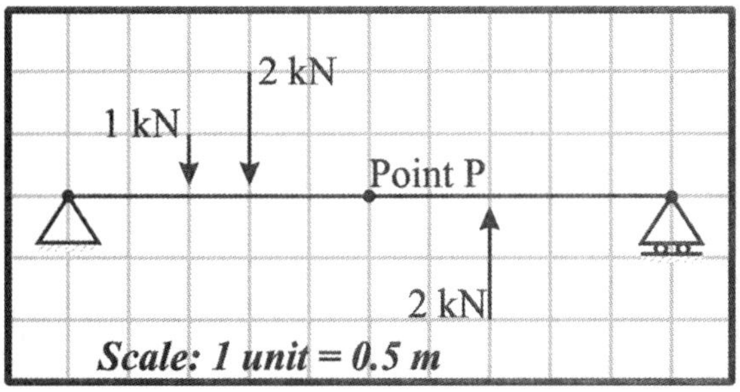

2 kN

1 kN

Point P

2 kN

Scale: 1 unit = 0.5 m

Step I: Determine the support reactions

Step II: Draw the free body diagram for the selected portion of the beam

Step III: Determine the values of the shear force and bending moment

$V =$ _____ $M =$ _____

Does the value of the shear force make sense?

Name: _____

Problem 4

Determine the shear force and bending moment at points A and B.

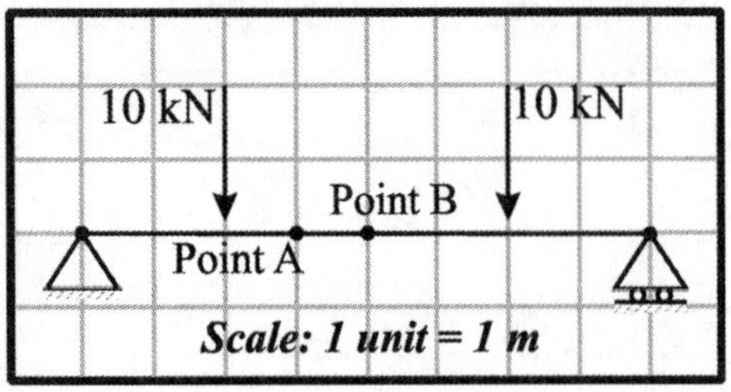

10 kN   10 kN

Point B

Point A

Scale: 1 unit = 1 m

Step I: Determine the support reactions

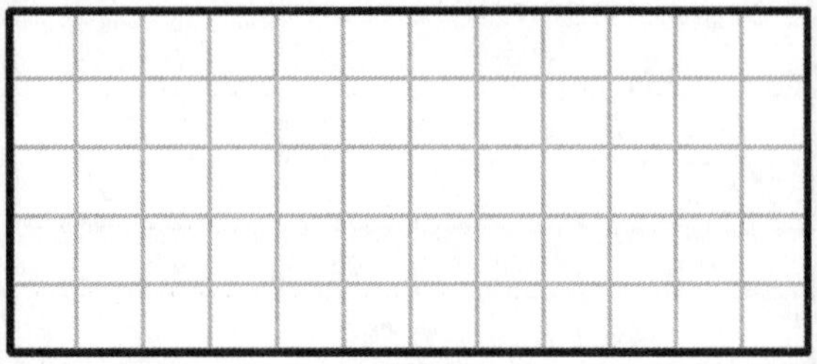

Step II: Draw the free body diagram for the selected portion of the beam

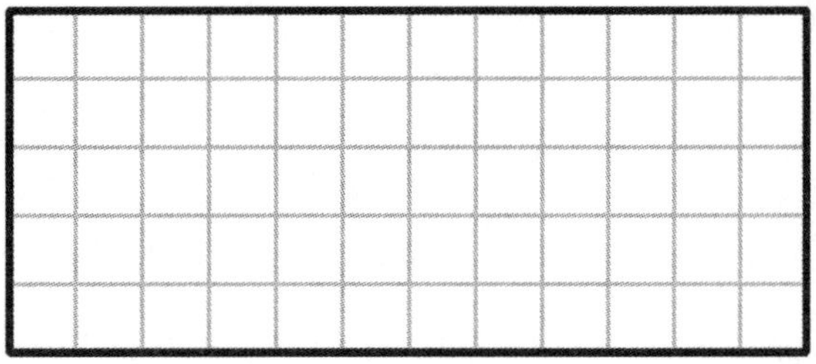

Step III: Determine the values of the shear force and bending moment

Point A $V_A =$ _____

$M_A =$ _____

Point B $V_B =$ _____

$M_B =$ _____

Does the value of the shear force make sense?

Name: _____

Problem 5

Determine the shear force and bending moment at points A and B.

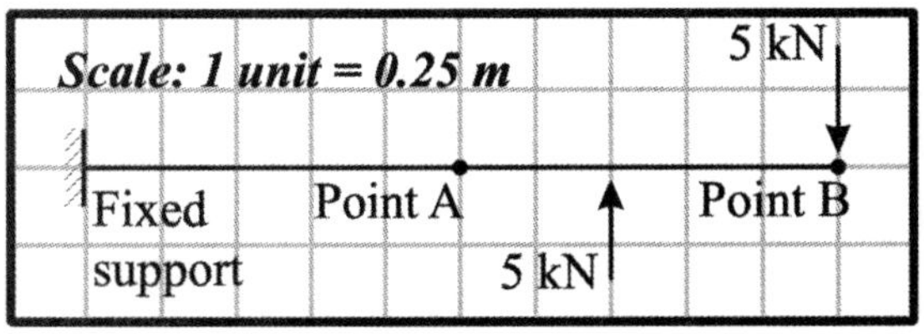

Scale: 1 unit = 0.25 m

Fixed support — Point A — 5 kN — Point B — 5 kN

Step I: Determine the support reactions

Step II: Draw the free body diagram for the selected portion of the beam

Step III: Determine the values of the shear force and bending moment

Point A $V_A =$ _____ $M_A =$ _____

Point B $V_B =$ _____ $M_B =$ _____

Can you skip step I and still solve this problem?

Name: _____

Problem 6

Determine the shear force and bending moment at points A and B.

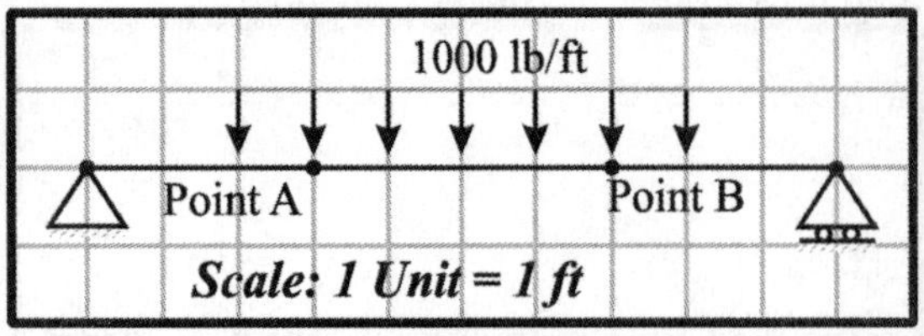

1000 lb/ft

Point A   Point B

Scale: 1 Unit = 1 ft

Step I: Determine the support reactions

Step II: Draw the free body diagram for the selected portion of the beam

Step III: Determine the values of the shear force and bending moment

Point A

$V_A =$ _____

$M_A =$ _____

Point B

$V_B =$ _____

$M_B =$ _____

Name: _____

Problem 7

Determine the shear force and bending moment at points A and B.

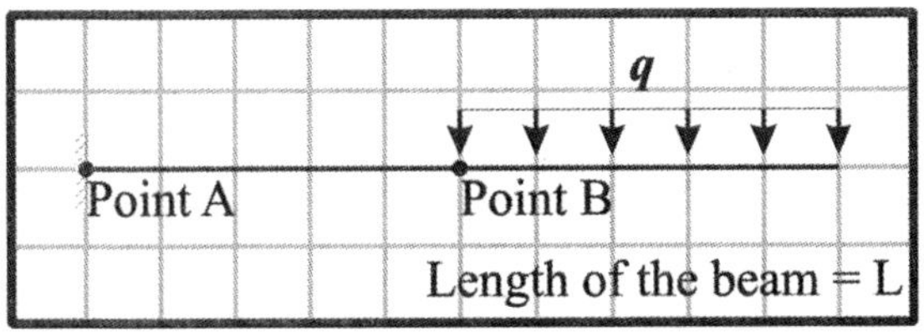

Step I: Determine the support reactions

q

Point A   Point B

Length of the beam = L

Step II: Draw the free body diagram for the selected portion of the beam

Step III: Determine the values of the shear force and bending moment

Point A   - $V_A =$ _____ $M_A =$ _____

Point B   - $V_B =$ _____ $M_B =$ _____

Name: _____

Problem 8

Determine the shear force and bending moment at points A, B, and C.

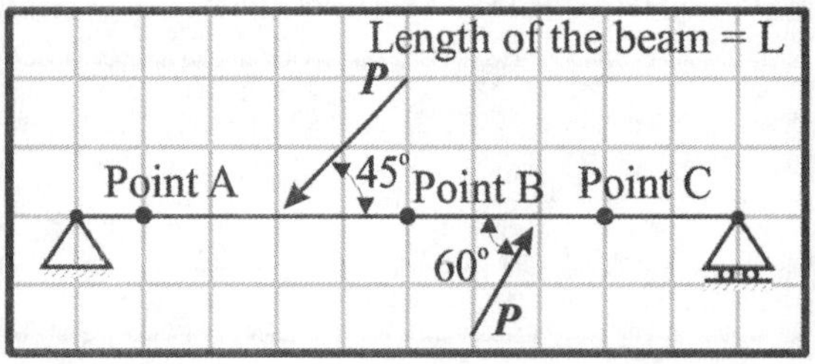

Length of the beam = L

P

Point A   45°   Point B   Point C

60°

P

Step I: Determine the support reactions

Step II: Draw the free body diagram for the selected portion of the beam

Step III: Determine the values of the shear force and bending moment

Point A

$F_A =$ _____ $V_A =$ _____ $M_A =$ _____

Point B

$F_B =$ _____ $V_B =$ _____ $M_B =$ _____

Point C

$F_C =$ _____ $V_C =$ _____ $M_C =$ _____

Name: _____

Problem 9

Determine the shear force and bending moment at points A, B, and C.

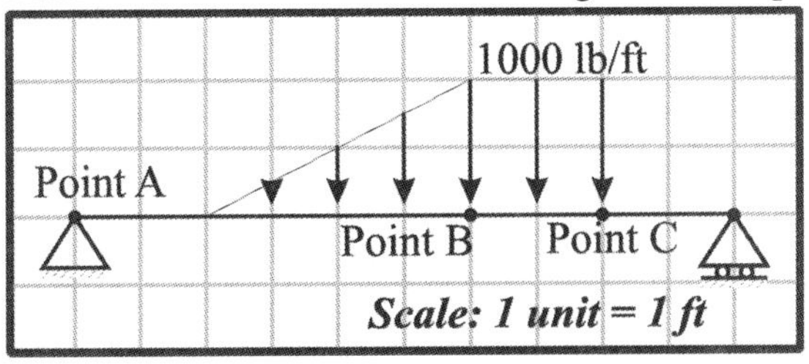

1000 lb/ft

Point A

Point B   Point C

Scale: 1 unit = 1 ft

Step I: Determine the support reactions

Step II: Draw the free body diagram for the selected portion of the beam

Step III: Determine the values of the shear force and bending moment

Point A

$V_A =$ _____ $M_A =$ _____

Point B

$V_B =$ _____ $M_B =$ _____

Point C

$V_C =$ _____ $M_C =$ _____

Name: _____

Problem 10

Determine the shear force and bending moment at points A, B, and C.

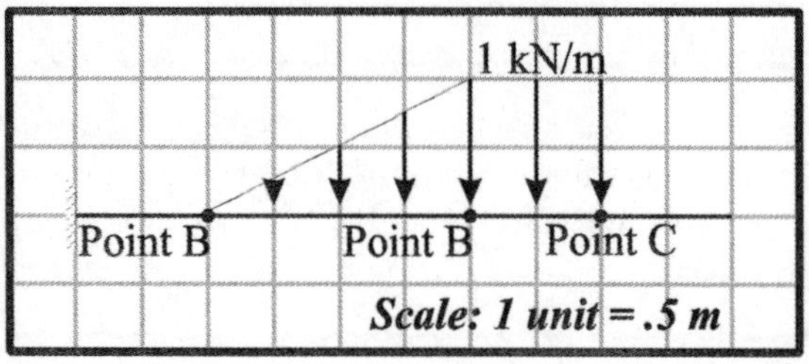

1 kN/m

Point B   Point B   Point C

Scale: 1 unit = .5 m

Step I: Determine the support reactions

Step II: Draw the free body diagram for the selected portion of the beam

Step III: Determine the values of the shear force and bending moment

Point A $V_A = $ _____ $M_A = $ _____

Point B $V_B = $ _____ $M_B = $ _____

Point C $V_C = $ _____ $M_C = $ _____

7.5. Sign Convention

Theoretically, it is acceptable to choose a sign convention arbitrarily as long as we follow it consistently. However, for practical reasons, we will adopt the following sign convention, which is consistent with most engineering applications. This sign convention helps in drawing shear force and bending moment diagrams.

a. Sign convention for shear force

A *positive* shear force tends to rotate the segment of the beam in a *clockwise* direction. Fig. 25 shows the shear forces acting on the two segments of a beam. The two shear forces are equal and move in opposite directions. However, both these forces are positive, because they attempt to rotate the beam in a clockwise direction.

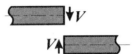

Figure 25. Positive shear force acting on two segments of a beam

b. Sign convention for bending moment

A *positive* moment that tends to deflect the beam with a concave curvature on the top. Fig. 26 shows two moments acting at a section of a beam. While they are equal in magnitude, they are opposite in direction. Both of these moments tend to bend the beam along a concave curvature facing up. Therefore, these moments are positive.

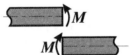

Figure 26. Positive bending moment acting on two segments of a beam

As shown in Fig. 27, a positive bending moment deflects the beam with a concave curvature facing upwards, creating an image of a smiling face or a beam holding water. On the other hand, the curvature for a beam subjected to a negative bending moment can be imagined as a sad face or a beam which cannot hold water.

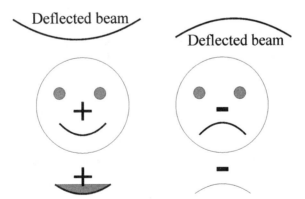

Figure 27. Sign convention for bending moments

7.6. Shear Force & Bending Moment Diagrams

Shear force and bending moment diagrams graphically represent the magnitude of the shear force and bending moment at successive points along the length of the beam. Engineers use shear force and bending moment diagrams to identify the maximum and the minimum values of the shear force and bending moment. These values are useful in calculating the stresses and estimating the possible failures. In this section, we will learn the steps for drawing the shear force and bending moment diagrams.

Drawing the shear force and bending moment diagrams involves the determination of the shear force and bending moment at several sections as a function of distance from the origin. Toward this end, divide the beam into segments in which the load is continuous. In these segments, draw sectional planes at an arbitrary distance x from the origin. Then, determine the shear force and bending moment at each sectional plane. The magnitudes of the shear force and the bending moment may be a function of x. The shear force and bending moment diagrams are the plots of the magnitude as a function of x (i.e., along the length of the beam).

Step I: Determine support reactions
   a.   Draw a free-body diagram of the entire beam.
   b.   Apply the equilibrium equations.
   c.   Solve for the unknown reactions

Step II: Identify sectional planes where the shear force and bending moment must be computed
   a.   Establish a coordinate system. We generally designate the left end of the beam as the origin; however, if it simplifies calculations, we can select any convenient location as the origin.
   b.   Identify points on the beam between concentrated forces, between concentrated forces and concentrated moments, and in the distributed loading regions.
   c.   Draw sectional planes through the identified points.

Step III: Compute the shear force and bending moment in the beam at each segment
   a.   *Derive the shear force and bending moment equations at each sectional plane*
      1.   For each sectional plane, divide the beam into two parts at the sectional plane.
      2.   Select the part of the beam that is easy to analyze.
      3.   Draw the corresponding free body diagram for the selected portion of the beam.
      4.   Write the shear force and bending moment equations to maintain equilibrium. Note that the magnitudes of the shear force and bending moment may be functions of x.
   b.   *Draw the shear force diagram*
      1.   Establish a set of coordinate axes with x as the abscissa and V as the ordinate. It is a good practice to draw the shear force diagram below the free body diagram.
      2.   Proceed from the left end. Start with zero shear force.
      3.   Using the shear force equations for each segment, plot the shear force diagram.
      4.   Since the beam is in equilibrium, the shear force at the right end must be equal to zero.
   c.   *Draw the bending moment diagram*
      1.   Establish a set of coordinate axes with x as the abscissa and M as the ordinate. It is a good practice to draw the bending moment diagram below the shear force diagram.
      2.   Proceed from the left end. Start with zero bending moment.
      3.   Using the bending moment equations, plot the bending moment.
      4.   Since the beam is in equilibrium, the bending moment at the right end must be equal to zero.

Example 4
Draw the shear force and the bending moment diagrams for the beam shown in Fig. 28.

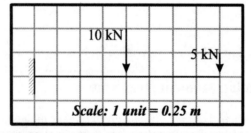

Figure 28. A cantilever beam with concentrated loads

Step I: Determine support reactions
a. Draw the free-body diagram for the cantilever beam.
Fig. 29 shows the free-body diagram for the beam.

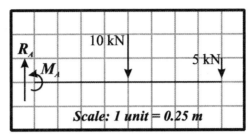

Figure 29. The free-body diagram of the cantilever beam

b. Apply the equilibrium equations.
The two equilibrium equations for the cantilever beam are

$$R_A - 10\,\text{kN} - 5\,\text{kN} = 0$$
$$M_A - 10\,\text{kN} \times 1\,\text{m} - 5\,\text{kN} \times 2\,\text{m} = 0$$

c. Solve for the unknown reactions.

$$R_A = 15\,\text{kN}$$
$$M_A = 20\,\text{kN.m}$$

Step II: Identify sectional planes where the shear force and bending moment must be computed
a. Establish a coordinate system
We designate the left end of the beam as the origin (refer to Fig. 30) and align the x-axis along the beam.
b. Identify points on the beam between concentrated forces, between concentrated forces and concentrated moments, and in the distributed loading regions.
We identify points P and Q between the concentrated forces.
c. Draw sectional planes through the identified points.

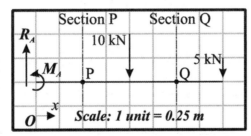

Figure 30. The beam with two sections

Step III: Compute the shear force and bending moment in the beam at each segment
a. Derive the shear force and bending moment equations at each sectional plane
Let us determine the shear force and bending moment at sections P and Q following the procedure outlined in section IV. Fig. 31 shows the free-body diagrams of the beam segments (at sections P and Q). The segments were selected to make the analysis easy.

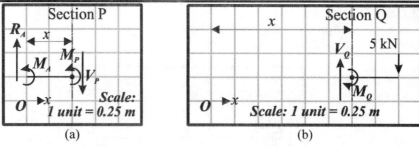

(a)   (b)

Figure 31. The free-body diagrams of the beam segments at sections P and Q, respectively

We choose the positive direction for the shear force V and the bending moment M in each segment. Note that the direction depends on the left or right segment of the beam. Now, for the first section at point P, we can write the shear force and bending moment equations as

$$V_P = R_A$$
$$V_P = 15 \text{ kN}$$
$$M_P = R_A x - M_A$$
$$M_P = 15x - 20 \text{ kN.m}$$

$$0 \leq x \leq 1 \text{ m}$$

For the second section, the shear force and bending moment equations are

$$V_Q = 5 \text{ kN}$$
$$M_Q = -5 \text{ kN}(2 - x)$$

$$1 \text{ m} \leq x \leq 2 \text{ m}$$

b. Draw the shear force diagram
The shear force takes two values, 15 kN when $0 \leq x \leq 1$ m and 5 kN when $1 \text{ m} \leq x \leq 2$ m. The shear force diagram is shown in Fig. 32. The magnitude of the shear force is zero at both ends.

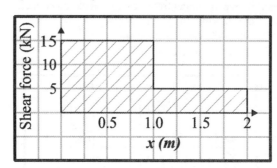

Figure 32. The shear force diagram

c. Draw the bending moment diagram
The bending moment is a function of x and varies linearly with x in each of these segments. Fig. 33 shows the plot of the bending moment. Note that the bending moment is -20 kN.m at $x = 0$, -5 kN.m at $x = 1$ m, and 0 at $x = 2$ m.

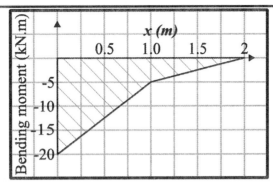

Figure 33. The bending moment diagram

Example 5
Draw the shear force and the bending moment diagrams for the beam shown in Fig. 34.

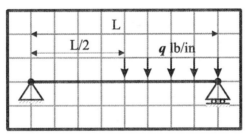

Figure 34. A simply supported beam with a uniform load

Step I: Determine support reactions
a. Draw the free-body diagram for the cantilever beam.
Fig. 35 shows the free-body diagram for the beam.

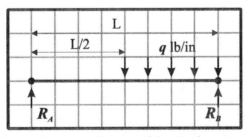

Figure 35. The free-body diagram of the simply supported beam

b. Apply the equilibrium equations.
The force equilibrium equation for the beam is

$$R_A + R_B - q \times \left(\frac{L}{2}\right) = 0$$

When taking the moment equation, we can represent the uniform load as a concentrated force whose magnitude is equal to $q \times \left(\frac{L}{2}\right)$ applied at a distance $\left(\frac{3L}{4}\right)$ from end A. If we can take the moments about the point A, we get the following moment equilibrium equation:

$$q \times \left(\frac{L}{2}\right) \times \left(\frac{3L}{4}\right) - R_B \times L = 0$$

c. Solve for the unknown reactions.

$$R_B = \frac{3qL}{8}$$

$$R_A = \frac{qL}{8}$$

The results make sense because the support closest to the applied force experiences a significant portion

of the applied force. Also, the total reaction force is equal to the applied force $\left(\dfrac{qL}{2}\right)$.

Step II: Identify sectional planes where the shear force and bending moment must be computed
a. Establish a coordinate system
We designate the left end of the beam as the origin (refer to Fig. 36) and align the x-axis along the beam.
b. Identify points on the beam between concentrated forces, between concentrated forces and concentrated moments, and in the distributed loading regions.
We identify points P and Q (see Fig. 36).
c. Draw sectional planes through the identified points.

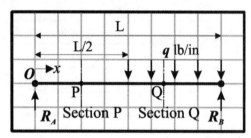

Figure 36. The beam with two sections

Step III: Compute the shear force and bending moment in the beam at each segment
a. Derive the shear force and bending moment equations at each sectional plane
Fig. 37 shows the free-body diagrams of the beam segments (at sections P and Q). The segments were selected to make the analysis easy.

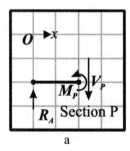
a

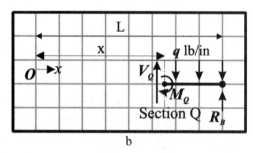
b

Figure 37. The free-body diagrams of the beam segments at sections P and Q, respectively

We choose the positive direction for the shear force V and the bending moment M in each segment. Note that the direction depends on the segment (left or right) of the beam. Now, for the first section at point P, we can write the shear force and bending moment equations as

$$V_P = R_A$$

$$V_P = \frac{qL}{8}$$

$$M_P = R_A x$$

$$M_P = \frac{qL}{8}x$$

$$0 \le x \le \frac{L}{2}$$

For the second section, the shear force and bending moment equations are

$$V_Q = -R_B + q(L-x)$$

$$V_Q = \frac{5qL}{8} - qx$$

$$M_Q = R_B(L-x) - q(L-x)\left(\frac{L-x}{2}\right) \qquad \frac{L}{2} \leq x \leq L$$

$$M_Q = \frac{3qL}{8}(L-x) - \frac{q(L^2 + x^2 - 2Lx)}{2}$$

$$M_Q = q\left(\frac{5Lx}{8} - \frac{x^2}{2} - \frac{L^2}{8}\right)$$

Note that in the bending moment calculation, we substituted the total uniformly distributed load $[q(L-x)]$ at the center of the distribution. The distance between section Q and the center of the distribution is $\left(\dfrac{L-x}{2}\right)$.

b. Draw the shear force diagram

The shear force takes a constant value $\left(\dfrac{qL}{8}\right)$ in the interval $0 \leq x \leq \dfrac{L}{2}$. The shear force varies linearly with x in the second interval $\dfrac{L}{2} \leq x \leq L$ and is given by $\left[\dfrac{5qL}{8} - qx\right]$. The shear force diagram is shown in Fig. 38. The magnitude of the shear force is zero at both ends.

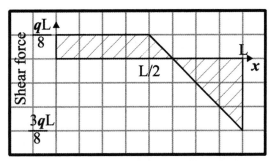

Figure 38. The shear force diagram

c. Draw the bending moment diagram

The bending moment is a function of x and varies linearly with x in the first segments. We can compute the bending moment at a few points. In the segment $0 \leq x \leq \dfrac{L}{2}$, the bending moment varies linearly. We can compute the bending moment at $x = \dfrac{L}{2}$ as $\dfrac{qL^2}{16}$. The variation in the second segment $\dfrac{L}{2} \leq x \leq L$ is nonlinear. To find the location where the maximum bending moment occurs, we must equate the first derivative of the bending moment equation to zero. We get

$$\frac{dM_Q}{dx} = q\left(\frac{5L}{8} - x\right) = 0$$

$$x = \frac{5L}{8}$$

We can find the magnitude of the maximum bending moment at $x = \dfrac{5L}{8}$

$$M_Q = \frac{9qL^2}{128}$$

Then plot the bending moment as shown in Fig. 39.

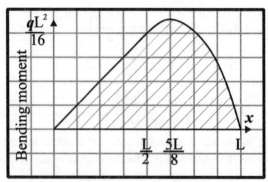

Figure 39. The bending moment diagram

Example 6

Draw the shear force and bending moment diagram for a simple beam with an overhang.

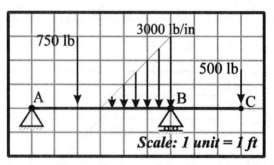

Figure 40. An overhang beam

Step I: Determine support reactions

a. Draw the free-body diagram for the overhang beam.
Fig. 41 shows the free-body diagram for the beam.

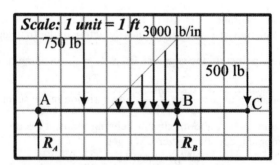

Figure 41. The free-body diagram of the overhang beam

We can replace the distributed load with a concentrated load whose magnitude is the area under the distributed load curve (shown in Fig. 42). We can apply the concentrated load at the center of the distribution (for the triangle, it is 1/3 of the distance from the base).

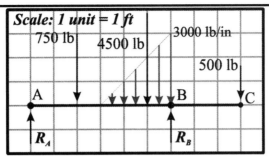

Figure 42. The free body diagram of the beam showing a concentrated load that is equivalent to the distributed load

b. Apply the equilibrium equations.
The force equilibrium equation for the beam is
$$R_A + R_B - 750 - 4500 - 500 = 0$$
$$R_A + R_B = 5750 \text{ lb}$$
If we can take the moments about the point A, we get the following moment equilibrium equation:
$$750 \times 2 + 4500 \times 5 - R_B \times 6 + 500 \times 9 = 0$$
$$28500 - R_B \times 6 = 0$$
c. Solve for the unknown reactions
$$R_B = 4750 \text{ lb}$$
$$R_A = 1000 \text{ lb}$$

Step II: Identify sectional planes where the shear force and bending moment must be computed
a. Establish a coordinate system
We designate the left end of the beam as the origin (refer to Fig. 43) and align the x-axis along the beam.
b. Identify points on the beam between concentrated forces, between concentrated forces and concentrated moments, and in the distributed loading regions.
We identify points P, Q, R, and S (see Fig. 43).
c. Draw sectional planes through the identified points.

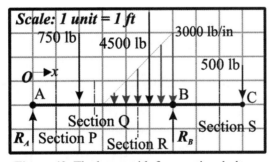

Figure 43. The beam with four sectional planes

Step III: Compute the shear force and bending moment in the beam at each segment
a. Derive the shear force and bending moment equations at each sectional plane
Fig. 44 shows the free-body diagrams of the beam segment at sections P. The segments were selected to make the analysis easy.

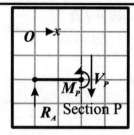

Figure 44. The free-body diagrams of the beam segments at section P

We choose the direction of the shear force and bending moment to be positive according to our sign convention. This strategy helps in directly plotting the magnitudes that we obtain from solving the equilibrium equations. The shear force and bending moments at this section (from the equilibrium equations) are

$$V_P = R_A = 1000 \text{ lb}$$
$$M_P = R_A x = 1000x$$

$0 \leq x \leq 2 \text{ ft}$

Fig. 45 shows the free body diagram for the left segment of the beam at section Q.

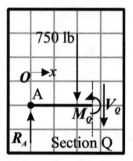

Figure 45. The free-body diagrams of the beam segments at section Q

The shear force and bending moments at section Q are

$$V_Q = R_A - 750 = 250 \text{ lb}$$
$$M_Q = R_A x - 750 \times (x - 2)$$
$$M_Q = 250x + 1500$$

$2 \text{ ft} \leq x \leq 3 \text{ ft}$

Fig. 46 shows the free body diagram for the left segment of the beam at section R.

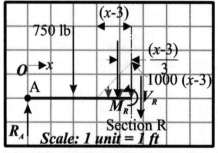

Figure 46. The free-body diagrams of the beam segments at section R

The shear force and bending moments at this section are

$$V_R = R_A - 750 - \frac{1}{2} \times (x-3) \times 1000 \times (x-3)$$

$$= 250 - 500\,(x-3)^2$$

$$M_R = 1000\,x - 750 \times (x-2) - 500\,(x-3)^2 \times \left(\frac{(x-3)}{3}\right) \qquad 3\,\text{ft} \le x \le 6\,\text{ft}$$

$$= 250\,x - 1500 - 500\,\frac{(x-3)^3}{3}$$

Note that in the bending moment calculation, we substituted the total uniformly distributed load $\left[\frac{1}{2}(x-3) \times 1000\right]$ at the geometric center of the distribution. The distance between section R and the center of the distribution is $\left(\frac{x-3}{3}\right)$.

Fig. 47 shows the free body diagram for the right segment of the beam at section S.

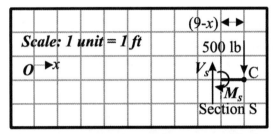

Figure 47. The free body diagram of the right segment of the beam at section S

Using the equilibrium equations, we get

$$V_S = 500\,\text{lb}$$

$$M_S = -500 \times (9-x) \qquad 6\,\text{ft} \le x \le 9\,\text{ft}$$

b. Draw the shear force diagram

We can create the shear force diagram by plotting these equations.

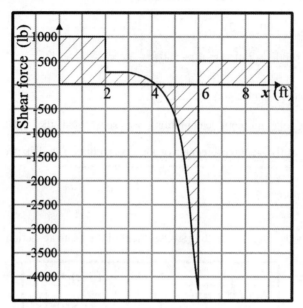

Figure 48. The shear force diagram

c. Draw the bending moment diagram

We can create the bending moment diagrams by plotting these equations.

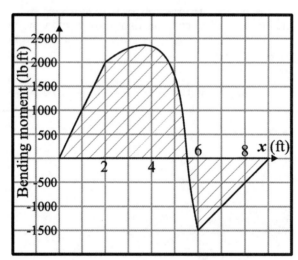

Figure 49. The bending moment diagram

Name:_____

Problem 1

Draw the shear force and the bending moment diagrams for the beam.

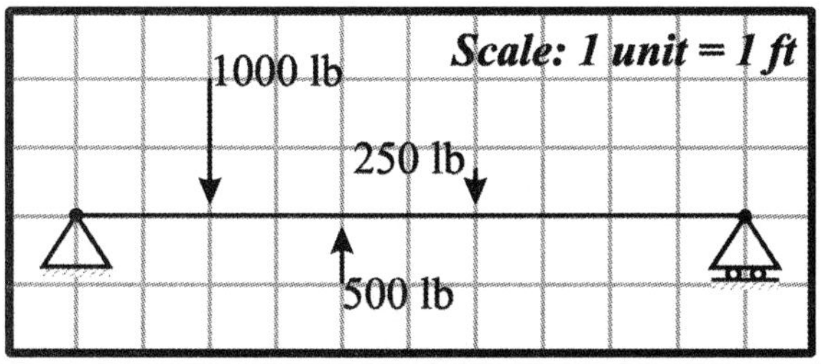

1000 lb

250 lb

Scale: 1 unit = 1 ft

500 lb

Name: _____

Problem 2

Draw the shear force and the bending moment diagrams for the beam.

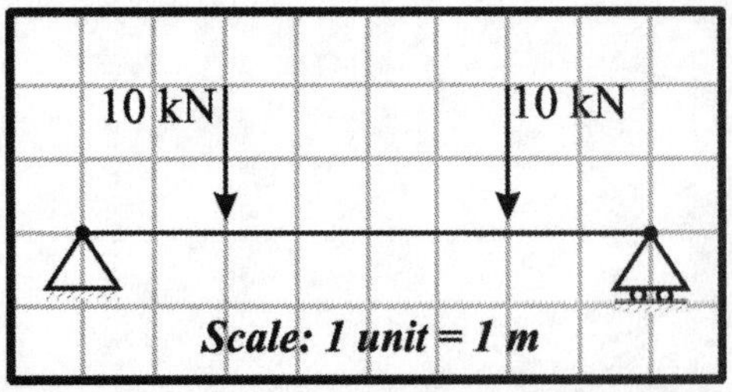

10 kN   10 kN

Scale: 1 unit = 1 m

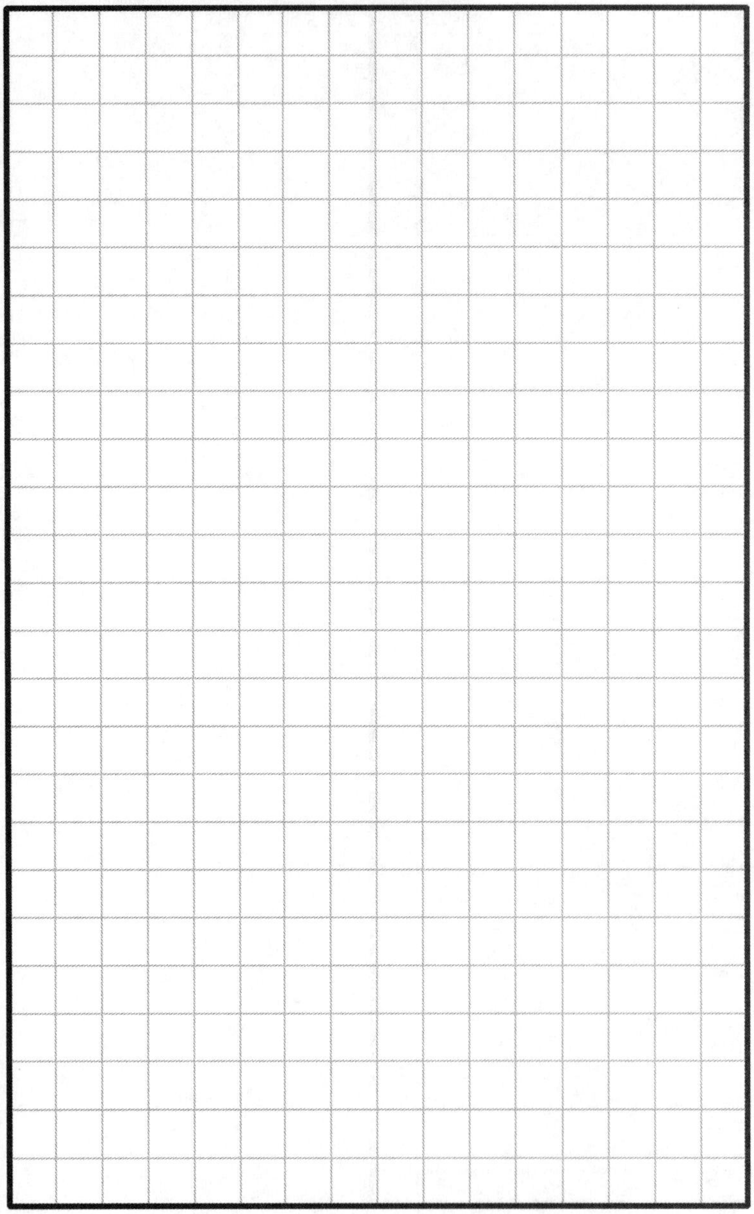

Name: _____

Problem 3

Draw the shear force and the bending moment diagrams for the beam.

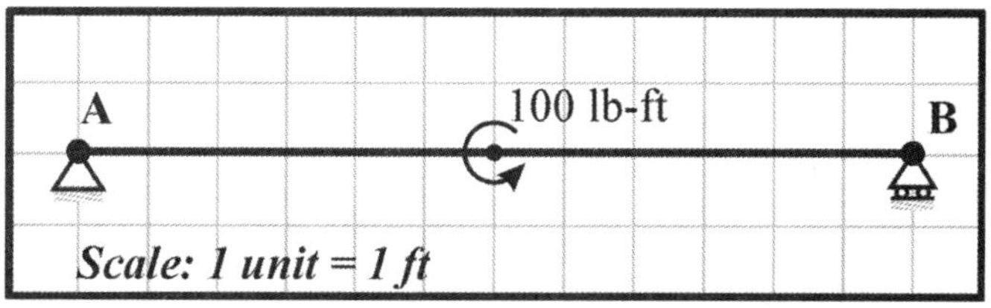

A   100 lb-ft   B

Scale: 1 unit = 1 ft

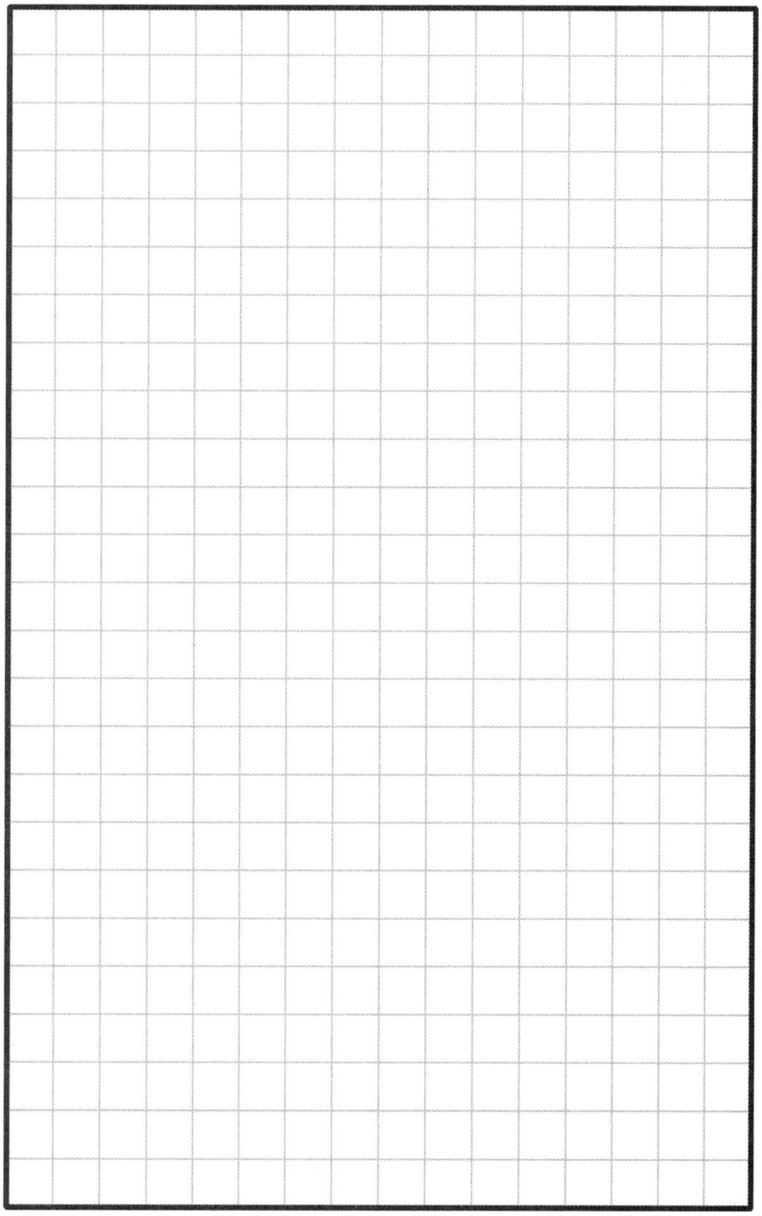

Name: _____

Problem 4
Draw the shear force and the bending moment diagrams for the beam.

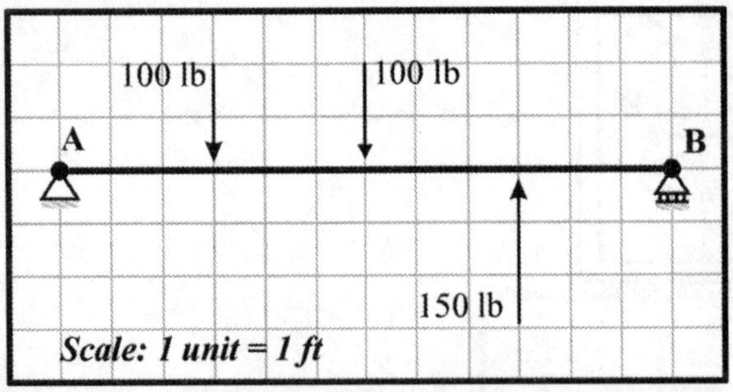

100 lb   100 lb

A   B

150 lb

Scale: 1 unit = 1 ft

Name: _____

Problem 5

Draw the shear force and the bending moment diagrams for the beam.

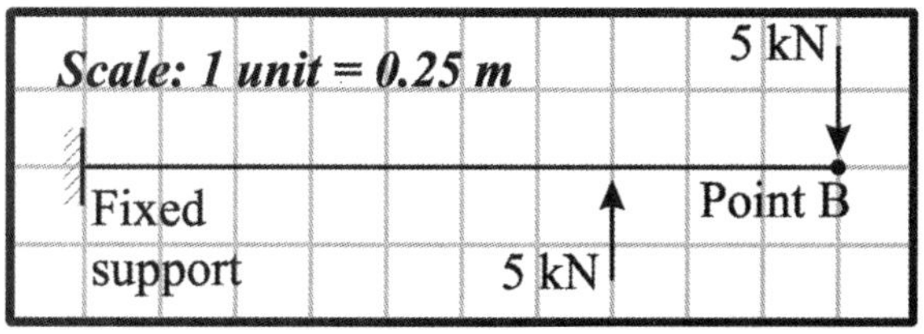

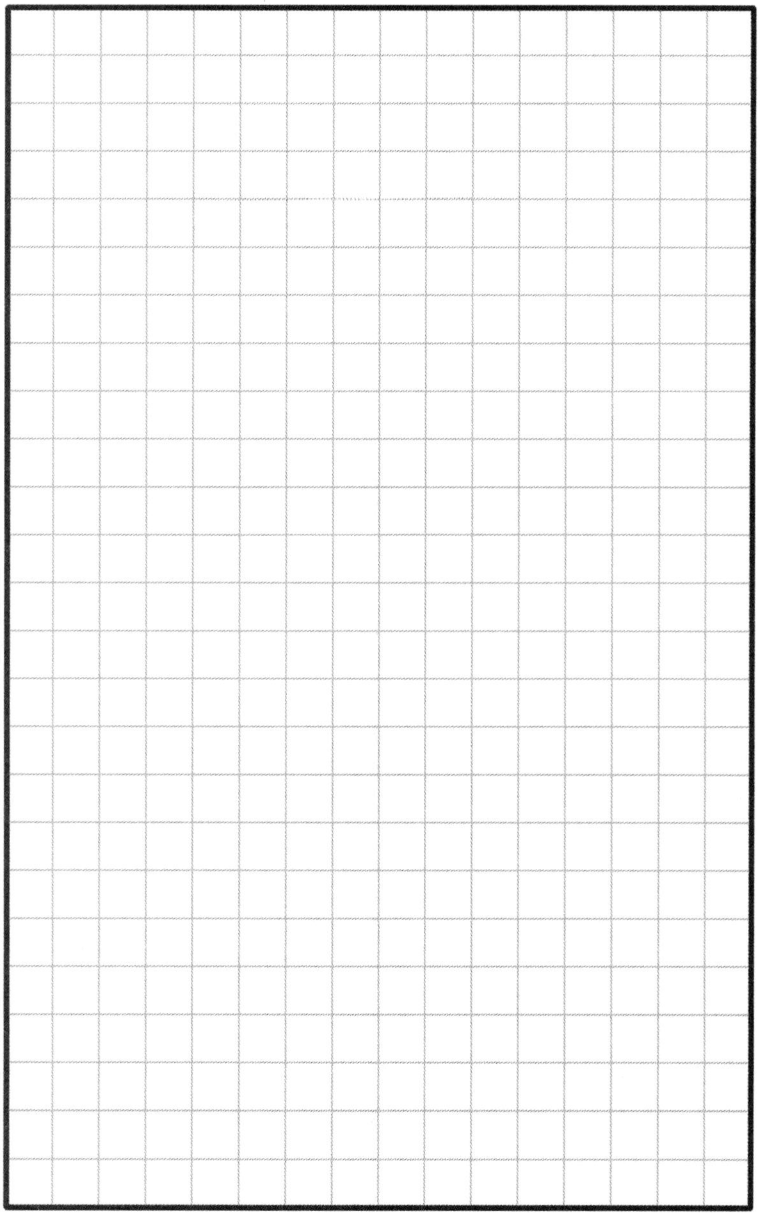

Scale: 1 unit = 0.25 m

5 kN

Fixed support

Point B

5 kN

Name: _____

Problem 6
Draw the shear force and the bending moment diagrams for the beam.

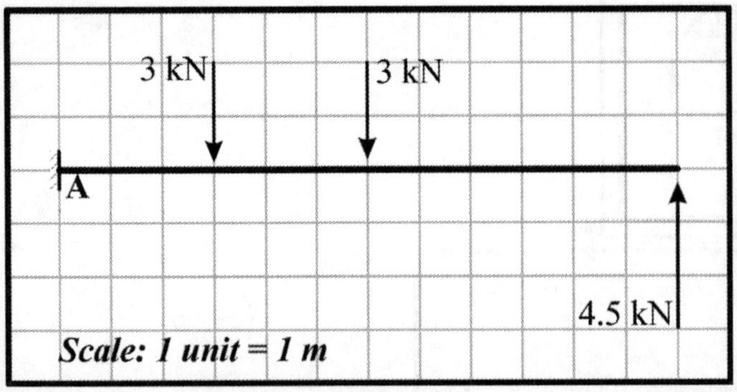

3 kN   3 kN

A

4.5 kN

Scale: 1 unit = 1 m

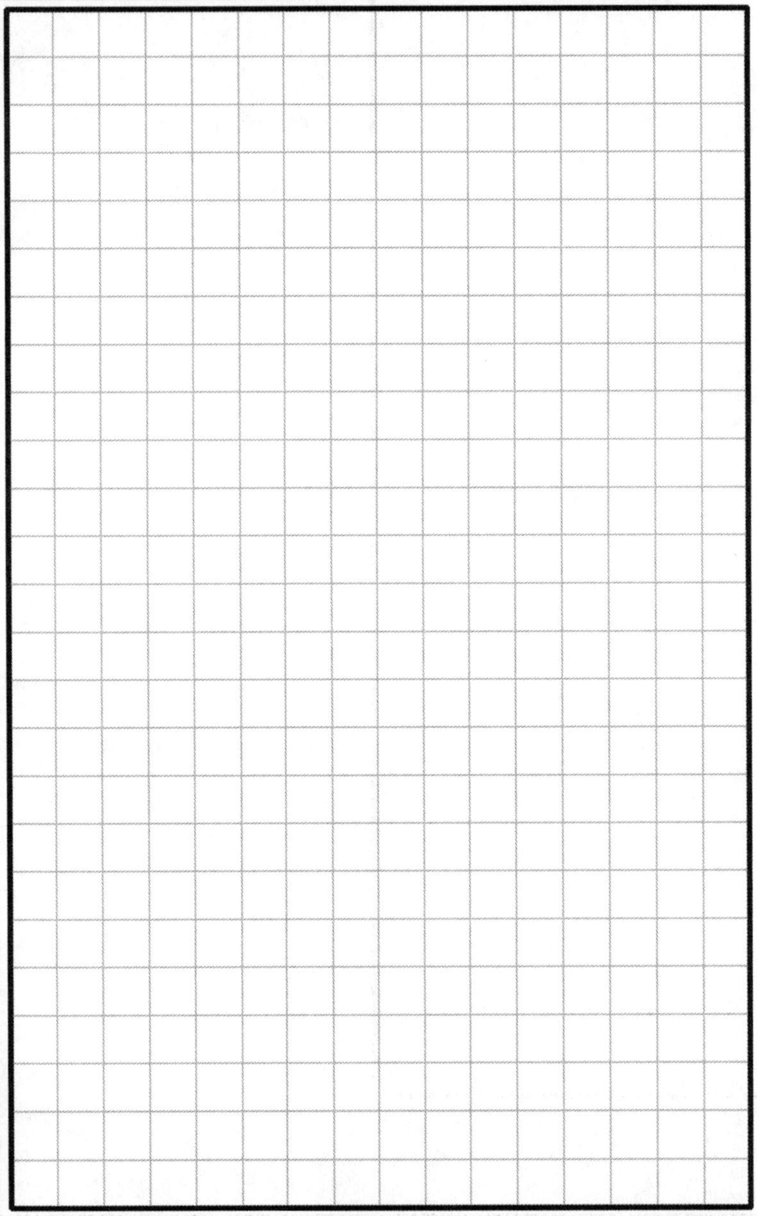

Name: _____

Problem 7

Draw the shear force and the bending moment diagrams for the beam.

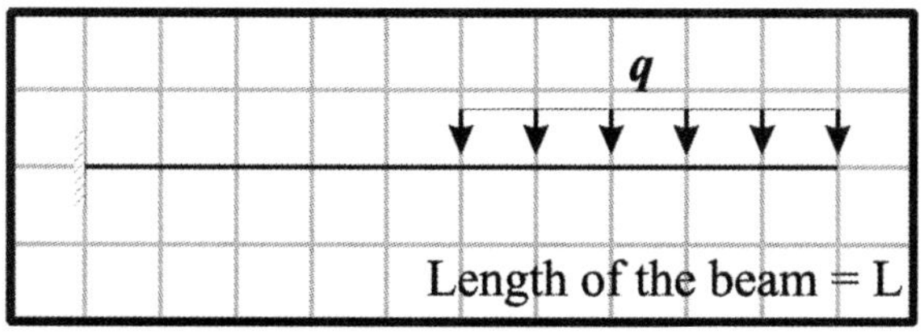

q

Length of the beam = L

Name: _____

Problem 8
Draw the shear force and the bending moment diagrams for the beam.

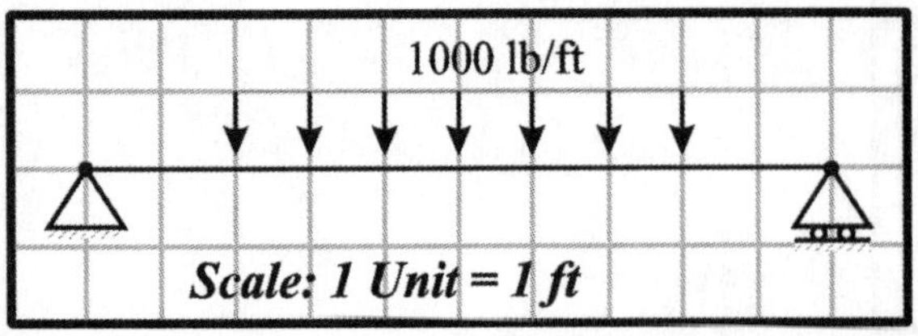

1000 lb/ft

Scale: 1 Unit = 1 ft

Name: _____

Problem 9

Draw the shear force and the bending moment diagrams for the beam.

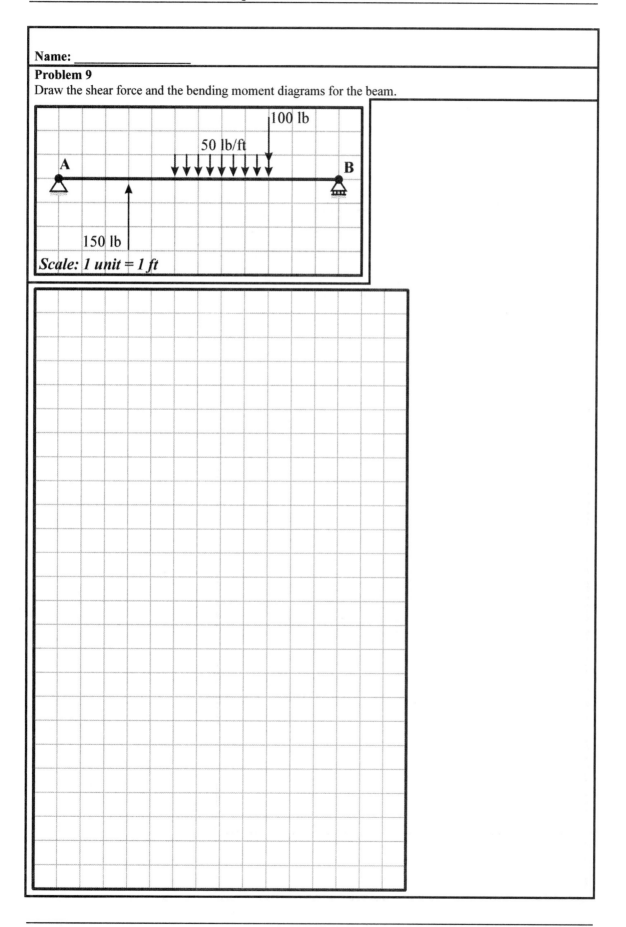

Name: _____

Problem 10
Draw the shear force and the bending moment diagrams for the beam.

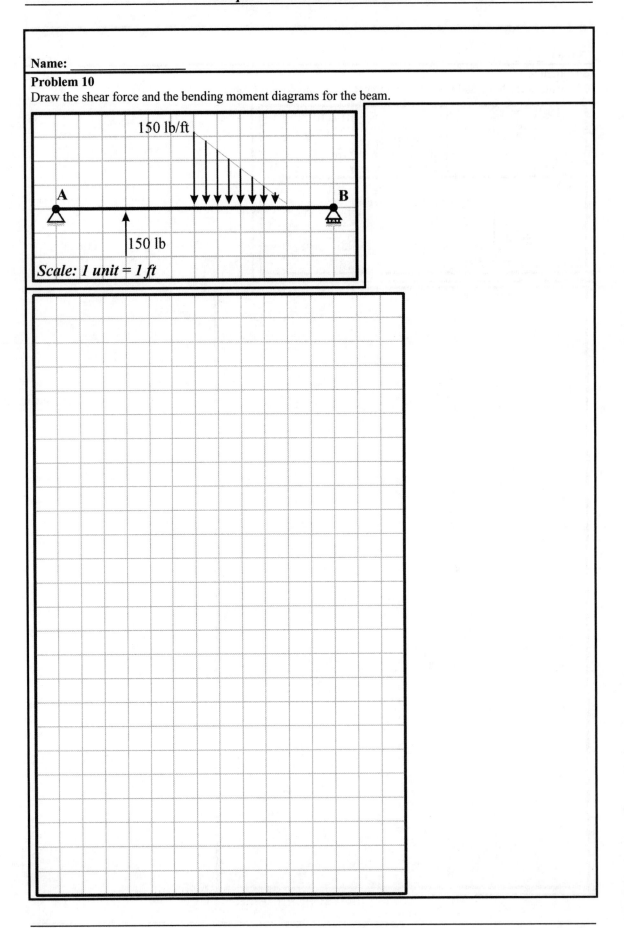

150 lb/ft

A

B

150 lb

Scale: 1 unit = 1 ft

Name: _____

Problem 11

Draw the shear force and the bending moment diagrams for the beam.

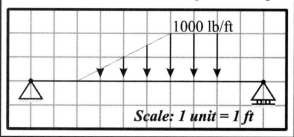

1000 lb/ft

Scale: 1 unit = 1 ft

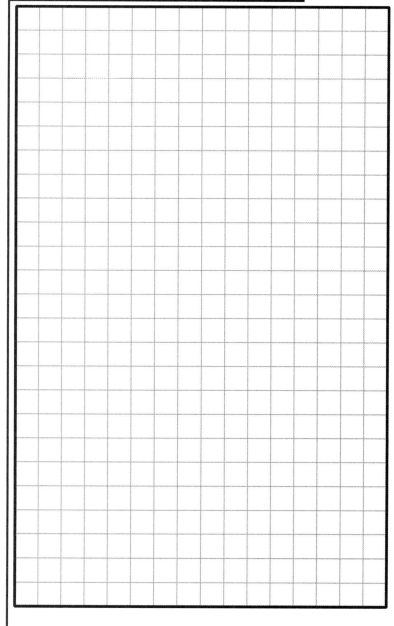

Name: _____

Problem 12
Draw the shear force and the bending moment diagrams for the beam.

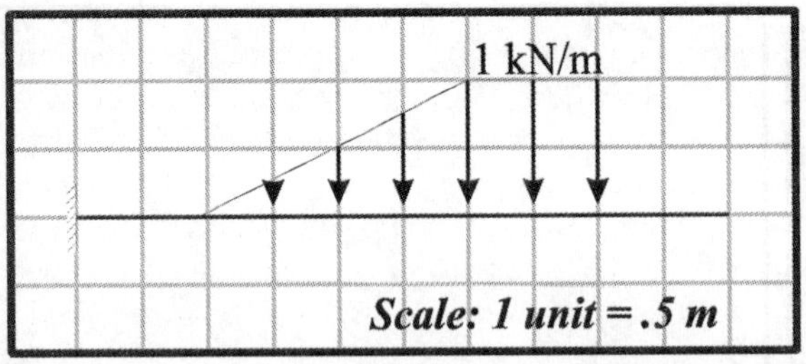

1 kN/m

Scale: 1 unit = .5 m

7.7. Alternative Approach for Creating Shear Force & Bending Moment Diagrams

a. Relationship between Shear Force and Bending Moment

The approach outlined in the previous section involves the identification of appropriate regions to add sectional planes and the computing of the shear force and bending moment at these sections as a function of x. For a beam with several loads, this approach can become tedious and cumbersome because it does not use the relationship between the shear force and bending moment effectively. In this section, we identify an alternative approach for creating shear force and bending moment diagrams based on their relationship. Before discussing this approach, let us identify the governing relationships.

Let us consider a beam with concentrated forces, concentrated moments, and distributed loads (refer to Fig. 50). In the figure, we identify five differential elements (small segments of the beam) for which we will correlate the shear force and bending moment to identify the relationships by drawing the free body diagrams and applying the equilibrium equations.

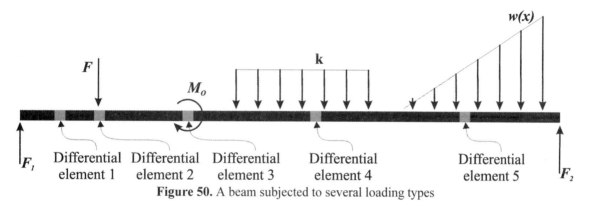

Figure 50. A beam subjected to several loading types

For differential element 1, the free body diagram is shown in Fig. 51. The free body diagram shows positive shear forces and positive bending moments on the left and right faces of the element. Note that there is no external load applied on this element.

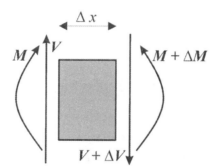

Figure 51. The free body diagram for differential element 1

Now, applying the equilibrium equations, we get

$$\Delta V = 0$$

$$\Delta M = V. \Delta x$$

$$\frac{\Delta M}{\Delta x} = V$$

From these equations, we can conclude that *when there is no external force applied on a given segment, the magnitude of the shear force remains unchanged, i.e. the trace of the shear force is horizontal. The slope of the bending moment curve is equal to the magnitude of the shear force. In other words, the change in the bending moment over a given segment is equal to the area under the shear force diagram in that segment.*

Fig. 52 shows the free body diagram for differential element 2. Similar to the previous element, the direction of the shear forces and the bending moments is positive. The primary difference from the previous element is the concentrated external load.

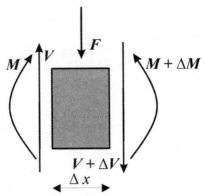

Figure 52. The free body diagram for differential element 2

Now, applying the equilibrium equations, we get

$$\Delta V = F$$

From these equations, we can conclude that *a concentrated force manifests as a vertical line whose length is equal to the magnitude of the force at the point of application in the shear force diagram.*

For differential element 3, the free body diagram is shown in Fig. 53. Note that the free body diagram shows positive shear forces and positive bending moments on the faces of the element and that there is a concentrated moment applied on the element.

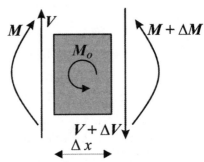

Figure 53. The free body diagram for differential element 3

Now, applying the equilibrium equations, we get

$$\Delta M = M_O$$

From these equations, we can conclude that *a concentrated moment manifests as a vertical line whose length is equal to the magnitude of the moment in the bending moment diagram.*

For differential element 4 with a uniformly distributed load, the free body diagram is shown in Fig. 54a. Fig. 54b shows the free body diagram of the differential element with an equivalent load. The equilibrium equations yield

$$\Delta V = F = -\mathbf{k} \cdot \Delta x$$

$$\frac{\Delta y}{\Delta x} = -\mathbf{k}$$

$$\Delta M = V. \Delta x - \mathbf{k} \cdot \frac{\Delta x^2}{2}$$

As $\Delta x \to 0$, the value of $\Delta M \to V. \Delta x$. Therefore, we end up with the familiar result

$$\frac{\Delta M}{\Delta x} = V$$

In other words, *at any point, the slope of shear force diagram is equal to the negative of the magnitude of the uniformly distributed load. The slope of the bending moment diagram is equal to the magnitude of the shear force.*

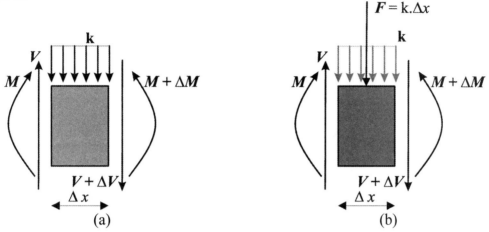

Figure 54. (a) The free body diagram with the uniformly distributed load.
(b) The free body diagram with an equivalent concentrated load

b. Creating Shear Force and Bending Moment
We use these relationships and insights to create the shear force and bending moment diagrams. The procedure is outlined below.

Step I: Determine support reactions
1. Draw a free-body diagram of the entire beam.
2. Apply the equilibrium equations.
3. Solve for the unknown reactions

Step II: Draw the shear force diagram
1. Draw a set of coordinate axes with *x* as the abscissa and *V* as the ordinate. It is a good practice to draw the shear force diagram below the free body diagram.
2. Proceed from the left end. Start with zero shear force.
   a. A concentrated force manifests itself as a vertical line in the shear force diagram. The direction of the vertical line (up or down) is the same as the direction of the force. The length of the vertical line is equal to the magnitude of the force.
   b. If there are no forces applied in a beam segment, the shear force diagram is a horizontal line for that segment.
   c. If a uniformly distributed load is applied, the slope of the shear force diagram is constant and is equal to the magnitude of the uniformly distributed load. The net increase (or decrease) in the shear force is equal to the total force applied by the distributed load.
   d. Since the beam is in equilibrium, the shear force at the right end must be equal to zero.

Step III: Draw the bending moment diagram
It is very important to note that the bending moment diagram is an integration of the shear force diagram (except when concentrated moments are applied).
1. Draw a set of coordinate axes with *x* as the abscissa and *M* as the ordinate. It is a good practice to draw the bending moment diagram below the shear force diagram.
2. Proceed from the left end. Start with zero bending moment.
   a. A concentrated moment causes a vertical line in the bending moment diagram. The direction of the vertical line (up or down) depends on the direction of the moment (clockwise - positive). The length of the vertical line is equal to the magnitude of the moment.
   b. If the shear force diagram for a beam segment is horizontal, the corresponding segment for the bending moment diagram will have a constant slope (whose magnitude is equal to the shear force).

    c. As discussed earlier, if a uniformly distributed load is applied to the beam, then the shear force diagram will have a constant slope. The corresponding bending moment diagram will be a curve whose slope increases continuously if the slope of the shear force diagram is positive.

*NOTE: DRAW DIAGRAMS FROM **LEFT** TO **RIGHT**.*

Condition	Shear force diagram	Bending moment diagram
Start and end points	The shear force is equal to zero.	The bending moment is equal to zero.
A concentrated force is applied at a point	A concentrated force manifests as a vertical line at the point of application. The direction of this vertical line (up or down) is the same as that of the external force. The length of the line is equal to the magnitude of the force.	The trace of the bending moment shows a discontinuity. The slope changes at this point.
No external force applied in a given segment	The magnitude of the shear force remains unchanged, i.e. the trace of the shear force is horizontal.	The slope of the bending moment curve is equal to the magnitude of the shear force. The change in the bending moment over a given segment is equal to the area under the shear force diagram in that segment.
A uniformly distributed force is applied in a given segment	The slope is equal to the magnitude of the uniformly distributed force. The net change in the shear force over the segment is equal to the total external force applied in that segment.	If the slope of the shear force diagram is positive, the slope of the bending moment diagram increases continuously, approaching a vertical line.
A concentrated moment at a point	No effect	A concentrated moment manifests as a vertical line at the point of moment application. The direction of the vertical line (up or down) depends on the direction of the applied bending moment (clockwise - positive). The length of the vertical line is equal to the magnitude of the moment.

Table 1. Simple rules for creating shear force and bending moment diagrams

Example 7 (Alternative approach to Example 4)
Draw the shear force and the bending moment diagrams for the beam shown in Fig. 55.

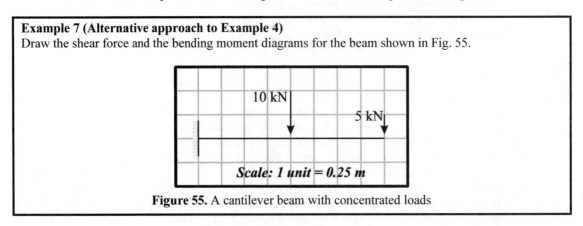

Figure 55. A cantilever beam with concentrated loads

Step I: Determine support reactions
a. Draw the free-body diagram for the cantilever beam.
Fig. 56 shows the free-body diagram for the beam.

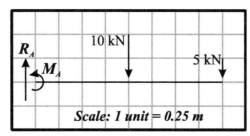

Figure 56. The free-body diagram of the cantilever beam

b. Apply the equilibrium equations.
The two equilibrium equations for the cantilever beam are
$$R_A - 10\ \text{kN} - 5\ \text{kN} = 0$$
$$M_A - 10\ \text{kN} \times 1\ \text{m} - 5\ \text{kN} \times 2\ \text{m} = 0$$

c. Solve for the unknown reactions.
$$R_A = 15\ \text{kN}$$
$$M_A = 20\ \text{kN.m}$$

Step II: Draw the shear force diagram
Figure 57 shows the step-by-step procedure for the development of the shear force diagram. Note that the shear force diagram starts and ends with zero shear force.

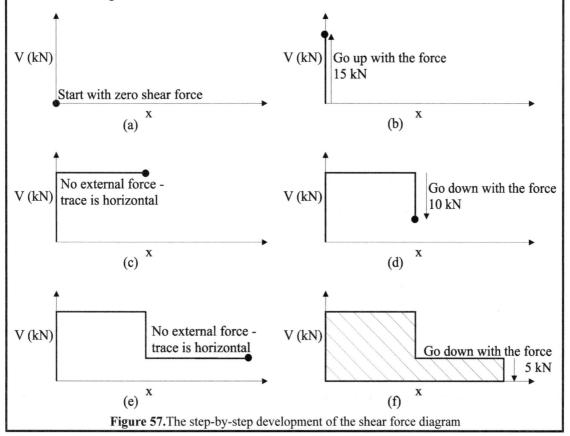

Figure 57. The step-by-step development of the shear force diagram

Step III: Draw the bending moment diagram
Fig. 58 shows the development of the bending moment diagram.

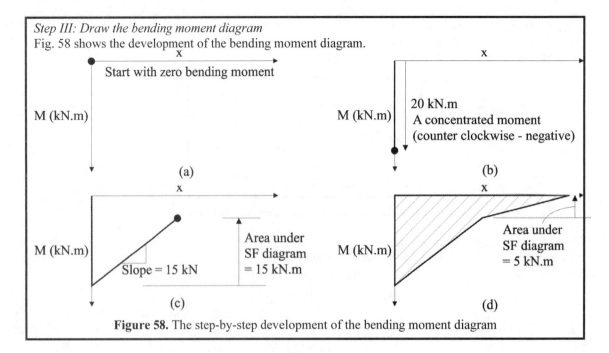

Figure 58. The step-by-step development of the bending moment diagram

Example 8 (Alternative approach to Example 5)
Draw the shear force and the bending moment diagrams for the beam shown in Fig. 59.

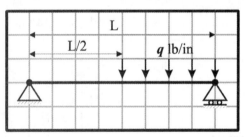

Figure 59. A simply supported beam with a uniform load

Step I: Determine support reactions
a. Draw the free-body diagram for the cantilever beam.
Fig. 60 shows the free-body diagram for the beam.

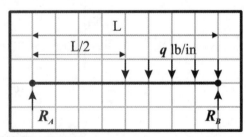

Figure 60. The free-body diagram of the simply supported beam

b. Apply the equilibrium equations.
The force equilibrium equation for the beam is

$$R_A + R_B - q \times \left(\frac{L}{2}\right) = 0$$

When taking the moment equation, we can represent the uniform load as a concentrated force whose magnitude is equal to $q \times \left(\dfrac{L}{2} \right)$ applied at a distance $\left(\dfrac{3L}{4} \right)$ from end A. If we can take the moments about the point A, we get the following moment equilibrium equation:

$$q \times \left(\frac{L}{2} \right) \times \left(\frac{3L}{4} \right) - R_B \times L = 0$$

c. Solve for the unknown reactions.

$$R_B = \frac{3qL}{8}$$

$$R_A = \frac{qL}{8}$$

Step II: Draw the shear force diagram
Fig. 61 shows the step-by-step procedure for the development of the shear force diagram. Note that the shear force diagram starts and ends with zero shear force.

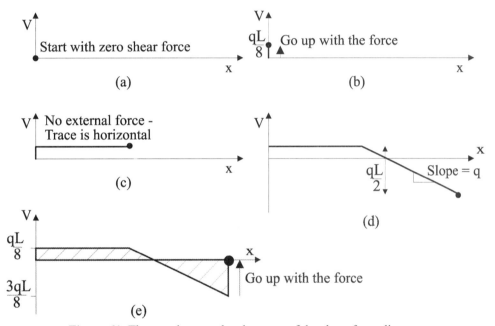

Figure 61. The step-by-step development of the shear force diagram

Step III: Draw the bending moment diagram
Fig. 62 shows the development of the bending moment diagram. When constructing this bending moment diagram, we start with zero bending moment. Until the midpoint $\left(x = \dfrac{L}{2} \right)$, the bending moment increases linearly. The slope of the bending moment diagram is equal to the magnitude of the shear force. Because the bending moment diagram is the integration of the shear force, it continues to increase until the shear force reaches zero. Using simple geometry, we can find the location of this point to be at a distance $\dfrac{L}{8}$ away from the midpoint. The bending moment continues to increase up to this point. We can compute the increase in the bending moment by evaluating the area under the shear force diagram. After reaching the peak, the bending moment decreases in a nonlinear fashion, with a slope decreasing to a value of zero.

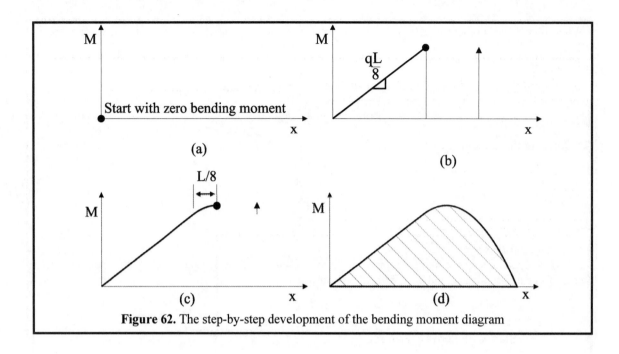

Figure 62. The step-by-step development of the bending moment diagram

Name: _____

Problem 1

Draw the shear force and the bending moment diagrams for the beam.

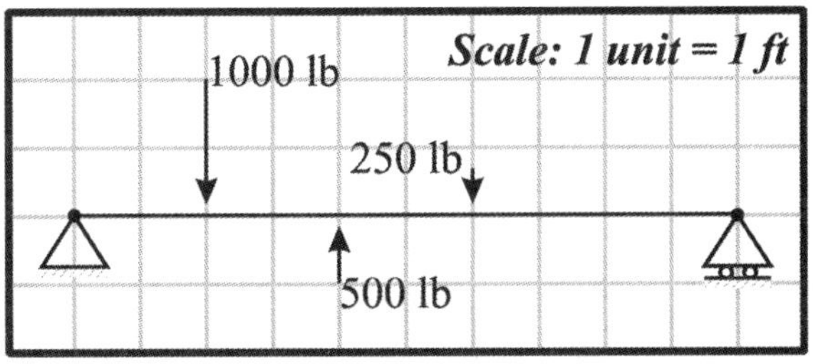

1000 lb

250 lb

Scale: 1 unit = 1 ft

500 lb

Name: _____

Problem 2

Draw the shear force and the bending moment diagrams for the beam.

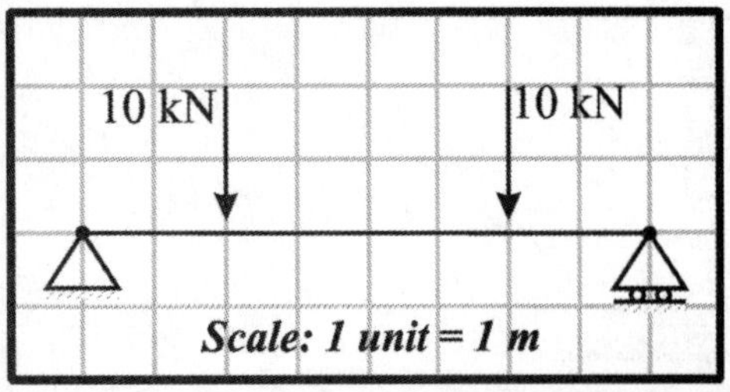

10 kN   10 kN

Scale: 1 unit = 1 m

Name: _____

Problem 3

Draw the shear force and the bending moment diagrams for the beam.

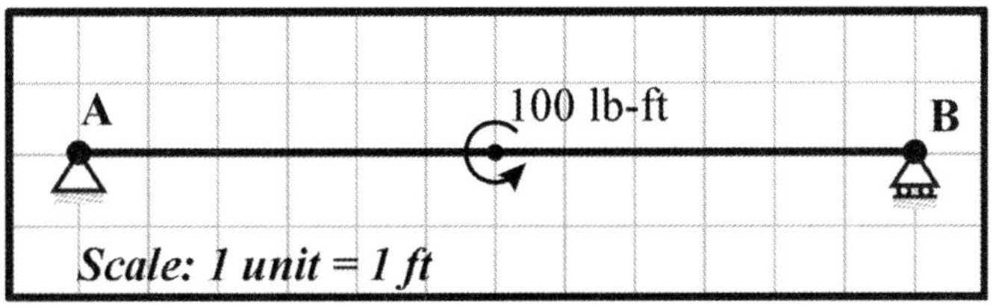

A   100 lb-ft   B

Scale: 1 unit = 1 ft

Name: _____

Problem 4

Draw the shear force and the bending moment diagrams for the beam.

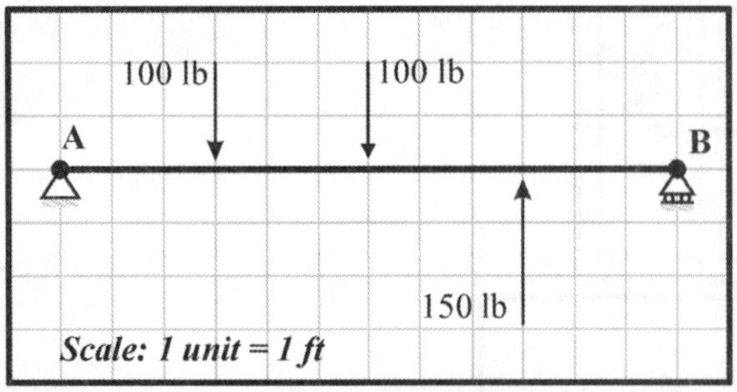

100 lb   100 lb

A

B

150 lb

Scale: 1 unit = 1 ft

Name: _____

Problem 5
Draw the shear force and the bending moment diagrams for the beam.

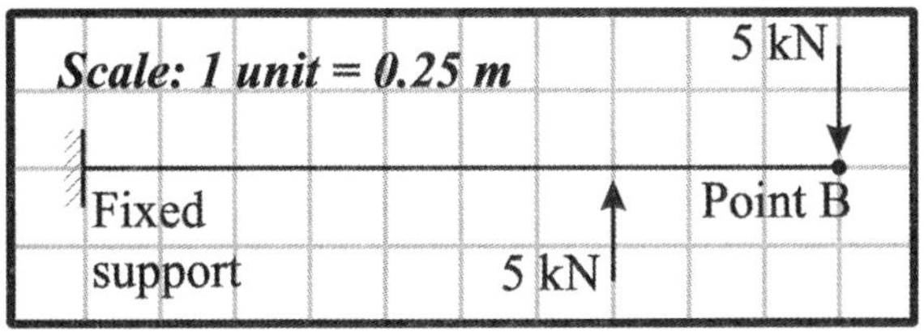

Scale: 1 unit = 0.25 m

5 kN

Fixed
support

Point B

5 kN

Name: _____

Problem 6

Draw the shear force and the bending moment diagrams for the beam.

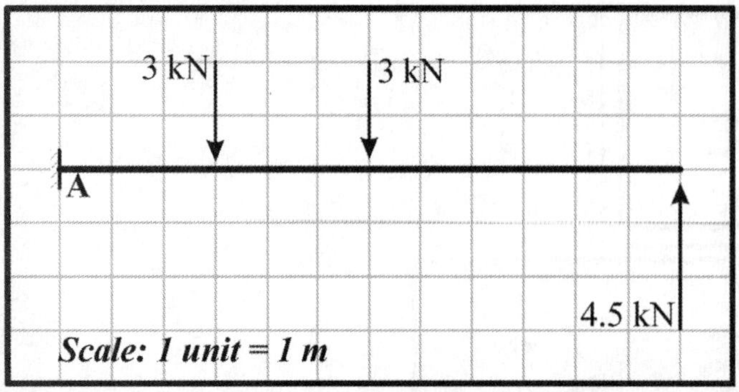

3 kN   3 kN

A

4.5 kN

Scale: 1 unit = 1 m

Name: _____

Problem 7
Draw the shear force and the bending moment diagrams for the beam.

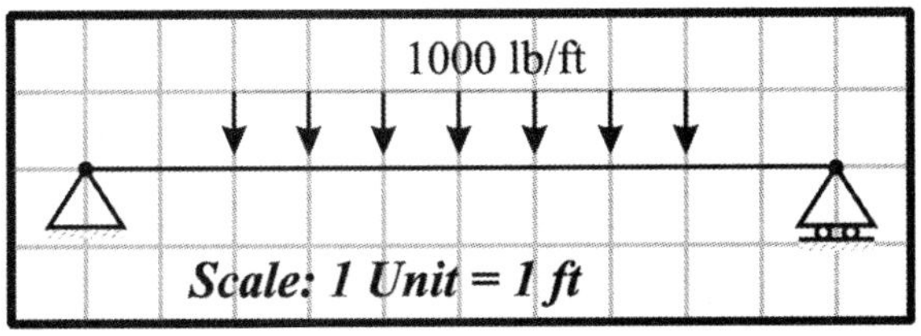

1000 lb/ft

Scale: 1 Unit = 1 ft

Name:_____

Problem 8
Draw the shear force and the bending moment diagrams for the beam.

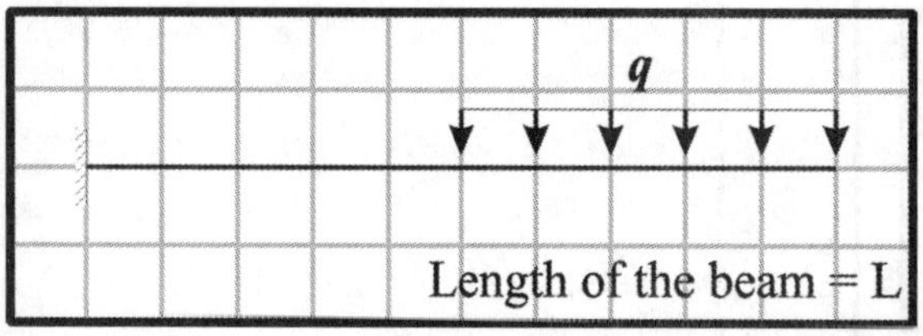

q

Length of the beam = L

Name: _____

Problem 9

Draw the shear force and the bending moment diagrams for the beam.

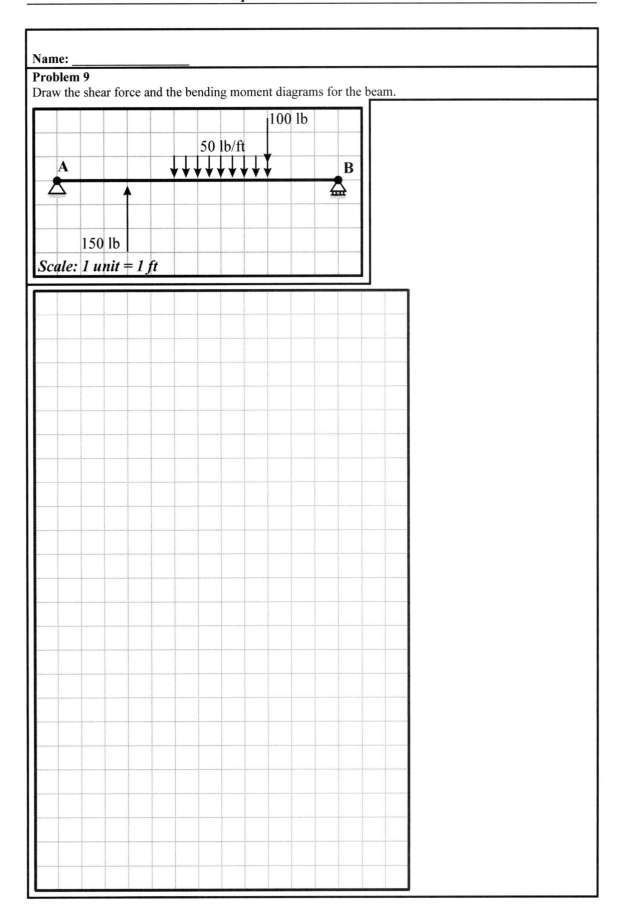

Name: _____

Problem 10

Draw the shear force and the bending moment diagrams for the beam.

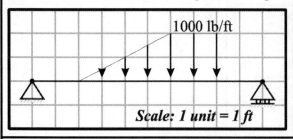

1000 lb/ft

Scale: 1 unit = 1 ft

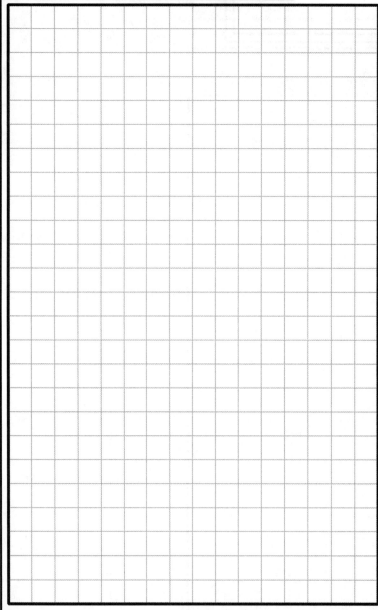

7.8. Numerical Approach for Creating Shear Force & Bending Moment Diagrams

In this section, the numerical approach is illustrated using a simply supported beam shown in Fig. 63. For this problem, before using the numerical approach, we must determine the reactions at the supports. By using the equilibrium equations, the reactions can be computed to be 80 lb and 120 lb respectively. The solution file – "Chapter VII – Simply Supported Beam.xls" - is on the CD

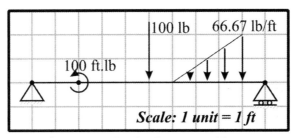

Figure 63. The simply supported beam

Step I: Discretize the beam

Discretization involves dividing the continuous beam into small segments or finite elements. The elements can be constant or variable in size, but have finite dimensions. The elements contact each other at nodes. In the numerical approach, we start by defining the coordinates of these nodes.

For the simply supported beam, the overall length is 10'. The beam can be divided into 20 elements whose size is 0.5'. The coordinates of the nodes will be 0, 0.5, 1.0, 1.5,...., 9.5, 10. We can create these coordinates in Excel by the following procedure:

a. To label column A, insert "x" in cell A1.
b. Insert the coordinates of node 1 – "0" – in cell A2.
c. Insert the coordinates of node 2 as "= A2 + 0.5" in cell A3. Note that the coordinates are written as "previous value of x + step" so that it can be propagated in the spreadsheet.
d. Select cells A3 to A22. Fill the formula in A3 down by selecting EDIT → FILL → DOWN command.

At the end of these steps, the spreadsheet should be similar to Fig. 64.

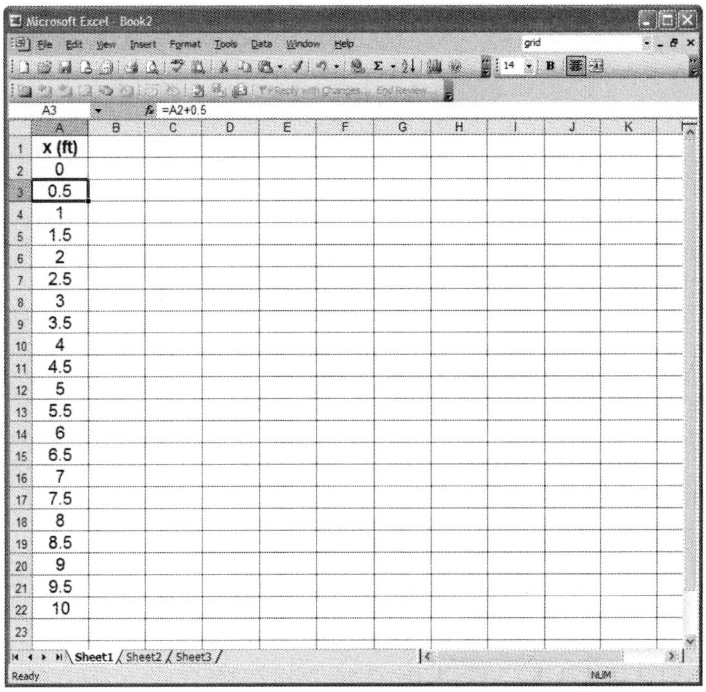

Figure 64. Excel sheet showing the coordinates of nodes

Step II: Apply forces and moments

This step involves applying the distributed and concentrated forces, and concentrated moments due to both applied loads and support reactions. We will continue to use the sign convention - an upward force and moment that creates a concave curvature facing upwards are positive. At the locations where the load is applied, there can be discontinuities in the shear force and bending moments. Therefore, the shear force/bending moment can assume two values at these nodes. To account for these discontinuities, insert additional rows at the locations where the loads are applied and specify the corresponding load. This step can be executed by the following procedure:

a.   Insert rows at x = 0, 3, 5, 6, 9, 10. The procedure for inserting a row is: Select the row → Right Mouse → Insert (refer to Fig. 65a). Insert the x-coordinates (same as the original value of x - 0, 3, 5, 6, 9, 10) (refer to Fig. 65b).

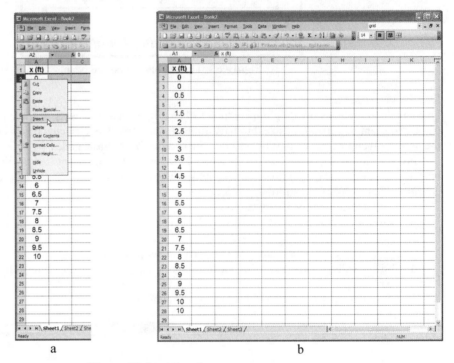

Figure 65. Inserting the rows

b.   Label columns B, C, and D as distributed force (DF), concentrated force (CF), and concentrated moment (CM) respectively.

c.   As the distributed force is not uniform, we need to find an appropriate equation to implement it in the spreadsheet. One possible equation is:

The magnitude of the distributed load at the current node =

The magnitude of the distributed load at the previous node +
Slope of the distributed load × Step size

We know that the load is distributed between x = 6' and x = 9'. The slope of the distributed load is - 22.22 lb/ft^2. The negative sign is due to the downward direction of the force distribution. Now, we can start applying 0 for the distributed load at x = 6. Note that we picked the second x = 6 (cell B18). The magnitude in cell B19 can be written as: "= B18 - 22.22 * (A19 – A18)". In this equation, (A19 – A18) provides for the step size. Select cells B19 to B24. Fill the formula in B19 down by selecting – EDIT → FILL → DOWN.

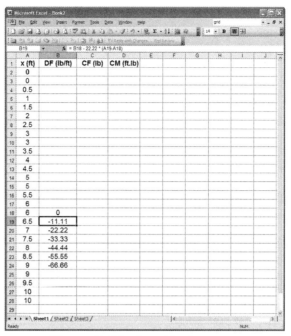

Figure 66. Distributed load

Clearly, the force distribution in the spreadsheet correctly correlates with the beginning and ending values of the distributed load. Also, it shows the discontinuity at x = 9.

d. The three concentrated forces act at x = 0, 5, and 10. We can consistently insert the load in the second row for the corresponding value of x (refer to Fig. 67).

e. The concentrated moment is applied at x = 3 (refer to Fig. 67).

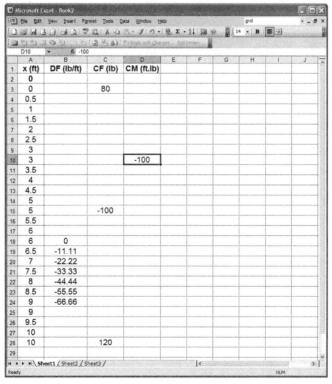

Figure 67. Concentrated forces and moment

Step III: Create the shear force diagram

We know that the shear force at x = 0 is zero. Now, as we step along the beam, the magnitude of the shear force at each node can be expressed as:

The magnitude of the shear force at the current node =

The magnitude of the shear force at the previous node +
The magnitude of concentrated forces applied during the step +
The resultant of the distributed force

The net distributed force can be viewed as the area under the distributed force curve. Mathematically, we can express it as

The resultant of the distributed force = Average distributed force × Step size

Now, the spreadsheet implementation involves

    a.   Label column E as shear force (V) by inserting V in cell E1.

    b.   Insert '0" for the magnitude of the shear force at x = 0 ("0" goes in cell E2).

         Now, the shear force in E3 can be written as: "= E2 + C3+ ((B2+B3)/2) × (A3 − A2)". In this equation,

             E2 corresponds to the magnitude of the shear force at the previous node

             C3 corresponds to the magnitude of the concentrated force applied during the step

             ((B2+B3)/2) × (A3 − A2) corresponds to the net resultant force where (B2+B3)/2) is the average height of the distribution and (A3 − A2) is the step size.

         Select cells E3 to E28. Fill the formula in E3 down by selecting – EDIT → FILL → DOWN (refer to Fig. 67). Note that the shear force does not go back to zero (due to small numerical errors).

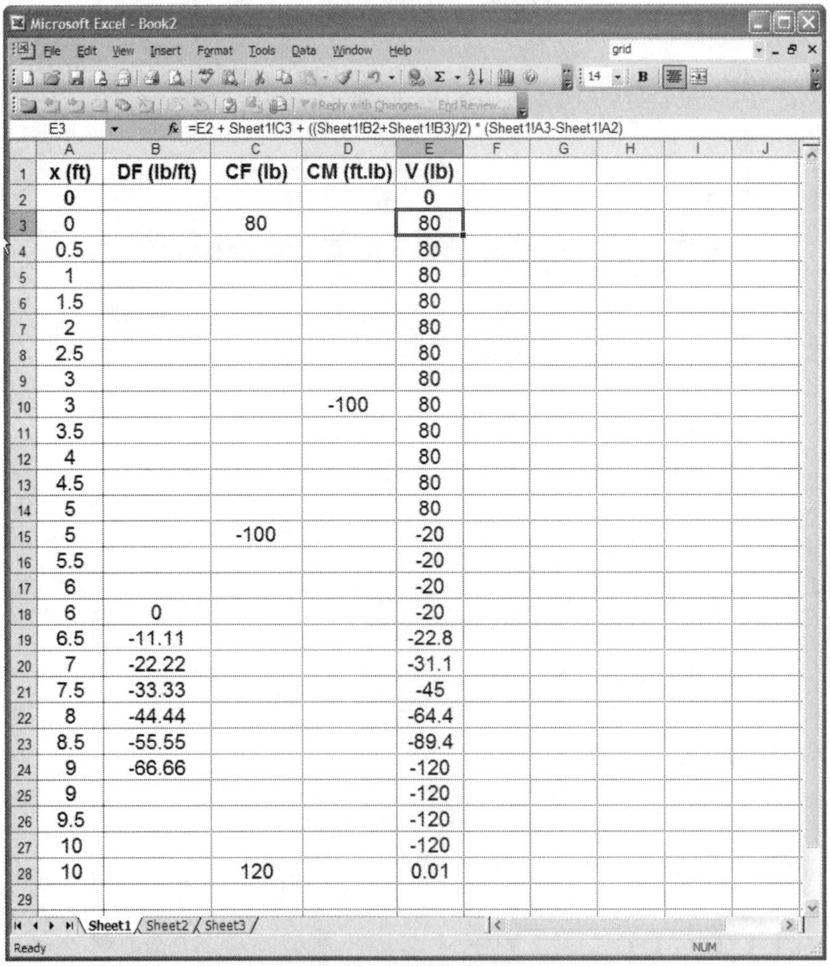

	A	B	C	D	E
	x (ft)	DF (lb/ft)	CF (lb)	CM (ft.lb)	V (lb)
2	0				0
3	0		80		80
4	0.5				80
5	1				80
6	1.5				80
7	2				80
8	2.5				80
9	3				80
10	3			-100	80
11	3.5				80
12	4				80
13	4.5				80
14	5				80
15	5		-100		-20
16	5.5				-20
17	6				-20
18	6	0			-20
19	6.5	-11.11			-22.8
20	7	-22.22			-31.1
21	7.5	-33.33			-45
22	8	-44.44			-64.4
23	8.5	-55.55			-89.4
24	9	-66.66			-120
25	9				-120
26	9.5				-120
27	10				-120
28	10		120		0.01

E3 ▾   *fx* =E2 + Sheet1!C3 + ((Sheet1!B2+Sheet1!B3)/2) * (Sheet1!A3-Sheet1!A2)

Figure 68. Shear force at different nodes

c. To plot the shear force diagram, select cells E2 to E28 → INSERT → CHART → XY Scatter → Scatter with data points connected by lines without markers (refer to Fig. 69) → Next → Series → Select the button next to X Values → Select cells A2-A28 (refer to Fig. 70) → Next → Provide chart title, value (x) axis and value (Y) axis (refer to Fig. 71) → As new chart → Shear force for name (refer to Fig. 72) → Finish (refer to Fig. 73)

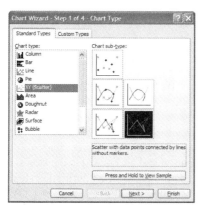

Figure 69. Chart type selection

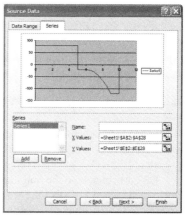

Figure 70. X-Value selection

Figure 71. Labels

Figure 72. Chart location

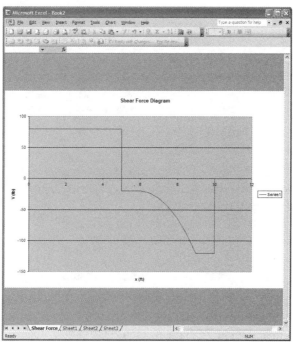

Figure 73. The shear force diagram

Step III: Create the bending moment diagram

We start the bending moment =0 at x = 0 is zero. Now, as we step along the beam, the magnitude of the bending moment at each node can be expressed as:

The magnitude of the bending moment at the current node =

The magnitude of the bending moment at the previous node +

The area of the shear fore diagram during the step +

The concentrated moment applied

The area of the shear force diagram can be expressed as

The area of the shear force during a step = Average shear force × Step size

Now, the spreadsheet implementation involves

a.   Label column F as shear force (V) by inserting BM in cell F1.

b.   Insert '0' for the magnitude of the bending moment at x = 0 ("0" goes in cell F2).

Now, the bending moment in F3 can be written as: "= F2 + ((E2+E3)/2) × (A3 – A2) + D3". In this equation,

F2 corresponds to the magnitude of the bending moment at the previous node

((E2+E3)/2) × (A3 – A2) corresponds to the area under the shear force diagram during the step. (B2+B3)/2) is the average height of the distribution and (A3 – A2) is the step size.

D3 corresponds to the magnitude of the concentrated moment applied during the step

Select cells F3 to F28. Fill the formula in F3 down by selecting – EDIT → FILL → DOWN (refer to Fig. 74). Note that the bending moment does not go back to zero (due to small numerical errors).

	A	B	C	D	E	F	G	H	I
1	x (ft)	DF (lb/ft)	CF (lb)	CM (ft.lb)	V (lb)	M (ft.lb)			
2	0				0	0			
3	0		80		80	0			
4	0.5				80	40			
5	1				80	80			
6	1.5				80	120			
7	2				80	160			
8	2.5				80	200			
9	3				80	240			
10	3			-100	80	140			
11	3.5				80	180			
12	4				80	220			
13	4.5				80	260			
14	5				80	300			
15	5		-100		-20	300			
16	5.5				-20	290			
17	6				-20	280			
18	6	0			-20	280			
19	6.5	-11.11			-22.8	269.3056			
20	7	-22.22			-31.1	255.8338			
21	7.5	-33.33			-45	236.8069			
22	8	-44.44			-64.4	209.4475			
23	8.5	-55.55			-89.4	170.9781			
24	9	-66.66			-120	118.6213			
25	9				-120	118.6213			
26	9.5				-120	58.62625			
27	10				-120	-1.36875			
28	10		120		0.01	-1.36875			
29									

F3 — fx =F2 + D3 + ((E2+E3)/2) * (A3-A2)

Figure 74. Bending moment at various nodes

c. To plot the bending diagram, select cells F2 - F28 → INSERT → CHART → XY Scatter → Scatter with data points connected by lines without markers → Next → Series → Select the button next to X Values → Select cells A2-A28 → Next → Provide chart title as Bending Moment Diagram, value (x) axis as x ft and value (Y) axis as Bending Moment ft. lb. → As new chart → Bending Moment (for name) → Finish (refer to Fig. 75)

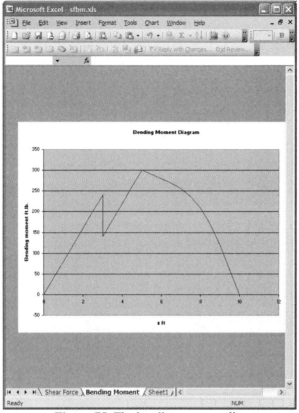

Figure 75. The bending moment diagram

Alternatively, most CAD packages allow the creation of the shear force and bending moment diagrams. The file "Chapter VII – Shear Force & Bending Moment Diagram" on the CD has instructions for creating the shear force and bending moment diagrams in ProMechanica.

Notes:

CHAPTER VIII

THE CENTROID AND THE MOMENT OF INERTIA

Learning Objectives

The material presented in this chapter will enable you to do the following:
1. Understand the concepts of the centroid, center of mass, and moment of inertia.
2. Determine the centroid of any geometry.
3. Compute the moments of inertia about axes through the centroid.
4. Transform the moment of inertia between two parallel axes using the parallel axis theorem.

8.1. The Centroid

a. Formulation of the Centroid

The centroid is a point that locates the geometric center of an object. The position of the centroid depends only on the object's geometry (or its physical shape) and is independent of density, mass, weight, and other such properties. The average position along different coordinate axes locates the centroid of an arbitrary object. To understand the concept further, let us find the centroid of a rectangle shown in Fig. 1. We can divide the object into a number of very small finite elements $A_1, A_2, \ldots A_n$. In this particular case, each small square grid represents one finite area. Let the coordinates of these areas be $(x_1, y_1), (x_2, y_2), \ldots, (x_n, y_n)$. Note that in Fig. 1, the coordinates x_1 and y_1 extend to the center of the finite area. Now, the centroid is given by

$$\overline{x} = \frac{\sum_i x_i A_i}{\sum_i A_i} \qquad\qquad \overline{y} = \frac{\sum_i y_i A_i}{\sum_i A_i} \qquad\qquad 1$$

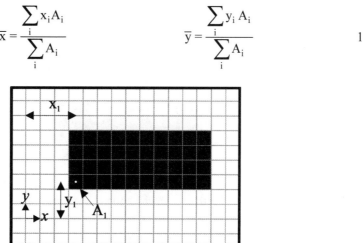

Figure 1. A finite element mesh of a two-dimensional surface

The calculations will result in the location of centroid C (see Fig. 2). Because point C is at the center of the rectangle, the results intuitively make sense. Now let us examine the properties of the centroid in more detail. Consider the moment due to the finite areas (instead of the forces) about two lines (AA and BB) parallel to the x- and y-axes passing through the centroid. Because the rectangle is symmetric about these two lines, the net moment will be zero. An important insight from this discussion is that the centroid always lies on the line of symmetry. For a doubly symmetric section (where there are two lines of symmetry), the centroid lies at the intersection of the lines of symmetry. With this insight, we can determine the centroid of several sections (see Fig. 3).

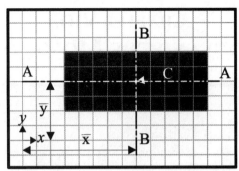

Figure 2. The location of the centroid

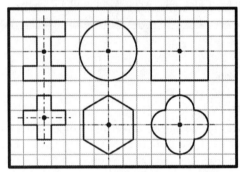

Figure 3. The location of the centroid for various symmetric geometries

Let us extend the symmetry argument by examining Fig. 4. Because the area is symmetric about line BB, its centroid must lie on this line. Now, the area is not symmetric about line AA. However, the four holes are equidistant from line AA, and the moments from the two holes on the top of line AA counteract that of the two bottom holes. Therefore, even though the area is not physically symmetric about line AA, functionally line AA can be viewed as the line of symmetry. Therefore, the centroid lies on the intersection of these two lines.

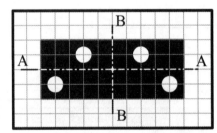

Figure 4. The location of the centroid

From common sense and the discussion so far, we can determine the centroid for doubly-symmetric sections by inspection. Equation 1 can also be used to calculate the centroid of composite sections. A composite section consists of the addition or subtraction of simple geometries. The calculation of the centroid for a composite section requires the following three steps:
1. Divide the composite geometry into simple geometries for which the positions of the centroid are known or can be determined easily.
2. Determine the centroid and area of individual components.
3. Apply eq. 1 to determine the centroid location.

The following example illustrates these three steps.

Example 1
Determine the centroid of the composite section.

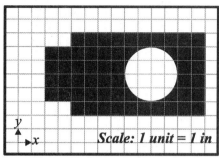

Figure 5. A composite section

Step 1: *Divide the composite section into simple geometries*
The composite geometry can be divided into three parts (refer to Fig. 6): two positive areas and one negative area (circular cutout).

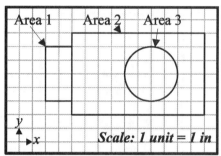

Figure 6. Parts of the composite section

Step II: *Determine the centroid and the area of individual components*
Table 1 provides the summary of the centroids of each area with respect to the reference coordinate system.

Part	Dimensions	Area (sq. in)	x	y
Area 1	2″×4″	8	3	5
Area 2	10″×6″	60	9	5
Area 3	2″ radius	-4π	10	5

Table 1. The centroid and the area of individual parts of the composite section

Step III: *Determine the centroid location*
To apply equation 1, Table 2 extends the previous table by adding the last two columns: $x_i A_i$ and $y_i A_i$.
The last row provides the sum of A_i, $x_i A_i$, and $y_i A_i$ respectively.

Part	Dimensions	Area (sq. in)	x	y	$x_i A_i$ (in^3)	$y_i A_i$ (in^3)
Area 1	2″×4″	8	3	5	24	40
Area 2	10″×6″	60	9	5	540	300
Area 3	2″ radius	-4π	10	5	-40π	-20π
		$\sum A_i =$ 55.434			$\sum x_i A_i =$ 438.34	$\sum y_i A_i =$ 277.17

Table 2. Computing the centroid of the composite section

Now, the centroid location can be computed by substituting the values into equation 1.

$$\bar{x} = \frac{\sum_i x_i A_i}{\sum_i A_i} \qquad \bar{y} = \frac{\sum_i y_i A_i}{\sum_i A_i}$$

$$\bar{x} = \frac{438.34}{55.434} = 7.91\,\text{in} \qquad \bar{y} = \frac{277.17}{55.43} = 5.00\,\text{in}$$

Let us carefully look at the value of $\bar{y}$ and locate the line it points to in Fig. 6. It locates a line parallel to the x-axis, and, in fact, the composite section is symmetric about this particular line. Thus, $\bar{y}$ indeed locates the line of symmetry. If we had examined the section more carefully from the start, we could have avoided the tedious calculations involving $\bar{y}$. Now, let us look at the value of $\bar{x}$. $\bar{x}$ for area 2 is 9". The addition of area 1 together with the removal of area 3 shifts the centroid of area 2 to the left, i.e., it reduces the value of $\bar{x}$. Therefore 7.91 in (< 9 in) makes sense for the value of $\bar{x}$.

Table 3 shows the locations of the centroid for some common sections.

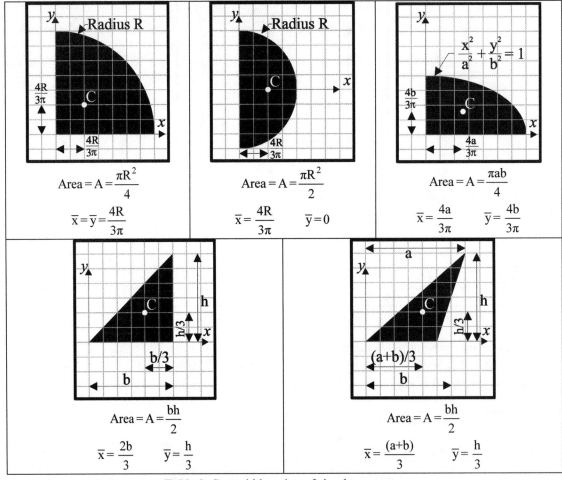

Table 3. Centroid location of simple geometry

b. Determining the location of the centroid using a Differential Element

Let us generalize the scope of equation 1 by reducing the size of the elements from finite to infinitesimal (miniscule) and changing the summation process to an integration process. If x and y are the coordinates of a differential element dA (see Fig. 7), the centroid of a two-dimensional surface is given by

$$\overline{x} = \frac{\int_A x \, dA}{\int_A dA} \qquad\qquad \overline{y} = \frac{\int_A y \, dA}{\int_A dA} \qquad\qquad 2$$

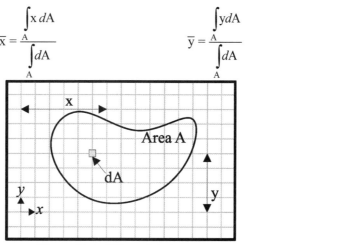

Figure 7. A differential element

The equation can be further generalized to a three-dimensional surface as

$$\overline{x} = \frac{\int_A x \, dA}{\int_A dA} \qquad \overline{y} = \frac{\int_A y \, dA}{\int_A dA} \qquad \overline{z} = \frac{\int_A z \, dA}{\int_A dA} \qquad 3$$

The same concepts can be used for determining the centroid of a line. The equation takes the form of

$$\overline{x} = \frac{\int_L x \, dL}{\int_L dL} \qquad \overline{y} = \frac{\int_L y \, dL}{\int_L dL} \qquad \overline{z} = \frac{\int_L z \, dL}{\int_L dL} \qquad 4$$

To determine the centroid of a volume, the equation takes the form of

$$\overline{x} = \frac{\int_V x \, dV}{\int_V dV} \qquad \overline{y} = \frac{\int_V y \, dV}{\int_V dV} \qquad \overline{z} = \frac{\int_V z \, dV}{\int_V dV} \qquad 5$$

Example 2

Determine the centroid of the quarter circle.

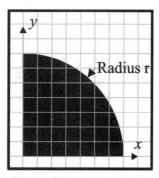

Figure 8. A quarter circle

The key step in solving this type of problems is to establish and define an appropriate differential element. Let us consider a vertical differential element with thickness dx and height h as shown in Fig. 9.

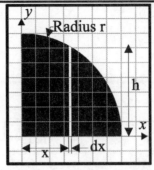

Figure 9. A vertical differential element in the quarter circle

The area of this differential element is

$$dA = h \cdot dx$$

Height h is a function of distance x. The relationship is given by

$$h = \sqrt{r^2 - x^2}$$

Because the section is symmetric about a line that is at 45^0 to the x- and y-axes, the centroid lies on this line. Therefore, $\overline{x} = \overline{y}$. We can now find $\overline{x}$ (or $\overline{y}$) for the centroid by applying equation 2.

$$\overline{x} = \frac{\int_A x\,dA}{\int_A dA} = \frac{\int_0^R x\sqrt{r^2 - x^2}\,dx}{\int_A dA}$$

We know that $\int_A dA$ is the area of the quarter circle $\left(\dfrac{\pi r^2}{4}\right)$. Substituting this value and integrating the numerator, we get

$$\overline{x} = \frac{\int_0^r x\sqrt{r^2 - x^2}\,dx}{\left(\dfrac{\pi}{4}r^2\right)} = \frac{\left[-\dfrac{\left(r^2 - x^2\right)^{\frac{3}{2}}}{3}\right]_0^r}{\left(\dfrac{\pi}{4}r^2\right)}$$

$$\boxed{\overline{x} = \frac{4\,r}{3\,\pi}} \qquad \boxed{\overline{y} = \frac{4\,r}{3\,\pi}}$$

Note that $\overline{x} = \overline{y}$ because of symmetry.

Example 3

Locate the centroid of the line whose equation is $y = 1 - x^2$ with x ranging from 0 to 1.

If we establish a differential element (see Fig. 10) whose length is dL at a distance x, the y coordinate of this element will be $\left(x, 1 - x^2\right)$.

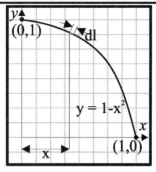

Figure 10. A differential element on the line

We can express the element length as

$$dL = \sqrt{(dx)^2 + (dy)^2} == \sqrt{1 + \left(\frac{dy}{dx}\right)^2} \cdot dx$$

If we differentiate the line equation, we get

$$\frac{dy}{dx} = -2x$$

Substituting the value of $\frac{dy}{dx}$ in the equation of the element length, we get

$$dL = \sqrt{1 + 4x^2}\ dx$$

Now, we can calculate the centroid using equation 4:

$$\overline{x} = \frac{\int_L x\, dL}{\int_L dL} \qquad\qquad \overline{y} = \frac{\int_L y\, dL}{\int_L dL}$$

$$\overline{x} = \frac{\int_0^1 x\sqrt{1 + 4x^2}\ dx}{\int_0^1 \sqrt{1 + 4x^2}\ dx} \qquad\qquad \overline{y} = \frac{\int_0^1 \left(1 - x^2\right)\sqrt{1 + 4x^2}\ dx}{\int_0^1 \sqrt{1 + 4x^2}\ dx}$$

Using the equations in Appendix A, we get

$$\overline{x} = \frac{0.8484}{0.9789} \qquad\qquad \overline{y} = 1 - \frac{0.6988}{0.9789}$$

$$\boxed{\overline{x} = 0.8667} \qquad\qquad \boxed{\overline{y} = 0.2861}$$

8.2. Center of Mass

The center of mass is a point that locates the average position of the mass of an object. For an object with uniform density, it coincides with the centroid. It is often called the center of gravity because the gravitational pull on an object can be represented as a concentrated force acting at this point. The concepts associated with the centroid easily extend to the center of mass. The equation for finding the center of mass of a volume takes the form of

$$\bar{x} = \frac{\int\limits_{m} x\, dm}{\int\limits_{m} dm} \qquad \bar{y} = \frac{\int\limits_{m} y\, dm}{\int\limits_{m} dm} \qquad \bar{z} = \frac{\int\limits_{m} z\, dm}{\int\limits_{m} dm} \qquad 6$$

For a three-dimensional surface of uniform thickness and density, the center of mass coincides with the centroid of the surface.

$$\bar{x} = \frac{\int\limits_{A} x\, dA}{\int\limits_{A} dA} \qquad \bar{y} = \frac{\int\limits_{A} y\, dA}{\int\limits_{A} dA} \qquad \bar{z} = \frac{\int\limits_{A} z\, dA}{\int\limits_{A} dA} \qquad 7$$

The same concepts can be used to determine the center of mass of a line. The equation takes the form of

$$\bar{x} = \frac{\int\limits_{L} x\, dL}{\int\limits_{L} dL} \qquad \bar{y} = \frac{\int\limits_{L} y\, dL}{\int\limits_{L} dL} \qquad \bar{z} = \frac{\int\limits_{L} z\, dL}{\int\limits_{L} dL} \qquad 8$$

Concept Questions

Name: _____

1. TRUE/FALSE: Using symmetry, we can determine that the centroid of the area is point A.

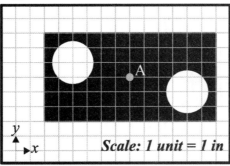

2. The coordinates of centroid with respect to the xy coordinate system is
   A. (0.7, 0.55)
   B. (0.7, 0.35)
   C. (0.55, 0.7)
   D. (0.35, 0.7)

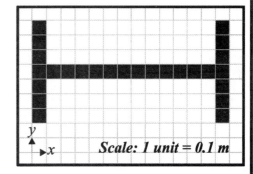

3. TRUE/FALSE: The location of the centroid depends on the mass properties of the object.

4. The approximate location of the centroid for the section is
   a. Point A
   b. Point B
   c. Point C
   d. Point D

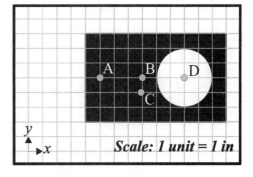

5. The approximate location of the centroid for the section is
   a. Point A
   b. Point B
   c. Point C
   d. Point D

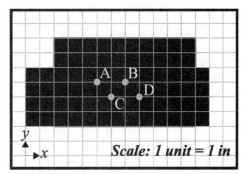

Name: _____

Problem 1

Determine the centroid of the section.

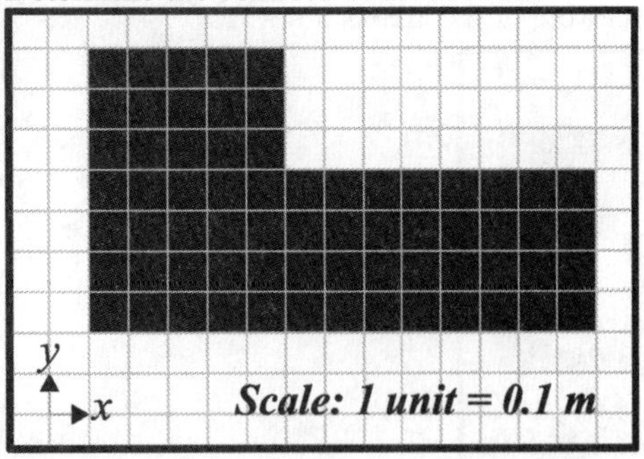

Scale: 1 unit = 0.1 m

Part	Dimensions	Area (sq. m)	x	y	x_iA_i (m³)	y_iA_i (m³)

Problem 2

Determine the centroid of the section.

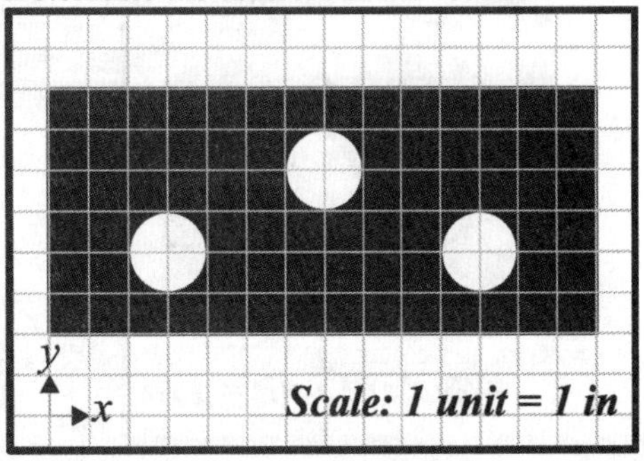

Scale: 1 unit = 1 in

Part	Dimensions	Area (sq. in)	x	y	x_iA_i (in³)	y_iA_i (in³)

Name: _____

Problem 3

Determine the centroid of the section.

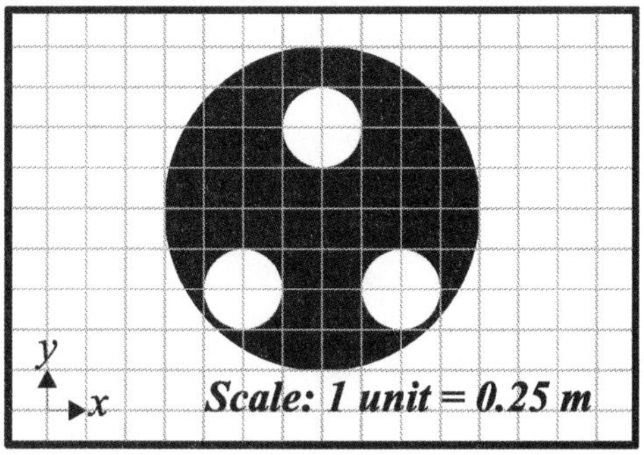

Scale: 1 unit = 0.25 m

Part	Dimensions	Area (sq.m)	x	y	$x_i A_i$ (m³)	$y_i A_i$ (m³)

Problem 4

Determine the centroid of the section.

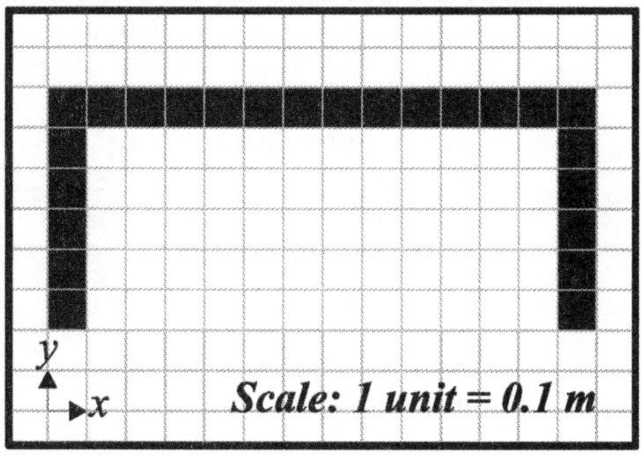

Scale: 1 unit = 0.1 m

Part	Dimensions	Area (sq. m)	x	y	$x_i A_i$ (m³)	$y_i A_i$ (m³)

Name: ____________________

Problem 5

Determine the centroid of the section.

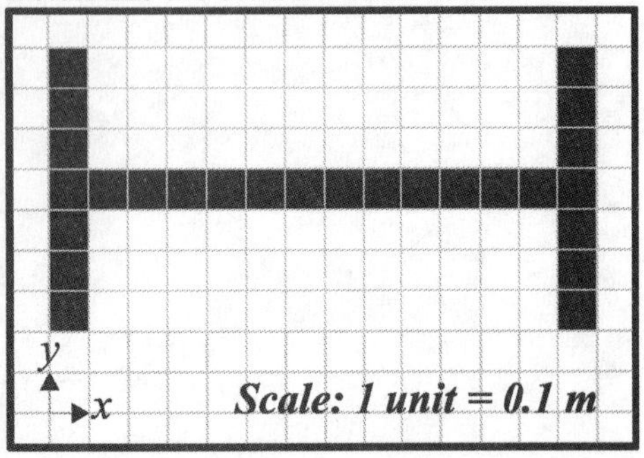
y
x
Scale: 1 unit = 0.1 m

Problem 6

Determine the centroid of the section.

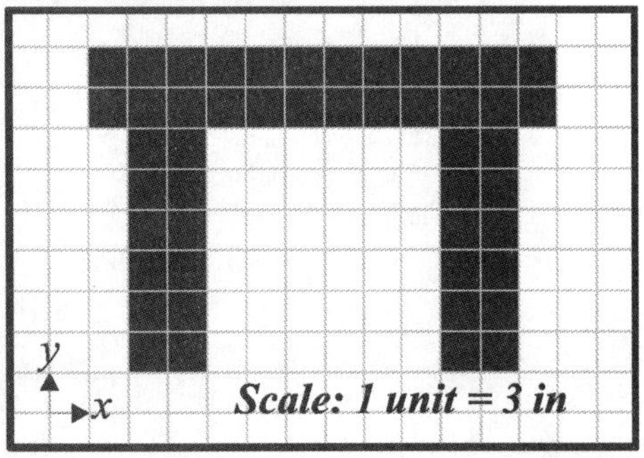
y
x
Scale: 1 unit = 3 in

Name: _____

Problem 7
Determine the centroid of the section.

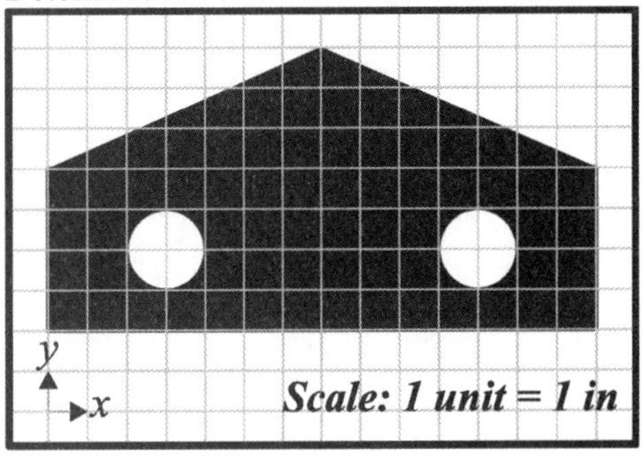

Scale: 1 unit = 1 in

Problem 8
Determine the centroid of the wing section.

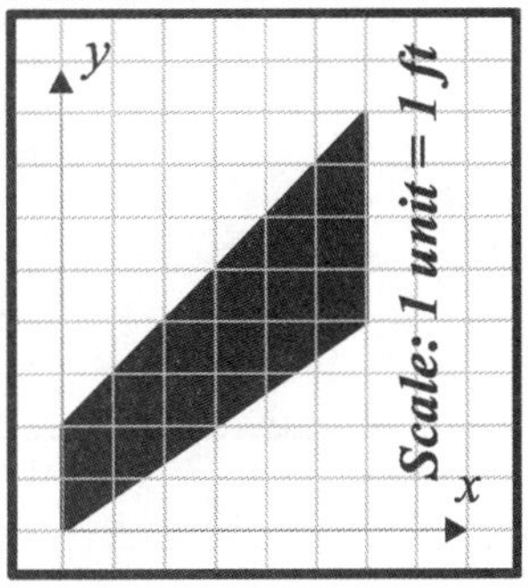

Scale: 1 unit = 1 ft

Name: _____

Problem 9

Determine the centroid of the section.

Scale:
1 unit = 2 in

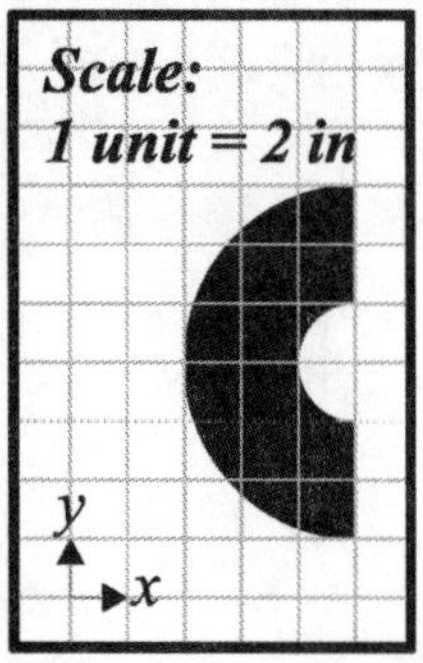

Problem 10

Determine the centroid of the section.

Scale: 1 unit = 0.2 m

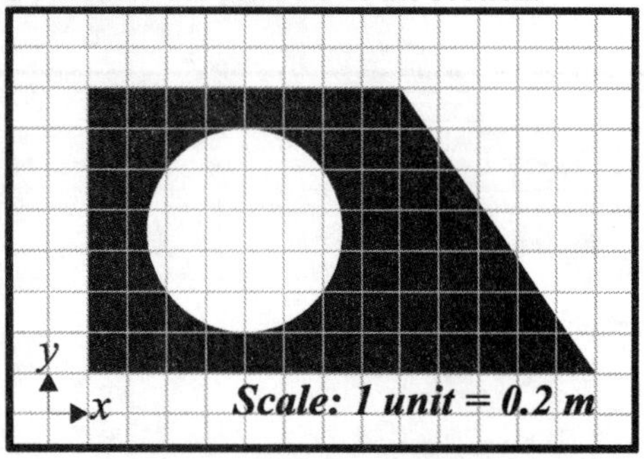

Name: _____

Problem 11

Determine the coordinates of the centroid using the differential element method. Compare the solution to that of Problem 8.

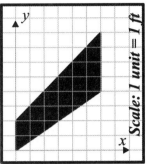

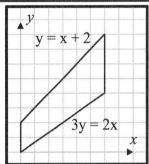

Problem 12

Determine the coordinates of the centroid for the quarter plate using the differential element shown in the figure. Compare the results with example 2.

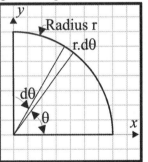

Name: _____

Problem 13

Determine the coordinates of the centroid of the area using the differential element method. Note that the curve is an ellipse that intercepts the x- and y-axes at 9″ and 4″ respectively. Use the equation for an ellipse $\left(\dfrac{x^2}{a^2}+\dfrac{y^2}{b^2}=1\right)$.

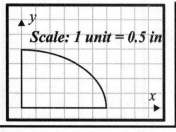

Problem 14

Determine the coordinates of the centroid for the triangle using the differential element method.

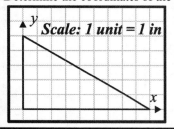

Name: _____

Problem 15

Determine the coordinates of the centroid of the cone. The height of the cone is 6″, and the radius is 3″. Use a cylindrical disc at a height z with thickness dz as a differential element. Begin by determining the radius and then the volume of this disc.

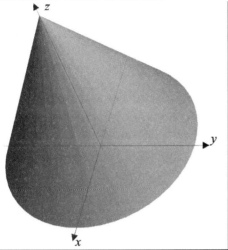

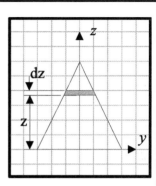

Problem 16

Determine the coordinates of the centroid of the hemisphere. The height of the radius is 3 m. Use a cylindrical disc at a height z with thickness dz as a differential element.

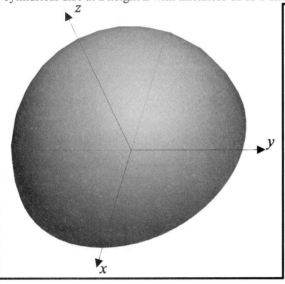

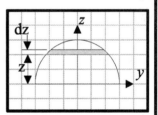

Notes:

8.3. Moment of Inertia

a. Formulation of Moment of Inertia

The moment of inertia comes in handy when solving a variety of structural analysis problems. For instance, the concept is useful for calculating stresses caused by torsional and bending loads. Table 4 defines the three moments of inertia of area A (see Fig. 11). The units of the moment of inertia are in^4, ft^4, or m^4. All three moments of inertia are always positive.

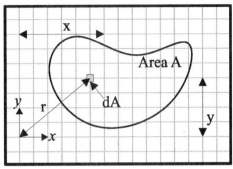

Figure 11. A differential element

Moment of inertia about x-axis:	$I_x = \int_A y^2 \, dA$	9
Moment of inertia about y-axis:	$I_y = \int_A x^2 \, dA$	10
Polar moment of inertia:	$J_O = \int_A r^2 \, dA$	11

Table 4. Moments of inertia of area A

Note that the polar moment of inertia is about the origin. Because $r^2 = x^2 + y^2$, the polar moment of inertia $J_O = I_x + I_y$. In addition to these three moments of inertia, we can define the product of inertia. The product of inertia can take both positive and negative values.

Product of inertia:
$$I_{xy} = \int_A x \, y \, dA \qquad 12$$

The moment of inertia is sometimes expressed in terms of the radius of gyration. The radius of gyration determines how the area is distributed around the centroid. It is given by

$$R_g = \sqrt{\frac{I}{A}} \qquad 13$$

We can obtain $R_{g\text{-}x}$, $R_{g\text{-}y}$, and $R_{g\text{-}O}$ by substituting I_x, I_y, and J_O respectively in equation 13.

Example 4
Determine the moments of inertia about the x- and y-axes. Also, determine the polar moment of inertia.

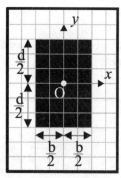

Figure 12. A rectangular section

Let us start by establishing a differential element as shown Fig. 13.

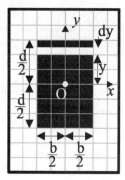

Figure 13. The differential element

The moment of inertia about the x-axis is

$$I_x = \int_A y^2 \, dA = \int_{-\frac{d}{2}}^{\frac{d}{2}} y^2 \left(b.dy \right) = b \int_{-\frac{d}{2}}^{\frac{d}{2}} y^2 \, dy$$

$$\boxed{I_x = \frac{bd^3}{12}}$$

Now, interchanging the dimensions b and d, we can get the moment of inertia about the y-axis:

$$\boxed{I_y = \frac{db^3}{12}}$$

The polar moment of inertia is the sum of the moments of inertia about the x- and y-axes $\left(J_O = I_x + I_y \right)$.
For the rectangular section,

$$\boxed{J_O = \frac{bd}{12} \left(b^2 + d^2 \right)}$$

b. Parallel Axis Theorem

In the previous example, we calculated the moment of inertia of the area about the x- and y-axes through the centroid. Often, we are faced with the task of computing the moments of inertia about another set of axes. In this section, we learn how to transform the moment of inertia about one axis to another parallel axis. Let the x'- and y'-axes pass through the centroid of area A.

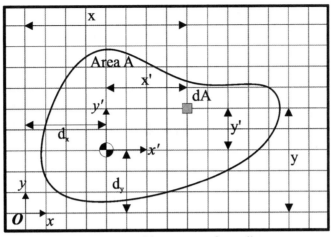

Figure 14. Area A with two sets of coordinate axes

Now, let us derive the moment of inertia about the x-axis, which is parallel to the x'-axis through the centroid.

$$I_x = \int_A y^2 \, dA$$

$$I_x = \int_A \left(y' + d_y\right)^2 dA$$

$$= \int_A y'^2 dA + 2 \int_A y' d_y dA + \int_A d_y^2 dA$$

$$= I_{x'} + 2d_y \int_A y' dA + d_y^2 \int_A dA$$

In the second term, $\int_A y' dA$ is equal to zero as the x-axis passes through the centroid. Substituting this value, we get

$$I_x = I_{x'} + A d_y^2 \qquad\qquad 14$$

Similarly, we can write

$$I_y = I_{y'} + A d_x^2 \qquad\qquad 15$$

Substituting these values into the polar moment of inertia,

$$J_O = I_x + I_y$$

$$J_O = I_{x'} + I_{y'} + A\left(d_x^2 + d_y^2\right)$$

$$J_O = J_C + A d^2 \qquad\qquad 16$$

Note that the moment of inertia about an axis through the centroid is the minimum. The parallel axis theorem is useful for computing the moment of inertia of composite sections. Table 5 shows the locations of the centroid for some common sections.

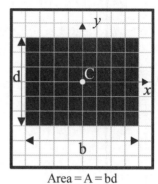

$$\text{Area} = A = bd$$
$$\bar{x} = 0 \qquad \bar{y} = 0$$
$$I_x = \frac{bd^3}{12} \qquad I_y = \frac{db^3}{12}$$

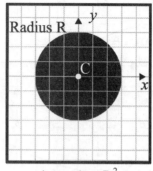

$$\text{Area} = A = \pi R^2$$
$$\bar{x} = 0 \qquad \bar{y} = 0$$
$$I_x = \frac{\pi R^4}{4} \qquad I_y = \frac{\pi R^4}{4}$$

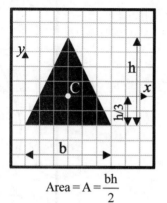

$$\text{Area} = A = \frac{bh}{2}$$
$$\bar{y} = \frac{h}{3}$$
$$I_x = \frac{bh^3}{12}$$

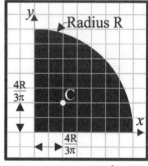

$$\text{Area} = A = \frac{\pi R^2}{4}$$
$$\bar{x} = \bar{y} = \frac{4R}{3\pi}$$
$$I_x = I_y = \frac{\pi R^4}{16}$$

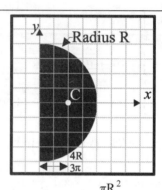

$$\text{Area} = A = \frac{\pi R^2}{2}$$
$$\bar{x} = \frac{4R}{3\pi} \qquad \bar{y} = 0$$
$$I_x = I_y = \frac{\pi R^4}{8}$$

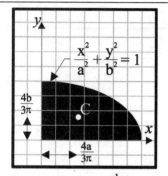

$$\text{Area} = A = \frac{\pi ab}{4}$$
$$\bar{x} = \frac{4a}{3\pi} \qquad \bar{y} = \frac{4b}{3\pi}$$
$$I_x = \frac{\pi ab^3}{16} \qquad I_y = \frac{\pi a^3 b}{16}$$

Table 5. Moment of inertia for simple geometry

Example 5

Determine the moments of inertia about the x'- and y'-axes about the centroid. Also, determine the polar moment of inertia.

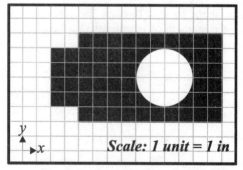

Figure 15. A composite section

Before we can compute the moments of inertia for the composite section, we must find the centroids of the individual sections. In Fig. 16, the composite section is divided into three areas. C_1, C_2, and C_3 are the centroids of areas 1, 2, and 3, respectively. C is the centroid of the composite section. The first half of table 6 is taken from example 1. As computed in example 1, the coordinates of the centroid are $(7.91, 5.00)$. In the table, $I_{x'}$ and $I_{y'}$ are the moments of inertia about the x'- and y'-axes passing through the centroid of each area. d_x and d_y give the distance between the centroid of each area and the centroid of the composite section along the x- and y-axes.

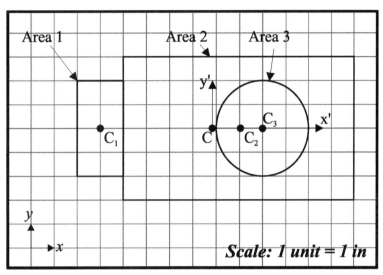

Figure 16. The composite section with the centroids of invididual components

Part	Dimen-sions	Area (sq. in)	x	y	$x_i A_i$ (in^3)	$y_i A_i$ (in^3)	$I_{x'}$	$I_{y'}$	d_x	d_y	Ad_x^2	Ad_y^2
Area 1	2″×4″	8	3	5	24	40	10.67	2.67	4.91	0	192.86	0
Area 2	10″×6″	60	9	5	540	300	180	500	1.09	0	71.286	0
Area 3	2″ radius	-4π	10	5	-40π	-20π	-0.785	-0.785	2.09	0	-54.89	0
Summation		55.43			438.34	277.17	189.89	501.89			209.26	

Table 6. Method of calculating the moment of inertia of a composite section

$$I_x = I_{x'} + Ad_y^2 \qquad\qquad I_y = I_{y'} + Ad_x^2$$

$$\boxed{I_x = 189.89 \text{ in}^4} \qquad\qquad \boxed{I_x = 711.15 \text{ in}^4}$$

$$J_O = I_x + I_y$$

$$\boxed{J_O = 901.04 \text{ in}^4}$$

Notes:

Concept Questions

Name: _____

1. The $x'y'$ coordinate system passes through the centroid and $I_{x'}$ is the moment of inertia about the x' axis. Similarly, I_x is the moment of inertia about the x axis. The relationship between the two moment of inertias is given by

   A. $I_x = I_{x'} + Ad_x^2$

   B. $I_x = I_{x'} + Ad_y^2$

   C. $I_{x'} = I_x + Ad_x^2$

   D. $I_{x'} = I_x + Ad_y^2$

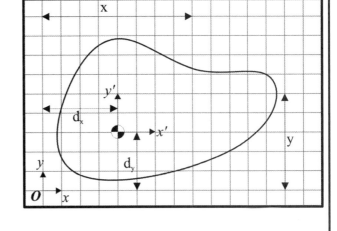

2. If b > d, then the following statement is true:
   A. $I_x > I_y$
   B. $I_x = I_y$
   C. $I_x < I_y$
   D. Can't be determined

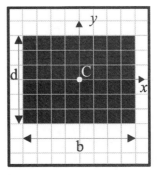

3. TRUE/FALSE: The minimum moment of inertia for an area occurs about the axis through the centroid.

4. TRUE/FALSE: The moment of inertia about any axis must always be positive.

5. TRUE/FALSE: The product moment of inertia must always be positive.

Name: _____

Problem 1

Determine the moments of inertia about the x- and y-axes and the polar moment of inertia about the centroid. Calculate using a differential element method.

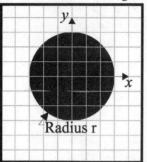

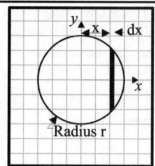

Problem 2

Determine the moments of inertia about the x- and y-axes and the polar moment of inertia about the centroid. Note that the curve is an ellipse that intercepts the x- and y-axes at 3″ and 2″, respectively. Use the equation for an ellipse: $\left(\dfrac{x^2}{a^2} + \dfrac{y^2}{b^2} = 1 \right)$.

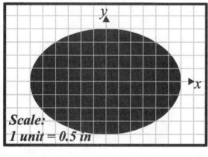

Name: _____

Problem 3

Determine the moments of inertia about the x- and y-axes.

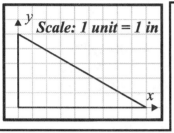

Problem 4

Determine the moments of inertia about the x- and y-axes.

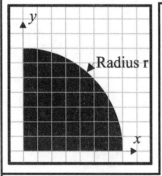

Name: _____

Problem 5

Determine the centroid for the section. Also, determine the moments of inertia about the x′- and y′-axes, and the polar moment of inertia about the centroid.

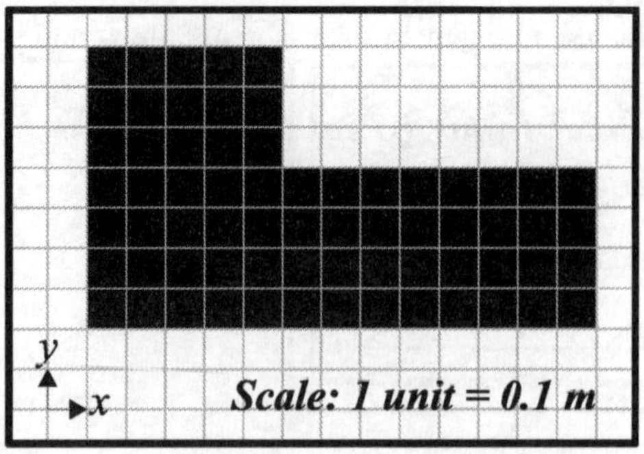

Scale: 1 unit = 0.1 m

Part	Dimensions	Area (sq. m)	x	y	$x_i A_i$ (m^3)	$y_i A_i$ (m^3)

Part	$I_{x'}$ m^4	$I_{y'}$ m^4	d_x m	d_y m	Ad_x^2 m^4	Ad_y^2 m^4

Name: _____

Problem 6

Determine the centroid for the section. Also, determine the moments of inertia about the x′- and y′-axes, and the polar moment of inertia about the centroid.

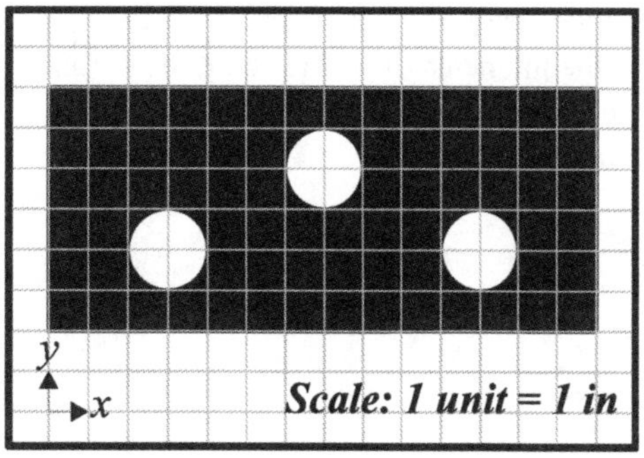

y

►*x*

Scale: 1 unit = 1 in

Part	Dimensions	Area (sq. in)	x	y	$x_i A_i$ (in^3)	$y_i A_i$ (in^3)

Part	$I_{x'}$ in^4	$I_{y'}$ in^4	d_x in	d_y in	Ad_x^2 in^4	Ad_y^2 in^4

Name: _____

Problem 7

Determine the centroid for the section. Also, determine the moments of inertia about the x′- and y′-axes, and the polar moment of inertia about the centroid.

Scale: 1 unit = 0.25 m

Part	Dimensions	Area (sq.m)	x	y	$x_i A_i$ (m³)	$y_i A_i$ (m³)

Part	$I_{x'}$ m⁴	$I_{y'}$ m⁴	d_x m	d_y m	Ad_x^2 m⁴	Ad_y^2 m⁴

Name: _____

Problem 8

Determine the centroid for the section. Also, determine the moments of inertia about the x′- and y′-axes, and the polar moment of inertia about the centroid.

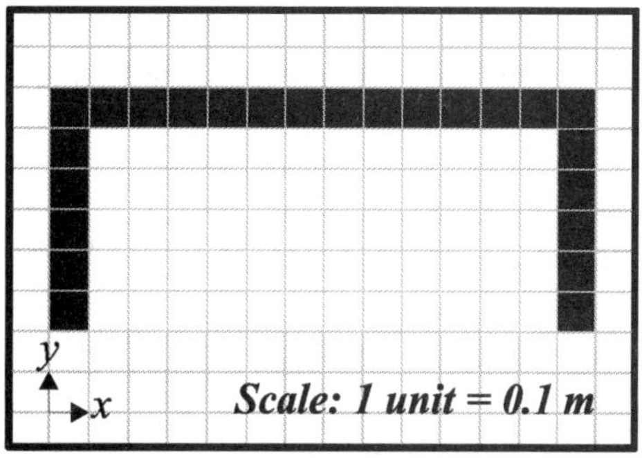

Scale: 1 unit = 0.1 m

Part	Dimensions	Area (sq. m)	x	y	$x_i A_i$ (m³)	$y_i A_i$ (m³)

Part	$I_{x'}$ m⁴	$I_{y'}$ m⁴	d_x m	d_y m	$A d_x^2$ m⁴	$A d_y^2$ m⁴

Name: _____

Problem 9

Determine the centroid for the section. Also, determine the moments of inertia about the x'- and y'-axes, and the polar moment of inertia about the centroid.

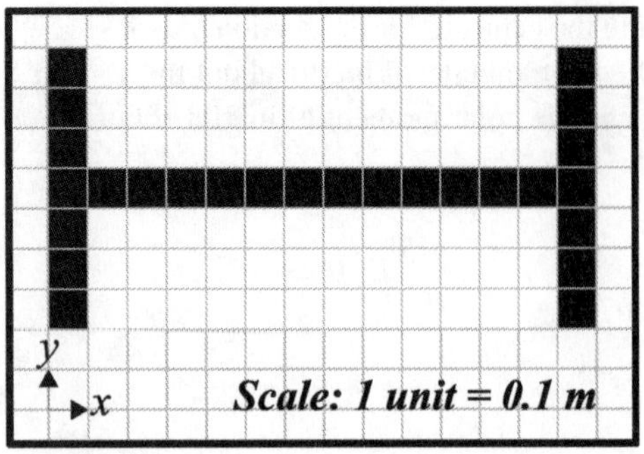

Scale: 1 unit = 0.1 m

y

x

Name: _____

Problem 10

Determine the centroid for the section. Also, determine the moments of inertia about the x′- and y′-axes, and the polar moment of inertia about the centroid.

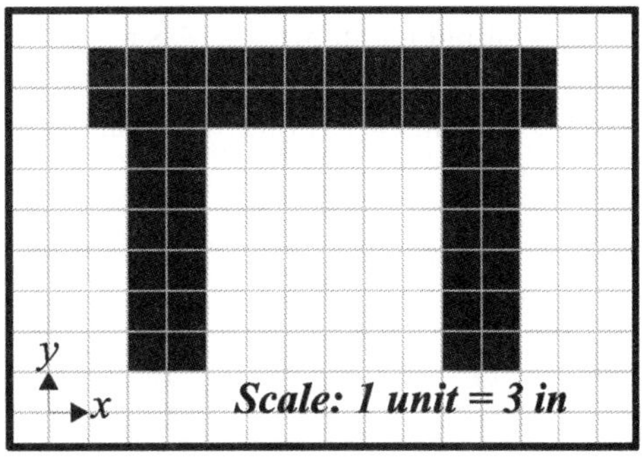

Scale: 1 unit = 3 in

Name: _____

Problem 11

Determine the centroid for the section. Also, determine the moments of inertia about the x′- and y′-axes, and the polar moment of inertia about the centroid.

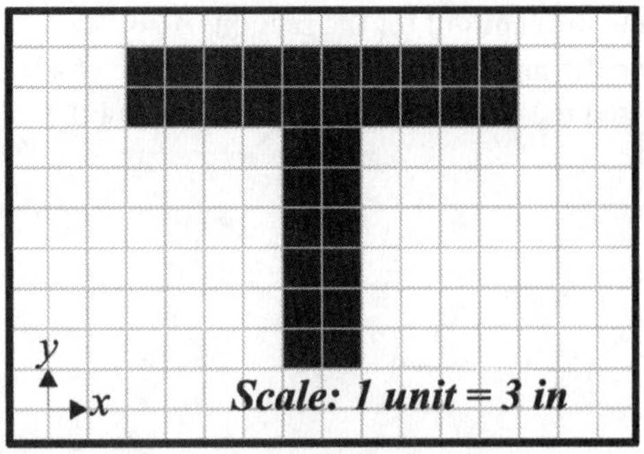

Scale: 1 unit = 3 in

Name: _____

Problem 12

Determine the centroid for the section. Also, determine the moments of inertia about the x′- and y′-axes, and the polar moment of inertia about the centroid.

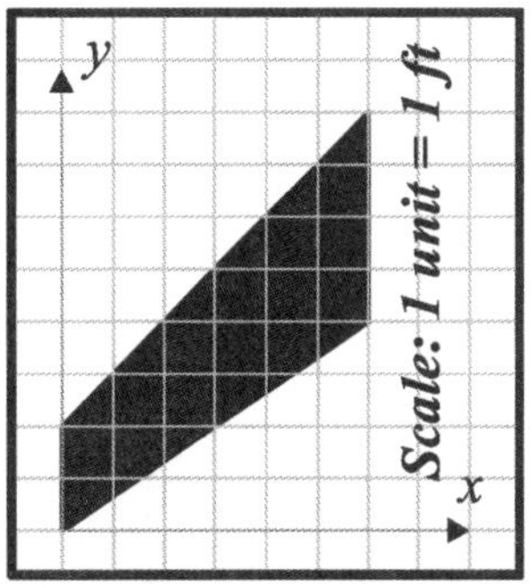

Notes:

Appendix A

Trigonometric Relations

Table of Integrals

Properties of Areas

Solutions to Selected Problems

TRIGONOMETRIC RELATIONS

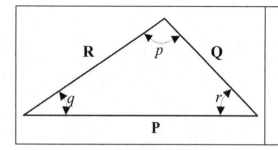

Sine law

$$\frac{P}{\sin p} = \frac{Q}{\sin q} = \frac{R}{\sin r}$$

Cosine law

$$P = \sqrt{Q^2 + R^2 - 2QR\cos p}$$

$$Q = \sqrt{P^2 + R^2 - 2PR\cos q}$$

$$R = \sqrt{P^2 + Q^2 - 2PQ\cos r}$$

$$\sin\theta = \frac{\text{Length of opposite side}}{\text{Length of hypotenuse}}$$

$$\cos\theta = \frac{\text{Length of adjacent side}}{\text{Length of hypotenuse}}$$

$$\tan\theta = \frac{\text{Length of opposite side}}{\text{Length of adjacent side}}$$

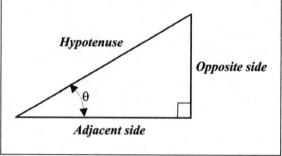

Note that hypotenuse is always the longest side in the right-angled triangle.

	0	30^0 or $\pi/6$	45^0 or $\pi/4$	60^0 or $\pi/3$	90^0 or $\pi/2$
$\sin\theta$	0	$1/2$	$1/\sqrt{2}$	$\sqrt{3}/2$	1
$\cos\theta$	1	$\sqrt{3}/2$	$1/\sqrt{2}$	$1/2$	0
$\tan\theta$	0	$1/\sqrt{3}$	1	$\sqrt{3}$	Infinity

$\sin^2\theta + \cos^2\theta = 1$

$1 + \tan^2\theta = \sec^2\theta$

$\sin 2\theta = 2\sin\theta\,\cos\theta$

$\cos 2\theta = \cos^2\theta - \sin^2\theta$

TABLE OF INTEGRALS

$$\int \sin x \, dx = -\cos x$$

$$\int \cos x \, dx = \sin x$$

$$\int e^{ax} \, dx = \frac{1}{a} e^x$$

$$\int x^n \, dx = \frac{1}{n+1} x^{n+1} \text{ for } n \neq 1$$

$$\int \frac{1}{x} \, dx = \ln|x|$$

$$\int \sqrt{(a+bx)} \, dx = \frac{2(a+bx)^{3/2}}{3b}$$

$$\int x\sqrt{(a+bx)} \, dx = \frac{2\sqrt{(a+bx)}\left(-2a^2 + bxa + 3b^2 x^2\right)}{15b^2}$$

$$\int \sqrt{(a^2 + b^2 x^2)} \, dx = \frac{\log\left(b\left(bx + \sqrt{a^2 + b^2 x^2}\right)\right)a^2 + bx\sqrt{(a^2 + b^2 x^2)}}{2b}$$

$$\int x\sqrt{(a^2 + b^2 x^2)} \, dx = \frac{(a^2 + b^2 x^2)^{3/2}}{3b^2}$$

$$\int x^2 \sqrt{(a^2 + b^2 x^2)} \, dx = \frac{bx\sqrt{(a^2 + b^2 x^2)}\left(a^2 + 2b^2 x^2\right) - a^4 \log\left(b\left(bx + \sqrt{(a^2 + b^2 x^2)}\right)\right)}{8b^3}$$

$$\int \sqrt{(a^2 - b^2 x^2)} \, dx = \frac{\tan^{-1}\left(\frac{bx}{\sqrt{a^2 - b^2 x^2}} + \right)a^2}{2b} + \frac{1}{2} x\sqrt{(a^2 - b^2 x^2)}$$

$$\int x\sqrt{(a^2 - b^2 x^2)} \, dx = -\frac{(a^2 - b^2 x^2)^{3/2}}{3b^2}$$

$$\int x^2 \sqrt{(a^2 - b^2 x^2)} \, dx = \frac{\tan^{-1}\left(\frac{bx}{\sqrt{a^2 - b^2 x^2}}\right)a^4}{8b^3} + \sqrt{(a^2 - b^2 x^2)}\left(\frac{x^3}{4} - \frac{a^2 x}{8b^2}\right)$$

PROPERTIES OF AREAS

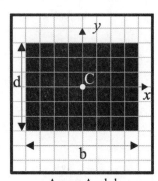

Area = A = bd

$\overline{x} = 0 \qquad \overline{y} = 0$

$I_x = \dfrac{bd^3}{12} \qquad I_y = \dfrac{db^3}{12}$

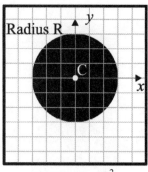

Area = A = πR^2

$\overline{x} = 0 \qquad \overline{y} = 0$

$I_x = \dfrac{\pi R^4}{4} \qquad I_y = \dfrac{\pi R^4}{4}$

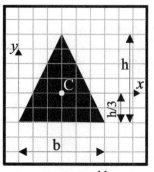

Area = A = $\dfrac{bh}{2}$

$\overline{y} = \dfrac{h}{3}$

$I_x = \dfrac{bh^3}{12}$

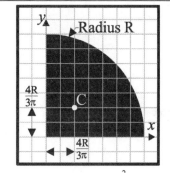

Area = A = $\dfrac{\pi R^2}{4}$

$\overline{x} = \overline{y} = \dfrac{4R}{3\pi}$

$I_x = I_y = \dfrac{\pi R^4}{16}$

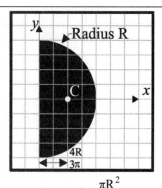

Area = A = $\dfrac{\pi R^2}{2}$

$\overline{x} = \dfrac{4R}{3\pi} \qquad \overline{y} = 0$

$I_x = I_y = \dfrac{\pi R^4}{8}$

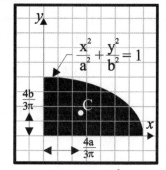

Area = A = $\dfrac{\pi ab}{4}$

$\overline{x} = \dfrac{4a}{3\pi} \qquad \overline{y} = \dfrac{4b}{3\pi}$

$I_x = \dfrac{\pi ab^3}{16} \qquad I_y = \dfrac{\pi a^3 b}{16}$

SOLUTIONS TO SELECTED PROBLEMS

Chapter I
Introduction
Exercise Set I
1. 4, 6, 3
3. 4.56 MN/m^2 (or 4.56 MPa), 765.6 MN.m/s, 54 mN
5. 87.56 kg
7. 76.6 ft^3, 305000 in^3
9. 28.6 m/s
11. 10 Mm^2/s^2
13. 7849 kg/m^3

Chapter II
Position & Force Vectors
Exercise Set I
1. 10,750 lb, 8.94^0
3. 1000 lb, 300 lb; 700 lb, 447 lb; -7 kN, 2.24 kN
5. 800 lb, 400 lb; 400 lb, 400 lb
7. 183 lb, 107^0
9. 1300 lb, 750 lb

Exercise Set II
1. 35.35 i + 35.36 j N; -100 i N; 15 i – 26 j N
3. 56.3^0; -45^0;141.3^0; 45^0
5. α = 22.68^0, β = 67.32^0, 34.55i kN
7. 49.6i kN; -100.2i kN
9. 45^0, 707 i + 707 j lb; 30^0, -100 i + 173 j N; 45^0, 3182 i - 3182 j lb;
   60^0, -2.6 i + 1.5 j kN; 15^0, 19.41 i + 72.44 j lb; 75^0, 33.7 i + 125.6 j lb
11. 40 i + 30 j, 50; -40 i - 30 j, 50; -5 i + 12 j, 13; 8 i - 15 j, 17; 7 i + 24 j, 25; -9 i - 40 j, 41
13. 1000 i lb; 1000 j lb; 514 i + 858 j lb; 800 i + 600 j lb; 528 i + 849 j lb; -707 i - 707 j lb
15. 82.28 N towards D

Exercise Set III
1. 90^0, 707 i + 707 j lb; 45^0, -100 i + 141 j + 100 k kN; 60^0, 2250 i - 3182 j + 2250 k lb;
   90^0, -2.598 i + 1.5 j kN; 65^0, 19.4 i + 32.1 j - 65 k kN; Cannot pick the angles arbitrarily
3. 2 i - j + 2 k, 3; -200 i - 300 j + 600 k, 700; -400 i +700 j + 400 k, 900;
   -60 i - 70 j + 60 k, 110; -2 i - 6 j - 9 k, 11;
5. 1.732 i + j + 3.464 k ft
7. 5 i + 2.89 j + 10 k kN
9. 121 lb
11. 537 lb
13. 28.3^0
15. 6200 lb, 29.9^0
17. 0.667 kN along r_{AB}, 0.535 kN along r_{AC}, 0.371 kN along r_{AD}

Chapter III
Equilibrium of a Particle
Exercise Set I
1. Person 5, 2.5w (including his own weight)
3. 3", 0.5", 3.5"
5. 4.95 kN, 9.81 kN, 4.95 kN, 9.81 cm
7. 0.4 kN, 0.4 kN, 1.8 kN, 0.4 cm
9. 1", 0.5"

Exercise Set II
1. 577 lb, 289 lb
3. -411 lb, 107^0 In the third quadrant
5. 5 lb
7. 750 kN, 900 kN

9. 113 lb, 144 lb
11. AA, 1061 lb
13. 1109 kg
15. 0.633 kN, 0.0805 m

Exercise Set III
1. 0.276
3. 5.48 lb
5. 5.87 lb, 4.13 lb

Exercise Set IV
1. 1237 lb, 1082 lb
3. 2940 N, 2940 N, 9652 N
5. 10,335 lb, 3337 lb
7. 1.8 kN
9. 120 lb, 70 lb, 70 lb
11. 400 lb
13. 400 lb, 0.956 ft

Chapter IV
The Moment Vector

Exercise Set I
1. -1050 ft.lb
3. -583 ft.lb
5. 0 ft.lb
7. -390 ft.lb
9. 1.03 kN

Exercise Set II
1. $-cF$, $-aF$
3. 0.5 kN.m, -13.5 kN.m
5. $-1050k$ ft.lb
7. $-580\ k$ ft.lb
9. $-4.02k$ kN.m
11. $-6080i + 4160\ k$ ft.lb, 7367 ft.lb

Exercise Set III
1. Total moment vector $-4i$ ft.lb, 0, $2k$ ft.lb
3. $-30i + 30j$ ft.lb
5. $-280i$ kN.m

Exercise Set IV
1. 0.75 kN.m
3. 1.945 kN.m
5. $1.944k$ kN.m
7. $-16i + 8k$ kN.m

Exercise Set V
1. Equivalent
3. Not equivalent
5. -300 lb @ 5' from point A
7. -1500 ft.lb
9. -4 kN @ 3 m from point A

Chapter V
Equilibrium of a Rigid Body

Exercise Set I
1. $P/3$, $2P/3$
3. 442 lb, 88.35 lb
5. 16.97 kN, 13.42 kN,
7. 0.8 lb, 0.577 lb

Exercise Set II
1. 7200 lb, 8 ft
3. 800 lb
5. 10,800 lb, 7.33 ft
7. 7,200 lb, 6 ft
9. 54 kN, 1.625 m

Exercise Set III
1. $R_{Ax} = 1060$ lb, $R_{Ay} = 530$ lb, $R_{Ax} = 530$ lb
3. -50 lb, -50 lb
5. 720 lb, 1080 lb
7. 7.95 kN, 8.55 kN
9. $R_{Ax} = 0$ kN, $R_{Ay} = 42$ kN, $R_{Ax} = 210$ kN.m
11. 10 lb
13. 5.34 cm
15. 125 lb, 625 lb
17. Will not tip
19. 3660 lb

Exercise Set IV
1. 25 kN, 25 kN, 50 kN
3. $W/2$
5. 5.86 kN, 12.1 kN, 12.1 kN

Chapter VI
Structural Design & Analysis
Exercise Set I
1. $F_{AB} = 500$ lb, $F_{BC} = -707$ lb, $F_{AC} = 707$ lb
3. $F_{AC} = F_{BC} = -707$ lb, $F_{AD} = F_{BD} = 500$ lb, $F_{CD} = 1000$ lb,
5. $F_{AB} = -2.5$ kN, $F_{AC} = 3.54$ kN, $F_{BC} = -3.54$ kN, $F_{CD} = 5$ kN, $F_{BD} = -7.07$ kN
7. $F_{AC} = F_{BE} = -7.07$ kN, $F_{CD} = F_{DE} = 5$ kN, $F_{AD} = -5$kN, $F_{AD} = F_{BD} = 0$
9. $F_{AB} = 8.75$ kN, $F_{AC} = -10.1$ kN, $F_{BC} = 5$ kN
11. $F_{AB} = F_{ED} = -300$ lb, $F_{BC} = F_{CD} = -300$ lb, $F_{AF} = F_{EH} = 424$ lb,
    $F_{BF} = F_{DH} = 0$, $F_{CG} = 200$ lb, $F_{CF} = F_{CH} = 141$ lb
13. 5 kN
15. 1414 lb

Exercise Set II
1. $F_{BC} = -300$ lb, $F_{FC} = -424$ lb, $F_{FG} = 600$ lb
3. $F_{EG} = -3.465$ kN, $F_{DF} = 3.175$ kN, $F_{EF} = 0.4653$ kN
5. $F_{DE} = 5$ kN, $F_{DB} = 0$ kN, $F_{AB} = -5$ kN
7. $F_{BD} = 354$ lb, $F_{CD} = 0$ lb, $F_{CE} = -790$ lb
9. $F_{BC} = -188$ kN, $F_{BG} = 39$ lb, $F_{FG} = 150$ lb

Exercise Set III
1. $R_{Ax} = F_{Bx} = 0$, $R_{Ay} = 133$ lb, $F_{By} = 133$ lb, $F_{Cy} = 67$ lb, $M_A = 1233$ ft.lb
3. $F_{Bx} = 0, F_{Cy} = 300$ N, $F_{By} = 300$ N, $M_A = 1500$ N.m
5. $R_{Ax} = 60$ lb, $R_{Ay} = 100$ lb, $R_{Bx} = -60$ lb, $F_{FD} = 283$ lb, $F_{Cy} = -100$ lb, $F_{Cx} = -200$ lb
7. 500 lb
9. $W_1 = 2F + W_2$

Chapter VII
Shear Forces & Bending Moment s
Exercise Set I
1. 10 kN, 20 kN.m
3. 1.6 kN, 0.5 kN.m
5. 0 kN, 3.75 kN.m, 0 or 5 kN, 0 kN.m

7. $V_A = \dfrac{qL}{2}$, $M_A = \dfrac{3qL^2}{8}$, $V_B = \dfrac{qL}{2}$, $M_B = \dfrac{qL^2}{8}$

9. 0 or 1667 lb, 0 ft.lb, 333 lb, 7332 ft.lb, 2333 lb, 4666 ft.lb

Exercise Set II

1.

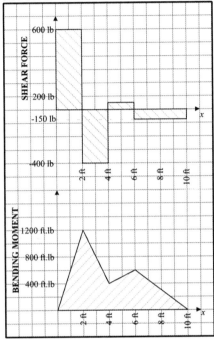

3.

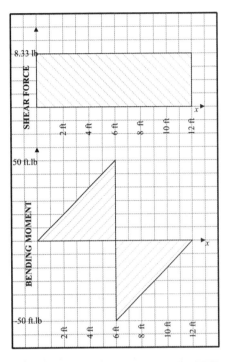

5.

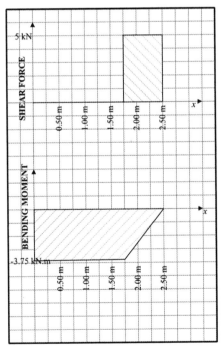

7.

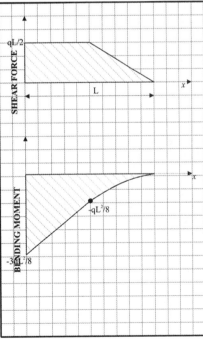

9.

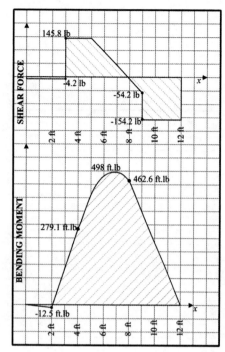

11.

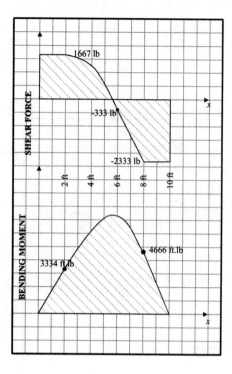

Chapter VIII
Centroid and Moment of Inertia
Exercise Set I

1. 0.6604 m, 0.4784 m
3. 1.75 m, 1.288 m
5. 0.7 m, 0.55 m (you can use symmetry)
7. 7", 4.89 "
9. 7.24", 8"
11. 3.333', 3.778'
13. $\dfrac{4a}{3\pi}$, $\dfrac{4b}{3\pi}$
15. 0,0,1.5"

Exercise Set II

1. $I_x = I_y = \dfrac{\pi r^2}{4}$
3. 93.75 in^4, 303.75 in^4
5. 0.02232 m^4, 0.09499 m^4, 0.1173 m^4
7. 0.6252 m^4, 0.6780 m^4, 1.303 m^4
9. 0.0058 m^4, 0.0737 m^4, 0.0795 m^4
11. 13180 in^4, 13820 in^4, 2700 in^4

APPENDIX B

STATICS
FUNDAMENTALS OF ENGINEERING (FE)
EXAMINATION STYLE PROBLEMS

1. A known force $\left(F_1 = 200 \text{ lb}\right)$ and an unknown force $\left(F_2\right)$ act on a hook. Determine the magnitude of unknown force if the resultant is along the x-direction.
- A. 245 lb
- B. 163 lb
- C. 283 lb
- D. None of the above

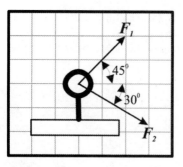

2. A block is in equilibrium on an inclined plane. If the coefficient of friction is μ, the friction force at the interface is equal to:
- A. $\mu W \sin\theta$
- B. $\mu W \cos\theta$
- C. $W \sin\theta$
- D. $W \cos\theta$

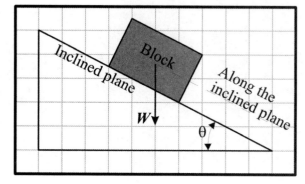

3. A car has front-wheel drive. If the car is accelerating, the direction of the friction force on the wheels:
- A. Front wheels in the forward direction, Rear wheels in the forward direction
- B. Front wheels in the forward direction, Rear wheels in the reverse direction
- C. Front wheels in the reverse direction, Rear wheels in the forward direction
- D. Front wheels in the reverse direction, Rear wheels in the reverse direction

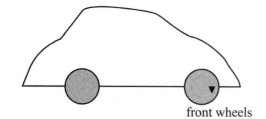

front wheels

4. The coefficient of friction is 0.75. The dimensions of the block are $a = 1''$ and $b = 1''$. If the angle θ is slowly increased, the block will first:
- A. tip
- B. slip down
- C. slide up
- D. May slip or tip with equal probability

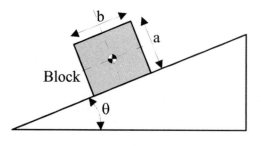

5. A force F is applied to the block. Determine the necessary condition for the block to tip.
- A. $F \geq \mu W$ and $F \geq \dfrac{a}{b} W$
- B. $F \leq \mu W$ and $F \geq \dfrac{a}{b} W$
- C. $F \geq \mu W$ and $F \geq \dfrac{b}{a} W$
- D. $F \leq \mu W$ and $F \leq \dfrac{b}{a} W$

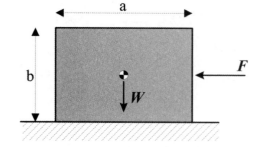

6. Two triangular wedges are forced together with force F. If the coefficient of friction is μ, at impending sliding the following condition must be true

A. $\sin\theta = \mu$
B. $\cos\theta = \mu$
C. $\tan\theta = \mu$
D. None of the above

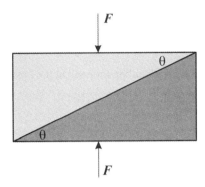

7. For the spring whose force vs. deflection diagram is shown in the figure below, the spring constant is

A. Zero
B. 12.5 kN/m
C. 25 kN/cm
D. Infinite

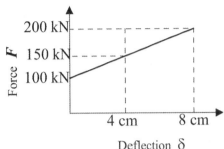

8. The effective spring constant for the spring assembly is given by

A. $\dfrac{k_b(k_a + k_c)}{k_a + k_b + k_c}$

B. $k_a + \dfrac{k_b k_c}{k_b + k_c}$

C. $k_a + k_b + k_c$

D. None of the above

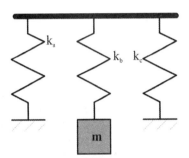

9. The effective spring constant for the spring assembly is given by

A. $k_1 + \dfrac{k_2 k_3}{k_2 + k_3} + k_4$

B. $\dfrac{k_1(k_2 + k_3)k_4}{k_1 + k_2 + k_3 + k_4}$

C. $k_1 + k_2 + k_3 + k_4$

D. None of the above

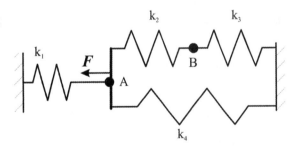

10. The moment at point P due to force F is 1 kN.m. The magnitude of force F

A. 4.5 m × 1 kN.m
B. 4.5 m × 1 kN.m × 3/sqrt(13)
C. 1 kN.m × 3/(sqrt(13) × 4.5 m)
D. 1 kN.m × sqrt(13) /(3 × 4.5 m)

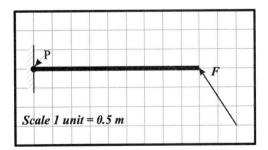

11. The bending moment at the base of the structure is:

    A. 12 kN.m
    B. 30 kN.m
    C. 50 kN.m
    D. $\sqrt{12^2 + 50^2}$ kN.m

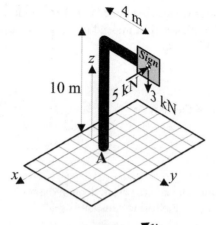

12. The couple due to forces at Points A and D at point B is

    A. 0 ft. lb
    B. $100\sqrt{41}$ ft.lb
    C. 400 ft.lb
    D. 900 ft.lb

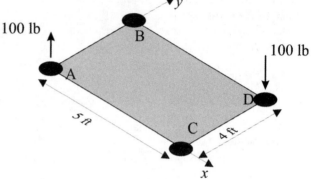

13. The tension in the cable AB is T. The moment of this tension about point O is:

    A. $T \times r_{OA}$
    B. $r_{AB} \times T$
    C. $r_{OB} \times T$
    D. None of the above

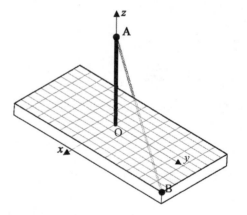

14. The magnitude of the couple due to the four forces is:
    A. 3 ft.lb
    B. 4 ft.lb
    C. 5 ft.lb
    D. 7 ft.lb

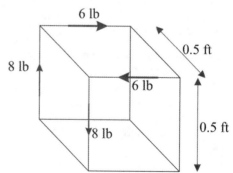

15. The reaction at point A is
   A. $0.5P + 0.25Q$
   B. $-0.5P + 0.25Q$
   C. -0.5 L $P + 0.75$L Q
   D. 0

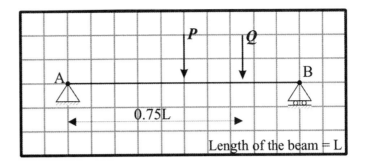

16. The hydrostatic pressure on the face of the dam at a depth x is given by ρgx where ρ is the density and g is the acceleration due to gravity. If the width of the dam is L, the height of the water level at which the dam will tip is equal to

   A. $\sqrt[3]{\dfrac{6Wb}{\rho g}}$

   B. $\sqrt[3]{\dfrac{6Wc}{\rho gL}}$

   C. $\sqrt[3]{\dfrac{6Wa}{\rho gL}}$

   D. None of the above

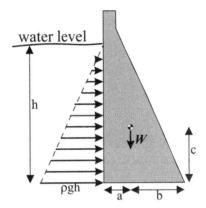

17. At tipping, the following statement is false:
   A. R_A and R_B are equal
   B. $P = 1.5 F$
   C. R_A is zero and R_B is equal to $P+F$
   D. R_A is equal to $P+F$

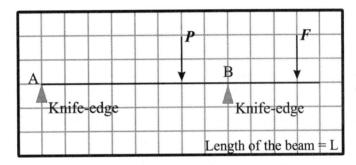

18. The number of zero-force members in this structure is:
   A. 6
   B. 8
   C. 10
   D. None of the above

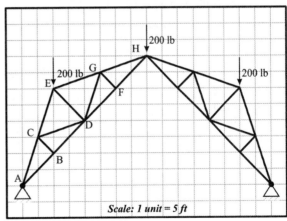

19. The load carried by member BF is:
   A. 0 lb
   B. 300 lb
   C. 600 lb
   D. None of the above

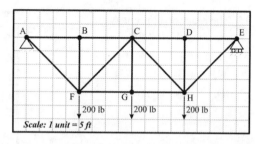

20. For a cantilever beam, the maximum bending moment occurs at:
   A. at the root (fixed support)
   B. at the tip (free end)
   C. at point B
   D. None of the above

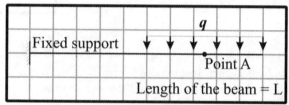

21. The shear force at point P is:
   A. 0 kN
   B. 5 kN
   C. 10 kN
   D. 15 kN

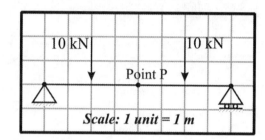

22. For the beam, the following statement is false:
   A. The shear force at point A is equal to the shear force at point B
   B. The bending moment at point A is equal to the bending moment at point B
   C. The bending moment at point B is larger than the bending moment at point A
   D. The bending moment at both supports is equal to zero.

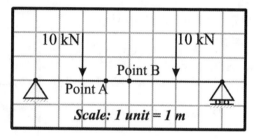

23. For the simply-supported beam, the following statement is true:

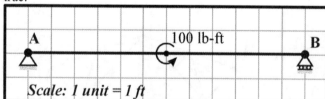

   A. The shear force along the beam is constant in magnitude and is equal to zero.
   B. The shear force along the beam is constant and is equal to $\left(\dfrac{100 \text{ ft.lb}}{12 \text{ ft}}\right)$
   C. The bending moment along the beam is constant and is equal to *M*.
   D. The maximum bending moment is 50 ft.lb.

24. For the beam, the following statement is true:

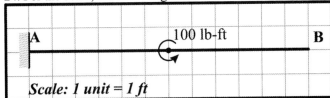

Scale: 1 unit = 1 ft

A. The shear force along the beam is constant in magnitude and is equal to zero.
B. The shear force along the beam is constant and is equal to $\left(\dfrac{100\ ft.lb}{6\ ft}\right)$
C. The bending moment along the beam is constant and is *M*.
D. The maximum bending moment is 50 ft.lb.

25. The maximum bending moment for the beam is:

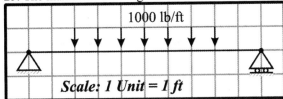

1000 lb/ft

Scale: 1 Unit = 1 ft

A. 15000 ft.lb
B. 10,500 ft.lb
C. 6,000 ft.lb
D. 0 ft. lb

26. The maximum bending moment for the beam is:

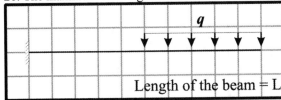

q

Length of the beam = L

A. $\dfrac{qL^2}{4}$
B. $\dfrac{3qL^2}{8}$
C. $\dfrac{qL^2}{2}$
D. $\dfrac{qL}{2}$

27. A skate board with the person in the middle can be viewed as a
    A. Simply supported beam
    B. Cantilever beam
    C. Balancing beam
    D. Simply supported beam with overhang

28. The center of gravity of the L-section is
    A. 3", 3"
    B. 1.864", 1.864"
    C. 0.336", 0.336"
    D. None of the above

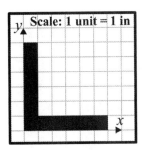

29. The moment of inertia of the hollow rectangular section about its centroid is
    A. 53.5 in^4
    B. 74 in^4
    C. 107 in^4
    D. None of the above

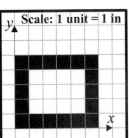

30. $(10i \text{ ft}) \times (80j \text{ lb}) =$
    A. 0
    B. 800 ft.lb
    C. 800**k** ft.lb
    D. −800**k** ft.lb

31. The unit vector for the force vector $F = 10i + 20j - 20k$ *lb* is:
    A. $i + j + k$
    B. $i + j - k$
    C. $\frac{1}{5}i + \frac{2}{5}j - \frac{2}{5}k$
    D. $\frac{1}{3}i + \frac{2}{3}j - \frac{2}{3}k$

32. If weight **W** is applied to point A, the following statement is true:
    A. Tension in cable AB > Tension in cable AC
    B. Tension in cable AB = Tension in cable AC
    C. Tension in cable AB < Tension in cable AC
    D. Tension in cable AB + Tension in cable AC = **W**

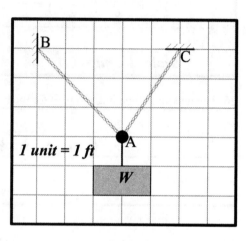

33. The equivalent load and its location for the overall load distribution is:

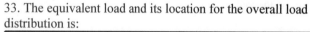
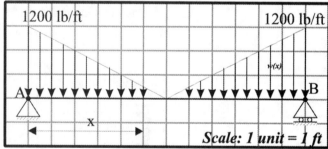

A. 28,800 lb and $x = 6'$
B. 14,400 lb and $x = 6'$
C. 7,200 lb and $x = 6'$
D. 7,200 lb and $x = 4'$

34. A 15 ft tall pole is supported by three cables. The pole is subjected only to vertical loading due to the tension in the cables. If the tension in cable PA is 500 lb, it is possible to determine the tension in cable PB

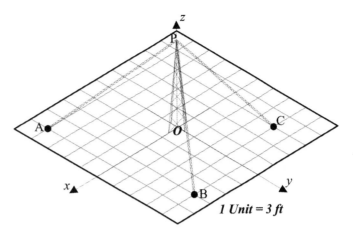

1 Unit = 3 ft

    A. Without any additional information.
    B. Only if the vertical load in the pole is also given.
    C. Only if the tension in cable PC is also given.
    D. Only if both the vertical load in the pole and the tension in cable PC are also given.

35. $(k \times j) \cdot i =$
    A. -1
    B. 0
    C. j
    D. $-j$

36. In a two-dimensional space, a rigid body has _____ degrees of freedom.
    A. One
    B. Two
    C. Three
    D. Four

37. Determine the load in member CD.

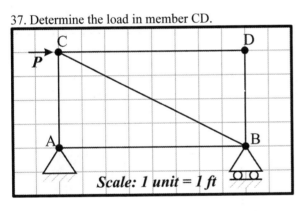

Scale: 1 unit = 1 ft

    A. 0
    B. $-P$ (tension)
    C. $\dfrac{\sqrt{80}}{8} P$ (tension)
    D. $-\dfrac{\sqrt{80}}{8} P$ (compression)

38. The direction of a vector is $\alpha = 0^0$, β and γ will be
    A. 0^0 and 0^0
    B. 45^0 and 45^0
    C. 90^0 and 90^0
    D. None of the above

39. A force whose magnitude 1000 lb is acting from point A (1, 1, 1) to B (4, 1, 5). The vector representation of the force is:
    A. $1000(3i + 4k)$ lb
    B. $1000(-3i - 4k)$ lb
    C. $200(3i + 4k)$ lb
    D. $200(-3i - 4k)$ lb

40. The magnitude of the resultant of two vectors whose magnitudes are 5 lb and 12 lb can not be:
    A. greater than 17 lb
    B. greater than 13 lb
    C. greater than 12 lb
    D. greater than 5 lb

41. Determine force F required to pull the block if the coefficient of friction is 1 between the blocks and 0.5 between the block and the ground:
    A. 0 lb
    B. 10 lb
    C. 20 lb
    D. 30 lb

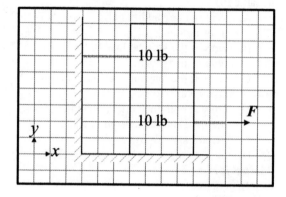

42. Determine the force required to pulley weight W.
    A. *F*
    B. 0.5F
    C. 2F
    D. None of the above

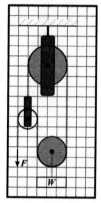

43. A person to lift himself up using the pulley arrangement. The weight of the person is 200 lb. The force required to lift himself is:
    A. 0 lb
    B. 100 lb
    C. 200 lb
    D. 400 lb

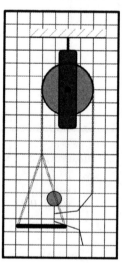

44. A 12 kN force is supported away from the wall. The magnitude of force reaction at point C, $R_C =$

    A. 8.485 kN
    B. 16.97 kN
    C. 6 kN
    D. 12 kN

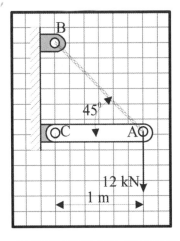

45. The number of zero-force members in this structure is:

    A. 4
    B. 5
    C. 6
    D. None of the above

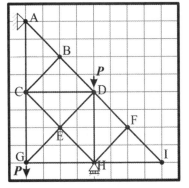

46. The moment due to force F is equal to
A. 20 ft.lb
B. 200 ft.lb
C. 2000 ft.lb
D. None of the above

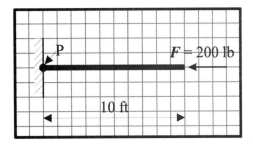

47. The coordinates of centroid with respect to the xy coordinate system is

    A. (0.7, 0.55)
    B. (0.7, 0.35)
    C. (0.55, 0.7)
    D. (0.35, 0.7)

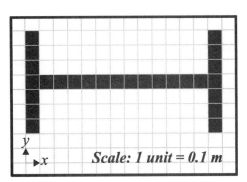

48. The $x'y'$ coordinate system passes through the centroid and $I_{x'}$ is the moment of inertia about the x' axis. Similarly, I_x is the moment of inertia about the x axis. The relationship between the two moment of inertias is given by

A. $I_x = I_{x'} + A d_x^2$

B. $I_x = I_{x'} + A d_y^2$

C. $I_{x'} = I_x + A d_x^2$

D. $I_{x'} = I_x + A d_y^2$

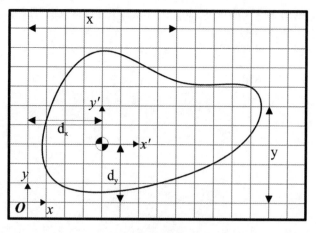

49. The car wheel hits the curb. The wheel can go over the curb, if

A. The magnitude of force F is large in comparison to the weight of the car

B. The magnitude of force F is small in comparison to the weight of the car

C. The magnitude of force F is equal to the in the weight of the car

D. None of the above – the wheel can not go over the curb.

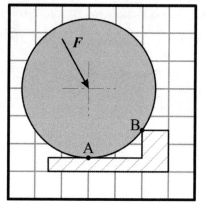

50. The resultant of three vectors whose magnitudes are equal (and nonzero) is zero. The following statement is false:

A. The three vectors lie in the same plane

B. The angle between any two vectors is 60^0 or 120^0

C. The vectors can be arranged to form an equilateral triangle

D. The angle between any two vectors is 90^0

ANSWER KEY:

1. C	11. D	21. A	31. D	41. A
2. C	12. B	22. B	32. C	42. C
3. B	13. C	23. B	33. C	43. D
4. B	14. C	24. A	34. A	44. B
5. A	15. A	25. B	35. A	45. B
6. C	16. A	26. B	36. C	46. B
7. B	17. C	27. A	37. A	47. D
8. A	18. C	28. B	38. C	48. A
9. A	19. A	29. A	39. C	49. D
10. D	20. A	30. C	40. A	50. D

Notes:

Notes:

Notes:

Notes:

Notes:

Notes:

Notes:

Notes:

Notes:

Notes: